MW00779417

A
HISTORY
of JEWISH LIFE
FROM EASTERN EUROPE
TO AMERICA

A
HISTORY
of JEWISH LIFE
FROM EASTERN EUROPE
TO AMERICA

Milton Meltzer

JASON ARONSON INC.
Northvale, New Jersey
London

For credits, see Acknowledgments on page 325.

First Jason Aronson Inc. Edition—1996

This book was set in 11 point Schneidler.

Library of Congress Cataloging-in-Publication Data

Meltzer, Milton, 1915-
    [World of our fathers]
    A history of Jewish life from Eastern Europe to America / Milton Meltzer.
        p. cm.
    Includes bibliographical references and index.
    Contents: World of our fathers—Taking root.
    Summary: Describes Jewish life in Eastern Europe in the nineteenth century, and the Jewish migration to America with the problems of adjusting to life in a new country in the face of prejudice and difficult living conditions.
    ISBN 1-56821-433-2
    1. Jews—Europe, Eastern—History—19th century. 2. Jews—Europe, Eastern—Migrations. 3. Jews—United States—Social conditions.
    4. Europe, Eastern—Emigration and immigration. 5. United States—Emigration and immigration. [1. Jews—Europe, Eastern—History,
    2. Jews—Migrations. 3. Jews—United States—Social conditions. 4. United States—Emigration and immigration.] I. Meltzer, Milton,
    1915-   Taking root. II. Title.
    DS135.E83M35   1996
    947'.0004924—dc20
                                                                    95-16065
                                                                        CIP
                                                                        AC

Manufactured in the United States of America. Jason Aronson Inc. offers books and cassettes. For information and catalog write to Jason Aronson Inc., 230 Livingston Street, Northvale, New Jersey 07647.

To Mary Richter and Benjamin Meltzer,
the young immigrants,
with love

Contents

Preface   ix

Part I   World of Our Fathers

1	Where They Came From	3
2	Order and Chaos	9
3	Doubly the Enemy, Doubly the Victim	19
4	Conscripts for the Czar's Army	26
5	The Useless Ones	36
6	I Was, with God's Help, a Poor Man	44
7	Making a Living in the Shtetl	51
8	The Sheyneh and the Prosteh	62
9	Study Is the Best of Wares	71
10	Fun and Feasts	80
11	Hasidism and Haskalah	87
12	Hebrew—or Yiddish?	96
13	What Is to Be Done?	107

14   1881—The Terrible Year   116
15   A Permanent Legal Pogrom   125
16   Zionists and Bundists   134
17   The City of Slaughter   143

PART II   TAKING ROOT

18   Less Than a Dog   160
19   To Go—or Not to Go   166
20   Crossing in Steerage   173
21   The Green Ones Arrive   182
22   Sheeny!   189
23   Tenements and Strangers   197
24   Cheese It—the Cops!   208
25   Peddlers and Pushcarts   213
26   Sweatshop   220
27   Where Children Slowly Roast   230
28   Run, Do, Work!   239
29   From Greenhorn to American   247
30   The Melting Pot Leaks   257
31   Settlements in the Slums   267
32   My Parents Don't Understand   275
33   Cahan and the Cafés   281
34   Actors and Poets   289
35   To Shake the World   299
36   The Door Closes   309

Bibliography   317
Acknowledgments   325
Index   327

Preface

W hen I was growing up in Worcester, Massachusetts, I had little sense of being a Jew. We lived in a mixed neighborhood of three-decker houses. There were other Jewish families on Union Hill, but there were many more who were Irish, Polish, Lithuanian, Swedish, German, Italian, Armenian in origin. Some were Protestant, more were Catholic. We played prisoner's base together and king of the mountain, and baseball and football and hockey. And we went to the same school. Many of their parents, like mine, had come from Europe to the Promised Land, so most of us were the first generation to be born in America.

My mother and father had met in New York, after emigrating from Europe. All I knew about their origins was that both came from what was then Austria-Hungary. The old maps showed it to have been a large, pasted-together empire, of many nationalities. It sprawled over much of Eastern Europe. Just which part, which town or village they were born in, I never learned until long after childhood. (And discovered only recently that my impression had been wrong.) Not that it was a secret. My mother and father simply did not talk about their life in the old country. And all wrapped up in myself, I never thought to ask. They were here, in Worcester, this was now, and I had no time for anything else. The past didn't interest me then (who would have thought I'd write history one day?) and the future stretched only as far as tomorrow morning. My mother and father had had a little schooling in Europe, I knew, but nothing that prepared them for anything but unskilled labor. Both had worked in factories before coming to Worcester. Now my mother was staying at home to raise a family of three sons. And my father tried to support us by washing windows.

I remember that they spoke only English. It was no doubt a faulty and accented English. They rarely used Yiddish. That must have been because they wanted us to grow up "American." And the faster we learned the American language, the better.

My father was not a believer. He did not go to the synagogue on the other side of the hill. I vaguely remember going with my mother once or twice on a high holiday. Still, I was prepared briefly for a bar mitzvah, the ceremony for boys reaching the age of thirteen. But it only meant that for several months a bearded old man came to our house after I came home from school, hammered a bit of Hebrew into my reluctant ears, and listened to me memorizing a set speech. As soon as that Saturday's ordeal passed, the lessons ended. I think now I was put through it because my mother was concerned with what her mother and father might think (they lived in far-off New York) if we hadn't done it. By the time my younger brother reached thirteen, she didn't even bother.

There were no books about Jewish life or history in our house (or about any other subject, for that matter). And being Jewish was never discussed. Until, that is, a neighbor told my mother that I was seen "fooling around" with the daughter of an Irish cop on the next block. Then my mother let me know (with a slap in the face) that this was a bad thing. Jew and non-Jew couldn't mix. "It never works out." Later, in high school, I fell in love with a classmate who happened to be Protestant. But she lived far away on the other side of town and I never asked her to come to my home. I spent a lot of time in hers, but by then I was old enough to conceal it better, or perhaps my mother was too beset by the Depression, which had come on, to think this mattered much. It did matter, to me, but in the end we each fell in love with and married someone else.

I left Worcester to go to a college in New York. From then on, I was on my own. My father died when I was a student. He never talked to me about his childhood. I don't know if he ever would have, even if I'd had the sense to ask the right questions. He was a silent man. I loved him, although I cannot remember a single conversation between us. My mother was far more talkative. She probably would have told me much about life in the old country that I'd delight in knowing now. But I never showed any interest in it. And by the time I was smart enough to want to know, it was too late. She was ten years gone.

If my own parents told me nothing about my people's past, then surely my teachers might have taught me something about it. They didn't. I think the Worcester schools were good ones—at least I thrived in them—but they too, like my mother and father, were hell-bent on Americanizing us. The classrooms were full of first-generation Americans, and the teachers took it as their business to mold us into true-blue citizens, loyal, faithful, patriotic. The only language that mattered was English. The only culture we heard about was Anglo-Saxon. The only history to study was American. Oh, a bit of British history was wedged in to let us know what our country had broken away from, and later there was some ancient history, Greek and Roman. But little in between. And certainly nothing about those countries so many of us sitting on the hard benches could trace our roots to.

As I went from grade school to junior high and then high school, I noticed that the proportion of immigrant children gradually dropped. Many left school to go to work. There were several high schools in the town; one specialized in preparing the "better" students from all over the city for college. When I entered it, I discovered there were far more boys and girls with Anglo-Saxon names than in the school I had come from. Some of these were excellent students; others seemed to be there only because their parents had the money to assure a college education. They dressed differently, spoke differently, behaved differently. I wanted to look like them, talk like them, act like them. They had an ease and assurance I envied. I worked hard at my studies, joined school clubs, made new friends. But the only one of the strangers I grew close to was the girl I fell in love with. And I never really felt at ease in her home or with her family.

I had too little knowledge of my past to find it solid ground to stand on. Nor could I penetrate the strange world of my new classmates. Who was I? From what did I come? To what did I belong? Only now did these questions begin to trouble me. I took a very long time, seeking the answers, all the while trying, like most immigrants and their children, to follow the American command to rise and assimilate.

I've learned something at last about my family's past. Not just my mother's and father's, but the life of the Jews in Eastern Europe from whom most of today's 6 million American Jews sprang. It is a world almost unknown to most of us, the world of our grandparents and great-grandparents. Who were they? What color and tension did their lives have? What concerns and what hopes? Getting to know those people—the places they lived in, the work they did, the enemies they feared, the customs and habits and values they lived by—we begin to know ourselves.

My grandfather, Samuel Richter, decided America was the place to raise his children, not Austria-Hungary. So he got up from the village of Skoryk, and left. Sounds easy, doesn't it? I never stopped, until recently, to imagine what it must have been like for a young father to make that decision. To quit the place he grew up in, to leave wife and children behind, to strike out across the unknown countries of Europe for a distant seaport, then to take steerage passage across the frightening Atlantic, and at the end of a harsh voyage, drop like some anonymous atom into the vast chaos of New York. Where would he find a place to sleep? What could he do to make a living? How would he make himself understood in a language he didn't know?

It was 1895 when Samuel Richter came to America. He didn't stay long; he went back in 1897. Why? I don't know. Too lonely? Unable to earn enough to bring the others over? But two years later, after fathering three more children (including a pair of twins), he decided to try again. And the next year, 1900, my mother, Mary, followed him. She was fourteen then, the oldest of her many brothers and sisters, a capable girl, with enormous energy and will. Together she and my grandfather earned enough to bring over the rest of the family in 1903.

Millions of others did it too, Jews like them and non-Jewish immigrants, chiefly Greek Orthodox and Roman Catholic, from all the countries of Eastern and Southern Europe, my father among them. Benjamin Meltzer was eighteen when he left the village of Havrilesht in the Austro-Hungarian province of Bukovina. He reached New York in 1897. He was the oldest of five brothers and two sisters. He came first, and alone. Later one of his sisters and two of his brothers joined him. But his mother and father (my grandparents) and one sister and two brothers did not come. He never saw them again.

Mary and Ben met in New York, married, and moved to Worcester, Massachusetts, where they raised three sons. My father died at the age of fifty-seven, my mother at seventy-seven. Nobody outside their family and small circle of friends ever heard of them. But the quality of their lives, the delights and disappointments, the ambitions and fears, the labors and illusions, are here, I hope, in this story of their immigrant generation.

I wrote this story of the Eastern European Jews because they are my people and I wanted to learn about them. But what happened to them, in many respects, is like what happened to all the other immigrants, whatever their origin. There were differences, of course, and most significant ones; each ethnic group has its own historical memory, real and imagined, and whether it is our own or not, it is worth exploring.

I

WORLD OF OUR FATHERS

1

Where They Came From

Half the Jews of the world lived in Eastern Europe in the year 1800.

That region isn't the Eastern Europe we identify today as the Soviet Union and the Communist countries west of it. In Jewish history, Eastern Europe was taken as the area bounded by the Rhine River on the west and the Dnieper on the east. Its northern extreme was the Baltic and its southern, the Black Sea.

Compared with Western Europe, it was backward. Its population was mostly peasants (many of them serfs until the 1860s), with some artisans and workers.

The Jews of Eastern Europe were *Ashkenazi,* with their own language, Yiddish. Over the centuries they had developed a unique group life. Their number grew rapidly, from one million in 1775 to five and a half million in 1875. In 1939, on the eve of Hitler's holocaust, there were seven million Jews in Eastern Europe; millions of others born there had gone to live abroad, the great majority in the United States.

Where did the Eastern European Jews come from? Why were so many living in this place, where legal and economic barriers made life for the Jews so much worse than elsewhere?

The true beginnings of Eastern European Jewry have been clouded by myth and legend. It is known that there were Jewish settlements in

Europe as far back as the time of the Second Temple (70 c.e.). But the centers of Jewish life were in Babylonia, Egypt, and Palestine. From the third to the tenth century, Babylonia was looked upon by Jews everywhere as their spiritual heart. Its large Jewish center developed a rich cultural life that helped maintain Jewish continuity in the Diaspora.

When the Moslem faith was carried abroad on Arab banners in the seventh century, Babylonian Jews migrated too. They settled in Palestine, North Africa, and several places in Western Europe. There is some reason to believe that Jewish settlements were started in the parts of Eastern Europe which later became Russia. They disappeared except perhaps for a few remnants, which may have lasted until the Middle Ages. The Mongol invasion of the thirteenth century wiped out any trace of them. Except for a lone Jew here and there, there was no Eastern European Jewry until the thirteenth century, when settlement started with people from Bohemia and Germany.

It was Western Europe that became the center of gravity for Jewish life in the Middle Ages. In the centuries that saw the decline of Roman power (350–650), many Jews engaged in farming. As freed slaves, or as poor immigrants seeking a better life, they bought small farms as soon as they could afford it. The incessant warfare and the decline of the cities made the life of a merchant or artisan precarious. So more Jews shifted from commerce to farming. Some became the owners of large estates in Spain, Italy, and southern France.

And then the tide was reversed and Jews were forced to abandon agriculture. The Church, which like everybody else used slave labor on its estates, issued decrees against Jews owning slaves. (Too many slaves were adopting Judaism as a quick path to the freedom Jews were bound by their faith to give fellow Jews in slavery.) Without labor it was impossible to farm the land. Nor could Jews take the religious oath of mutual defense that obligated feudal landlords to protect one another from roving marauders or voracious neighbors. Except for the minority who converted to Christianity to keep their lands, most Jews were forced to give up agriculture.

Luckily, the warfare between the Christians and the Moslems gave the Jews an opening to another way to make a living. The interchange of goods between East and West had been crippled when the Moslems gained control of the eastern coast of the Mediterranean in 650. Because the Jews were not a part of that quarrel, both sides were willing to do business with them. Jewish merchants could come and go freely, using their fellow Jews along the commercial routes to establish trading stations.

"Jew" and "merchant"—in the popular mind the two terms soon came to mean the same thing. But as soon as Christians and Moslems worked out a sort of peace, the Jews no longer monopolized trade. Christians were drawn to where the profits were, and Venetians and other Italians soon rivaled the Jewish merchants. Jews partnered with Christians and together they expanded international trade.

Serving the economic needs of medieval society, the Jews were protected by the kings and nobles who knew their value and had a stake in their success. As the old towns of Roman days revived and new towns sprang up along the trade routes, the Jews once more came to live chiefly in the urban centers. These were relatively small—perhaps a few thousand Christian families and fifty Jewish families. The Jews could live where they liked, often on streets together with Christians. All Jews lived under the regulations imposed by the Jewish community. Life centered on the synagogue and the cemetery. Leadership came from the elders, who had the authority to judge civil suits between Jews and to levy fines.

It was only in Spain that the Jews of medieval Western Europe experienced a "Golden Age." With the Moslem conquest of Spain came freedom from the slavery they had known under the harsh rule of the Visigoths. Jewish writers of the Middle Ages identified Spain as the Sepharad where Obadiah (verse 20) had prophesied the exiles of Jerusalem would find refuge. The Jews of this Iberian corner of Europe thus came to be known as the *Sephardim*. The contrasting term, Ashkenazim, arose at the same time: Jewish communities had prospered in the Rhineland towns and medieval rabbis began to speak of Germany as Ashkenaz (Genesis 10:3 and Jeremiah 51:27). Gradually the Jews of northern Europe came to be called Ashkenazim to distinguish them from the Sephardim.

Jewish merchants contributed greatly to Spain's rising power and wealth. Prosperous Jews and Moslems alike were proud to foster culture. Hebrew scholarship flowered side by side with the Moslem and the two cooperated in studies and teaching. The cultures intermixed through translation of one another's works. Jewish philosophers, poets, physicians, mathematicians, astronomers, geographers, cartographers, diplomats, translators, and financiers helped fertilize the soil from which the intellectual life of Europe would be reborn.

But beyond the peninsula the Jews of Europe enjoyed no Golden Age. They were only tolerated in the medieval centuries. Under the Church's influence, the state made Jews outcasts. King, noble, or bishop controlled their lives. Shut off from the land, they were also excluded automatically by the Christian guilds from the many crafts and trades they had practiced. As the economies developed, the Church eased its restrictions on commercial activity. Trade became more respectable and Christians who had been eyeing the profitable world of trade began to displace the Jews as merchants. The Jews had to turn to banking and finance (the Church still forbade Christians to receive interest) and by 1250 they so dominated the field in many countries that "money lender" and "Jew" became as synonymous as "merchant" and "Jew" had once been. But as this sphere too became enticing, the Church's restrictions relaxed and Christians again replaced Jews. Most medieval Jews knew nothing but poverty; they endured through their tough loyalty to Jewish life and their conviction that it was the only one certain to bring salvation to mankind.

It is worth noting that everywhere, as a country's economy advanced, Jews were permitted only a smaller and smaller role in it. Forced out of Western Europe, they pioneered the commercial development of Eastern Europe. When they were no longer considered essential to the economy, their Christian rivals called them avaricious and heartless—the image perpetuated by Shakespeare's Shylock—and then took over their functions.

The Crusades, which began in 1095, convulsed the medieval world and were a catastrophe for the Jews. The romantic tales of chivalrous knights fighting to reclaim the Holy City of Jerusalem from the unbelievers omit the horror that accompanied the holiness. For two hundred years the Jews who lived along the path of the eight Crusades felt the murderous effect of armed zeal. What, said the Christian preachers, march to redeem the Holy Land from the infidel and leave untouched these Jewish dogs in our midst? So they sacked and burned the Jewish communities, raped their women, massacred their people. Greed as well as piety inspired the Crusaders. A Jewish merchant or moneylender killed meant goods that could be seized or a debt that could be canceled.

It was in 1215 that the Church's Fourth Lateran Council decreed Jews must wear distinctive dress—a large hat on the head, or a yellow or crimson circle over the heart. They became plainly marked targets for mobs who saw the Jew as the "Christ-killer." Made public pariahs, they seemed certain to be headed for expulsion or extermination. For the first time, stories were spread that Jews murdered Christian children and used their blood for the Passover ritual. (Pagans had accused the early Christians of the same crime of ritual murder.)

But the elimination of the Jews did not happen all at once. As long as their money could be drained into royal treasuries, they were tolerated. Once they lost that value, they were thrown out: from England in 1290, from France in 1306, from the German countries in the fourteenth and fifteenth centuries, from Spain in 1492.

The shock of expulsion from Spain was the greatest Jews had known since the destruction of the Second Temple. Many Jewish communities of Western Europe disappeared, their people driven to martyrdom, to forced conversion, to emigration. Only a small number of those who fled survived to reach their destination.

What of the Jews who were allowed to remain in Western Europe? After Spain expelled its Jews, the idea spread that Jews must live apart from Christians. Like all people who hold something in common, Jews tended to live near one another. But the choice had been theirs. Now they were compelled to live in a ghetto, behind walls and locked gates. The law forced the Jew to live there and nowhere else, while the Christian could live anywhere but in the ghetto.

Generation after generation—from 1500 to 1800—the Jews were labeled the instrument of Satan and subjected to degrading regulations. They were cut off from the mainstream and isolated. The rights and privileges they had known when they were a vital part of European development were taken away from them. Declared unwanted, they were made unnecessary. "It is impossible," says the Catholic historian Frederick M. Schweitzer, "to narrate medieval Jewish history as anything but a nightmare of horrors—injustice, massacre, expulsion, forcible conversion, contempt, hatred. In a word, it was a perpetual state of terror, one that was not alleviated but deepened with the passage of time."

By 1600 the ghettos had sunk into a squalid darkness. The infinite variety of Jewish life enjoyed in the days of freedom narrowed into rigid custom. Intellectual life could only stagnate in the ghetto. The world outside heaped contempt upon the Jew; it was inevitable that fear and suspicion of everything beyond the walls should color the ghetto Jew's attitude. Although Italy and Germany were the chief enforcers of ghetto existence, the ghetto attitude spread to Jews in other lands.

The birth of Protestantism in the sixteenth century only intensified the evil. Luther fueled the flames of bigotry when he called for the extermination of the Jews. And Catholicism, defending itself against the new Protestant heresies, charged that the Reformation was the product of Jewish influence. It seemed that both wings of Christianity measured religious zeal by how harshly the Jew was treated.

The Jews expelled from Western Europe went in many directions. The English, French, and German refugees headed for Prussia, Austria, Poland, and Lithuania. The Sephardic Jews scattered widely—to the Ottoman Empire (Turkey), to Palestine, to northern Italy, to Holland. And some to the New World, where they settled first in Brazil and the West Indies, and then in North America. Now the Diaspora was worldwide.

But the major migration was from west to east. By 1500 the center of the Jewish world had shifted east of the Rhine. The East European era in Jewish history had begun.

2

Order and Chaos

The Jews making new homes in Eastern Europe felt optimistic. First of all, they were welcomed. Poland and the other Slavic countries were beginning to stir economically. They were poor compared to Western Europe, but they were moving up. Their cities were growing. There was a need for Jewish hands and a need for Jewish enterprise. A Jew could earn his bread and eat it in peace. Such security after the hatred and terror suffered in the West drew a deep sigh from a sixteenth-century rabbi of Cracow. "If it could only stay this way until the Messiah's arrival!" he wrote.

The Polish Jews were largely artisans and tradesmen. They practiced many crafts and moved freely in the channels of commerce. As far back as 1264, one of Poland's rulers, Boleslav the Pious, had issued a charter protecting Jews from mistreatment and regulating their relations with the government and with Christians. The charter made it possible for Jewish communities to function under Talmudic law. Later, in 1344, Casimir the Great had expanded the royal safeguards for Jews.

With life, property, and freedom to worship protected, the Jews increased rapidly. By the seventeenth century there were hundreds of thousands in Poland and Lithuania. In many towns they were a majority of the population. Usually they lived in separate quarters, but these were not the walled-in ghettos of the West. They were chosen freely because the people wanted to enjoy the traditional Jewish communal life. Here they could be Jews at home and Jews outside their homes without fear or shame.

Under such favorable conditions the Jews developed a middle class. They were a useful bridge between the owners of the large estates and the peasants who worked the land. They served as agents for the nobles, operating their estates or taking charge of such sources of revenue as inns and taverns. In eastern Poland, particularly on the Ukrainian steppes, Jews herded livestock, planted and fished, and helped make spirits, potash, and flour. They took a major role in trade, distributing farm produce, bringing in textiles and luxuries from abroad, and selling Poland's furs and raw materials. They marketed merchandise throughout the villages and towns, and took part in the fairs vital to the country's commercial growth. As credit became more important to Poland's economic life, the Jews lent money to all classes from king to peasant. (Non-Jews too engaged in the same business.)

Lacking an official system for collecting taxes and tolls and managing state properties, the Polish government put this essential function in the hands of "tax farmers." These private individuals paid the government a fixed sum for a fixed period to carry on the profitable occupation. Jews and non-Jews, burghers and noblemen, took up the business. The Church opposed giving Jews such authority over Christians but couldn't prevent it.

The Jews were not Poland's only immigrants in this period. German Christians entered too, and in large numbers. Part of their baggage was hatred for the Jews and the conviction that these people had no rights any non-Jew was bound to respect. The German settlers competed with the Jews as merchants and artisans and, where they could, tried to limit Jewish influence. The Church backed such moves to restrict Jews who would not be converted to Christianity. It sought to pressure the government in this direction and to prejudice the peasants and the townfolk against their Jewish neighbors.

But because the kings and nobles felt they could not do without the Jews' economic services, the opposition did not get very far. True, the charge of ritual murder was often revived and there were some bloody outbreaks in the cities. But the villages where many Jews lived were quiet. The terror unleashed against the Jews of the West during the sixteenth century did not sweep over Poland. Now and then Jews were banished from one city or another. Still, under royal Polish protection, Jewish immigrants continued to arrive from Western Europe.

The refugees brought with them the patterns of communal life that had developed widely among medieval Jews. A governing body called the kahal headed the Jewish community. It maintained a synagogue and cemetery, a ritual bath, a hospital and home for the aged, and distributed charity funds to sustain the needy. Poland's rulers allowed the kahal to manage Jewish affairs. It collected the taxes for transmittal to the government. Since the richer paid the greater part, they came to exercise the greater power. Committees took care of economic, legal, and educational matters. The Jews had their own judicial system, appointed their own rabbinical judges, and enforced their own decisions. The great fairs which dominated Polish economic life provided the opportunity for the lay and religious leaders of Jewry to meet regularly. These meetings led to the formation of a Parliamentary Council of the Four Lands, which grew into a complex instrument for governing the affairs of all the Jews in the kingdom.

It was their community organization that helped the Jews to develop their economic strength. It protected Jewish commercial interests in two ways. It acted for all Jews in dealing with the world outside—the kings, nobles, and burghers—seeking to win from them privileges or agreements. At the same time, it tried to reduce competition among the Jews themselves and to maintain fair trading practices within Jewry and in dealings with non-Jews.

The expansion of commerce spurred the growth of handicrafts. In the early 1600s Jewish merchants saw the possibilities of trade in ready-made clothing. They sold craftsmen raw material on credit. The tailors made up the garments and sold them back to the merchants at a low price. (This was the putting-out system, an early stage in capitalism.) The use of credit enabled many Jews to enter the garment trade. The second most important industry for them was baked goods, but they spread into many other trades too, both light and heavy.

Soon the craftsmen were numerous enough to organize their own guilds, like those of the Christians. Their aim was to better their economic position by controlling competition. Cracow's seven Jewish master barbers (Sender, Shmerl and his brother, Hirsch, Hayyim, Moses, and Jehiel) formed a guild in 1639. Unlike the barbers of today, they also did a good deal of minor surgery. These passages from their guild laws indicate their concerns:

> 1. First, they are obligated to make a weekly collection for charity among their members, receiving as much as the generous instincts of each one prompts him to give.
> 2. No barber may keep in his shop more than one apprentice to teach the trade to. This apprentice must bind himself for three successive years. During the first two years the apprentice shall under no circumstances be permitted to bleed a patient; and even in the third year he shall not be allowed to let blood except when his master is at his side. This is in order that he may practice and accustom himself to the work properly, and not faint or become slipshod in his profession. . . .
> 5. The above mentioned barbers have also bound themselves not to raise prices and thus impose a burden upon the people of our community, but will accept the fee that people have been accustomed of old to pay for bloodletting, cupping, hair cutting, and the healing of bruises and wounds, so as not to give rise to any complaint against themselves on the part of the people of our community. On the other hand they will not cheapen or lower—God forbid—their fees by being too liberal, and forgoing that which is their just due by accepting less than one Groschen net from everyone for cupping. Whoever will transgress by treating the matter of fees lightly will always have to give to charity, as an unquestioned obligation, a half a gulden, not to mention other punishments, and both he and anyone he may send will be prevented from doing any more work. . . .
> 11. The seven barbers above mentioned have also agreed that there shall be brotherliness and friendship among themselves, and that during the three festivals they will have a good time, enjoy themselves to the full, and be glad and merry of heart. . . .

The scholarship of Polish Jews won recognition far beyond the borders of the country. Jews abroad sent their sons to study the Talmud in Polish yeshivas. The Talmud was not only a sacred religious work but a practical guide to everyday life. Its scholars held sway in the religious schools and also in the public assemblies and kahal councils. The increasing complexity of economic and social life provided students of the Talmud with new legal problems to test their creativity.

By a natural process, the language of the Jews of Poland became Yiddish. Jews everywhere had always spoken the language of their homeland—Arabic, French, Italian, Spanish, whatever it was. They also knew the languages of the Bible and their sacred writings—Hebrew and Aramaic. In medieval Germany the Jews had spoken a Middle High German, with a Hebrew admixture. They continued to use it when they migrated eastward, now mixing in Slavic words too. By the sixteenth century this Yiddish tongue had become the common speech of Jews throughout Eastern Europe. A popular literature in Yiddish flourished, with Cracow as its publishing center.

Compared with the agony they had known in the Western countries, life in Poland was calm for the Jews. They were now the largest Jewish community in Europe. The Roman Catholic clergy continued to harass them, but still they prospered. Then overnight, in the year 1648, everything changed. Civil war broke out in Poland. Greek Orthodox Cossacks from north of the Black Sea rose up in revolt. They were led by Bogdan Chmielnitsky, who united the Ukrainian peasants and the Tatars against the "heretical" Roman Catholic Poles and the "unbelieving" Jews. It was a war of extermination. The Cossacks had been badly treated by their Roman Catholic Polish lords. The Ukrainian peasants blamed the Jewish tax farmers for the heavy burden placed on them to satisfy the greedy demands of the Polish nobles. Economic grievances and religious hatred combined to bring the Jews catastrophe.

On June 10, 1648, the Cossacks moved on the town of Nemirov in Podolia. Here many Jews from the countryside had gathered for protection under the fortress walls. Nathan Hannover, a Polish rabbi, describes what he saw happen:

> When the Jews saw the troops from afar they were frightened, though as yet they did not know whether they were Polish or Cossack. Nevertheless the Jews went with their wives and infants, with their silver and gold, into the fortress and locked and barred its doors, ready to fight them. What did those scoundrels, the Cossacks, do? They made flags like the Poles, for there is no other way to distinguish between the Polish and the Cossack forces except through their banners. Now the people of the

town, although they knew of this trick, nevertheless called to the Jews in the fortress: "Open the gates. This is a Polish army which has come to save you from your enemies, should they appear."

The Jews who were standing on the walls, seeing that the banners were like the flags of the Polish forces and believing that the townspeople were telling them the truth, immediately opened the gates to them. No sooner had the gates been opened than the Cossacks entered with drawn swords, and the townsmen too, with swords, lances, and scythes, and some only with clubs, and they killed the Jews in huge numbers. They raped women and young girls; but some of the women and maidens jumped into the moat near the fortress in order that the Gentiles should not defile them and were drowned in the water. Many of the men who were able to swim also jumped into the water and swam, thinking they could save themselves from slaughter. The Russians swam after them in the water. Some of the enemy, too, kept on shooting with their guns into the moat, killing them till finally the water was red with the blood of the slain.

Rabbi Hannover's father died in the slaughter that year and he himself was murdered later. Six thousand Jews were killed in Nemirov. Those who escaped fled to Tulchin, only to be handed over to the Cossacks by Polish nobles who thought to buy their own safety with Jewish blood. After killing the Jews, the Cossacks killed the Poles.

The wars went on for ten years—Cossacks, Tatars, and then Muscovites and Swedes invading Poland and Lithuania one after another. The Muscovites too massacred Jews, or drove them to the Russian interior, where they were made to convert or sold into slavery. Poland was forced to give up most of the Ukraine to Russia. Hundreds of Jewish communities were wiped out. Hundreds of thousands—over one third of the total Jewish population—died by sword, famine, and pestilence. All Polish Jewry was impoverished. A tide of refugees swept westward, a tide that would persist under persecutions extending into the twentieth century. Jewish suffering in wave after wave of pogroms reached a peak unparalleled until the time of Hitler. "Now, at least," wrote one Jewish scholar, "every single Jew knew without any doubt that the Messiah was coming, for he had to come."

The "deluge" is the name given this period in the history of Poland. The uprisings and wars were ruinous. Anarchy and corruption ruled the country. And the worse things were for Poland, the worse they were for the Jews. Competition between Jew and non-Jew became the more intense, and persecution and pogrom the more frequent. The enormity of the national disaster made Jews feel hopeless about their prospects here on earth. As in the past, whenever the hardships of their lives as Jews deepened, they turned to mysticism and asceticism.

The study of *Cabala*—Jewish mysticism—became popular again. Jews took the troubles of the time as proof that the messianic era was near, for it had been foretold that the Messiah's coming would be preceded by war and pestilence. In 1648 Sabbatai Zevi, a magnetic young Jew of Smyrna, announced himself as the Messiah and declared the millennium would begin in 1666. The Jews of Europe, desperate for a miraculous deliverance from persecution, welcomed the news with frenzied joy. In that year, as he had promised his adherents, Sabbatai Zevi came to Constantinople to force the Sultan of Turkey, ruler of the Holy Land, from his throne and to lead the dispersed remnants of Israel back to Mount Zion to establish the Kingdom of God. But the sultan clapped him into a dungeon and offered him the choice of converting to Islam or losing his head.

Sabbatai Zevi turned Mohammedan. His apostasy was a betrayal, a shattering disillusionment for his followers. They sank into deeper despair. They had learned how to live as Jews in the Diaspora—the Talmudic texts taught them that—but was it enough? How long must they wait for deliverance? The messianic fervor indicated many could no longer resign themselves to accept this life. In the anarchy which had seized Poland, the moral strength of the community leaders and the rabbis was crippled. They were helpless in the face of such widespread disaster.

Just now, when their spirit was failing, a religious movement began which had a great and profound effect upon the Jews. Its founder was Israel ben Eliezer, known among his followers as the Besht (from the first letters of the three Hebrew words *Baal Shem Tov*, Master of the Good Name). He was born about 1700 in the province of Podolia, at the foot of the Carpathian Mountains. He started to preach his philosophy of faith among the common people, using their language and voicing their needs. He moved among the village Jews, proclaiming his mission of love and joy. "My teaching," he said, "is based on three kinds of love: love of God, love of the Torah, and love of man."

An ecstatic mystic, he saw the world as a wondrous emanation of God. God was everywhere, and his presence made the world full of beauty and melody and joy. Man was God's handiwork, and man should live not in tears and despair but with joy and hope and faith. No matter what his afflictions, man was meant by God to laugh, sing, and dance. This was the purest and highest form of prayer. One worshipped God not by prayer or ritual but by simple acts of loving kindness to one's fellow men. In loving man, the faithful demonstrate their love for God.

Love of God to the Baal Shem was higher than all forms of religious worship, even the study of the Torah. To the Talmudists it was shocking to hear the Baal Shem teach that doing good in life was more meritorious in God's eyes than living up to the strict letter of the 613 precepts of the Torah. But too much rationalism, said the Baal Shem, was a threat to true religion.

His optimistic movement, called Hasidism (the word means pietism), penetrated deep into the hearts of Jews throughout Eastern Europe. Its warmth and humanity were a dynamic countercurrent to the dry, formalistic Judaism that had prevailed since the 1500s.

Out of Hasidism came a new kind of leader, the zaddik (saintly man). He appeared at a time when the mass of Jews longed for a messianic figure, someone who could intervene with God on behalf of His children. Long ago Talmudic law had taken away the crown of priesthood and in its place put the crown of learning. The rabbi, after this change, functioned as the learned man who answered his people's questions.

But the zaddik or rebbe was more than a guide to his followers. He was like a priest who transmitted the people's petitions to God. The zaddik was the focal point of the Hasidic community. His province became the human concerns of the shtetl—work, business, conscription, poverty, sickness, worry, fear. He heard complaints, gave consolation, inspired hope, prescribed joyful love of God. Dynasties of zaddikim developed as leadership came to rest on hereditary authority. A visit to the zaddik at his court was considered to be of great importance. Followers were always close by, but they came especially on the holidays to observe his conduct, listen to his words, and sing and dance with their fellow Hasids.

Martin Buber saw their role this way:

> Through the zaddik all the senses of the Hasid are perfected, not through conscious directing, but through bodily nearness. The fact that the Hasid looks at the zaddik perfects his sense of sight; his listening to him, his sense of hearing. Not the teachings of the zaddik but his existence constitutes his effectiveness.

In that same generation another leader arose who saw the problems of the Jews from a different point of view. Elijah ben Rabbi Solomon, born in Vilna in 1720, was as devoted to his people and their faith as the Baal Shem. A child prodigy, he took the path of restoring vitality to the study of the law. The faith, hope, and joy of worship which Hasidism offered he took for granted. Rather than modify the traditional Judaic attitude toward study, he called for the fullest development of the Jewish mind as the way to find an answer to his people's needs. He refused rabbinic posts and gave all his time to study. Soon he was recognized as the unofficial spiritual leader of Eastern Europe's Jews, and became known as "the Gaon," a term old Babylonia had applied to the heads of the academies. The Gaon wanted prayer to be simplified. He was against useless show of mental agility. He urged concentration on the true meaning and usefulness of rabbinic wisdom. And as a rationalist he wanted to restore the harmony that for centuries had existed between Judaism and secular learning. He studied astronomy, physics, mathematics, philosophy, and music. He thought the mastery of secular knowledge could help enrich life and broaden the Jew's understanding, not only of Judaism, but of the world he lived in. "Every lack of knowledge in secular subjects," he said, "causes a hundredfold lack in the study of the Torah, for Torah and knowledge are joined together."

The Jews of Eastern Europe were torn between these two movements; between the Hasidim and their opponents, called the Misnagdim. The masses of southern Poland and the Ukraine formed the base of the Hasidic movement. Northern Poland, with its intellectual tradition, became the stronghold of the Gaon. When the Hasidim began to make inroads in the north, the rabbis met and excommunicated the entire sect, forcing it underground.

The bitterness of the conflict seemed to threaten all Jewry. Just then, the world outside intervened. The kingdom of Poland vanished, dismembered in three stages that lasted over a quarter of a century. After many generations of self-government within their own communities, the Polish Jews found themselves to be the new "Jewish problem" in three strange countries.

3

Doubly the Enemy, Doubly the Victim

The partitioning of the country speeded the process of change among Poland's million Jews. It did not happen overnight, of course, and it was another quarter century before the boundaries of the states they fell under became fixed.

The first partition began when the Russian troops of Catherine the Great moved into Poland during the Ukrainian uprisings of 1768. The Prussian ruler, Frederick II, fearing the invaders would grab all Poland, proposed the country be divided among the Austrians, the Russians, and himself. When the knife fell in 1772, Russia got the biggest slice—Polish Livonia and White Russia—and about 1.3 million of the inhabitants. Austria got a third of the partitioned land and about half the population. Prussia contented itself with the smallest piece, West Prussia.

A year later Russia forced another partition, this time dividing with Prussia about half of what remained of Poland. In 1795, after the failure of an insurrection for Polish freedom led by Kosciusko, Poland disappeared altogether, carved up once more. Now Russia had her first common frontiers with her fellow partitioners, Austria and Prussia.

After Napoleon won his victory over Prussia in 1806, he altered the map of Eastern Europe again. He carved the semi-independent Duchy of

Warsaw out of the portion that had belonged to Prussia since 1793. At the Congress of Vienna the map was redrawn once again. Most of the Duchy of Warsaw, the central part of Poland, became the so-called Kingdom of Poland, attached to Russia. In 1831, when another Polish uprising failed, it was converted into a province. Controlling three fourths of the old Poland, Russia harbored the greater part of Eastern Europe's Jews. All the provinces she had taken during the three partitions (among them the regions of Minsk, Volhynia, Podolia, and Lithuania, with Courland and Bialystok acquired later) were incorporated into Russia proper. From these parts the Jews spread into southern Russia, the Black Sea coast, Bessarabia, and the interior.

Russia's history had begun in the ninth century when Vikings rowed down the rivers from the Baltic to the Black Sea and founded the Principality of Kiev. Within a century, Christianity became the official state religion. It was a slave-trading society. In the twelfth century, colonizers who had cleared the wilderness and wiped out the natives established the Principality of Moscow. From the thirteenth to the fifteenth century, the invading Mongols ruled Russia. After they were driven out, the first independent Russian state was set up, with Moscow as the capital city, and the title of Czar or Caesar came into use for the Russian monarch. Peter the Great (1682–1725) dragged Russia into the Western world, transforming the country's culture, expanding her frontiers, and building the new capital, St. Petersburg, as his window to the West. Catherine the Great, in adding much of Poland to the empire, brought almost a million Jews into a country that had traditionally feared and hated outsiders ever since the Mongol invasion. It was not Jews alone who were distrusted—they were so few until her time—but Mohammedans, Roman Catholics, nonbelievers.

The Jews entered Russian life as the modern age began for the Jewish world of Europe. Although a few had slipped through the gates earlier, until the arrival of eighteenth-century rationalism, the bulk of the Jews remained prisoners of the ghetto. The ideas of the secular enlightenment, the promise of liberty, equality, and fraternity, were a brilliant attraction to Jewish youth. Outside the dark ghetto the world sparkled with philosophers and scientists, artists and musicians, universities and museums. What was a young Jew starved for culture to choose? Ghetto

Judaism or Christian enlightenment? But there was a third choice, a choice dramatized by Moses Mendelssohn.

Born in 1729 to a poor Torah scribe in the ghetto of Dessau, Germany, Mendelssohn made his way to Berlin at fourteen and studied philosophy, mathematics, and languages. While he prospered as a businessman, he earned a great reputation for his critical essays in philosophy. The lion of the intellectual salons, he became Europe's most celebrated Jew. His acceptance in Gentile society led young Jews to dedicate themselves to modern education in the hope they too would achieve a great place in Western culture.

In the same years that the Baal Shem Tov and the Gaon of Vilna were speaking to the needs of Eastern Europe's Jews, Moses Mendelssohn and his followers were seeking to liberate their people from the shackles of the ghetto and to revive the Jewish spirit. The movement was called the Haskalah, or Enlightenment. Jews must be prepared to meet the challenge of the modern world. Mendelssohn translated the Pentateuch into German to make it easier for his fellow Jews to study the Bible. The Haskala wanted the Torah to be taught alongside philosophy and science, and all of them to be used in the search for universal truths. It argued for separation of church and state. It believed religion was the individual's concern. The Jewish community ruled by Talmudic law was like a state within the state, Mendelssohn said, and he warned that modern nationalism would not tolerate that.

Soon after Mendelssohn's death (1786), the French Revolution exploded. Napoleon's armies breached the walls of Europe's ghettos. But inside those ghettos, Jewish communal life, with its own rabbinical laws, courts, and administration, was going on as before. Napoleon believed this to be a feudal remnant that had no place in the new political state. He forced the Jews to convoke an assembly—the first Sanhedrin since the destruction of Jerusalem. He instructed the rabbis to renounce the ghetto's Talmudic laws and pledge allegiance to the state and its laws. This the assembly did, leaning on the Talmudic injunction that the laws of the host state were the laws of the Jews, so long as no law violated freedom of religion. Thus Napoleon broke ghetto power and overnight made the Jews citizens, with all the rights and duties of the dominant majority.

It meant a great change for the Jews in the Diaspora. Now they were no longer a minority nation within each country but individual citizens of the state. The new democratic regimes said, in effect, there is no need for Jewish self-government when we guarantee the protection of our minorities. The Talmud, which had been the judicial bulwark of the Jewish communal governments in the Diaspora from Roman through feudal times, seemed endangered. And so too, as events proved, was Jewish identity, for emancipation demanded the renunciation of any Jewish identification but the religious. More and more young Jews deserted the ghetto to warm themselves in the bright sun of Western culture.

But it was different in Eastern Europe. Here, in Russian Poland and the neighboring lands, Jews lived under a benighted government and among backward peoples. Most of Russia's population was rural in 1800. Scarcely 4 percent of the people lived in towns. The upper class, the gentry, were only 1 percent. They included almost everyone with a secular education as well as plenty of ignoramuses. The clergy were another 1 percent. Then, in overlapping categories, there were the military, the merchants, the officials.

The status of the gentry and the peasantry was hereditary by law. The gentry and the clergy were privileged classes, for they were exempt from conscription, taxation, and corporal punishment. The landed gentry had the additional pleasure of levying all three of these upon the peasants on their own estates.

The czars cared nothing for ideals or the rights of man. Their feudal society might have been smashed and the country modernized if Napoleon's campaign against Russia had succeeded. But it failed and the old classes stayed in power. Only a few of them had been educated in Western Europe; the rest were far behind. The Jews had little to learn from the non-Jews. They could draw only upon their own cultural resources and their ancient tradition of learning. They did not feel lonely or isolated, for their number was far larger than in Mendelssohn's Germany. Since there was little to envy or emulate in the Russian world, they did not burn to be accepted as equals by the Christians.

The three states that had swallowed up Poland—Russia, Prussia, and Austria—contained among them nine-tenths of Europe's Jews. Their monarchs formed the Holy Alliance at the Congress of Vienna in 1815. With Napoleon's defeat, the Alliance set out to restore whatever the French Revolution had overthrown. They meant to stamp out radical ideas and put the throne and the Church in the place of freedom. Their ideal was a strong national state that would force the minority peoples under its rule to assimilate. As Christian monarchs, they would not tolerate non-Christians. Jews they considered both alien and anti-Christ, hence doubly their enemy, doubly their victim.

Russian policy toward the Jews was changeable and contradictory. Sometimes the government headed in two directions at once; at other times it suddenly reversed itself. Whatever the policy of the moment, it rested solely on force. Usually it met passive resistance from the Jews. The Russian officials charged with carrying out policy might ignore or reinterpret it, either because they were bribed or because they had their own notion of the right policy.

While the government berated the Jews for their separatism, it did its best to keep Jews out of Russian society unless they converted. In effect, the Russian way of "solving the Jewish problem" was to treat this people like the plague, a plague that must be quarantined. In the vast interior of Russia, there were few middle-class people to develop the country's vast resources. It would have been to the government's advantage to encourage the Jews to settle throughout Russia and put their energies to work serving its economic needs. But the merchants of Moscow wanted no competition from Jews. So orders went out barring Jews from living in the interior cities. Czar Alexander I decided to confine the Jews within an even smaller area. He mapped a Pale of Settlement that permitted Jews to live only in a prescribed region—parts of Lithuania, the old Polish provinces, White Russia, and the Ukraine. It was the ghetto again, but on an outsize scale. The rigid policy of segregation was designed to save the "Holy" Russian people from contamination by the Jews.

In all three states of the Holy Alliance the policies on the Jews were similar. Prussia and Austria, like Russia, set up pales of settlement to keep the Jews out of their interior. They treated the small number of rich or assimilated Jews one way (they were "useful") and the vast mass of the poor Jews quite another (they were "useless"). They forced Jews out of the villages and cut down their trade with the people. Sometimes they tried to switch Jews into different occupations, especially agriculture, but usually they made a mess of it. Jews have to be made more "useful," they would cry, by which they meant, made to pay more and higher taxes. As their states tended toward a degree of modernization, influenced by the spreading demand for democracy and freedom, the notion of graded emancipation was introduced. The rich Jews were allowed a taste of equality and the poor Jews none. By and large, Russia lagged behind the others when it came to any liberal practices.

The Pale of Settlement was only one part of the Jewish Statute of 1804. The statute was Russia's first comprehensive legislative program for the Jews. It was the product of many sources—high officials, the gentry, proposals sent in by Jews and non-Jews, a special committee, and the example of Prussian laws. It ended up a contradictory mishmash. It called for the expulsion of the Jews from the villages; allowed Jewish children to attend the general schools and Jews to open their own secular schools (with either Russian, Polish, or German as the required language); permitted Jews to buy or rent land for farming; gave Jewish merchants, artisans, and manufacturers permission to live temporarily in the interior, including Moscow and St. Petersburg. It also affirmed the Jews' traditional right to local self-government, with the *kehilla*'s jurisdiction limited to religious affairs.

One provision of the czar's statute obliged Jews to acquire surnames. Up to then the Jews of Eastern Europe had generally been known by their Hebrew names. (In ancient and medieval times, however, Jews had assumed the Greek, Roman, Arabic, Spanish, Gallic, or German names of the regions they lived in.) When there was more than one Jew in the locality with the same name, the name of the father was added. Thus, Aaron the son of Benjamin could be distinguished from Aaron the son of Gideon. When there were two Aarons and each had a father named Benjamin, the occupation of each was often used to make the distinction. Thus, Aaron the blacksmith was differentiated from Aaron the cobbler. Many Jews in Eastern Europe had nicknames tied to personal peculiarities, perhaps to help establish identity. Sometimes the street or town where a man lived, or the name of his wife or mother, was inserted to pin down his identity. Thus "Zalman, Leah's," meaning Zalman, the husband of Leah, might be the way this Zalman was known in a town where a number of men were named Zalman.

The Russian officials did not dictate how family names were to be chosen. "Each family selected the name it liked best," said Dr. Benjamin Lee Gordon in his autobiography. "When Dr. Solomon Mandelkern visited me . . . he told me that he well remembered the time when the ukase came forcing the adoption of a surname. It arrived on a holiday, and there were *mandlen* (almonds) on the table; hence his father's choice. The names Diamond, Gold, Silver, Stein, etc., were adopted by the Jews themselves. In Austria, however, the Jews had no right to select unapproved names. A list of such names was submitted to them, including some very offensive ones, such as Eselkopf, Rundskopf, Ochesenschwanz, Lumpe, Fresser, Schnapser, Grokerklotz, and Wantz."

In the next few years the government banned Jews from holding any leases on land, from selling liquor or keeping taverns, saloons, or inns. (The nobility had blamed the miserable state of the peasantry on the Jewish tavernkeepers.) At one blow a great number of Jews were deprived of their traditional means of livelihood. Expelling Jews from the villages was postponed a few times and, when finally ordered, proved impossible to carry out. So it was put off once again.

In 1818 the government said it was ready for a Jewish advisory body, to be elected by the Jewish communities. The advisers may have had advice to offer, but no one listened. Meanwhile, Jews were ordered not to hire non-Jewish domestics, and their dealings with the village landowners were further limited. Again the order to expel the Jews from the villages came down, was postponed, came down again, was postponed again. In 1823 the now classic drama of a ritual murder trial was staged, this time in the town of Velizh, and two years later the impotent Jewish advisory body was dissolved.

This marked the end of the reign of Alexander I. As the historian Ronald Hingley summed him up, he was a man who "mouthed highminded abstractions about equality and brotherly love, while contriving to sponsor the continued enslavement and repression" of his subjects. His reign was a busy time for legislative and administrative measures dealing with the Jew. What the Jew learned from it was that he could count on nothing. The government's actions were inconsistent and unpredictable. How could he know where it was safe to live? Or by what trade or profession he could earn his bread? The czar said yes today and no tomorrow. And the next czar?

4

Conscripts for the Czar's Army

The next czar was Nicholas I. Made a colonel in his cradle and a general at the age of twelve, he was interested in little but military matters. A notorious martinet, he never wore civilian dress. He inherited a corrupt and disorganized state desperately in need of reform. Educated Russians, most of them army officers, had organized a conspiratorial movement. It did not want simply a palace coup, replacing one despot with another. Rather it had the revolutionary goal of changing the system of government, putting a republic in its place, or at least a constitutional monarchy. The plotters struck in December 1825, when Alexander I died. Badly led, they were dispersed by artillery. Nicholas arrested three thousand Decembrists, as they were called, hung five of their leaders, and exiled hundreds to Siberia.

The answer Nicholas gave to the cry for reform was not more freedom but more discipline. That, and a new national anthem:

God save the Czar!
Mighty and powerful,
May he reign in glory over us,
Reign that our foes may quake.

O Orthodox Czar!
God save the Czar!

He clapped civil servants, professors, and students into distinctive uniforms, elaborated a system of censorship, and created a secret political police called the Third Section. A systematic campaign of thought control began. Nicholas trusted no one but himself. His rigid discipline crushed initiative and silenced criticism. Under the thirty-year rule of this "Iron Czar" (1825–1855) the governmental system could only continue to rot and crumble.

While still a Grand Duke, Nicholas had made a tour of Russia. He returned convinced that the Jews he had seen were nothing but "leeches." As czar, his first move against this "internal enemy" was typical—a military measure. Nicholas ordered military conscription for them in 1827, and at a rate double that of the Christian population. And why not double? Weren't they taxed doubly in other respects?

For Jews to be allowed into army service in other countries was considered a privilege (by the Jews, as well). But the term of service in the Russian Army was then twenty-five years. And Nicholas's motives for conscripting Jews were hardly democratic. He wanted to reduce the number of Jews by forcing them to change their religion. If the Jewish soldiers were Russified in their long service, he hoped those who survived would Russify other Jews when they returned home.

Military service normally began at the age of eighteen. Nicholas thought that was late to begin ridding the Jewish soldier of his "superstitions." He lowered the age for Jewish conscripts to twelve, thus imposing on the children an extra six years of preparation for army life.

During the years from twelve to eighteen, the children were farmed out to Russians in the remote interior, where ordinarily Jews were not allowed to set foot. There they worked the soil and were trained in the proper faith. Then at eighteen they began their twenty-five-year service.

Upon the Jewish kahal was imposed the burden of supplying the young conscripts. (No one volunteered, of course.) Each kahal appointed deputies to do the recruiting. As the season for recruitment approached, many of the children and young men marked for service disappeared. A Yiddish folk song recalls it:

Az aleksander pavlovitsh iz meylech gevorn,
Zenen yidishe hertser freylech gevorn, oyvey, oyvey!
Der ershter ukaz iz aropgekumen oyf yidishe zelner,
Zenen zich ale tselofn in di puste yelder, oyvey, oyvey!

When Nicholas I became king,
Jewish hearts became "gay," oh, woe!
The first decree for Jewish soldiers was issued,
Then all fled to the wild woods, oh, woe!

Into the forest or across the border they fled, hunted like animals. In
hiding they lived a nightmare, waiting for the whisper of an informer.
Since the physically unfit were rejected, another route of escape was self-
mutilation. Men amputated fingers and toes, deafened their ears, blinded
their eyes, rather than enter the hated service. Mary Antin, who came
from Polotzk, wrote of still another way out:

> It was always possible to bribe conscription officers. This was a
> dangerous practice—it was not the officers who suffered most in case the
> negotiations leaked out—but no respectable family would let a son be
> taken as a recruit till it had made every effort to save him. My grandfather
> nearly ruined himself to buy his sons out of service . . .
> If it were cowardice that made the Jews shrink from military service
> they would not inflict on themselves physical tortures greater than any
> that threatened them in the army, and which often left them maimed for
> life. If it were avarice—the fear of losing the gains from their busi-
> ness . . . they would not empty their pockets and sell their houses and
> sink into debt on the chance of successfully bribing the Czar's agents . . .

Resistance to the draft meant the Jewish community had trouble
meeting its quotas. The czar was ruthless: for every missing Jew he
ordered three others to be taken. Anyone who hid a runaway or helped
him escape was himself punished by military service, and his community made to pay a heavy fine. If the deputies failed to fill their quota,
they could be fined or inducted.

The czar's elaborate conscription law with its ninety-five clauses
gave many openings for corruption. Parents could save their own sons
by supplying a substitute who had to be a Jew. It meant a ready market
for kidnappers. Another clause let a town turn in as a recruit any Jew

caught away from home without a passport. Jewish gangsters roved the highways and invaded the inns, attacked lone Jews, tore up their papers, and delivered them for a price to the nearest recruiting station.

Many parents tried to keep the birth of their sons a secret. They did not register the newborn. Such unregistered boys were known as *malochim*—angels. They lived, but yet, because of the government's cruelty, they did not exist.

Luckless parents had to stand by and see their children herded off to the eastern provinces and Siberia. It was like mourning for the dead: they would be gone at least a quarter of a century, if not forever. The Hebrew writer I. L. Levin, who saw such a transport start on its long journey, described the scene:

> Near a house stood a large and high wagon, to which a pair of horses were harnessed. Soldiers brought out children from the house, one after another, and deposited them in the wagon. Soon it was packed to capacity. Children were sitting or lying on top of each other like herring in a barrel. Fathers, mothers, and relatives stood around. A person who has not seen the agonizing parting of parents from their little children and who has not heard their helpless lamentations that penetrate to heaven does not know real tragedy. One father gives his boy a little book of Psalms. Another hands his son phylacteries. From all sides are heard admonitions: "Remain a Jew; no matter what happens, hold fast to Jewishness!" Mothers wring their hands, the hopeless tears never stop, moans of agony and cries of despair resound. I was then nine. I kept looking at the sky. I felt that now, at any moment, God must perform a miracle. He must rain down pitch and tar upon the murderers. He must scatter them, so that the imprisoned children could return to their mothers. . . . But the sky remained calm, and the wagon began to move to the accompaniment of piercing cries and shouts.

The officers in charge were instructed to carry the children by wagon. But sometimes they pocketed the transport money and soon after leaving the village would drive the children on foot the rest of the way. The records show such journeys on foot to the remote regions could take a full year, the children slogging month after month through dust, mud, snow, ice, beaten with the knout, starving, sickening, dying. The Russian revolutionary Alexander Herzen, while serving a sentence in

exile, once came across such a group of Jewish children. He spoke to
their transport officer:

> "Whom are you escorting and to where?"
> "As you see—a horde of damned little Jews, eight to ten years of age.
> At first, they were supposed to be driven to Perm; then the order was
> changed. We're driving them to Kazan. I took charge of them for a
> hundred versts. The officer who handed them to me said, 'It's a misfor-
> tune—a third of them remained on the road (the officer pointed his finger
> downward). Not half will reach their destination. They die like flies!' "
> The children were lined up in proper formation. It was one of the most
> terrible sights I have ever witnessed. Poor, unfortunate children! The 12-
> and 13-year-old lads were still holding up, somehow. But the little ones, of
> eight and ten! . . . No brush could create such horror on canvas . . . Pale,
> exhausted, frightened, they stood in their clumsy army overcoats, eyeing
> pitifully and helplessly the soldiers who lined them up roughly. Their lips,
> their eyes, indicated how feverish they were. Gusts from the Arctic Sea
> blew in. Without care or help they were marching on—on toward their
> graves. . . .

Even children as young as eight were taken. If they weren't married,
they could be snatched off the street and sent into the army at any age.
Jews had to find a way out, and boys still at the age to be playing marbles
were married to little girls. Folk humor includes a story about a Jew who
saw such a child playing on the street and asked him why he wasn't at
school. The child answered, "I don't go to school any more. I was
married yesterday."

"If you got married yesterday and are now the head of a family, why
aren't you wearing long pants?"

"Yesterday I got married, so I wore the pants; today my little brother
is getting married, so he's wearing the pants."

What happened to the Jewish children who reached the distant
barracks? They were formed into battalions and their religious retrain-
ing begun. Every means was tried to induce them to convert. The local
priest worked on them, and when he failed, as he usually did, the
noncommissioned officers turned to force. A favorite method was to
make the child kneel on the barracks floor when bedtime came. If he
consented to be baptized, he was allowed to sleep in his bed. If not, he

was kept on his knees all night, until he collapsed. The stubborn ones were beaten or tortured. If they refused to eat pork, they suffered more beatings. They were fed on salted fish and then denied water unless they agreed to baptism. Most of the younger ones gave up and were baptized. The older children often endured the whippings, the hunger, the thirst, the sleeplessness, refusing to betray their faith. Some who would not yield were whipped to death, some were drowned.

"The Gentiles used to wonder at us," said Mary Antin, "because we cared so much about religious things—about food, and Sabbath, and teaching the children Hebrew. They were angry with us for our obstinacy, as they called it, and mocked us and ridiculed the most sacred things." When her cousin was taken as a soldier, his company was briefly stationed in Polotzk. "I saw my cousin drill on the square, carrying a gun, *on the Sabbath*. I felt unholy, as if I had sinned the sin in my own person. It was easy to understand why mothers of conscript sons fasted and wept and prayed and worried themselves to their graves."

Zalman Shazar, a writer who later became president of Israel, tells of the poet Yaakov Shalom Katzenelenbogen, called Yashak, who came from Shazar's home town of Steibtz. Two weeks after he was conscripted, Yashak fled from the army and, still in his uniform, came straight to the Shazar home:

> He had not given a thought to what might happen to him, but as soon as we learned that he had gone off without leave and that everyone, including the police, had seen him rushing through the streets of the town, we understood the grave danger to which he was exposing himself. The family had not even been able to discuss where best to hide him, when the police appeared; and the police, two Christian constables and their Jewish assistants, had not even crossed our threshold, when Yashak jumped through a window and ran out. He fled, and the police raced after him. Panic-stricken, the townspeople watched the young man they were so fond and proud of—this prodigy of traditional and modern learning . . . running for dear life down the streets, pursued by two corpulent armed policemen, who blew their whistles and shrieked: "Catch him! Catch him!" while after them, running and stumbling and ostensibly shouting, trailed the Jewish policeman with the shiny tin badge on his chest. The vague phrase, "running away from the army,"

had suddenly become terribly concrete for all us onlookers; it was like a deer fleeing from hunters in a forest.

Naturally no one of all the townspeople so much as lifted a finger to catch the fugitive; but they did nothing to help him either: fear of the authorities was simply too strong. They stood there petrified, staring at the ghastly spectacle. Only the Jewish policeman turned aside for a second and slipped into our house, whispering something to my sister and hastily returning to the chase. A few minutes later my sister handed me her little valise packed with some of her clothing and told me to carry it to the shed in her friend's yard. All this while Katzenelenbogen was still running like an arrow speeding through the air along the synagogue street straight to the market, with the policemen at his heels. In the market place he jumped onto the railing of my uncle's house and from the railing into the courtyard and from the courtyard into the garden, the policemen whistling and shouting after him all the time. And then in the garden he climbed on the fence, jumped up into a tree and then into another tree—and vanished.

Half an hour later Reuvele the waggoner drove his carriage in leisurely fashion through the town. His passengers were three girls: one was my sister; the second, her friend, the daughter of our wealthy man and granddaughter of Yashak's mother's new husband; and between them sat an elegant young lady, dressed like the daughter of a Polish nobleman—with a hat and parasol. Along the synagogue street, then across the Nieman River, the carriage travelled, heading toward the tar furnaces that belonged to our wealthy man.

From those tar furnaces young Katzenelenbogen made his way to the border, and from the border to Lvov, and from Lvov to London. We were never to see him again. . . .

An organization to rescue children forced into military service was created by Rabbi Menaham Mendel Schneersohn, head of the Habad dynasty of Hasids for nearly forty years. Where his underground railroad could not operate, he instituted a secret program to steel the children's resolve to remain faithful Jews.

The Jewish soldiers who survived knew little but humiliation and cruelty in service. As a rule they were not trained for combat but made to serve as orderlies or musicians. It was a lonely life, separated from family and community. Even if they adapted to this alien world, they could never win promotion to commissioned officer. A high proportion of those who completed their service ended it as invalids, and returned to civilian life still second-class citizens. In Western Europe, army service brought the Jewish soldier equal rights. Not in Russia.

Morris R. Cohen, who became a distinguished philosopher, wrote of his childhood in the town of Neshwies. He recalled the frequent visits to his home of the water carrier . . .

> . . . an old man who had been a soldier under Czar Nicholas. He had been taken away from home as a very young boy, kept in some sort of non-Jewish institution until he was 18 and then served 25 years in the Russian army, his regiment participating in the Crimean War. After his discharge he returned to Neshwies, married, and on his meager earnings as a water-carrier, brought up two adopted children of whom he frequently spoke. Whenever he came to the house to deliver water, he and my grandfather would exchange stories—often the same ones—but I listened with rapt attention to the discussion between the two old men in regard to former days—the incidents of the Crimean War, of the Polish uprisings of 1832 and 1836, of the Turkish War of 1878, and what happened to the Jews during these and other days. . . .

The burden of military service fell upon the poorer Jews. Merchants, shop superintendents, rabbis, graduates of Russian schools were spared duty, although they had to pay a thousand rubles if exempted. In one town the poor Jews smashed the windows of the rich because they saw the deputies were recruiting none of them.

When the czar's conscription plan turned the kahal into police dogs tracking down recruits, it created professional informers. These *moserim* became a plague. They threatened to inform against the kahal whenever it took steps to avoid or lighten the draft by such measures as false registration. They demanded bribes in return for silence.

A gang of these informers operated in Minsk. One of their victims was the father of Ephraim Lisitzky, who tells what happened:

> When it came time for my father to serve in the hated Russian army of the Czar, his widowed mother, whose sole support my father was at the time, hit on the idea of changing his elder brother's name, and entering him in the town's death records. This imaginary death earned my father the right, as the firstborn, to be exempted from military conscription.

Unluckily for him, however, my father passed from the frying pan of military service into the fire of the informers. Those scoundrels learned of my grandmother's ruse after a few years, and proceeded to make my father's life miserable. Under the threat of denouncing him to the authorities, they extorted money from my father. They visited our home from time to time. Loudly, banging their fists on the table, they would yell: "We're assessing you so much and so much. You deliver it by such and such a date or we turn you in!" Vainly my father and mother pleaded with them to have mercy; they had to hand the money over on the scheduled day—money they had saved by stinting on food or pawning their few possessions.

One day the informers dropped in on my mother when she was alone and told her they were holding my father at one of their hideouts, and they would hand him over to the police if she didn't pay up within an hour. My mother was pregnant at the time, in the seventh month. Her heart constricted with anxiety—where was she to get the money? At the moment she went into labor, knelt, and gave birth—to a live child, for once. But she was alone in the house, and fainted during the birth. When she regained consciousness, the infant was dead. My mother recovered physically from this ordeal, but she lost her mind. She pounded the wall all day with her fists, screaming to heaven, throwing dishes at the good women of the neighborhood who came to calm her. She rained blows on the head of my father as well as her own father, who had been summoned from his home in Slutzk. After a short while she came to herself, but the depression never left her until the day she died.

The blackmailers terrorized communities to the point where assassination became the victims' only means of self-defense. In the neighborhood of Ushitza in 1838 the court indicted eighty of the Jewish elders for murdering two informers. Twenty were sentenced to convict-labor gangs. A few fled before the trial, among them Rabbi Israel Rizhiner, who later founded the rabbinical dynasty in Sadgora, Bukovina.

Evasion of the draft caused such a shortage of Jewish recruits that the furious Nicholas I added new and harsher conscription laws in the early 1850s. He fined the entire Jewish community when they sheltered a fugitive. If a recruit was missing, almost anyone could be taken in his place—the family's father, a relative, or a kahal elder. The czar gave them a terrible choice: either turn kidnapper to replace the missing one, or yourself put on the hated gray uniform and serve as a penal soldier.

In that swamp of force and fraud created by the Russian government, the Jews became demoralized. It was risky to stay in your community and risky to leave. You could be drafted at home and kidnapped on the highway. Any friend might be an informer, any stranger a bandit. Jew was turned against Jew.

The Jewish sense of insecurity in a Gentile world was ancient. Under the terrible new pressures exerted by the czars, it was projected even beyond death. There is a traditional bit of Jewish humor about a young Jew facing conscription into the czar's army. A friend tells him to be cheerful:

> There's really nothing to be depressed about, if you consider the chances sensibly. You're being taken into the army! Well, one of two things will happen: either there's a war or there isn't. If there isn't, what have you to worry about? But even suppose there is a war, one of two things will happen: either you'll be sent to the front or you won't. If you're not, what is there to worry about? But even suppose you're sent to the front, one of two things will happen: either you'll be wounded or you won't. If you're not, what is there to worry about? But even suppose you're wounded, one of two things will happen: either you'll recover or you won't. If you recover, what is there to worry about? But even suppose you don't recover, one of two things will happen: either you'll be buried in Jewish earth or you won't. If you're buried in Jewish earth, what is there to worry about? But even suppose you're not buried in Jewish earth? Well then, well then . . . well then, brother, you're certainly in one hell of a fix.

5

The Useless Ones

So consuming was the hatred of Nicholas I for the Jews, one wonders that he found time for anything else. In his thirty-year reign he issued six hundred decrees against them. Not content with new ideas for persecution, such as his military-conscription plan, he dug up ancient anti-Jewish regulations and applied them mercilessly. The sweeping Jewish statute he announced in 1835 was largely a mass of medieval measures whose rusty edges his bureaucrats polished and sharpened. The Pale of Settlement was shrunk again, thus increasing the number of rural places Jews could not settle in. Synagogues could not be placed near churches. Jews could not use Hebrew or Yiddish in documents or commercial papers. They could not hire Christian domestics unless they segregated them from the Jewish help.

To the recruiting law, which was designed to "save" Jewish souls, Russia added a new means of "redeeming" Jewish spiritual life. The police began a censorship drive against Jewish books. The Jewish books printed in Russia—mostly religious—had been strictly supervised by censors who were apostate Jews. Now the government decided that such books coming in from abroad might be dangerous too. Jews were ordered to bring in to the police all books that had not been screened.

Thousands were being forwarded to St. Petersburg when the Czar decided it would be easier to burn all "harmful" books on the spot. The books that "trustworthy" rabbis had passed were sent to Vilna or Kiev for the stamp of approval or the touch of the match.

Looking abroad, government officials noted that the Prussians and the Austrians were trying other methods of eliminating the "religious fanaticism and isolation" of their Polish Jews. The czar's council pondered what was wrong at home. The Talmud, they concluded, was the root of the evil. It fostered disdain for the Gentiles and made the Jews look to their kahal for authority, rather than to the official government. Jews were educated by those fanatical *melamdim* who preached intolerance of others. And the traditional clothing worn by the Jews further separated them from the Christian community.

As to measures already tried within Russia, the council gave them poor marks. Conscription was having little effect on Jewish morals or manners. Expulsion from the villages had failed too. Jews were so martyr-minded they could endure the worst persecution. Something different was needed.

The council knew just what medicine to give this stubborn people. First, a cultural dose: set up special schools for its children and eliminate both the cheders and the *melamdim;* ban the wearing of the traditional garb; reform the rabbinate. Then take away Jewish autonomy by abolishing the kahal and reforming the special Jewish tax system. Finally, punish the "useless" Jews (the petty traders and the poor) by taking away the few rights they had and raising their recruitment quota.

Nicholas I was impressed. He told his ministers to launch the program.

To prepare the Jews for school reform, a propagandist was needed to sell them on the czar's good intentions. A German Jew, Max Lilienthal, who ran a Reform school for Jews in Riga, was summoned for the task. But how to convince parents that the government wanted to help their children when those same children were being forced by the thousands into the army? It stood to reason that to baptism in the barracks the czar meant to add baptism in the schools.

When Lilienthal finished his impossible mission to the Pale, he reported that the educational plan would be difficult but not hopeless. A few crown schools for Jews were opened with both Christian and Jewish teachers, supervised by the same mix on local boards. The government's secret intention of ultimately closing the cheders and forcing all the Jewish children into schools under Christian control soon leaked out. The Jews' response was passive resistance.

Meanwhile, the czar began cutting down Jewish communal authority. Self-administration was taken over by the police and the municipal councils—except for the functions of dragging recruits into the army and collecting taxes. These the czar left to the gutted kahal. Reform, Nicholas-style, only added to the harshness of Jewish life.

It is hard to understand how any sane official could have thought otherwise. In dealing with the miserable living standard of the Jews, Nicholas turned to police methods for a solution. It was like putting traffic cops in charge of economy. His police snatched Jews out of the villages, threw them into the cities, ordered them out of the borderland, herded them into the interior.

The senseless back-and-forth movement left some Jews still in the villages, but scarcely a tenth of the total Jewish population. They served the village gentry as grain merchants, tavernkeepers, brokers. But the masses of Jews were funneled into the cities, where they competed desperately with one another for work. Shopkeepers, artisans, and laborers—everyone but a handful of rich merchants—made poor livings, if any. A sensible program to establish masses of Jews as farmers would have helped considerably to improve Jewish economic life. But Nicholas I made only erratic gestures in that direction. About twenty thousand Jews settled on the land, too small a fraction to affect the lives of Russia's 2 million Jews.

In the last years of Nicholas I, Western Europe saw a second emancipation. In 1848 the people of France, Germany, Austria, Italy swept away the reaction that had dominated their countries for some three decades. And Jews joined the revolutionary movements that promised political freedom and civil equality to all.

But the absolutism that was overthrown in the west remained in iron control of Russia. The czar's spies were everywhere, nosing out the faintest whiff of reform. It was plain the autocracy would not tolerate a liberal constitution. It was satisfied with a police state.

In 1850, pushing its assimilation program, the government ordered Jews to stop wearing their traditional clothing. The men were also ordered to cut off their earlocks and the women to stop shaving their heads on the eve of marriage. It was a historical about-face. In the Middle Ages the Jews had been compelled to wear the traditional garb. Now they were compelled not to.

When many Jews refused to obey the edict, the police were unleashed. They inspected Jewish women to see if they had natural hair under their wigs, and they caught men on the streets, snipped off their earlocks, and shredded their long gaberdine coats. Resistance to these imperial orders was especially strong among Hasidic Jews, who fought fiercely to retain Jewish customs.

As the reign of Nicholas I neared its end, another ritual murder trial was staged, this time because of the death of two Russian boys in Saratov. The investigation dragged on for years, resulting in a finding of insufficient evidence against the indicted Jews.

In Austria the 1848 revolution placed Jews on a political seesaw. Their freedoms rose and fell with the fortunes of liberalism. But with the 1867 constitution they won civic equality and political representation. Jews flocked into the state schools and the universities, entering law and medicine in large numbers. With the ending of censorship, the Jewish press flourished. Out of Vienna and Lemberg poured many journals devoted to business, politics, scholarship, and the arts. By 1870 Austria's Jewish population exceeded 600,000.

For Russia, hope of freedom dawned when Nicholas I died in 1855. In St. Petersburg, wrote Peter Kropotkin, "men of the educated classes, as they communicated to one another the news, embraced in the streets." For Russia's Jews it was good news too. Their Haman had died at last. They had no reason to expect much from his son, Alexander II. The training of the heir to the throne did little to encourage originality or independence of thought. As a young officer of the Guards, however, Alexander had disappointed his father by taking scant interest in military affairs. This, together with a kindly disposition, made his father feel that Alexander lacked the qualities essential for a czar.

When Nicholas I died, Russia was in the midst of the Crimean War, the product of his territorial ambitions in southeastern Europe. Alexander's first year on the throne was given to carrying on the war until the fall of Sevastopol, when he negotiated a peace. His father had sacrificed all human concerns to make Russia an invincible military autocracy. But the Crimean fiasco showed how badly led and badly organized the Russian

Army was. It was beaten on its home territory by invading French and British forces that were themselves stupidly generaled.

Enlightened public opinion insisted that social reforms were needed to wipe out the humiliation of defeat and to restore Russia's prestige. The educated classes were eager to help with the work of reform. The new czar, while giving up none of his autocratic power, moved gradually toward reform.

In 1861 he freed about 30 million serfs. He acted against strong opposition from serf owners, who feared losing property without compensation. A long debate took place over the questions of how much land the peasants should get, what land, and how it should be paid for. Conditions differed widely among the 50 million peasant slaves; nearly half belonged to the state, not to private owners. In the end the freed serfs got about the same amount of land they had formerly cultivated for their own maintenance. The landlords were paid by the state, which then exacted payments from the peasants on an installment plan stretching over forty-nine years.

Alexander also modified censorship, liberalized educational policy, and encouraged education for all classes. For a while he even restored autonomy to the universities. Russia was decades behind Western Europe in the great technological changes of the industrial revolution. Alexander encouraged the development of Russia's natural resources and the building of a great railway network to tie his vast regions together. He reorganized the army and navy, set up a new judicial system on the French model, introduced a new penal code and a simplified method of civil and criminal procedure. He granted local self-government with elective assemblies to the rural districts and the larger towns.

When the czar emancipated the serfs, it was reasonable to expect he would free the semi-enslaved 2.5 million Jews. But the Jewish question was not met head-on. It was dealt with in bits and pieces, and again with contradictory policies. Instead of the club, the czar tried the carrot. He continued military conscription of the Jews, but with several modifications. The drafting of children was stopped. But the evil done for decades was not atoned for. The Jewish child-soldiers who had converted were not sent home. They were placed instead in the care of Christians.

Recruitment of Jews would be equalized with that of the general population, the government said. But the heaviest burden was still placed on the "nomadic and unproductive" Jews—that is, the "useless" ones so labeled under the old categories. The changed regulations were less conducive to the practice of kidnapping or of drafting "penalized" Jews.

The Jews took advantage at once of the new educational openings. If they had higher education they could now live outside the Pale, enter certain professions, and hold office. Jewish children went to the state schools in greater and greater numbers. By 1872 they were 15 percent of all students in the Pale. Many went on to the universities, chiefly to study law or medicine. It was thrilling to find themselves free of the old bonds. A Jewish lawyer, V. O. Harkavy, told how he and his friend felt when they were enrolled at Moscow University in 1864:

> When we came out of the old university building, we crossed to the other side of the street and, respectfully doffing our hats, bowed before the sanctuary that had opened its doors to us and we embraced each other. Proudly we walked home, eager to shout to everyone we met: Have you heard? We are students. All at once it was as though the alienation from the Christians around us had gone. We felt like members of a new society. . . .

Alexander's goal was clear: to merge the Jews with the Russian people, "insofar as the moral condition of the Jews will permit," as he put it. He was following the same path as his father, but using different tactics. Nicholas had segregated the "useless" Jews, piling penalties upon them for a mode of life he, not they, was responsible for. At the same time he made no concessions to the "useful" Jews. Alexander maintained the same categories, only, instead of punishing the "useless," he dangled promises before those who would be obediently "useful."

The Jews who had already prospered were delighted to be promised some privileges. A group of wealthy St. Petersburg merchants pointed out to the czar that equal rights given to Jews in the West had hastened their assimilation. Logically they should have asked him to grant full equality to all Russia's Jews. Instead, they suggested that if certain rights and privileges were granted to "the best among us"—meaning themselves, of course—it would help carry out the government's goal. Thus, they accepted the czar's separation of their own people into those who deserved to live like humans and those who didn't.

On that principle the government marked three grades of Jews as "useful"—the top class of businessmen, the university graduates, and the artisans. Their wealth, education, and skill could help develop commerce and industry, as well as the military machine. Under Alexander II Russia had extended its domain to the Pacific. It was now a vast colonial empire, covering about a sixth of the earth's land surface. The Jewish businessmen were allowed to move out of the Pale and into the interior cities. Their families and a few artisans and domestics could accompany them. (The privilege of leaving the ghetto cost them a heavy tax for many years.)

Jewish university graduates could apply for permission to live outside the Pale and to hold government posts. Later, in 1879, this privilege was extended to Jewish pharmacists, dentists, male nurses, and midwives. The government debated for almost ten years what to do about the Jewish artisans. Finally, Alexander decreed that artisans, mechanics, distillers, and artisans' apprentices could settle throughout the empire. But so many restrictions and qualifications were added that this opened only the smallest hole in the great ghetto wall. Few artisans managed to get out. It was rather the traders, disguised as artisans, who slipped through into the interior, where competition was less fierce. To stay out of jail they bribed the police. When caught, they were exiled.

Casting about for other ways to Russify the Jews, Alexander II revived the idea of abolishing the centuries-old institution of the cheder and the *melamed*. In 1855 it was decreed that within twenty years all teachers or rabbis must be graduates of a government-run rabbinical seminary or institution of higher learning. But the cheders and the *melamdim* went on in their accustomed way, resisting every attempt to change them. In 1873 the government gave up the idea of closing the cheder. Instead, it closed the two seminaries and the hundred state schools that were supposed to remake all Jews into Russians.

It was but another example of the puzzling maze of regulations covering the Jews. Visitors to nineteenth-century Russia could rarely understand them. "This, however, is not surprising," wrote Francis Palmer, an Englishman who managed large estates in Russia. The regulations, he said, "can hardly be understood in Russia itself, in consequence of the system by which new regulations and edicts are frequently issued by the Government without revoking others—sometimes of quite a contradictory nature—already in force. The result is that the new edict is often found to be altogether unworkable, but instead of being recalled, it is allowed to remain while yet another is added. The consequence of this is that the local administrations, while carrying out the intentions of the Government in their general principles, do not really execute the actual letter of the law."

6

I Was, with God's Help, a Poor Man

Like millions of other Eastern European Jews, Selman Waksman was raised in a shtetl. The shtetls—the word means small town—were essentially marketplaces, the regional centers for trading goods and services. They were country towns made up of innkeepers and distillers, peddlers and artisans, shopkeepers and wholesalers. Not to mention the *luftmenschen,* the people "living on air"—beggars, hangers-on, dreamers. The shtetl's population might be largely Jewish, wholly Jewish, or mixed, with a strong Jewish minority.

Selman Waksman was born in Novaia-Priluka, a town in the Russian Ukraine. It had been the birthplace of his mother and of her mother too. Selman, who grew up to become a microbiologist and a Nobel prize winner, never forgot what Novaia-Priluka was like:

> It was a bleak town, a mere dot on the boundless steppes. It was flat and surrounded by wide, forestless acres. In summer, the fields of wheat, rye, barley, and oats formed an endless sea. In winter, snow covered the ground, and the frosted rivers carried the eye to the boundless horizon, where the skies met the earth somewhere far away. Only the slow-flowing rivers and brooks, with occasional groves of oak and chestnut, broke this continuity of land and sky. The earth was black. . . .

It was a small town. Very few of its inhabitants obtained from life more than a bleak existence, and even that required hard, continuous struggle. In spite of the abundant crops and the well-fed herds of cattle and sheep, of swine and horses, and the hard-working people, life was materially poor, since the resources went to fill the coffers of the landlords, the Czar and his retinue, and the police. . . .

Many of the houses in town were attached to one another, in rows of fifteen or twenty. . . . Most of the houses consisted of a large living room with a lime-washed earthen floor, a small bedroom, and usually a small kitchen, the major part of which was occupied by a thick-walled clay stove. This stove served many important functions: for baking the weekly supply of bread, for preparing the daily meals, for heating the house, and occasionally offering extra sleeping quarters for guests or members of the family. Its broad, flat, clay-coated surface could often be offered, especially in winter, as a welcome resting place to the visitor or to the youngsters of the family. Occasionally, the house had a cellar or garret, both serving to enlarge the living quarters of the household or to provide extra storage space for casks of pickled vegetables, fruits and homemade beverages.

Here and there on the outskirts of the town was a house somewhat more impressive than the others. A tin-covered roof, a slightly larger structure containing more than the usual three rooms, a wooden fence, and often an adjoining small garden were the meager niceties that indicated the wealthier inhabitants. . . .

Several parallel rows of whitewashed, straw-thatched adobe houses surrounded a large open square, with a well at one corner. Here, on religious festivals or on market days, the peasants from various villages would come to trade, to sell their agricultural produce, and to buy manufactured goods. They also came to meet friends and to make merry. Returning to their villages in their creaky, ungreased, horse- or ox-drawn wagons in summer, and in their smooth-running sleighs in winter, they left the square full of garbage and refuse. Then for several days, peasant women cleaned up the debris with their longhandled brooms made of reeds and rushes growing close to the local brook, and again the square was bare.

There was always such a market square in the towns of the Pale. Michael Charnofsky pictures his Warshilovka:

The center of the town had one square block of stores built of brick, about ten stores on each side. The four corners had the biggest stores and the others were smaller sizes for shoemakers, for capmakers or tailors, or novelties and other small businesses. But the corner stores were the big businesses. One was a big hardware store, the second a big grocery, the third sold yard goods, and the fourth farm implements.

Every other Sunday was *yarid* (market) day at Warshilovka. Hundreds of peasants would come from the surrounding villages and farms to trade:

> They would first go to church, and that part would be jammed with people. The main attraction was the numerous beggars. Two lines formed. Between the lines walking to the gate the beggars would sing religious songs and the people would give them money. . . . On the yarid day the streets would all be filled with different articles and livestock. On one street there would be wagons all laden with oats, hay, wheat, corn and buckwheat; another street (called *Lebediga-Gasse,* the Life Street) would be all cows, sheep, goats, pigs, and horses. The other streets had amusements in tents. The main business was done around the stores.

The great majority of Russia's Jews lived in such towns, scattered in the thousands over the Pale of Settlement. Of the 7 million Jews in Eastern Europe toward the end of the nineteenth century, about 5 million lived under the czar. The rest were next door in Rumania, Hungary, and Austro-Hungarian Galicia.

The Pale of Settlement, which ran about a thousand miles in length and three hundred miles across, corresponded roughly to what are now the Soviet republics of Lithuania, Byelorussia, the Ukraine, and the eastern part of today's Poland.

While the Jews were only about 5 percent of Russia's population, they made up perhaps a fourth of the people who lived in the towns. In contrast with the Jews, only a small portion of the other people of Russia lived in or near enough to towns to be affected by urban life. Francis Palmer observed that about four out of every five Russians lived in regions "that modern life and thought as yet hardly touched to any appreciable extent."

The towns were islands in a sea of poor, illiterate peasants. But were the people in the towns any better off? Take the town in White Russia that Morris R. Cohen had lived in as a boy in the 1880s:

Anyone accustomed to the American standard of living who might have come to Neshwies in those days and walked through its unpaved and unlighted streets, looked into its small, unventilated and often over-crowded wooden houses, devoid of all plumbing or the simplest precautions against contagious diseases of an epidemic character, would have pronounced the town unbelievably poor, dirty, criminally ignorant as to hygiene and altogether lifeless. Indeed, he would have wondered how its six to eight thousand inhabitants managed to live at all. . . .

About the dirt and material poverty of the town there could be no doubt. It was miles from the nearest railway station. There were no factories or large industries to sustain its economy. So far as anyone could tell, the town lived on trade with the peasants who brought to its markets their wood, potatoes and grain and took back salt, nails, kerosene, and sometimes linen goods, shoes and other "luxuries," besides a little money to help pay their taxes. The stationing of a cavalry regiment must have added to the commerce of the town, though the military supplies came in wagons from the outside world, and the officers and soldiers did not seem to have very much money to spend.

A very serious handicap was the meager water supply from the few wells. There was a pond at the outskirts of the town. But as the stables of the cavalry regiment bordered on it, people did well not to drink its water, except after boiling. They supplemented the amount they bought from water-carriers by gathering in the rain in simple, primitive ways. Thus, every time it rained, pots and pails were put out to catch the water that came over the massive buttresses of the military barracks.

This lack of water made people helpless against the frequent fires which in the summer would sweep away many houses—none of them insured. I remember that every time the weekly portion of the Pentateuch began with Numbers, chapter 9, "Thou shalt kindle," we expected a fire. In one of these, the young son of a former neighbor of ours and his blind grandfather whom he was leading through a street were caught and burnt to death. When such fires broke out we used to pack up our belongings in a few bundles, carry them to a nearby field, and wait between hope and fear. . . .

A town "renowned for its poverty" was Slutzk, in the province of Minsk. "My grandparents spent their whole life fending off poverty," wrote Ephraim E. Lisitzky, "but poverty refused to desert its old friends. This house of theirs, with its clay floor, mildewy and spider-webbed walls, its sooty ceilings, dripping filth whenever the oven was lit—where could poverty find a finer residence?"

Poverty—the word is repeated again and again in the memoirs of shtetl dwellers. Samuel Schwartz, who came from Nagyzöllös in Austria-Hungary, puts it this way:

> When I say poverty I mean a situation such as is hardly thinkable in our land of plenty [America]. It was nothing unusual to have been occasionally without bread in the house. To obtain it, we either had to borrow a slice from a neighbor or buy a loaf on credit. It often happened that there was not a match in the house to kindle a stove or light the petroleum lamp, if there was wood in the stove or kerosene in the lamp. . . .
>
> Most of the time our home consisted of one or one-and-a-half rooms and kitchen. The latter was shared most of the time with another tenant. If you ask how we managed—well, we just managed; even if I told you, you would not understand. . . . Our food was sparse and simple. . . . We often did not have enough wooden spoons with which to consume it when we were all together. Our bread was made of coarse corn meal, not the fancy corn bread we know here as a delicacy, but a huge coarse loaf. . . . A piece of white bread was a rare treat. Potatoes, beans and other vegetables furnished the diet. Milk was a rarity, as were eggs. Meat was only for *Shabbos*. . . .

Israel Wolwolff, who lived in Mitterkiefke, recalls that even with everyone in the family working—father, mother, children—all they could manage for food was bread and vegetable soup, "and for Friday—the big day—a soup made of meat and bones, which father would bring home especially for the Sabbath meal." The *kugel* and *challah* his mother prepared especially for the Sabbath were foods they did not taste all week long.

The most common diet was potatoes and herring. Sometimes not even herring was possible, and poor Jews lived on bread and potatoes. "My parents didn't actually starve," said one Jew, "but were always on the brim of starvation."

There were plenty of Jews who did starve. The Englishman Sir Moses Montefiore, touring Russia in 1846, wrote in his diary that he had never seen such poverty as among these Jews. At Willcomin, near

Vilna, he said he learned that in the previous year one Jew out of four had died of hunger. Tevye, the dairyman created by Sholem Aleichem, says, "I was, with God's help, a poor man." In the shtetl the Jews "may not take their poverty to heart," said Maurice Samuel, "but they are aware of it; it fills the house, it is the continuous undertone in their lives, it lurks in all the conversations of the grown-ups. It is a presence and a personality—*dallus,* poverty—referred to with a sort of affection, born of long familiarity. . . ."

The homes of the peasants, who lived close by the Jews in the small shtetls or on the outskirts of the larger ones, often looked better. In *Life Is with People,* the classic study of the Jewish small towns of Eastern Europe, Mark Zborowski and Elizabeth Herzog offer this explanation:

> The poorest peasant spends his spare time puttering about his home, repairing the door, the fence, the whitewashed walls. The impoverished city dweller accepts the condition of his home as part of the state of things, beyond his jurisdiction.
>
> The general appearance of neglect declares in addition the fact that the house is viewed as a temporary shell. "My shtetl" is the people who live in it, not the place or the buildings or the street. "My home" is the family and family activities, not the walls or the yard or the broken-down fence. A shtetl family that has lived in the same house for generations would detest and resist the idea of moving away. Yet, essentially, the house remains a temporary dwelling, inhabited for a brief moment of history. It is not part of the family entity, to be cherished and tended. Doctrine teaches that only the mind and the spirit endure—"life is a hallway to heaven"—and even the least soulful Jews of the shtetl, through force of circumstances if not of conviction, treat their physical dwelling places in accordance with this teaching.
>
> A long history of exile and eviction strengthens the tendency to regard the dwelling place as a husk. True, it is not unheard of or even uncommon for a shtetl family to inhabit the same house for a hundred years. Yet at any moment the fatal decree may strike and they may be tossed from the homestead into the deep dust of the road. Daily activities are pursued as if today's condition would continue forever; but the setting in which they are placed is slighted as if it would be snatched away tomorrow.

The economic life of town and countryside in the Pale were closely interwoven. "But not so the cultural life," says Selman Waksman.

The inhabitants, the Jews and the Ukrainian peasants, were two distinct peoples, different in racial origins, in historical background, in religion, in habits and customs, in communal life, and even in their very languages. Though they formed an interdependent economic system which dominated the region as a whole, spiritually the two peoples might have lived in different worlds.

The Jews in the shtetl were an island culture. They lived as a minority within the culture of the majority. That majority conditioned the life of the minority. Whatever happened to it was bound to have an impact upon the Jews' life. The two groups recognized different values, followed different customs, were often subject to different laws. In a political climate controlled by the czar's innumerable edicts, the people of the shtetl could expect nothing but bad weather.

Living for the most part as a majority in the shtetls, the Jews went on with their own traditional life. They paid little attention to the changing politics of Eastern Europe. What they knew about the non-Jewish world they learned in the course of making a living.

7

Making a Living in the Shtetl

How did the Jews of the shtetl make a living?

Take Warshilovka, a small town near the city of Vinittsa in the Ukraine. The district was called the breadbasket of Russia; its orchards grew the best fruits; yet poverty was widespread. Warshilovka had only three streets, two hundred Jewish families, and two dozen Gentile families. The town's only industry was a mill where rope was spun out of flax, then made into horse harnesses. The harnesses were shipped to the big cities of the Ukraine.

From Michael Charnofsky, who was brought up in Warshilovka, comes these vignettes of people struggling to make a living there:

Chaim Laiser was six feet two inches tall; he was thin, with no flesh on his body. His cheekbones stuck out like two horns, a long nose was between them, and his two eyes were sunken, leaving two big holes in the face. Bones, bones all over, pinched with hunger. His wife Sonia was short, only five feet five inches; she was thin and lightweight, but on the go all the time—cleaning, preparing, watching over her family. Moishe, the eldest son, and Berke, the second son, were just like the father. Even though they were yet very young their arms and feet were just like sticks, and their bodies—you could count every bone, and you wondered when they would break in half. The two daughters were not so bad. Their faces were filled out and on their bodies was some flesh.

Chaim Laiser was in the *sichke* business. He had a machine that cut straw into small, half-inch pieces. He would fill up big sacks and sell them to people to mix with the oats to feed their cows, goats and horses. The machine was located in the center of the barn, with a long arm to harness the horse to. The horse would walk in a circle around the machine and turn the knives that cut the straw. In one day he cut enough sichke to supply all his customers who couldn't afford pure oats and had to fool their cows, goats and horses by mixing oats with sichke. With what he made out of his business he was able to buy one pood of flour, to bake bread for the family for the week.

Because Laiser had no pasture for his horse and couldn't afford to feed him all week for the one day's work, he arranged with Noah the water carrier to let him use the horse the other days of the week in return for feeding it. At harvest time Laiser helped peasants in return for potatoes, onions, eggs, and a chicken for the Sabbath. In the winter Charnofsky's father gave Laiser a few weeks' work. With his pay Laiser bought kindling wood, without which his family would have frozen to death.

At Passover time the village women brought him the dough they had rolled because he had a big oven. He baked it into matzos for them, getting enough money to make matzos for his own family.

When the orchards ripened, Laiser worked from early morning until nightfall, picking fruit for half a ruble a day. In two months he went from cherries to plums, pears, and apples. That was his "prosperous" season. When fall came, he chopped wood for the townfolk. Charnofsky would hear him say, *"A sach milluches and wainig bruches."* ("Many trades but not much luck.")

Women worked just as hard in Warshilovka. Zelda Baron was a widow left with eight children, the oldest only twelve and the youngest three. She had to make a living for them all. She got up before daybreak and by the kerosene lamplight woke each child in turn, washed it, dressed it, and served them all breakfast. She had a cow of her own; it gave her milk and she thanked God for it every time she fed the children.

When the sun was up and the people came out to do business, she tended to her own. She had a basement rented from a store on the square and she kept fruit there, bringing it out to a stand on the street each morning. Her two oldest boys helped her.

When yarid came—it was twice a month, on the second and fourth Sundays—the streets were jammed, and there was competition from the peasants who brought their own fruit to sell. Zelda sat all eight of her children behind her fruit stand and appealed to the crowds to buy her fruit. "I must support my eight children; my husband is dead. Buying my fruit will help me. The children must eat." She repeated it all day long, and it worked. She bought food with what she earned and twice a week baked bread and cooked the potatoes and beans needed for the next few days. For the Sabbath she prepared a big lung and liver the butcher would save for her because he knew she couldn't afford choicer meat. Her children didn't starve but they were always hungry.

Moisha Zadels made his living as the town usurer, lending money to Jew or Gentile. He made loans only on articles the borrower brought him: copper or brass utensils, clothing, watches, rings, pillows, featherbeds, quilts, blankets, whatever. He set the price for each article and there was no arguing with him. "If he loaned ten rubles he would take two rubles off for the interest and give you only eight rubles to pay back in ten months, one ruble a month. On the last payment he would return the article."

Most of the town's Jews and many of the peasants were in hock to him. He was strict: fail to pay and you were hit with double interest. If you still didn't come up with the money, you lost your article. About twice a year he would load his wagon with such articles and sell them in Vinittsa.

Moisha was miserly: he never gave to charity and but little to the synagogue. No one liked him, everyone avoided him. In the synagogue no one would sit next to him. He was never called to the Torah, never given an honor. He didn't seem to care.

He got his reward when his house burned down one cold winter night. He lost all his own cash and property, and the fire consumed all the articles people had pawned. The borrowers stopped paying because he had nothing to return to them. Moisha and his family became one of the many poor families of Warshilovka.

There were water carriers in every town. Ephraim Lisitzky remembered seeing his father at the trade.

From early morning till late at night he shuffled along the streets and alleys of Minsk, loaded down with his yoke and two pails, going from house to house, carrying water for a paltry fee. In the summer he would come home late at night, blistered from the sun and soaking with sweat; in the fall he would be drenched from head to foot; and in the winter he would appear at the table frozen, rime-bearded, and coated with ice. He would sit down, miserably fatigued, and groan through supper. He would fall asleep over the grace after meals, his head slumping on the table, the last word of the grace crumbling from his lips.

My father had been a yeshiva student in his youth. Necessity had forced him to become a water-carrier, but he had never become reconciled to his lot . . . Sometimes, on the way to or from cheder, I would see my father coming toward me, the yoke across his shoulders. His face would redden with humiliation, and he would turn into the nearest courtyard. . . .

Uncle Reuben, another of Lisitzky's family, was an itinerant tailor.

He walked from village to village sewing shortcoats, trousers, and other clothing for peasant families. Every Sunday he would put a small, hand-operated sewing machine on one shoulder, and a bag on the other shoulder with the rest of his sewing implements, bread for the week and, of course, prayer shawl, phylacteries, and prayer book. Thus loaded, he would set out on his rounds of the farms.

When he had a job to do for a peasant, he would settle down in the farmhouse, eating the bread he had brought along from home together with the potatoes the peasant wife baked in the hearth. He would share the peasant's bed of boards, which served for the whole family. The peasants were fond of Uncle Reuben. He never cheated them, his prices were reasonable, and he never kept for himself the leftovers from the material they supplied him with. And during his visit he regaled them with news of the great world and edifying stories from the holy books. He was treated as an honored guest. When Uncle Reuben was ready to leave, the peasants would give him bunches of onions and garlic, bags of beans and peas and millet and spilt, and similar country gifts. For his part, Uncle Reuben liked the peasants, too. He spent most of his time in their households, and felt like one of the family.

The mother of Israel Wolwolff was one of the countless women in the Pale who labored endlessly to help support the family. His father sold glass and sieves, and with horse and wagon would travel from village to village, returning Friday afternoon for the Sabbath after having earned $1.50 or $2.00 during the week. Israel recalls how one day . . .

> . . . a wagon arrived with a sack of flour weighing 200 pounds. This proved the beginning of the *knish*-baking business for mother. She started immediately to bake knishes to be sold—in that way hoping to contribute to the family larder. At this time of my life I was attending public school, and after school hours I used to help my mother, who had a stand where she sold her knishes. I would come to relieve her so that she could go home and make more of her wares. Towards evening, when the day's business was over, and all my knishes were sold, I would go home also. In the evening my mother would knead the flour and prepare the dough for the next morning. At dawn she would fill the squares of dough with potatoes and buckwheat, and then bake them in the oven. By morning the knishes were all ready for marketing.

Israel's young mind was alert for other ways to help his father and mother. He bought matches wholesale from a village store and paid a peasant ten kopeks to take him with him when he drove the seven miles to another village for the market held on alternate Sundays. He had to rise early enough to get to the market two hours before dawn, when buying and selling began. He would put a rope around a case of matches, tie it to his shoulder, and drag the case through the aisles between the merchants and farmers, crying, "Who will buy my matches?"

When the day's business ended at two in the afternoon, he rode back home. After counting all his expenses, he found his profit was about $1.50. "When I came home in the evening I would give my mother $1.00 and keep the remainder for myself. With this I would buy a top or marbles, and sometimes candy. I was then a grown man of eight years."

He sold matches for six months, then rock salt for another six months, till adults complained the child was undercutting them. He kept on trying. Next it was rabbit skins, then a smoked, dried fish which came in bales. Now he had an assistant, his seven-year-old brother Hyman. All the while he continued to help his mother sell knishes on weekdays, for his own merchandising was limited to Sundays. He drove calves for a cattle dealer, once chasing them three hours through a rainstorm over a distance of seven miles. He did odd jobs for the owner

of a dress-goods store close by his mother's knish stand, and by the time
he was eleven, the owner was taking him along on business trips to the
big market in Karillov, one hundred miles off. "At home I was an
important person. I had money to do with as I pleased and could give it
to whom I pleased—a big man of eleven years!" But he began to realize
what little future there was in this buying and selling to keep your head
barely above poverty. One day he would manage to get to America.

Simche and Molke were another couple who had a hard time in
Warshilovka. Molke explained to her three biggest children that they
must help earn some money; their father couldn't do it alone. She
learned to make *kvass,* an iced punch sweetened with saccharine and
colored a bright red. They would sell it to the peasants at the biweekly
yarid during the hot summer months. She poured the drink into three
big tubs, covering the tops with a white sheet, leaving an opening to fill
the glasses. Then she put a board across each top to display the drinking
glasses. The family was ready for business:

> Chaim, Fishel, and Mailech, nine, eight and seven years old, were at
> their post selling kwass. They learned to call out loudly, "Kwass, kwass!
> Drink kwass!" And their business went better every time. Once when
> Molke's brother was in town and heard the boys sell their kwass he
> thought of a new way, even more appealing, to call out. *"Kwass frontzsky
> he govoreet po Russkie kwass kwasok Kwassachock chto kwass piea tho shunke no
> biea."* This meant: "French kwass that speaks Russian. He who drinks
> this kwass doesn't beat his wife." The peasants loved this song and at
> times they gathered around the place listening to them call out about the
> kwass. This really worked up the business, until the boys brought home
> close to two dollars each and Molke could afford to buy meat twice a
> week and cook a wonderful dinner for all . . .

Life Is with People gives the flavor of the shtetl's marketplace:

> Bargaining is raised to a fine art. For Jew and peasant alike, to pay the
> price asked or to refuse to modify the first price named would be contrary
> to custom. If it is an important negotiation between men, like the sale of a
> cow or a horse, the ceremonial of transaction involves the stretching out
> and withdrawing of hands, the seller striking his palm against the palm
> of the buyer, the buyer pulling away until agreement is reached when
> they shake hands and thus seal the bargain.

When the buyer or seller is a woman, which is often the case, the procedure is more verbal and much more vivacious. The acquisition of a Sabbath fish may take on all the suspense of a pitched battle, with onlookers cheering and participants thoroughly enjoying the mutual barrage of insults and exhortations. Points are scored through technique and finesse, and the process of bargaining has as much interest and zest as the final result. . . .

The marketplace was where Jew and non-Jew came together. The non-Jew was the farmer. The Jew, officially barred from owning farmland, was the town dweller. Apart from meeting in the market and at scattered business negotiations, they lived in different worlds.

Business was usually done in a friendly way.

The peasant will have his special peddler for small purchases, his special customer for eggs or potatoes. He will give first preference to this Jew, loyally repulsing other offers. The Jew will try to buy his grain regularly of one peasant. A sturdy business relationship is built up between them. At the same time, each distrusts and fears the other. It is not that each knows the other will try to cheat him in bargaining, for this is merely a part of the market game, a game that belongs to Eastern Europe and is as native to the peasant as to the Jew. . . .

Beneath the surface dealing there lay a sense of difference and danger.

Secretly each feels superior to the other, the Jew in intellect and spirit, the "goy" in physical force—his own and that of his group. By the same token each feels at a disadvantage opposite the other, the peasant uneasy at the intellectuality he attributes to the Jew, the Jew oppressed by the physical power he attributes to the goy. . . .

The Jews sometimes had to flout regulations to make a living. A license was needed to sell certain things and people often didn't have one. What might happen then? *Life Is with People* tells:

Illegal selling of *bagel* is viewed as a respectable way for an "orphan" to help his widowed mother. When she has baked a fresh batch of the crusty, ring-shaped rolls, her six- and seven-year-old sons will take them out to hawk on the streets, packed in a basket covered with a piece of clean linen. They will sell as many as they can to anyone lucky enough to have a penny. Suddenly the alarm will be sounded in a whisper, "The 'sixer' (policeman)!" At once the children will disappear from the street; no one has seen or heard of them. Half-eaten bagel will suddenly be shoved into pockets or market bags. When the "sixer" is well out of the way the frightened boys will peek out to be reassured, and perhaps consoled by a sweet from some sympathetic passer-by. Everyone knows that if they were caught they would be beaten, and their baskets would be taken away with the bagel—of which the constabulary is very fond— and the precious linen cover. That they are guilty of selling without a license is a matter of concern to the government, but certainly not to their customers or to those who only wish they had a penny for a piping-hot roll. . . .

Ephraim Lisitzky's grandparents both worked to support their nine children. Six of them were girls who came to the marrying age one right after another. The dowry drain must have been unbearable. Grandfather drove a dilapidated droshky harnessed to a skinny nag, and passengers took him only if no other droshky was in sight. What his grandmother did to help out, Ephraim could not forget:

> Summers, she hired out to work in the vegetable gardens on the outskirts of Slutzk alongside other poor women. She left at sunrise and spent all day spading, furrowing, weeding, and picking. She returned home at sunset, her back bent, her whole body aching and gritty. Home, she would cut up some cucumbers and onions, toss the slices into a cucumber brine whitened with buttermilk, and serve the dish with dry black bread. Sitting down to eat with the family, she would rest her weary head on her arm and fall asleep, forgetting all about her hunger.
>
> In the winter, Grandmother sold potatoes, frozen apples and pears, chickens, geese and similar commodities. She stayed in the market all day. When she came home her dress was frozen stiff, her body a piece of solid ice. Thawing out at the oven, she set a pot of water on the fire, threw in some slices of potatoes, groats, and onion, sprinkled on salt and pepper, and prepared the famous Slutzk *krupnik*. . . . After supper, she cleared the dishes from the table to make room for the pile of feathers from the fowls she had accepted to pluck for a few pennies. She plucked until midnight. Every now and then she would doze off, her head nodding—but her fingers miraculously worked of their own accord.

Between Purim and Passover Grandmother worked in a matzo bakery. Every day during that period she stood over the dough crib from dawn until midnight, kneading dough. Two days before Passover she returned home, her hands as puffed up as the dough she had kneaded, her back so twisted she could hardly straighten up without cracking her bones. Groaning, she cleaned the house, made the utensils *kosher* for Passover, and prepared meals. The first night of Passover, Grandmother's groans mingled with Grandfather's sad chanting of the Passover *Haggadah* at the *seder.*

Reb Eliahu and Reb Shloime were two men Zalman Shazar singled out in the little town of Steibtz, where he came from. They were the *shochtim,* ritual slaughterers:

> Though for decades, both in the slaughterhouse outside the town and in their own courtyards, they had slaughtered cattle for the butchers and fowl for the housewives and heard the cows groaning and seen the chickens writhing at their feet and flashed their rigorously sharpened knives and stained their long coats with blood—for all that, strangely enough, the two of them were the kindest of men and so gentle that they seemed incapable of hurting a fly.
>
> Reb Eliahu was the veteran shochet of the two, but he was much more than a shochet. The town wits used to say that he had so many occupations you could people a whole community with him. Besides being a slaughterer, he was the reader in the Old Synagogue, he blew the *shofar* on the High Holy Days, he was the chief *mohel* performing circumcisions in the town, and he was renowned as a matchmaker, having good connections with the best matchmakers in the country and serving all the wealthy families of the vicinity. He took the place of a Government-appointed rabbi, keeping a register of births and arranging certificates. In addition to all this, he spent hours every day cutting gravestones and carving ornamental designs on them: hands lifted in blessing in the case of a member of the priestly class; pitchers of water for libation in the case of a Levite; chopped-down trees to indicate young lives that had been prematurely ended. And he carved rhymed eulogies in verse of his own composition on the stones: the Hebrew was most elegant and the letters at the beginning of the lines gave you the names of the dead.
>
> He had still another truly unique occupation—nowadays we would say he operated an employment agency for rabbis. . . . Clearly, Reb Eliahu's sources of income were many; some hard, some easy, some

conventional, some unconventional. But the end result of them all was
that he had the greatest difficulty in providing for his wife, his sons and
daughters and sons-in-law and their children. All his long life he was a
poor man. But he was a very dignified and serene poor man, a wise and
gentle one. . . .

Steibtz was a simple town, not distinguished for its learning or its
charity. There were dozens of other places, just as ordinary, in the
province of Minsk or beyond in the Pale. Yet there was one thing about it
that Zalman Shazar wanted everyone to know:

It was without doubt a center of work—a town of laborers, strong-
armed and muscular men. Though Koidenhove had its Hasidic rabbi,
it had no river. Though Mir had its renowned yeshiva, it had no railroad.
Steibtz had both. It lay on the banks of the River Nieman, which rose at
nearby Pesuchna and was covered with rafts floating all the way to
mighty Koenigsberg. And a railway line passed through Steibtz on the
way from Brisk in Lithuania to Moscow. The noisy, bustling river bank
in Steibtz was one of its unique features, too. The entire stretch, from the
iron bridge to the ferry over the river, was shaded by trees and covered
with parts of boats under construction, rafts ready to be launched, piles of
lumber of all sizes and types, heaps of withes used like ropes to bind
the rafts.

From dawn till the stars came out workers toiled and sweated here.
Often after reading conventional discussions of Jewish "parasitism" in
the Diaspora, I have found myself wanting to beg the pardon of these
long-gone workers of Steibtz whom I knew in my youth. I remember
them patching holes in the sides of the boats with rope and fiber; lying on
their backs on the ground under larger boats, with huge wooden hammers and long iron files in their hands, closing up cracks from the
morning to late hours of the night; hammering away and singing while
the breezes blew from the turbulent river. Not all of them were young.
There were white-bearded ones, too, with large families, fathers with
children and sometimes grandchildren.

How horrified the whole town was that ghastly night when the
scaffolding snapped and a boat fell on the workers, and Berel Chashe-
Breinas was pulled out from underneath crushed to death, still holding a
hammer in his hand! And that accusation of parasitism—fruit of the
earnest desire to reform the Jewish economic structure—how totally
undeserved it was in your case, carpenters and boat builders of Steibtz;

planers of boards and fasteners of rafts; carters that worked along with your horses to drag logs from the woods and throw them into the Nieman; transporters of barrels of tar to the boats; loaders and unloaders, tossed by rain and storm and wind during the long, long hours of your working day!

8

The Sheyneh and the Prosteh

Chaim Laiser, Uncle Reuben, Simche and Molke, Reb Eliahu—they lived by the old saying, "If no bread, then no Torah." The common toast they all knew was *"Gezunt un parnosseh"*—"Health and livelihood." And everybody in the shtetl, of whatever age or sex, pursued *parnosseh*. The scholar too, for study was considered "work for the Creator," and the scholar was busy at it from first light till long after dark.

Those who lived by trading on some scale—the merchants, dealers, storekeepers—took pride in not working with their hands. They considered themselves to be the sheyneh, the fine Jews. They were a small minority. The great mass of others were petty middlemen of all sorts, artisans, or unskilled workers.

The widespread impression of the Eastern European Jews as "nonproductive" middlemen isn't borne out by the facts. In the Russian Pale, the Jews were only 4 to 6 percent of the population, but 21 percent of all factory workers were Jews. In Galicia, a fourth of the people working in industry and the crafts were Jews, some two and a half times their share in the general population. There was actually a smaller proportion of Jews engaged in commerce in Russia than in the countries of Western Europe. But inside Russia and Galicia most of the middlemen were Jews.

And that fact made it easy to charge that Jews were nothing but middlemen or, as the anti-Semites put it, "parasitic peddlers" and "unproductive hucksters."

Ignored was the historical background: that what the Eastern European Jews did to make a living was restricted by government decrees handed down over hundreds of years. They could not own or operate the sources of raw materials, they could not travel freely, they could not live on the land or in large cities. The effect was to force the majority into the position of middlemen, buying and selling goods and services.

Ignored too were the considerable number of Jews who worked with their hands. Some trades became identified with Jews—tailor, cobbler, blacksmith, limeburner. In some places only Jews were certain kinds of laborers—teamsters, porters, coachmen, loggers, water carriers.

Few Jews were in agriculture, because the law prevented them from owning farmland. While 90 percent of the Russians were tilling the soil in the 1870s, less than 5 percent of the Jews were. The best many could do was to rent an orchard and hope for a good crop they could sell to a dealer. The law did not bar Jews from owning cattle, and dairymen were common in the shtetl. Some had their own cows. Others bought milk from a farm and sold it to the shtetl. A lucky few had a horse to pull the delivery wagon; most had to carry the milk pail on a shoulder pole, often for miles.

The Jews who did manage to engage in farming had to do it by leasing the land. Hirsch Abramovitch has described the arrangements made by Jews in the villages of Lithuania. From absentee owners they leased estates ranging from a hundred to several hundred acres, or even more. They paid the rent in advance, generally for six months. Sometimes the terms called for a share of the farm products as well.

The Jewish lessee usually didn't till the soil himself but spent all his time in the field managing the estate. He hired tenant farmers to work for him, giving them huts, groceries, and a patch of land for their own use. Sometimes a sharecropper system was used instead, with the land sublet in return for half the crop. A capable manager did better with his own hired help. The incompetent lessee wound up in bankruptcy.

But even with good management, few Jewish farmers got rich this way. It took the labor of the whole family to make any kind of a living from a leased farm. The women milked the cows, made the cheese and butter, cared for the garden, cooked not only for the family but for the day laborers and the unmarried yearly workers. They also baked the bread, raised the chickens, and watched the ducks. They prepared the feed for the cattle, spun and wove the wool and flax into cloth, and sewed the clothing for the household. And on top of all that, they raised the family, most likely a big one.

The children all helped too, both with the household tasks and the barn and field labor. There was always something that needed doing from dawn until far into the night.

The Jewish farmers raised food, but their families didn't eat much of it. Borsht was the main dish, eaten twice a day. There was cooked barley, and cereals, and once in a while pancakes. Rarely did they eat meat during the week; that was a Sabbath special, with the meat bought in the town. At the end of the winter, in the calving season, they would have a calf slaughtered, eat some of it, and salt the rest. In late autumn it would be a sheep, and then meat was on the table every day of the week—for a while.

No matter what a Jew did to make a living, it was his *gesheft,* his business, and it was important. But some ways of making a living were esteemed more than others, not only because of the income they brought, but because of the degree of respectability attached to them. It was better to be one's own boss, no matter how shaky the business, than to work for another. Better, too, to be a salesman than a worker. For the salesman used his head, while the worker used only his muscle. In *Life Is with People* the distinction is explained:

> The shtetl folk feel that "head," *kop*—and especially *"yiddisher kop"*—is the chief capital in any enterprise, and sometimes the only one. Yiddisher kop is identified with *seykhel,* "brains" or "good sense." Every human being has seykhel but "yiddisher seykhel" is of a special kind and quality. It is characterized by rapidity of orientation and grasping of a problem, intuitive perception, and swift application to the situation.

Such distinctions divided the shtetl socially, partly on the basis of economic position and partly on that of religious status or learning. The artisans in some communities were shunted off to their own synagogue. Within the synagogue people were seated by their social standing. The concept of *yichus,* which had to do with the family's position, again not altogether linked to wealth, contributed to where Jews stood in the community.

The two classes were, from another angle, the intellectual aristocrats and the less learned plebians. In the first class were rabbis, teachers, cantors, students. They spent their time in prayer and study, and looked down upon manual labor as degrading. Fathers felt bad when they had to agree to a son's taking up a trade. They took comfort from recalling what the Gaon had said: that if a man was not fit for pure scholarship, he should be taught a trade and thus enabled to support his more gifted fellow Jews.

The prejudice against working with one's hands was deep-rooted. In his memoirs, the Yiddish poet Eliakum Zunser tells of the humiliations endured by his boyhood friend, Motke Kochel, the son of an innkeeper in Vilna. Motke couldn't study the Talmud for endless hours. He would slip out of the classroom, hide in the attic of the inn, and with wood or clay shape human figures. His father beat him savagely for breaking the divine commandment against the making of graven images. But he would not give up his carving. They fought bitterly over it until at last his father took Motke out of school and apprenticed him to a wood carver. Motke worked for years in the Vilna ghetto, carving what none of his neighbors understood or wanted—until at the age of twenty a government official's wife saw his work, recognized his genius, and sent him to the Imperial Academy of Art in St. Petersburg. He won international renown as the sculptor Mark Antokolsky.

Because he worked with his hands, young Motke was linked in his father's mind with the prosteh, the unschooled, the laborers, the artisans, the people destined to do nothing but the dirty work. Yet it was not the occupation itself which brought the negative label but its status in culture and education. If a man who worked with his hands had learning and manners, then he was not prosteh. And the son of prosteh parents could always acquire learning and rise to become one of the sheyneh. Hillel, the great sage, came from a poor family and started life as a water carrier.

The sheyneh thought of the prosteh as loud, violent people, hardly a cut above the crude peasants. The prosteh in turn had their stereotype of the sheyneh, calling them hypocritical pedants who might have a

Jewish head but not a Jewish heart. Yes, scholars sat on their behinds and studied day and night, but workers sweated the week long to make the holy Sabbath possible.

But both—the sheyneh and the prosteh—lived by the same code, as *Life Is with People* points out:

> In both groups the dominance of the traditional pattern is accepted in a spirit ranging from affirmation through grumbling to resistance. Proportions differ, and the negative response is higher among the prosteh, yet any prosteh father longs to have a son become a learned man, even though he may swear that scholars are parasites living on the toil of honest fellows like himself. . . .
>
> Moreover, while each group harbors a stereotype of the other, each sees the other as an essential partner in the life of the community. One is the man of action, the other the man of thought. The man of learning or of wealth is constant adviser and constant helper. The prosteh not only do the heavy work but in time of violence they are strong-armed defenders. And violence is no stranger to the shtetl.

Because of the nature of their work, the prosteh were in closer touch with the peasants. For them the peasants were the outside world. And by the same token, the outside world saw the shtetl through what they knew of the prosteh. To most Jews in the shtetl, Gentile meant the peasant. And for the peasant, Jew meant the prosteh.

In a portrait of Swislocz, written by one of its sons, Abraham Ain, we get a sense of the economic life of a large shtetl. Swislocz was in the district of Grodno. There were nearly two thousand Jews living there in the 1870s, when the first leather factory was opened. Soon there were eight factories, all owned by Jews, employing forty to fifty workers each, and another dozen or so smaller shops with six to twelve workers.

About 70 percent of the town's Jews made their living from the factories. They were divided into dry and wet tanneries. The leather they produced from horse hides was sold to merchants all over Russia and used to make leggings and uppers for shoes and boots. It took three months to convert a hide into leather. The wet work was mainly unskilled, and most of the workers were non-Jews. The skilled labor of the dry factories was done mostly by Jews. No machinery was used in either type of operation; it was hard work. The lighter labor was done by boys. Most of the town's Jewish boys entered the factories between twelve and fourteen, or were apprenticed to artisans.

Until the early 1900s working conditions in the leather industry were terrible, Ain wrote. The workers put in a fourteen- or fifteen-hour day, six days a week, and the wages were very low. Not until the Bund, the socialist organization of Jewish workers, was formed in 1897 did life improve. Two general strikes in Swislocz made the difference.

There were a hundred Jewish artisans in Swislocz. The largest group were shoemakers (twenty-two), then came tailors (sixteen), bakers (eleven), joiners and blacksmiths (nine each), and a scattering of cop-persmiths, tinsmiths, bricklayers, glaziers, watchmakers, carpenters, locksmiths, potters, driers, harness-makers, and bookbinders. There were several Jews who shifted from one kind of calling to another, doing whatever paid at the moment, and some who were indirectly involved in agriculture on a small scale.

Swislocz had about sixty stores, most of them small. A dozen were run by women whose husbands had other trades. The rest were the sole support of the families owning them. The few big stores catered to the landowners, the officials, and the leather manufacturers. Until the sale of liquor was made a state monopoly in 1898, there were about a dozen Jewish tavernkeepers. Several Jews dealt in grain, and some were in the timber business. The big timber men hired managers and loggers; the others did all the work themselves. The better logs were floated down the Narew to the sawmills or to Germany. The others were cut up for railway ties or firewood.

In the town of Bilgoray in Lublin province, where the novelist I. J. Singer was born, the making of sieves was the local industry. These were shipped to all parts of Russia and abroad. In Singer's memoir of his childhood, he tells of the Jewish sievemakers.

The peasants made sieves only during the otherwise empty winter months, but the several hundred Jewish families in Bilgoray who were engaged in this trade worked at it all year round. The women collected the horse hair from which the sieves were fashioned, then cleaned and washed it. The men sat before the looms like so many spiders trapped between the poles and ropes and did the weaving. It was unhealthy work that caused consumption after twenty years or sooner. Most of the sievemakers worked from before daybreak until well into the night. Bent over their looms, they grew hunchbacked and purblind, their lungs torn from coughing, their faces drained of blood. And their wives wasted away with them.

But for all their effort they barely made enough to feed their families. The few wealthy contractors who gave out the work paid next to nothing for the long hours of labor, and it often happened that after a family had slaved for a whole week there was no money left with which to celebrate the Sabbath and they were forced to go begging from door to door. I remember how ashamed they seemed when they came to Grandmother's kitchen. She gave away loaf after loaf of bread, for which they thanked and blessed her. Afterwards, Grandmother railed against the Hasidim who included in their ranks these contractors and some of the worst exploiters and bloodsuckers in town. The street on which the sievemakers lived was a pocket of filth, disease, and poverty, while the contractors grew only fatter and sleeker from day to day.

There were some Jewish entrepreneurs who reached the heights in Eastern Europe's business world. Pauline Wengeroff, born into such a family of upper-class Jews in 1833, in Bobruisk, White Russia, described them in her memoirs. As a contractor, her father played a great economic role in the first half of the nineteenth century, erecting fortifications for the czar, building roads and canals, and supplying the army. When Pauline married Hanan Wengeroff she went to live in the town of Konotop. "My father-in-law, the richest man in town, held the government's wine and liquor concession. I remember the way the house was furnished—the large rooms, expensive furniture, beautiful silver, carriages and horses, servants, frequent guests."

A little later her husband got the liquor concession in Lubny. In 1859 her husband's father, grandfather, and another partner obtained the leasehold on liquor for the province of Kovno. Her husband was put at the head of the office. This was in the early years of the reign of Alexander II, when it was possible, she wrote, "for the Jews to attain an unexpected influence in commerce and industry. Never before or after did the Jews in St. Petersburg live in such wealth and distinction as then, when a good part of the financial affairs of the capital were in their hands. Jewish banking houses were founded. Corporations headed by Jews were organized. The stock exchange and the banks grew to immense proportions."

A few years later the Wengeroffs moved to St. Petersburg.

The society we became part of consisted of distinguished and cultivated people, most of whom lived a carefree existence in wealth and
luxury.

The St. Petersburg Jewish community had a magnificent synagogue
and even two rabbis—one modern and seminary-trained, the other Orthodox. But the Jewish community had abandoned many Jewish customs and traditions. The more fashionable even celebrated Christmas.
Only Yom Kippur and Passover were observed, but in an up-to-date way.
Some Jews drove to the synagogue in their carriages and ate in the
intervals between the Yom Kippur service. Passover was kept, even
among the most progressive. It remained a festival of remembrance,
joyful because it recalled not the exodus from Egypt, but one's own
childhood in the shtetl. The seder was observed, in a highly abbreviated
form. Even baptized Jews kept the seder. Though they did not themselves
make the holiday feast, they welcomed invitations from their not-yet-
baptized friends.

These were the customs of the upper stratum of Jewish Petersburg. To
live in this milieu and remain impervious to it required a strong character
and religious fidelity which my husband lacked. Yet here in Petersburg, I
had often witnessed the strong feeling of solidarity among these Jews
who had given up traditional Judaism. Jews in trouble with the authorities anywhere in Russia used to turn to the Petersburg Jewish community
for help. Petersburg Jews spared neither money nor time. They appealed
to the highest authorities on behalf of the oppressed Jews. Their concern
was natural and understandable. This Jewish solidarity became prover-
bial all over the world. Even the baptized Jews were not immune to it.

In 1871 the Wengeroffs moved once more, now to Minsk, where
Pauline's husband was made vice director and then director of the
Commerce Bank. "Once again we lead a comfortable and prosperous
life," she wrote.

A glimpse of another Jewish aristocrat's life comes from a memoir of
Baron David Günzburg, written by his daughter Sophie. Baron David,
born in Kamenets-Podolski in 1857, belonged to the third generation of a
family of financiers. His grandfather Joseph, permitted to settle in
Petersburg, founded a bank there bearing his name. The founder's son
Horace handled the affairs of the Grand Duke of Hesse-Darmstadt, a

high officer of the Russian Army. In gratitude the Duke bestowed the title of baron on Horace and extended it to the entire family.

Horace brought up his sons in a religious and traditional spirit, Sophie said. Her father David, one of the sons, was an intellectual and a noted linguist. He learned a new language almost every year and had mastered thirty-four by the time of his death. He inherited a library of ten thousand volumes and built it to more than fifty thousand, making it one of the largest and finest private collections in the world. Although David was Russia's leading authority on Middle Eastern languages and history, as a Jew he was denied a professorship in the University of St. Petersburg. He opened a school of his own, with the right to confer degrees, and taught most of the subjects himself. He served in two czarist ministries, was active in Jewish community affairs, wrote books and articles, and even gave his children Hebrew lessons every morning at seven.

David, like his father Horace, served the Jews as their friend at the court. Denied so many legal rights, the Jews were forced to depend upon men of influence to get their case before the czar. Such men were called *shtadlanim,* and the Günzburgs were the first to fulfill that role. David, Sophie wrote, "used to intercede with the authorities in crucial matters, thwarting plans (which somehow became known to him) for violence against Jews, freeing an innocent Jew from prison, obtaining residence permits, providing an accused Jew with a fair defense lawyer. He never sought favors for himself. . . . Two or three rooms in a small suite [in the Günzburg home] were set aside to house Jews refused residence permits in the capital city. Here they lived in hiding until my father could obtain proper documents for them. They did not leave the house; food was brought into their rooms by our servants."

Jews such as Samuel Solomonovich Poliakov did much to build the railroads that spread across Russia in the 1860s and 1870s. While their enterprise brought them great wealth, the extension of the railroads into the Pale meant a painful readjustment for a great number of other Jews. Jewish innkeepers, drivers, and middlemen of the villages and small towns were deprived of their livelihood and forced to move elsewhere or to change their way of making a living. Zunser wrote a song about their troubles—"*Sogt Kaddish nokh der Velt*" ("Dirge for the World")—in which the coming of the railroad and the telegraph are blamed for bringing about cataclysmic changes in the world they were used to.

9

Study Is the Best of Wares

While living with his grandfather in Neshwies, young Morris Cohen went to cheder for six days in every week. The schoolday began at eight in the morning and ended after six, except for Friday, when the boys were dismissed a little earlier. There were few vacation days in the year, only the holiday weeks of Passover and Succoth. Looking back at his childhood in the old country, Professor Cohen recalled what he learned in cheder:

> I was taught to translate the Bible into the vernacular—Yiddish. This was a great joy, especially when we came to the narrative portions of the Book of Genesis and later to those of Judges, Samuel, and Kings. These were my first story books as well as my introduction to history, and to this day the Biblical stories have an inexhaustible liveliness for me, as if I had actually lived through them.

> My first rebbe in Neshwies was exceedingly poor, had four children and was very much harassed. In his irritation, he omitted the usual ritual of deliberate punishment, the letting down of the trousers and the application of the strap. Instead he lashed out his blows at the least provocation, and sometimes . . . even without provocation. . . . The cheder was located on a quiet street, and the long rectangular back yard

was covered with grass. I remember especially one late afternoon as the long shadows were fading with the setting sun, I ran around in the yard with a feeling of great elation. . . .

In the winter, we had to stay in the cheder until after dark and so had to light our way home by carrying lanterns. For a long time the possessing, the cleaning, and the carrying of the lantern, appealed to me as a thrilling adventure. For the rest there were few organized games among us inside or outside of the classroom. . . .

After two years in my first cheder I was sent to another rebbe, Reb Nehemiah, who was a *maskil,* that is, one who believed in bringing some of the beauty of Western learning into Hebrew studies. Indeed, he gave private lessons in grammar to advanced pupils who came to his house late in the afternoon or evening . . . But we, the regular pupils, were taught nothing but the traditional curriculum, the Pentateuch with the Commentary of Rashi and a few other books of the Bible. Only in an occasional comment would our rebbe's learning open up for me glimpses of the great outside world of geography and history. I remember particularly his explanation of the origin and evolution of boats and of the Franco-Prussian War of 1870 . . .

My mother, who never forgot her disappointment at not having succeeded in her ambition to learn the art of writing, was determined that I should not be similarly handicapped. So she had a letter written to her father that he should see to it that I receive instruction in the art of writing Yiddish. To this my grandfather replied, "My dear daughter, I am giving your son Torah—the substance of life. The trimmings come later."

In Swislocz, said Abraham Ain, boys of five were sent to cheder, which was usually in the teacher's home. They were taught the alphabet and reading for the first year and a half, then promoted to a higher grade, where they studied the Pentateuch and the rest of the Bible. The next step was the Talmud. Some teachers also gave the boys writing and arithmetic. By the age of ten, a Jewish boy knew a little of the Bible, could write Yiddish and do some arithmetic, and was studying the Talmud. Some boys were only part-time cheder students and gave several other hours a day to learning Russian, arithmetic, and writing.

Boys whose parents couldn't afford the fee went to a Talmud Torah, where the tuition was low or free. Bible and Talmud classes were mixed with reading, arithmetic, Yiddish, and Russian. Girls did not start their education until seven or eight. They were taught to read and write

Hebrew and Yiddish, and to do arithmetic. At the age of thirteen or fourteen they were usually apprenticed to seamstresses. The poorer girls became domestics.

It was not until about 1900 that a general public school, running through the fourth grade, and a modern Hebrew school were opened in Swislocz, for all Jewish children.

This tradition of elementary education—centered on the Bible and Talmud—was almost universal for shtetl Jews. As early as three, and up to thirteen, boys went to school, no matter what their social or economic position. The conviction that Jewish education was for everybody went back to Rashi, the commentator on the Torah and Talmud who lived in the eleventh century. It was Rashi, said Abraham Joshua Heschel, who "democratized Jewish education; he brought the Bible, the Gemara, and the Midrash to the people, and made the Talmud a popular book, everyman's book. . . . Scholarship ceased to be the monopoly of the few and became widely disseminated. In many communities, the untutored became the rare exception."

Uncle Reuben, the itinerant tailor of Slutzk, is an example of this.

> Every day Uncle Reuben awoke before dawn, washed his hands, and recited the daily portion from the Psalms. Later he went to the synagogue where he said the morning prayers and stayed on to study a chapter from the *Mishnah*. On his returning home he would open the thick leather-bound prayer book whose pages had yellowed with age and handling, and recite an additional prayer, comprising excerpts from holy writings, assigned for each day of the week. Then he would eat breakfast, and sit down to work. He sewed, as he prayed, with great dedication; he was meticulously precise, anxious to do credit to his friends, the peasants.
>
> At one in the afternoon, Uncle Reuben would stretch out on the sofa, and nap briefly. Then he would wash his hands again, open the Midrash *Rabbah,* and study the portion of the week. He had a hard time walking the muddy roads of Polesia on his rounds of the villages; but the intricate paths of the Midrash were even harder. En route he would stumble over strange words, lose his way, wander in circles, and finally stop and look desperately around. Where in the world was he! Suddenly, Uncle Reuben's face would light up. "Aha!" He had found his way out of the morass of the Midrash.
>
> Back to the synagogue he went for the afternoon prayers, studied *The Well of Jacob,* said the evening prayers, and listened to the news from the

shopkeepers and the young men who read the modern Hebrew papers. After the evening meal he read a chapter from a popular inspirational book using both the original Hebrew and the Yiddish translation in the margins. The women of the household would stop talking at their chores and listen to his loud singsong.

It is like the shtetl depicted by Mendele Mocher Sforim in one of his stories, "Shloime Red Khayims." He calls it . . .

a place of learning of old standing, where practically all the inhabitants are scholars, where the House of Study is full of men and youths busily pursuing their studies . . . where, at dusk, between the *Minha* and the *Maariv* services, artisans and other simple folk gather around the table to listen to a discourse on the Midrash, the Bible . . . and similar ethical and philosophical works. . . .

Heschel asks:

What other nation has a lullaby to the effect that "study is the best of wares"? At the birth of a child, the school children come and chant the *Shema* in unison around the cradle. The child is taken to school of the first time wrapped in a *tallis.* Schoolchildren are referred to as "sacred sheep," and a mother's pet name for her little boy is *"mayn tsadikl"* (my little saint). Hence, one is ready to sell all household belongings to pay tuition. Women work all their lives to enable their husbands to devote themselves to study. One shares his last morsel of food with a yeshiva *bokher.* And when the melancholy sweet tone of Talmudic study penetrates the poor alleys, exhausted Jews on their pallets are delighted, for they feel they have a share in that study. . . . Study was a song of longing, a pouring out of the heart before the Merciful Father, a sort of prayer, a communion and an ardent desire for a purified world.

The teaching in the cheder used none of the educational methods we call progressive today. The process of learning was endless repetition. The little child had to memorize the strange Hebrew words and their meanings. He learned only the elements of reading and the prayers. Then he advanced to the second cheder, where he studied the *khumesh* (Pentateuch), learning to translate whole sentences and to understand the text. Here he worked with Rashi's commentary, going into interpretation and hidden meanings. In the next stage, the highest cheder, he undertook independent study under the guidance of a teacher more highly qualified than the elementary *melamed*. Here the study of the Talmud covered all kinds of problems, ancient and modern, religious and secular. The boring mechanical mode the youngster had begun with was now replaced by the true excitement of learning, when the mind and imagination are stretched to their full capacity. The boy was ten or eleven at this point and everyone watched closely to see if he had the intellectual power to become a Talmudic scholar. If he did, he was sent on to the highest institution of learning, the rabbinical academy called the yeshiva.

The old one-room cheder was a "unique juvenile madhouse," says Maurice Samuel. It was supposed to be the child's second home, and the *melamed* a person to be cherished like one's father. But almost no Jew who has left a memoir of those early days mentions a rebbe with affection. Eliakum Zunser describes the bedlam in the cheder, the scolding, the spanking, the slapping, the beating with the indispensable *kantchik* (cat-o'-three-tails). In Sholem Aleichem's stories the boys speak of their teachers as "the Murderer" or "the Death-Angel."

In his novel, *The Brothers Ashkenazi*, I. J. Singer etches in acid a *melamed* in Lodz who taught older children.

Reb Boruch Wolf is famous for his cruelty not less than for his piety and learning. Besides, he overworks the boys. He holds them in the schoolroom from early morning till late at night. On Thursday, which is repetition day, he works with them beyond midnight and sometimes until the morning hours. He crams into the children not only the Talmud with all its accepted commentaries but all kinds of super-commentaries on the commentaries themselves. . . . He wants the boys to learn early how to carry on the heavy burden of Torah and Jewishness.

He never teaches the boys the interesting parts of the Talmud, the legends and stories and adventures of the great teachers in Israel. These he considers fit only for women, or for anti-Hasidic Jews, or for others with weak heads. . . . He avoids those tractates of the Talmud which deal with bright and cheerful things, like holy days, festivals and jolly customs. . . . His learning is as dry and bony and harsh as his own old body. He hates the simple and straightforward, the obvious meaning of a text or inter-pretation. If it isn't complicated, it isn't learning to him.

The Yiddish writer I. L. Peretz, who grew up in the 1850s in Zamoscz, a town in Russian Poland, gives a more affectionate picture of his cheder teacher:

He, too, was small in stature and frail. Though he was an angry little man, quick to fly into a temper, he didn't whip his pupils. His hands would tremble, and he would call to his wife: "Henneh, grab hold of the oven-rake and split the head of the ignoramus!"

Henneh, however, remained placidly in her seat near the oven, going on with her plucking of chickens or knitting of socks.

But if his angry command had to do with me, she would reply: "Listen, don't you dare touch Leibish! I'll tell Rivele on you!"

To eke out a living, Henneh peddled onions and green vegetables from house to house. Rivele, my mother, was one of her customers and the two women were fast friends.

"What a wonderful woman Rivele is!" said Henneh. "A female saint. She denies herself and her family necessities in order to give to the poor. And in such amounts! And this murderer wants to hit her Leibishl!"

"Nu! Nu!" grumbled the rebbe. "But don't forget to tell her what a rascal he is!"

Zunser warned young men thinking of becoming *melameds:*

May God give you a better profession than teaching; but if, alas, you are doomed to teach, conduct yourselves differently. Little creatures need character training above all. So don't let a child hear oaths and curses, because these will burrow into its head like worms into a young apple. Children are wards entrusted to you, and you are paid by fathers and mothers to guard these wards against harm and to implant into them good habits. If a child sees you behaving badly, if it hears falsehood and deception within your walls, the seeds of corruption enter its soul and the beautiful flower will become a prickly thorn.

But there was another side to it, Maurice Samuel points out:

Though children were willing to play tricks on the Rebbi now and then, we never meet with genuine rancour. A Rebbi was looked upon as a natural calamity; it was in the nature of things that he should be impatient, unsympathetic, handy with the kantchik. Children learned to accept his cruelties with something like good humour, and in this they were training themselves for life as Jews. They would have much to put up with from a surrounding world more impatient, more unsympathetic, and handier with the whip than even their Rebbi.

Samuel asks why the cheder, with its traditional method of teaching that remained the same generation after generation, did not cripple the children's minds. "How is it that they did not become idiots, but on the contrary maintained an astonishingly high level of intelligence and, what is more, actually learned what they were taught?"

He thinks it is because today we tend to exaggerate the sensitivity of children and to underestimate how resilient the human being is at all ages. People endure when they accept the situation, he believes. "The readiness to endure is half the trick of enduring, and those who have not known the better do not lose half their strength whimpering over the worse." Because the children in the Eastern European cheders "took for granted what they had to face in the way of training, they were immune from most of the negative effects."

There was, too, he adds, the important fact that children and parents agreed on the worth of what the cheder was teaching. "Boys were learning in cheder that which their fathers knew and cherished. They were treated as children but they were challenged as adults."

The yeshivas of the nineteenth century drew hundreds of boys from all over Eastern Europe. They were located not in the old centers of learning—Lublin, Cracow, Lemberg—but in the shtetls, the centers of Jewish spiritual life. The yeshiva at Volozhin, the outstanding center of Torah scholarship, was founded in 1802. Others developed in such small towns as Eyshisok, Mir, Slobodka, Telz, Slonim.

Education in the yeshiva rested on independent study, with the teacher used as a guide. The student relied upon himself in his deep analysis of the Talmud. The approach was to examine commentary and interpretation, always moving from the various texts back to the Biblical passages that were their ultimate sources.

The study of the Talmud was called *pilpul*, which is defined in *Life Is with People* as . . .

Pepper, and it is as sharp, as spicy, as stimulating as its name implies. It involves comparison of different interpretations, analysis of all possible and impossible aspects of the given problem, and—through an ingenious intellectual combination—the final solution of an apparently insoluble problem.

Penetration, scholarship, imagination, memory, logic, wit, subtlety—all are called into play for solving a Talmudic question. The ideal solution is the *khiddush,* an original synthesis that has never before been offered. This mental activity is a delight both to the performer and to his audience. Both enjoy the vigor of the exercise and the adroitness of the accomplishment. And at the same time, both relish demonstrating their ability to perform on so lofty and esoteric a level. When two accomplished scholars engage in pilpul, they will be surrounded by an admiring group that follows each sally in eager silence, and later will discuss the fine points with each other—possibly working up a new argument about which scholar carried the day.

The yeshiva teacher was respected as much as the rabbi. He was paid not by the parents of the students, as in the cheder, but by the institution. Most of the yeshiva *bokhers* (yeshiva boys) were the sons of poor parents. The Jewish community undertook to support not only the yeshiva itself, with the salary of its head and the high cost of books, but each student attending it. It was a widespread custom for students to eat in a different house every day of the week. Funds were raised throughout Eastern Europe for these purposes. Every Jew felt obliged to support the study of the law, and the small towns took great pride in their yeshivas.

No degree was given to mark the end of a phase of study. How could you complete study when "the Torah has no bottom?" A diploma was given after a few years in the yeshiva to show that the student had a right to function as a rabbi. He got no scholarly degree or title. A learned man, whether a self-taught cobbler or a yeshiva-trained intellectual, was respectfully called Reb, meaning "my teacher." The study of the law never ended. It could be interrupted for a time by circumstances, but the good Jew explored the limitless law as long as he lived, part of his day while working for a living, and all of the day after retirement.

Every shtetl had its men who did nothing but study the Talmud, night and day. The highest honors of the community went to them. They had *yichus,* they were the "beautiful Jews." If a youth showed promise of being such a scholar, everyone would help provide the opportunity for study. The father would support his son, sisters their brother, a father-in-law his son-in-law. Charnofsky offers a snapshot of such a man in Warshilovka:

> Zalman Yankew David was a man in his early forties, but he had the appearance of a man in his seventies. Zalman never worked in his life. He was a Talmud student. He always prayed, he always learned, he was almost always at home or in the synagogue. He sat over a *mishnaes*, a *gemura*, a *tillum*, or other such books, reading and studying. He only took time out for eating two meals a day and sleeping and teaching his own three sons the great learning of God, the Talmud, the Torah, and everything that he knew a Jew should learn.
>
> Zalman was well educated. He knew most of the tillim by heart. He could converse with rabbis about the deep Jewish learning, and would show them many interpretations that contradicted the holy books. He could have been a rabbi but had no such desires.
>
> When Zalman married, his wife knew and her father knew that he would never support a family. But his father-in-law wanted him in the family. He said that Zalman was gold and diamonds to a family, so he provided full support for him and his wife.
>
> When the father-in-law died, Zalman's wife, Ruth, took over. They already had three children that were growing up, and the needs were big. So she decided to sell *crellin* (beads) to the peasant women at the local yarids, and to travel to the nearby yarids. . . . Ruth worked hard. . . . But Ruth was happy. She knew that her husband had to sit at his learning and prayers and that he was shaping and building an afterlife for her and himself and the children. She thought of the *Gan Aden* and of how wonderful it would be there, with no worries, no conflicts, no disagreements, where only people with *treiag mitzvas* (613 good deeds) would be admitted. Her husband would have all of those and would be accepted without a doubt. It was worth all her efforts, all her hard work. . . .

The study of the Talmud has long been considered to be of the highest religious and social value. It is a tradition that goes back to the days of the Second Temple. "Thou shalt study in it day and night" was like a commandment. And Jewish society has always had unlimited admiration for one who followed scholarship as the pathway to God. The sage and the scholar became the aristocrats of the Jewish world. In modern times, that prestige, authority, and position have been accorded by Jews not only to those learned in religious studies but to people of intellectual attainment in secular culture.

10

Fun and Feasts

The most fun the Jewish children of Warshilovka had came during the winter when the Bug River froze solid. Not that it didn't provide fun in the summertime too. Then they swam in the river. But they couldn't boat on it; that was strictly forbidden by their overcautious parents. The Jewish children watched enviously as the peasants rowed or paddled up and down the stream that flowed through their town.

In the winter, the Bug froze so deep, horse and sleigh crossed the ice without fear of breaking through and people walked across freely. The youngsters turned out for skating. Charnofsky remembered the joy it gave.

Most of the time we all made our own skates. We took a piece of wood as long as the shoe, put a couple of holes across the width with two strings in to tie to the shoe, and a wire across the length. This made a very good skate, and all we had to do was break it in. When the wire got shiny, the skates were perfect for skating. Our sleds were also homemade. That was easy—even mothers could make sleds for their children. No one ever knew that there were so many children in town until the sleigh-riding came along. Of course the rich children also came out with a servant and a brand-new sled, bought ready-made, or with ready-made skates. We admitted that they had the nicest sleds and skates, but no one was jealous, for we were all out for a good time. The younger children would roam around the market place with their sleds but not for long, because they would get too cold.

The bigger children with their skates would go to the Bug. The skating was real exercise, and everyone was warmed up. Everybody was trying his best to outdo the other one. They skated in rings, and they skated holding hands. Then there was a great straight race that went for miles up and back. . . . It was at this time that the Gentile and Jewish children would mix, and there were no objections from anyone. In fact, one couldn't tell the difference. They all had red cheeks, sparkling eyes, smiling faces, and sportsmanlike feelings—all alike, only some better skaters than others. . . . When the full moon was out and reflected on the white snow and ice, and the frost was mild, our fathers would go out with us, and they too had a good time.

Play was regarded by the shtetl as a concession, says Maurice Samuel, not a right. He describes what was permitted.

On Passover you had games of chance with Brazil nuts; on *Chanukah* you could play cards, or a game resembling "put and take," with little, four-sided spinning tops, on which were inscribed letters recalling the miracle of the unspent oil in the Temple in the days of the Maccabees; on the Thirty-third Day of the Omer (*Lag b'Omer,* between Passover and Pentecost) there was actually an outing into the fields! On *Purim* . . . there was a play—to be exact, one of two plays, and perhaps even both: the drama of Esther and *The Sale of Joseph.*

That joyous day in the fields that took place on Lag b'Omer is described in *Life Is with People.*

This is the one day of the year when the boys, with their melamed, go out into the fields and woods to enjoy the outdoor world that otherwise is nonexistent to the cheder. Each brings his lunch in a package, and all the mothers vie to give the best *"naseray"* and the most savory tidbits, so that they will not "be ashamed" when all the food is opened and pooled in a common meal. The boys play outdoor games, long caftans flapping about their legs, earlocks bobbing as they run and jump, or shoot at a target with bows and arrows. The melamed, who all the year round bars the cheder door against any spirit of play, accepts the antics of this day as part of the approved regime. How happily he accepts it is "something else again" for occasionally it furnishes an opportunity to work off accumulated resentments against the presiding authority of the schoolroom. Excess in this direction is usually checked, however, by the realization that tomorrow the melamed will again reign in his own realm. . . .

Even in cheder the children enjoyed some happy hours. One of them came at twilight, when the *melamed* went to shul (synagogue) for prayers. In winter, the children sat in the darkness (candles were too costly to burn) and, while waiting for their teacher's return, passed the time telling stories.

Crowding together against the winter cold and the fear of the wonders they are describing, they tell each other tales in which themes carried over from pagan myths jostle with folklore rooted in the Talmud. In the melamed's absence the strict program of Hebrew erudition is broken into by a medley that mingles biblical miracles with the spirits and demons shared by all the folk, Jews and peasants alike. The boys tell each other in turn about the spirits who throng the shul after midnight, and the tricks they play on anyone who has to sleep there—so that a beggar would rather sleep on the floor of the humblest house than enjoy the honor of a bench in the shul. They tell about the devils who haunt the woods at night, the *sheydim,* and how some of them even get into the shtetl streets when it is very dark. They tell about the *dybbuk* who enters the soul of a person so that he becomes possessed and speaks with a voice not his own, uttering blasphemies that would be far from his true mind. They tell of Lilith, Adam's first wife, who steals children; and of children kidnapped from their parents by gypsies, or by wicked men who deliver them into Army service. Children of Hasidim will repeat tales their fathers bring from the rebbe's court, about the miracles wrought by "wonder man."

Sometimes shtetls had special celebrations. In Shklov, a village of White Russia on the Dnieper, the Burial Society—its members were all Hasidim—gave an annual bean feast. It was the only reward its members got for a whole year's hard work—washing the dead and preparing them for interment, putting on their shrouds, carrying them to the graveyard, and burying them. In hot weather or cold, in rain, snow, or ice. The money the society collected paid for shrouds for the poor, for upkeep of the cemetery, and for the lone sexton's salary. What was left went into the bean feast. It took two days to prepare it. Zalman Schneour gives this mouth-watering description of the feast held in the synagogue:

First, the breaking of bread. For that, each member of the burial society got a large white roll, and half a loaf of fresh cornbread. Then to drink each other's health everyone was given a bottle of brandy. And to keep it company, a plate of chopped goose-liver, with a few spoonfuls of freshly melted goose-dripping over it, as an appetizer.

The first course was a slice of carp weighing about a pound, stuffed, and full of onions and pepper, trimmed with soft and hard roe, and swimming in horse-radish, colored and sweetened with beetroot. Next, at least a quarter of a fat goose, roasted in its skin, with all the fat on it. And the gizzard and wings, or a stuffed neck and the feet. And to go with it, a big sour cucumber, and a baked apple.

And to raise a thirst, each member of the burial society got a big stack of thin dry toast, with a thick layer of powdered spices on it and pepper and salt, or ginger. This was eaten between courses, munched so loudly that it set the palate on fire, till it had to be quenched with whatever was going in the way of drink, cold beer or dry cider.

After that came a quarter of a pudding, each the size of a big drum, made of noodles, and bound with eggs and goose fat, goose brains, onions and more fat. Each pudding was crisp and brown on the outside, like a walnut, and inside soft and yellow like calves' brains. These puddings were famed all over Shklov. The wealthiest inhabitants never enjoyed anything so rich and tasty. With the pudding went a mountain of pancakes, made with cinnamon and spices. Or dumplings. With fruit in them. Ordinary people would have called them fruit pies. But for the members of the burial society they were just dumplings.

Then the servers brought sacks of winter apples, slung over their shoulders, and handed them round to the guests. Could any of our generation have eaten all that?

Of all festivals the Sabbath was the first. The people of the shtetl worked all week to reach the Sabbath and celebrate it. To them life and religion were inseparable, and the Sabbath was the most beautiful sign of God's grace, of His gift to them. One of Sholem Aleichem's draymen tells what it meant to him:

When the Sabbath comes I'm a different man, do you hear? I get
home betimes on Friday afternoon, and the first thing of course is
the baths, if you know what I mean. There I sit on the top row of
the steam room and get myself scalded from head to foot. That puts a
new skin on me. Fresh as a newborn babe I dance home, and there on the
table are the two old brass candlesticks, shining like stars, if you know
what I mean, and the two big Sabbath loaves; and there, right beside
them, are the winking Sabbath fish, sending out a smell that takes you
by the throat. And the house is warm and bright and fresh and clean in
every corner. So I sit down like a king, and open the Good Book, and go
twice over the week's portion. Then I close the Book, and it's off to
the synagogue.

What a homecoming after that! When I open the door and sing
out "Good Sabbath" you can hear me at the other end of town. Then
comes the benediction by candlelight, and the drop of good old whiskey,
that sings right through me, if you know what I mean, and then the
Sabbath supper—the shining fish, and the golden soup, and the good
old yellow carrots in honey. That night I sleep like a lord, if you know
what I mean.

And where am I going in the morning? Why, to the synagogue, of
course, as I'm a man and a Jew. And back from the synagogue it's the real
Sabbath meal again, the grand old chopped radish, and the good old
onion, and the jellied calf's foot, if you know what I mean, with a proper
smack of garlic. And when you wake up after your Sabbath afternoon
nap, and your mouth's dry, and there's a sourness in your belly, if you
know what I mean, what's better, I ask you, than a quart or two of cider?
Then, when you're good and ready, and fresh and strong, you sit down to
the Good Book again, like a giant, and off you go! Chapter after chapter,
eh? Psalm after psalm, at the gallop, like the mileposts on the road, if you
know what I mean. . . .

Just how the Sabbath was prepared for and enjoyed by such a
struggling shtetl family as Simche's and Molke's is depicted in detail in
Jewish Life in the Ukraine.

For this holy day Molke would buy thirty pounds of flour to bake
challah. She would have dough to take off to make noodles for soup and a
kugel, to make *poplickes* (pancakes) for the children and enough twisted
challahs to last through the Sabbath. Then she would get some fish and
horseradish, for without fish the Sabbath would lose one custom. Then

of course there was meat or, if there was enough money, chicken. She would also have a *tzimmes* of carrots, and when Simche came home, usually Friday about noon, if he had had a good week and could afford it, he would go out and buy a bottle of wine. . . .

Molke at sunset would light four candles stuck in candelabra, put on a clean, ironed dress and a silk kerchief on her head, turned in back of her ears. With satisfaction, a sense of accomplishment and devotion, she would put her hands over the lighted candles, close her eyes and *bentsh licht* (say her prayers to open the Sabbath). The children would stay near her, and it seemed as if a divine spirit filled the room. When she ended she said, "Good Shabbos" and the children answer, *"Humain"* (so it should be).

When Simche returned from the synagogue he would repeat "Good Shabbos" and everybody would say "Humain." The table was set; the candles threw a dim light over the room. The white tablecloth glimmered and the lights showed two challahs covered with a hand-embroidered cloth, the bottle of wine and glasses around it—knives, forks, spoons, all were on the table. Simche washed his hands, opened the bottle, filled the bigger glass, put it in the palm of his hand, and said khiddush, the blessing of God for the Sabbath. He then took a drink and handed the glass to Molke. She took a sip and gave each child a sip, beginning with the oldest. Then Simche uncovered the challah and cut a piece, made a *moitza,* and sat down.

Everybody started with the fish, then soup, meat, or chicken, with kugel made of the noodles, and last the tzimmes, made of carrots sweetened with sugar. Between the courses Simche and the children would sing zmiros, a sort of thanksgiving prayer in song. Every one of the boys tried to be louder than the others and Molke would sit, her face shining brightly, and help in the harmonizing. From time to time she would say humain, and the children would follow suit. As the candles got low and began to go out only the kerosene lamp was left burning, until Vassil's son, the peasant friend of the family, would come to turn it out. Molke would hand him a big piece of challah. No Jew was allowed to turn out fire on the Sabbath.

In total darkness Simche and Molke would sit after the children were in bed, and talk about the next world and how a Jew has to prepare for it, how much good he had to do to his neighbors, to his friends, and even to his enemies to gain enough mitzvas to go right to heaven. . . .

They sat talking until they tired and went to sleep. And when the Sabbath was gone and the grim week started, it was again the start of a struggle to make enough to live on. . . .

The word for week was *vokh,* but it meant more, it meant everyday life, it meant hard work, it meant the return from the heavenly joy of the Sabbath to the world where one was "misunderstood, despised, and often hated." The people of the shtetl, it was said, lived from Sabbath to Sabbath, the one day each week that made all Jews equal and every man a king.

11

Hasidism and Haskalah

It was always *schwer zu sayn a yid*—hard to be a Jew—in Eastern Europe. To be a Jew meant to face difficulties and dangers every day. Could a Jew escape that condition? Some tried. They had two paths open to them. One was to desert Judaism and convert to another religion. The other was to remain a Jew but to try to change Jewish life so as to eliminate all its difficulties and dangers.

The great mass of Eastern European Jews took neither path. They accepted the challenge of being Jewish and remained loyal. The options nineteenth-century Russia gave them only a small minority accepted. The government let Jews assimilate to the middle class without forcing them to convert to Christianity. And thousands who had the education and the financial means did. In every community the government also imposed, as we have seen, an official Jewish structure to carry out the czar's notions of what the Jews needed. Jews who accepted that structure took their legal problems to secular courts, sent their children to government schools, and looked to the government rabbis for spiritual leadership. But so few embraced this imperial Judaism that it was said Jews on the government payroll exceeded the Jews who acknowledged their authority.

Most of the Jews gave their allegiance to the kahal, despite the czar's attempts to abolish or weaken it. The kahal expressed basic and ancient Jewish concepts of religion and social welfare. It was the outgrowth of Jewish collective life. The government, in trying to destroy it, only succeeded in strengthening it by making membership a courageous and voluntary act. Every Jew who insisted, in defiance of the czar's anger, on remaining within the Jewish collective multiplied the Jewish will to survive. They did not want to assimilate. They cherished their own institutions. They were Jews and they meant to go on living as Jews.

Loyalty to Jewish identity freely given did not mean, however, that there was no conflict within the Jewish community. The old joke, that wherever there are two Jews there are three synagogues, reflects the discord and dissension within the Jewish world.

For many years Eastern European Jewry was divided by the two hostile camps of Hasidism and Haskalah. Both, as we have seen, rose in the eighteenth century, Hasidism as a revolutionary movement of religious renewal, the Haskalah as the enlightenment. In the beginning, rabbinic Judaism, which for centuries had dominated Eastern European Jewry, felt itself under siege from both camps.

Hasidism, which rapidly won the great majority of shtetl people, seemed the main danger at first. It met violent resistance from the rabbinical scholars and from the sheyneh of the shtetl. The Misnagdim believed Hasidism was such a terrible apostasy that they used denunciation, jailing, and ostracism against it. There was a time when each group placed marriage with the other on a level with marriage to a non-Jew.

Yet the principles of both were complementary, two aspects of the Jew's relationship to his God, rooted in the same Covenant. The Hasid stressed God's compassion, mercy, and understanding; the Misnagid divine justice and the Jew's obligation to fulfill his duties. By the early nineteenth century, Hasidism and rabbinic Judaism found the boundary lines between them blurred. The Hasids moved from anti-intellectual extremism back to the ancient tradition of respect for learning. They became proud not only of their leaders' magic powers but of their knowledge of the sacred books. The courts of the zaddiks became centers for both the learned and the unlearned, the prosteh and the sheyneh.

While the two movements did not merge, they managed to reconcile their differences. The shtetl world, knowing and needing justice and compassion, rationalism and emotionalism, learning and faith, was able to absorb both movements.

Hasidism was by no means monolithic. There were many variations within the movement, influenced in part by the personalities of the different Hasidic leaders and in part by social and economic differences. *Life Is with People* concludes, however, that the character of the regional divisions of Eastern Europe seemed to have the greatest influence upon patterns of Hasidism.

The Ukrainian Hasids were the prosteh and the uneducated. Their leaders were rarely scholarly, and their followers believed blindly in the magical powers of the zaddikim. The traditional conflict between the rational, scholarly Misnagid and the emotional, untutored Hasid persisted in the Ukraine until the Russian Revolution destroyed that world.

The Lithuanian Jews resisted the Hasidic movement. Known as cool skeptics, the *Litvaks* turned a deaf ear to the ecstatic songs of the Hasidim, and laughed scornfully at the tales of miracle-working rebbes. Nevertheless, says *Life Is with People*,

> . . . little by little, the ethical aspect of the teachings of Besht, the ideals of love for God and Israel, penetrated even into the Lithuanian shtetl and contributed to the formation of a strangely intellectualized Hasidism. Rabbi Zalman Schneour of Lady, 'The Old Rov,' was the founder of this form of rationalistic Hasidism, completely devoid of the magical component and based on three principles: *Khokhma, Bina, Death*—intelligence, understanding, knowledge. The first letters of the three words form the word *Khabad,* which is the official name of the movement, although it is also known as the Lubavitsher Hasidism, because the dynasty originated by 'The Old Rov' officiated in the shtetl of Lubavitsh. In Khabad-Hasidism, the mystical relationship of man and his Creator is intellectualized to the maximum and the Hasidic principles of love and compassion toward human beings arh based not on emotional sentimentality but on rational principles of ethics and philosophy.

In the Polish shtetls the zaddik was often a famed scholar whose following observed every injunction of the *Shulkhan Arukh,* the huge compendium of rabbinical law. The Polish Hasids attended the zaddik's court, but at home they studied the law and saw to it that their children did too, in cheder.

What helped Hasidism and rabbinic Judaism find an accommodation was the common threat they faced in the Haskalah. The enlighteners argued that Judaism, like Christianity and Mohammedanism, was a universal religion that was not the possession of a particular people. The Jews in the Diaspora had long ceased to be a people, they held, because a people must live in its own country. There was no longer any nationhood linked to Judaism; rather you were a Frenchman or a German or a Pole "of the Mosaic faith."

From this idea flowed the conviction that Jews should abandon those differences which were not organic with their "universal religion" and insist upon assimilation with the non-Jewish society they lived in, adopting its culture, language, patriotism.

In Western Europe many young followers of the enlightenment swiftly left the Jewish fold altogether. In Eastern Europe the Haskalah met strong resistance because of the special national character of Jewish life. The Jews there felt a much greater bond as a distinct people. Their devoted study of Talmud and Cabala, their Hasidism, their economic separation from the Gentile world, their self-government in the kahal, their Yiddish language—all these welded an ancient identity they fought to continue.

The enlighteners tried to batter down Jewish nationalism by claiming that assimilation was inevitable for the Jews; they would be wise to welcome it because it would free Jewry from all its suffering. Anti-Semitism would vanish, they promised, and together with the Gentiles, the Jews would rise to a higher realm of morality and culture.

All through Eastern Europe the early advocates of the enlightenment saw it as a ticket of admission to Gentile society. In Poland, Haskalists criticized traditional Jewish values and customs. They adopted the fashionable Western short jacket, shaved earlocks and beard, and abandoned religious observances. They preferred to be called not Jews but "members of the Polish nation of the Jewish persuasion." They pressured the state to impose reform upon the more stubborn Jews. In Galicia, Joseph II said he would grant the Jews the privilege of religious tolerance, but only if they would become less Jewish, that is, give up the harmful teachings of the Talmud. He started a secular school system for Jewish children with German as the language of instruction. This pleased the Haskalists, who thought German was the natural tongue for Western culture.

In Russia, as we have seen, the small number of prosperous Jews whose activities drew them close to high government circles praised Russian culture. They too, like the Poles, looked to the government to force reform upon Jewish education and religion, and pleaded for the emancipation of such deserving Jews as themselves. Several of these first *maskilim* converted to Christianity.

Watching these developments in Poland, Galicia, and Russia, the traditionalists and the Hasidim concluded the Haskalah was suicidal for Jews. They viewed modernism and secularism as powerful weapons in the hands of enemies. Feeling themselves under siege, they withdrew behind the walls of tradition.

It was the Jews in the larger communities, the centers of trade and commerce and finance, who seized most eagerly upon the new general education. Most of them were literate in Hebrew or Yiddish, and knew as well the local language—German, Polish, Russian, Ukrainian, Lithuanian, or Lettish. They needed education to engage in foreign trade, and their commercial activities pulled them beyond the limits of their own town. Such Jews were among the first to be urbanized when the Eastern European cities were still in their infancy.

The maskils were of many kinds. In Galicia their leading figure was Nachman Krochmal (1785-1840). Faithful to Jewish identity, he used modern scholarship to extend the Jews' intellectual frontiers. The Hebrew press and Hebrew scholarship enjoyed a revival of several decades under maskil influence. In Galicia the merchant-scholars were violently opposed to Hasidism. Joseph Perl went so far as to call in the imperial police to break up Hasidic prayer meetings. On their side, the traditionalists were also guilty of invoking state power against other Jews. When a Russian maskil was on his way to Berlin in pursuit of greater secular knowledge, the traditionalists were said to have got the Prussian government to refuse him a passport because they feared he would desert Judaism while abroad.

To the young Russian and Jewish intellectuals of the mid-nineteenth century the crowning of Alexander II promised liberation from despotism. The Yiddish poet Eliakum Zunser spoke of the czar's early reign as the Golden Epoch of Russian Jewry. He idealized Alexander II, believing in his good will and trusting him to take down all the legal fences that shut the Jews in. Young Jews shared the faith of the Russian intelligentsia in a coming emancipation. They rushed from the Pale to enter the czar's high schools and universities, where they expected to help create a cultural renaissance. The Russian writers who shaped the radical minds of that generation—Chernishevsky, Pisarev, Dobrolyubov— were read avidly by Jewish youth too. The intellectual power that had been dedicated to the study of Talmud turned to the study of science, philosophy, social reform.

"Russification" was the slogan of the day as the government pro- claimed its desire to merge the Jews with the "indigenous" population. But how would this be done? Would the Jews achieve an equality which allowed them their difference? Or would it be an equality that cost them their independent national identity? The czar meant to do it by interfer- ing with the internal life of the Jews. And some maskils went along to the point of allying themselves with government agents to put down the "fanaticism" of the "dark masses" in the shtetls. Rabbis and teachers certified by the state inevitably served the czar's interests and ended up using the police against the Hasidim. They censored Hasidic books and restricted the movement of the zaddikim. The breach widened between the Jewish intellectuals and the Jewish masses, who felt only contempt for those who pushed the czar's assimilation campaign.

The spread of secularism stiffened the resistance of Orthodoxy to all change. The effect upon both rabbinic Judaism and Hasidism was to make them repressive and inflexible. Let a Jew move the slightest distance from the prescribed path and he might be accused of sinning. If he cut his earlocks, if he preferred the shorter coat, if he read a modern book, he was a heretic.

Nevertheless, there was change. Against rabbinic opposition, even the Jewish educational system permitted small innovations. The late nineteenth century saw some secular subjects introduced, and modern teaching methods began to be applied.

The enlighteners built their strongholds at the two ends of the Pale—the ancient city of Vilna in the north and the new metropolis of Odessa in the south. To the port rising on the Black Sea came a group of Jewish merchants from Brod, the Galician town. In the 1820s they started the first school of Jewish general education in Odessa. Lacking traditions, the city became Europeanized before other Jewish communities. Vilna's enlightenment began in the 1830s with two writers who shaped the new

Hebrew style—Mordecai Aaron Ginsburg and Abraham Baer Lebensohn. The circle that grew around them was not concerned with assimilation; it struggled to build a solid foundation for the rebirth of Jewish literature.

In the shtetl, as well as in the larger towns, the Haskalah made its approach to the learned through the use of Hebrew, "the sacred language." This was the medium the Talmudic scholars used; they would not read Yiddish or the other secular languages. The enlighteners published newspapers, magazines, books, and pamphlets in Hebrew, with the aim of broadening the horizon of Jewry. The intellectual appeal reached young scholars and some of their elders too.

In *The Brothers Ashkenazi*, I. J. Singer describes Feivel, the ragdealer of Lodz whose passion was rationalism. He spent all his earnings on the literature of the Haskalah. Young people gathered secretly in his house to read the "evil books." Pale and terrified students pored over the modernist writings and felt the foundations of their old life dissolving under them. One of Feivel's disciples was thirteen-year-old Nissan, the son of Reb Noske, a teacher of the Talmud. Singer pictures the feverish devotion of young Nissan to the new learning.

> He read day and night, running frequently to Feivel for new material, stealing candles from the synagogue to be able to study when everyone else in the house slept. He read without system whatever Feivel gave him, Mendelssohn's modernist commentary on the Bible, Maimonides's *Guide to the Perplexed*, German translations which he only half understood, articles in the modernish Hebrew periodical *Ha-Shahar*, stories and poems and treatises by Smolenskin, Mapu, and Gordon, rationalist essays by Krochmal and Adam HaCohen, fantastic travel books, Hebrew treatises on astronomy and higher mathematics, of which he understood nothing, but which attracted and fascinated him because they represented that great, brilliant, forbidden world which was opposed to everything held sacred by his father. From Mendelssohn he passed on to Solomon Maimon, and from him to Spinoza and Schopenhauer. He mumbled the German words to himself, caught part of their meaning, tried to guess at the rest, lived in a fever of intellectual effort and wild hopes. And with all this he still managed to learn the weekly lesson set by his father. . . .

The Haskalah made far deeper inroads upon the cities than the shtetls. But almost no shtetl was without an enlightened soul. True, probably only one, and he spotted by his fellow Jews because he subscribed to a newspaper. Even though they cried shame upon him for reading such ungodly stuff, they pestered him for the news.

Looking back on the Haskalah, the writer called the father of Yiddish literature, I. L. Peretz, showed small regard for its accomplishments. In his *Memoirs* he wrote:

> Enlightenment also signified "education," principally linguistic. For example, "What is the word for 'boots' in all languages?"; a few songs on the theme: "The four seasons of the year"; Fishman's Hebrew grammar; Stern's *"Wie haben zie geshlafen?"* (How did you sleep?); my officer-teacher of Russian who repeated again and again *prechastia, de prechastia* (the Russian participle and gerund); the declamations: "By the light of the moon" and "I would raise my voice with force, if I would know"; and the fact that Isaac, the only one of my schoolmates who graduated from the gymnasium, was away at that time studying medicine—that was the sum total the Enlightenment contributed to our Jewish way of life!

In another place, Peretz said:

> The Enlightenment didn't throw any significant light in any direction. It failed to inspire us with hope, or to provide us with a philosophy that we could live by. Hastily, and without sufficient thought, we leaders took over a foreign formula. The resulting trend was not consonant with the Jewish way of life and thought. It was a misdirection. We didn't know for sure where it meant to go, but certainly it traveled on the wrong road—the wrong road for us Jews!

Peretz mentioned his fellow townsman Abraham Goldfaden—the first Yiddish dramatist—as "the most hopeful herald" of the enlightenment. Goldfaden thought the Gentile was "panting to greet us and take us in, in one universal brotherhood of man. But, from what we could see in Zamoscz, they hadn't yet stretched out the hand of friendship far enough to be noticed."

With rapid strokes Peretz sketched in the local Polish intelligentsia, with whom the enlightenment leaders thought the Jews should become brothers. One example serves to show Peretz's scorn:

There's Dr. Skrashinsky, who is good-natured when he's not drunk or in a bad temper because he is not yet drunk. He's an old "intellectual." He, too, has a wife, and three daughters, and they, too, are ugly rather than beautiful. After graduating from medical school and becoming a doctor, he closed his medical books forever, never to open them again. He leaves all medical problems to others. What has happened in the medical profession since he left college, is no concern of his. What he learned there is enough for him. On his rounds in the hospital, he passes rapidly between the rows of beds, casts a glance here and there, asks the patients to stick out their tongues, to turn their heads now to the right, now to the left—and out he goes. The medical aide follows him into the office. There Dr. Skrashinsky hastily and impatiently writes out some 30-odd prescriptions. This is concluded with the ejaculation: "Son of a bitch!" He hands the prescriptions to the assistant, and that's the end of his day's work.

At least in Zamoscz, he concluded, "the Jews were exhorted by the enlighteners to assimilate with the city riffraff and the backward peasants." As for himself, he added, the enlightenment caused only "a momentary romantic stir in our lives," and then it passed.

12

Hebrew—or Yiddish?

Peretz had nothing good to say for the enlightenment, at least while in one mood. Yet from the Haskalah came a new Jewish literature of which he himself was a proud part. Poets, novelists, dramatists, folklorists, historians, journalists created an original literature out of the treasures of their ancient culture and the vitality of their contemporary life. An extraordinary feature of this new literature was that it functioned in two languages—Hebrew and Yiddish.

At the beginning of the literary renaissance, Hebrew and Yiddish were intense opponents. The early Haskalists despised Yiddish. To them it was the tongue of the ignorant masses and of the Hasidic courts. Not a language, really, only a jargon. It was like a shameful brand the long exile had burned into the Jewish people. The Haskalists revived the ancient Hebrew tongue and used it to carry on their war against ghetto medievalism and separatism.

Their enemies, the Hasidists and the Talmudists, fought bitterly against the spread of modernized Hebrew. To them the sacred tongue was destined for religious study and nothing else. To use it any other way was an offense, like cutting off the earlocks or shortening the gaberdine.

Their everyday language was Yiddish, the language identified with Sholem Aleichem's Kasrielevky. But the tongue was used far beyond the shtetl. About two thirds of the world's Jews at that time spoke or understood Yiddish. It is a language often described quite misleadingly, says Maurice Samuel, "as an offshoot of Middle High German with an admixture of Hebrew and Slavic. Etymologically nine-tenths of the words commonly used in Yiddish are in fact of German origin, but the tone and spirit of the language are as remote from German as the poetry of Burns is from the prose of Milton."

The formation of Yiddish began perhaps a thousand years ago, when Jews from northern France settled along the Rhine and adopted the local German dialects, bending them to their own old speech patterns. The new Yiddish dialect was influenced at once by elements of the Hebrew and Aramaic that were the languages of Jewish religion and scholarship. Slavic tongues too came to modify Yiddish later on, as did the speech of other regions Diaspora Jews lived in. By the sixteenth century Yiddish writing flourished in Italy, where Ashkenazic Jews had settled. A century later Amsterdam Jews were publishing Yiddish books and the first Yiddish newspaper. Not until the mid-nineteenth century, however, would Yiddish literature be more than a vehicle for entertainment and for instructing those shut off from Hebrew, chiefly women and the less literate men.

The pioneer champion of Haskalah in Russia was Isaac Baer Levinsohn (1788–1860) of Kremenets. He used the Hebrew language to renew Jewish life, proclaiming the value of manual labor as both a physical and spiritual cure for ghetto Jewry. His book *The House of Judah,* published in 1828 in Vilna, dealt with Jewish life in Russia. The young devoured the message: to seek knowledge, to study not only Hebrew systematically but Russian too, and to learn the skills needed to till the soil.

Nachman Krochmal used Hebrew to examine the Jewish past critically. His *Guide for the Perplexed of the Age* compared Israel's historical path with that of other peoples and found the mark of Jewish individuality to be its absolute spirit, with both faith and reason its essential manifestations. Jewish nationhood was indestructible, he believed, and its unique genius would yet make great contributions. He saw the revival of Hebrew language and literature as the way to develop Judaism's character.

The poets of the Haskalah turned to the Bible as a rich literary source, giving new meaning to its lore, applying its humanist values to their own life and times. The kings and prophets, the peasants and shepherds of old Judea, spoke in many a narrative poem to the modern Jews of Eastern Europe. One of the most popular of such writers was Abraham Mapu (1808–1867) of Kovno. His historical romances were the first novels in modern Hebrew literature. Implicit in his vision of ancient Palestine, with its Hebrew culture deeply rooted in its own soil, was the contrast with life in the czarist Pale. His intricately plotted love stories, packed with intrigue and adventure, inspired readers with a consciousness of how great and noble Jewish life had been–and could be.

Another Hebrew writer produced by Vilna was Judah Leib Gordon (1830–1892). In his epic poems and dramatic monologues he satirized the ugly, stagnant side of Jewish life and attacked the rigid orthodoxy, the ignorance, the bigotry that choked progress and growth. He was not content to worship ancient glories; his aim was to draw upon the best of the old traditions to meet the challenges of modern society.

Like Gordon, Moses Leib Lilienblum (1843–1910) insisted that contemporary society demanded reforms of the Jewish people. His autobiography, *The Sins of Youth,* published in 1876, was one of the most influential books of its time. In his dismal picture of ghetto life in Lithuania, he called for the young to be educated for a useful life. Unless they were, he warned, they would desert the Jewish world. His book was a cry for rabbinic Judaism to recognize the need for inner change, to let outdated customs go, to clear the path for religion to adjust to life.

The Hebrew novelist and editor Peretz Smolenskin (1842–1885) came from the Russian province of Mohilev. After a brief stay with Hasidism, he took up secular learning, mastering modern European languages while earning his way as a Hebrew teacher. Refused a permit to publish a Hebrew journal in Russia, he began issuing his monthly, *Ha-Shahar,* from Vienna in 1869. He believed Jews had a national identity that transcended their religion. He used the Hebrew language to strengthen Jewish nationalism among his people. Samuel Leib Citron, who knew Smolenskin, said "there was not one yeshiva in all the Russian Pale to which Smolenskin's *Ha-Shahar* had not found its way. The young people devised cunning ways to deceive their guardians. They read *Ha-Shahar* on the Gemara and under the Gemara and sat up nights with it. . . . The Orthodoxy considered *Ha-Shahar* as unclean, feeding on poison emanating from the anti-divine, while the young people looked upon it with piety and love, as something sacred. . . . [It] revolutionized their minds, undermined old ideas infested with traditional moldiness, stimulated them to new ideas. It brought light into the most dismal Jewish byways, rescuing thousands of talented young people who otherwise would have exhausted their talents in sterile pastimes."

But as the nineteenth century wore on, a reaction to the Haskalah set in among the writers themselves. We saw it in Peretz. Smolenskin was another to confess its failures. The wave of assimilation had swept many young people away from Jewish identity. Anti-Semitism was on the rise, and pogroms broke out in several parts of Russia. If the slavish imitation of Western ways continued, Smolenskin said, it would end in national suicide. Jewish survival depended upon the recognition of the Jewish people, not only as a religious community, but as a national entity. Jewish history proved, he said, that the religious idea and the national concept were one and inseparable. His modern novel, *The Wanderer in Life's Way*, took his hero through the stages he himself had undergone, and climaxed with the hero dying in defense of Jews during the Odessa pogrom of 1871.

Early in the 1860s a Jewish press emerged, chiefly in Vilna and Odessa. Some of the papers appeared in Hebrew, some in Yiddish. They advocated Haskalah, fought against anti-Semitism and for equal rights for Jews, and tried to modernize the Jewish way of life. Russian censorship crippled their efforts, and few lasted long. By 1871 all were silent, except for Smolenskin's monthly, which reached Russian Jews from Vienna.

As Jewish nationalism mounted, Hebrew as a spoken tongue revived. It had been confined chiefly to the book, but now, powered by the new written literature, it became the core of the Hebrew renaissance. On the tongue and in print it became the vernacular, with dusty clichés cleared out and nineteenth-century modernity introduced.

Swiftly, within two generations, it was renewed as a living language developing with and from Jewish life. Later, with the rebirth of Israel, it would become the language spoken by all the people, used in every aspect of daily life, in schooling and in business, in science and in politics, in war and in peace. Hebrew became a language with a rich secular literature, a literature that could produce a Nobel laureate.

The pioneer of spoken Hebrew was Eliezer Ben Yehuda (1858–1922). He gave all his energy to its revival, using his skills as philologist and editor to adjust Hebrew to the needs of everyday life. His *Dictionary of Ancient and Modern Hebrew* is the indispensable classic in this field.

It was in poetry that the new Hebrew spirit found its greatest expression. The most important pioneering work was done by two poets who broke free of outworn Hebrew rhetoric and created an idiom that came more simply and naturally to a modern Jew's tongue. Chaim Nachman Bialik (1873–1934) was the new poetry's most powerful voice. Born in the Ukraine, he became the channel for the aspirations of the Jewish masses. He wrote in both Hebrew and Yiddish, taking from the traditional Jewish culture his diction and symbols. He made available to modern Jews the riches of all the older sources, from Bible and Talmud through the rabbinic literature and the secular Jewish poetry of Arabic Spain. With his strong historical sense, he brought out their timeless and universal humanism.

Bialik's contemporary, Saul Tchernichovsky (1875–1943), born in the Crimea, wrote lyric and epic poetry in Hebrew. He portrayed the martyrdom of both medieval and modern Jewry. He found the bond of common humanity in the widest range of characters. He sought the regeneration of the Jewish people in labor, in cultivation of the sense of beauty, and in the rebellious and heroic spirit of ancient Israel. His work in translation was of equal value, bringing into Hebrew the poems and plays of Homer, Sophocles, Shakespeare, Goethe. For their seminal influence on Hebrew poetry, Bialik and Tchernichovsky have been compared with William Carlos Williams and Ezra Pound.

A little younger was the poet from White Russia, Zalman Schneour (1886–1959). He defied the old conventions in vigorous modern Hebrew, and resurrected the sensual life in verse and fiction. The social upheavals of his time were at the heart of his work. He exalted resistance to injustice and hymned the historical struggle of exiled Israel to retain its identity among the nations.

But it was through Yiddish, the language of the shtetl, that writers reached their greatest audience. In poems, novels, plays, short stories, they mirrored the lives of the shtetl Jews, sparked a revolt against inertia and dogmatism, and drew readers on to new horizons. The Yiddish literature grew in soil fertilized by deep social change, for by the 1880s the Jewish masses had begun to awaken, to take their fate in their own hands. They moved into cities and entered the working class as industrial capitalism took hold in Russia. They organized trade unions, went on strike, reached out for education and culture.

Among the early writers to meet their needs were Isaac Meir Dick (1814–1893) and Eliakum Zunser (1836–1913). Dick's realistic stories and romantic novels were best-sellers, popular especially with women who bought his penny booklets at the market or from wandering peddlers. His critical picture of traditional Jewish life was enjoyed particularly for the folk humor embedded in it. Zunser, like Dick born in Vilna, was known as Eliakum the Bard. His poems, satires, and essays recorded the responses of the Jews in the Pale to life under the czars. Zunser's work too was circulated in penny paperbacks and his poems were recited, sung, or chanted in the home. Like Dick, his goal was to teach ethical conduct and to plant new ideas in his readers' minds.

In 1875 a humorous Jewish weekly appeared. Called *Yisrolik,* it was edited by Isaac Joel Linetsky (1839–1916) and Abraham Goldfaden (1840–1908). Linetsky had written a novel attacking Hasidic practices, and Goldfaden was known for a collection of Yiddish songs. Soon Goldfaden reached new audiences with his plays and musical comedies, establishing the first modern professional Yiddish theater.

In the last quarter of the nineteenth century three writers appeared whose work earned Yiddish literature worldwide recognition. They were Sholem Jacob Abramowitz (1836–1917), known by his pen name, Mendele Mocher Sforim; Sholem Rabinowitz (1859–1916), who wrote as Sholem Aleichem; and Isaac Leib Peretz (1852–1915). Each wrote in Hebrew too, but it is for their Yiddish creations that they are supremely valued.

The oldest of the group, Mendele, was born in Kapulye in the Lithuanian Pale. He passed an examination for teachers in government-sponsored schools and got a job in a Jewish school in Kamenets. In 1858 he moved to Berdichev, where marriage brought him a wealthy father-in-law who supported him while he wrote. In 1864 his first Yiddish story was serialized. When his father-in-law lost his money, Mendele, now with a family of seven, could barely pay his rent on his earnings from his books. Baron Horace Günzburg became his patron for a few years, until Mendele was hired as principal of a Jewish school in Odessa. The job supported him for the rest of his life.

Mendele stripped the folk language of its heavy Hebrew idioms and shaped it into a flexible instrument for his stories on the Jews penned up in the Pale. His first literary experiments were all in Hebrew, but one day he asked himself:

> What good does the writer's work and thought serve him, if they are of no use to his people? For whom was I working? The question gave me no peace but placed me in a dilemma. Yiddish, in my time, was an empty vessel, filled only with ridicule, nonsense, and the twaddle of fools who could not speak like human beings. . . . People were ashamed to read Yiddish, not wanting to show their backwardness. . . . The Hebrew writers, concerned only with the style of sacred language, uninterested in the people, despised Yiddish and mocked it. . . . My concern for Yiddish conquered my vanity and I decided, come what may, I would have pity for Yiddish, that rejected daughter, for it was time to do something for our people. . . .

When he wrote his first Yiddish story—it was in 1863—Mendele adopted the pseudonym that means Mendele the Bookseller. His work, as one critic said, "has a kind of dual feeling: every line echoes with disdain for the Jewish life that is past and every chapter ends on a note of sadness that cries out with compassion." In his stories he kept telling people to live better.

> The life of the Jews, although it seems outwardly ugly and dark in color, is inwardly beautiful; a mighty spirit animates it, the divine breath which flutters through it from time to time. . . . Israel is the Diogenes of the nations; while his head towers in the heavens and he is occupied with deep meditation concerning God and His wonders, he himself lives in a barrel.

Critical though Mendele was of Jewish life in the Pale, he loved and identified with the tragicomic characters who crowded his bitter novels. Total commitment as a Jew did not require him to romanticize the

Jewish world he sprang from. Half a century of creative work earned him the title of the grandfather of modern Yiddish literature.

Sholem Aleichem was one of Mendele's great literary offspring. (This pen name means "Peace be unto you" in Hebrew, and is a traditional greeting among Jews.) Born in Voronov in the Ukraine, at seventeen he became a teacher of Russian, and at twenty-one a government rabbi. He married a landowner's daughter and went into business to make a living until he quit in 1903 to give all his time to writing. He published his first Yiddish story at the age of twenty-four. It was the first droplet in a powerful flood that would fill twenty-eight volumes of his collected works.

In his own lifetime Sholem Aleichem became the kind of public literary figure that Dickens and Mark Twain were. Like them, he was both a popular entertainer and a major artist. But unlike them he came from a much more homogeneous culture. He could speak for his shtetl society and be recognized as their one true voice, the voice of the Jewish people as a whole. As Irving Howe and Eliezer Greenberg put it:

> Sholem Aleichem gave to the Jews what they instinctively felt was the right and true judgement of their experience: a judgement of love through the medium of irony. Sholem Aleichem is the great poet of Jewish humanism and of Jewish transcendence over the pomp of the world. For the Jews of Eastern Europe he was protector and advocate; he celebrated their communal tradition; he defended their style of life and constantly underlined their passionate urge to dignity. But he was their judge as well; he ridiculed their pretensions, he mocked their vanity and he constantly reiterated the central dilemma, that simultaneous tragedy and joke, of their existence—the irony of their claim to being a Chosen People, indeed, the irony of their existence at all.

Sholem Aleichem's world is peopled with the ordinary Jews of the shtetl, but the three most representative ones are Tevye the Dairyman, the philosopher of the heart; Menachem Mendel, the *luftmensch*; and Mottel, the cantor's son. Tevye is no nebbish: his instincts are healthy; he knows what is good in this world and what is bad. His defeats do not destroy him. Unable to reshape the world, he uses humor to sweeten it. In Sholem Aleichem's stories about children, he introduced something new into Yiddish literature. He portrayed young boys who resisted

being pushed so soon into their father's world of study and prayer, with
its crowded, dismal atmosphere, its burdens of Torah and mitzvas,
its eternal worry about making a living. The humorist showed deep
insight into childlike feeling. He shared with the child the gift of carefree
laughter.

Sholem Aleichem's stories poured out of him inexhaustibly. What
kind of Yiddish style did he use? Not, says Maurice Samuel, what we
would call a writer's.

> He was a speaker. He chatted about his world. Or put it this way: he
> let his world flow through him, as though through a funnel. He uses
> ordinary language; his stories, people, and townlets have the quality of
> anonymity; they are not thought up; they happen to be there, and
> Sholem Aleichem calls our attention to them, casually. It is all one long
> monologue, the recital of a pilgrimage. Certainly it is all transfigured by
> the passage through his mind, but it is not distorted. The bad is there
> with the good, the hateful with the heartening. . . .

When Maurice Samuel was a young man, he met Sholem Aleichem
on the porch of a New Jersey beach hotel. It was shortly before the
writer's death, and Samuel never forgot the encounter.

> I, a youngster of twenty, sat and stared at him, who was already a
> living legend among his people. A slightly gnomelike elderly little man,
> with a clever, wrinkled face, kindly, satirical eyes, and a gentle voice, full
> of tenderness and slyness. Even in repose his face suggested irrepressible
> amusement, as though invisibly on the tip of his nose a joke were ever
> balanced neatly on its center of levity. You would have taken him for
> a Hebrew-teacher, a small town rabbi, perhaps even for a wise old
> shopkeeper given to books and close observation of his customers; cer-
> tainly an attractive, even a fascinating personality, full of years and suf-
> fering and accumulated comment on life, but not, in heaven's name, a
> literary genius.

Peretz was born at a time when the Hasidic tradition was under
attack from the new trend of secular thought that was gaining ground
among Eastern European Jews. He began to write in Yiddish while still
an adolescent, but his first work to be published was a book of poems in
Hebrew. For the next ten years he did little writing while practicing law.

Then the government disbarred him when a competitor denounced him as a socialist. Needing money, he turned again to writing, this time in Yiddish. "In that language," he said, "are hidden the weeping of our parents, the outcries of many generations, the poison and the bitterness of history. It contains the dearest diamonds—Jewish tears which become hardened before they had dried." Diamonds, but his writing never made him any money to speak of.

In 1890, financed by a rich Warsaw Jew, Peretz toured many shtetls in the Pale to gather economic and cultural data for a report on the life of Polish Jews. Returned from his investigation, he was hired as book-keeper by the Jewish Civic Center of Warsaw, a job he held until his death. He did all he could to strengthen the Jewish community. The city's Jewish literary life centered on his home.

As an intellectual, Peretz did not reach the mass audiences of the more popular Mendele and Sholem Aleichem. He linked the folk voice of the past with the Jewish renaissance, using a pithy, idiomatic Yiddish. He fought against assimilation and for a dynamic Judaism. His earlier writing is electric with city rhythms and social revolt. Later he reshaped Hasidic tales into parables that reflect the dilemmas of the modern intellectual. His influence upon Yiddish writers has been compared with that of Pushkin upon Russian and Emerson upon American culture.

A glimpse of Peretz at home in Warsaw has been left us by Jehiel Isaiah Trunk. The young writer, newspaper-wrapped story in hand, heart pounding, rang the famous man's doorbell. When it opened,

There stood before us a short, stout figure, with graying short-cropped hair. A long yellow mustache concealed his mouth; the ends of the mustache drooped over the corners of his lips and trembled upon his cheeks. He wore a silk smoking jacket. His shirt collar was open and revealed a short, rather heavy neck. He wore pince-nez, with half lenses. He raised his limpid eyes to us and asked what we wanted.

They spoke in Yiddish, Trunk explaining that he had brought a story for Peretz to read. Then the young man looked around the second-floor apartment.

Peretz's home overwhelmed me, everything seemed to me full of poetry and fame. His study was a large light room, though the old fashioned windows, set with small panes of glass, seemed somewhat countrified. In the center of the room stood large wooden bowls of full-grown oleander plants, which filled the room with flaming crimson, a crimson that seemed dewy in the light of the sun pouring in. The windows of the study showed a generous portion of sky because there was no building opposite, only the tall factory chimney just opposite the window at which Peretz's desk stood. The desk itself was covered with large vases of flowers that overshadowed everything else, making it seem like a fragrant flowerbed. The walls were densely hung with drawings and photographs, including portraits of Peretz in various poses. . . .

After Peretz read the young writer's story, he said,

"You have interesting ideas . . . but you don't know Hebrew. You think in Yiddish and translate yourself into Hebrew. No, this has no point, why don't you write Yiddish? Doesn't it suit you, a son-in-law of the Priveses, to write in the language of the common herd?"

Trunk promised to bring him something in Yiddish, and then Peretz said he'd like to read him something he'd written that day. Trunk recalled the effect it made on him.

It was a prose poem, "Cain and Abel." I would not today rank it among Peretz's best work. But at that moment I considered it the greatest spiritual experience of my life. Peretz's voice was unlike any I had ever heard, at once crusty and tender, metallic as gold and sweet as the subtlest honey. In this voice Peretz could express with mastery his emotions and turbulence, his longings and his unquieted temperament. He could threaten like an enraged lion and be gentle as the most peaceful dove. . . .

Peretz gave guidance to many such young writers. "To be Jewish," he said, "is our only way to be human. . . . To find the essence of Jewishness in all places, all times, in all parts of the scattered and dispersed world-folk; to find the soul of all this and to see it lit with the prophetic dream of a human future—that is the task of the Jewish artist."

13

What Is to Be Done?

On a spring day in 1866, Alexander II was returning from a walk in the Summer Garden in St. Petersburg. A young student standing nearby took out a revolver and pointed it at the czar. As he pulled the trigger, someone shoved his arm aside. The bullet missed its target. The student, Dmitri Karakozov, was immediately seized and turned over to the police.

Karakozov, the son of an impoverished noble family, had been expelled from two universities. He was a member of "Hell," a terrorist cell in a student revolutionary organization. Disgusted with endless radical talk, he wanted action. The Russian masses seemed deaf to propaganda; they needed to be roused from their torpor by an act of revolutionary violence, he decided. When his group refused to join him, he set out to assassinate the czar by himself.

Karakozov missed, but his shot reverberated throughout the empire. Russians crowded churches to give thanks for the czar's deliverance. In theaters, audiences interrupted the performance to demand everyone sing "God Save the Czar." Messages of joy at the czar's escape poured in from the local assemblies and from governments abroad. The public contributed funds to erect a chapel on the sacred spot where the czar had stood when fired at. Over the entrance was placed the message TOUCH NOT MINE ANOINTED.

The gallows quickly put an end to Karakozov's young life. His act gave government reactionaries the chance to pull the brake on the reforms initiated by Alexander II. The abolition of serfdom, the intro- duction of local government councils, and a new court system were more than enough, they insisted. They seized upon the attempted assassination as proof of what they had argued all along: reform had gone too far and anarchy now threatened the regime. To stop it dead, the czar must expand the police, clamp censorship tighter, revise the educa- tional system, and intensify Russification.

Tired of trouble, and longing for protection, Alexander II gave full rein to reaction. He set up a commission to investigate the assassination attempt. It failed to find any widespread revolutionary organization. But a handful of terrorists was enough for the investigators. They concluded the universities were producing students with no respect for law and order and that the people themselves were fed up with the decline in authority.

In May 1866 the czar proclaimed his new course. His policy would safeguard religion, property rights, and public order. "Orthodoxy, autoc- racy, and nationality"—they were more solidly enthroned than ever. Any talk of a constitution for Russia or of political freedoms was now a crime against the state.

The key members of Karakozov's revolutionary group were caught and sentenced to hard labor and imprisonment in Siberia. Several leftist publications were closed down. Hundreds of other radicals were rounded up and often sent into exile without trial. Political prisoners were treated so harshly that dozens died, committed suicide, or went insane in prison. Often when suspected revolutionists were acquitted by the courts, police rearrested them and forced them into exile. Certain acts against the state, especially terrorism against officials, were placed under military courts, which could impose the death penalty.

Karakozov was one of those angry young men who despaired of any basic change in Russian life. The number of radical intellectuals had grown in the late 1850s and early 1860s as Alexander's relaxation of controls allowed some freedom to discuss social and economic ques- tions. But the radicals thought the czar's reforms trivial, promising no real improvement for the empire's suffering millions.

One of the powerful influences on youth's emotion and thought was a novel called *What Is to Be Done?* Published by Chernishevsky in 1864, it became the bible of the radicals. It held out the vision of a socialist society and advocated workers' cooperatives and women's liberation. Its heroine, Vera Pavlovna, wants independence and equality in her sexual life, and at the same time a career. She sets up cooperatives of seamstresses that divide profits equally among the workers and also educate them. The leading male character, Rakhmetev, trains himself like a Spartan in selfless devotion to his future revolutionary mission.

The official view of such young radicals is reflected in the records of the political police. They describe Vera as a woman "with hair cut short, wearing blue glasses, slovenly dressed, loath to use comb and soap, and living in common law matrimony with one or more members of the male sex, who are equally repelling."

The radicals were encouraged at first by the distrust the peasants showed for the czar's emancipation program. The former serfs struggled against the restrictions and obligations still imposed upon them, and even used armed force against authority. In Kazan province in 1861 they refused to obey the officials. Troops came in and killed or wounded 350 peasants. The rural unrest encouraged the radicals to demonstrate, and many more students turned to socialist thinkers as their guide. Manifestos poured off underground presses, addressed to peasants, soldiers, and students, calling for open revolutionary activity in response to the government's repressive measures. What the people needed, one said, was "land and freedom." When St. Petersburg University was shut down because the government thought it a hotbed of revolution, Herzen's journal, *The Bell,* urged the expelled students "to go to the people." That phrase became one of the most famous slogans of the Russian revolutionary movement. Another manifesto called "Young Russia" urged youth to place itself at the head of the masses and lead them to a revolution, a revolution that would wipe out the institutions of state, family, and church, and under a dictatorship build a new Russian society based on socialism and the peasant commune.

Turgenev's novel of 1862, *Fathers and Sons,* creates in the character of Bazarov a young radical taken as typical of his generation. Opposite such a youth the novelist poses his weak and ineffectual elders, members of the gentry class to which Turgenev himself belonged. The critic

Pisarev considers Bazarov a positive hero because as a nihilist he negates the traditions and values of the older generation. His example, Pisarev writes, would help free the sons from the superstition and ignorance that crippled their fathers.

That same year the first revolutionary organization was founded, taking the name of "Land and Freedom." It survived scarcely twelve months, but it set the example for a movement that would prepare the people for revolution.

The conflict between fathers and sons had broken out in Jewish life before Turgenev wrote his famous novel. When a young man or woman in the shtetl chose to abandon Orthodoxy, it meant a break with family and home. They usually went one of two ways. Some gave up their Jewish identity to merge with the revolutionary movement. They saw that the czar's minor reforms had not solved the Jewish question. Only a tiny part of the Jewish population had seen its lot eased. And as reaction intensified control, the dream of Jewish emancipation faded. Only a revolution gave hope for liberation. The young Jewish radicals were captivated by the call to "go to the land"; the revolt would begin through work with the peasant.

Others left Judaism to become part of the secular Yiddish world, joining one of the political or cultural movements within it. Some who repudiated their Jewishness later came back to it, after discovering that Russian revolutionaries too could be anti-Semitic, that socialism would not necessarily give the Jews full equality and liberate them from persecution.

It was part of the tragic war between the generations, one side totally committed to Orthodoxy, the other side blind to historical Judaism, national as well as religious.

At the end of the 1860s, the government sent to officials throughout the empire a manual on how to cope with the "internal enemy"—the Jews. It was based upon the writings of Joel Branfman, a Jew from Minsk who converted to Christianity and turned spy and informer for the government. In essence, the manual insisted the government must destroy the Jewish community and all its institutions or Russia would be taken over by the Jews' worldwide "secret government."

Soon after, a pogrom against the Jews broke out in Odessa. Greeks and Jews alike had built Odessa into a prosperous city. But the two groups were strong commercial rivals. The Greeks decided to scare their competitors out through a pogrom. They excited the Russian populace with a rumor that the Jews had desecrated a church. The pogrom began on Easter Sunday, 1871. Mobs of Greeks and Russians ran wild in the streets for three straight days, beating up Jews and smashing and looting hundreds of their homes and shops. It ended on the fourth day when the government finally intervened. An "investigation" concluded that the violence against the Jews was only a "crude protest" of the masses against the "exploiters."

About the same time, one of the czar's numerous commissions on the Jews decided that whatever remained of Jewish self-government must be eradicated. Schools, mutual-aid societies, community organizations—all must go. But the Pale of Settlement had to be continued. A commission spokesman warned how dangerous it would be to let the Jews outside the Pale because "the plague that now affects only the western provinces will engulf the entire empire." This concern for quarantining the Jewish "plague" had proved for years to be quite elastic. The historian Simon Dubnow points this out in relation to the Jews and agriculture.

> During the reign of Alexander I and Nicholas I colonization was encouraged in the barren southern steppes. But under Alexander II, when Novorussia was no longer in need of artificial colonization, and the farmland was needed for its "own" peasants, the government ceased to encourage Jewish colonization. Shortly after, the Jews were deprived of the largest tracts of land, which were in turn distributed among Russian peasants.

Anti-Semitism was forming into an explicit movement and shifting from the religious to the political sphere. Conservative forces in Russia, like those in Germany and France in the same period, pumped up the Jewish issue. They exploited anti-Semitism as one day Hitler would, if far more skillfully. The folklore of anti-Semitism deposited in the minds of the peasants over the centuries was brought to the surface by vicious men whose aim was to turn the poison to political account.

The revolutionary rumblings in Russia exposed dissatisfaction with the way things were. Instead of honestly facing its internal problems, the government used diversionary tactics. On the powerless minority of Jews was laid the responsibility for the evils the people were suffering from.

In high governmental and social circles anti-Semitism became more and more blatant. Edicts and exclusions continued. A military-service law added new discriminatory measures against the Jews in the 1870s. In the Russo-Turkish War of 1877–1878, many Jews died to emancipate their "brother Slavs." The government gave no praise to their sacrifice; instead, from all the military provisioners who were abusing their contracts, it singled out a Jewish firm for public attack. At the Congress of Berlin in 1878, the participating nations favored granting the Jews of Rumania, Serbia, and Bulgaria equal rights. But the Russian delegate fought against it.

A Catholic priest defrocked for "unheard-of crimes and a corrupt life" published a book *On the Use of Christian Blood by Jews.* The government bought copies to distribute among the Russian police. In 1878, another ritual murder trial was staged, against nine Jews in the Caucasus. They were exonerated, but the popular superstition about ritual murder was once again spread on the pages of the Russian press.

The Jewish question in Russia was not isolated from other problems, of course. As Henrik Sliosberg, one of the Jewish lawyers who fought hardest against czarist anti-Semitic persecution, pointed out:

> Jews were not the only ones denied civic rights; actually 90 percent of native Russian peasants were without rights. There was high-handedness not just toward Jews alone, but toward other nationals as well; the Jews, however, received the hardest blows from Russian reaction, and the persecution of Jews became the barometer of the political outlook at any given time.

Renewed oppression by the czar drove still more young Jews into the revolutionary movement. Many joined the Populists, a socialist group that saw the peasant commune as central to the ideal society they wanted to build. Students from the universities, the technical schools, and the high schools made up the bulk of the Populists. Many were from the upper classes and the clergy, with a proportionately large number of Jews among them. These sons and daughters were the first generation raised on secular lines, knowing little of Jewish tradition. Some were hostile to everything Jewish. They feared their Jewishness would block them from "going to the people." They often came from families which had assimilated. Fighting for a revolutionary new society meant entering a world in which all religions would disappear. There would be no Jews, no distinction between themselves and everyone else.

That they felt so inferior is due in part to the Russian literature they were raised on. Pushkin, Gogol, Lermontov, Dostoevsky, Turgenev could not depict Jews as anything but vile creatures. Russian fiction, drama, and poetry portrayed the Jew as dirty, dishonest, contemptible; as parasite, opportunist, fiend. The Jew would do anything for money, betray anyone for his own advantage. He deserved only the worst treatment. Sensitive as they might be to all other human souls, when it came to the Jew, the Russian writers saw him as subhuman. Nor did the socialist theoreticians to whom the young radicals looked for guidance offer any opposing view. Neither Marx nor Bakunin had a good word to say for the Jew, rich or poor. Rather, their "scientific" opinions only strengthened the self-hatred of young Jewish revolutionaries.

In the beginning, the Populists believed the overthrow of czarism would be a simple thing to do, perhaps even bloodless. They had only to bring light to the "dark people." Once shown their true interests, the peasants would make the revolution.

The young Jewish radicals were fascinated by this messianic vision of a kingdom of heaven on earth. Morris Winchevsky, recalling his feelings then, said, "We were all Narodniki and the peasants were our brothers." But the peasants—four-fifths of the population—were largely illiterate, while most of the Jews, no matter how badly off, could at least read and write and be reached through the printed word in Yiddish. One of the Jewish Populists, Aaron Liberman, tried to convert the Jewish masses to socialism with a Hebrew monthly. The government banned it in Russia and it soon went bankrupt.

Since the peasants could not read the revolutionary word, the radicals had to make them hear it. Following Herzen's "To the People!" about two thousand Populist students took to the countryside in what became known as the "mad summer" of 1874. They penetrated deep into Russia, expecting to find peasants waiting for the word to rise up against the czar and seize the land.

But the ex-serfs, though they lived in terrible poverty, were bound by deep religious faith and an almost instinctive loyalty to the czar. Not the czar but landlords and officials were their enemies, as they saw it. When the call for revolutionary action came, they did not respond. Instead, they led some of the radicals, especially those already anti-intellectual, toward a mystical belief that in the rural folk there resided an innate wisdom from which the Populists could learn.

Most of the young radicals, their naive faith shaken, soon became disillusioned. But the Populist movement was not destroyed. It changed, finding other approaches to revolution. By 1878 a new secret society was active, reviving the name "Land and Freedom." It set up a tighter organization and stricter discipline. An attempt at a political demonstration in St. Petersburg was swiftly crushed by the police. The leaders were arrested and thrown into the Peter-Paul fortress. Such old ways of working, it was apparent, were no longer effective.

The new way was to be terrorism. Basically, a policy of frustration. The masses had shown themselves indifferent to making a revolution. If they would not help themselves, the enlightened few must do it for them. But how? Through the direct method of terror. Assassinate the most unpopular leaders of the government, the reasoning went, and the regime would collapse, giving way to the new order.

It was not a fresh idea. Terror had been tried sporadically in Russia for the past quarter of a century. But these young revolutionaries meant to do it differently, in a systematic and sustained way.

It began early in 1878. The first target was the St. Petersburg police chief, General Fedor Trepov, who had ordered flogging of an imprisoned revolutionary for not taking off his cap when the chief passed. In January Vera Zasulich shot Trepov, but lacked the skill to more than wound him. To the government's consternation, a jury acquitted her because of Trepov's reputation for cruelty and she disappeared underground.

Educated Russians openly showed their sympathy for Zasulich. In the next few months there were serious strikes in St. Petersburg. Zasulich's act was followed by more attempts on the lives of officials, with the terrorists resisting arrest and sometimes shooting it out with the police who raided their hideouts. That summer the chief of the czar's Third Section of gendarmes was himself assassinated. Now government and public alike were convinced an army of terrorists was operating. In actuality, their total number, scattered in small groups, was probably no more than a thousand. Ignorance and fear led the government to launch a massive campaign against sedition and terrorism. Officials were given the power to expel undesirables, exile the dangerous, shut down periodicals, and try in military courts any civilians suspected of acts of terrorism. Relentlessly the czar's men raided, arrested, expelled, jailed, executed. They could not help but be indiscriminate under such orders, and the innocent were caught as often as the guilty were missed.

The sweeping attack only heightened the terror. In 1879 Prince Dmitri Kropotkin was killed. His assassin was Gregory Goldenberg, a young Jew. When Goldenberg was arrested many months later, he was tricked into talking to an informer-cellmate and gave away names, methods, and other details of his terrorist group. When he realized what he had done, he hanged himself in his cell.

The mounting use of terror caused a split in the Land and Freedom society. One group, calling themselves the Black Partition, determined to go on with propaganda work in the villages. They put their trust in reason and persuasion. The revolution would be justified only if it were the work of the people for whose benefit it was supposed to take place. The others, impatient at the slow work of education and frustrated by the Russian conditions which defeated most attempts at reform, formed the People's Will. It was a tiny, highly disciplined group of professional revolutionaries ready to justify any means by the one end—revolution.

The two groups divided funds and materials amicably and went their separate ways. The refusal of the Black Partition to adopt conspiratorial methods made it easy for spies to penetrate their group. The police smashed their printing press early in 1880 and the leaders fled abroad.

The wave of terror and the dissatisfaction with the government's conduct of the war with Turkey produced a political crisis for the czar. The educated classes wanted to return to the reforms of the 1860s and even asked for constitutional government. The ruling circle was shaky, uncertain, divided over how best to meet the serious challenge. If the revolutionary danger was as great as it seemed, would it be better to make concessions to the people? Or better to crush the opposition with even more violence?

14

1881—The Terrible Year

In August 1879 terrorists of the People's Will sentenced Alexander II to death. For nearly two years they carried on a desperate campaign with but a single objective—to kill the czar. They made no preparations for the seizure of power. They gave no thought to what might happen upon the czar's death. Their only hope was that the people would rise up and take their fate into their own hands.

Three times they planted dynamite to blow up the imperial train. Each time something went wrong. Then they turned to another scheme. They placed dynamite under the floor of the czar's dining room in the Winter Palace. The charge was set to go off just as a state dinner was about to begin. The explosion occurred on time, but the czar's entry had been delayed. The victims were eleven guardsmen killed and fifty-six others wounded as the walls and floors caved in.

Government morale was shattered, the citizens in panic, many fleeing the city. St. Petersburg was put under a state of siege, with armed guards patrolling the streets, curfew imposed, and the royal family in hiding.

The czar appointed a commission with dictatorial powers to root out sedition and made General Mikhail Loris-Melikov its head. A few days

116

later, a terrorist tried—but failed—to kill the general. The young man was arrested and hanged within forty-eight hours.

Loris-Melikov pressed the czar to make reforms in domestic policy. The terror, he argued, was the diseased outgrowth of deep dissatisfaction among the people. Peasants, students, the clergy, local officials—all were embittered because they felt the government did not listen to their needs. The czar, he said, should get rid of tyrannical and corrupt officials, relax the censorship, and revive the spirit of the early years of his reign. Alexander was impressed. He moved to liberalize the government. Meanwhile, police informers and agents provocateurs helped hunt down scores of terrorists. Twenty-one were executed. It was the price they paid for six unsuccessful attempts on the czar's life in a span of eight months.

The reforms made by the czar were superficial. He abolished the Third Section but transferred its gendarmes to the state police and continued their old functions. As terrorist activity diminished, the mood of crisis passed. The czar listened agreeably to a scheme for expanding his State Council so as to give his rule the appearance of broader popular participation.

As his advisers drafted a manifesto announcing the changes, the terrorists were completing plans for another assault upon Alexander. Director of the operation was Andrey Zhelyabov, the son of serfs. Early in 1881 he and Sophie Perovskaya, a daughter of aristocrats, took an apartment in St. Petersburg for the plotters to work from. They watched closely the czar's movements about the capital: he followed a fixed routine on Sundays. Now they could design his death.

They rented a cheese shop and at night mined their way beneath it to a point under the street the czar's carriage nearly always passed over. They chose Sunday, March 1, for the day of execution. If his carriage took the usual route, he would be blown to pieces by the underground cylinders of dynamite. If that failed, bomb throwers stationed in several places would have their turn.

Meanwhile, the police started to grope their way toward the heart of the People's Will. Zhelyabov was picked up on suspicion. But the terrorists had allowed for that possibility; they could go on without him. Suspicious neighbors told the police something strange was going on at the cheese shop, and on February 28 they raided it. They failed to detect the concealed entrance to the tunnel where the dynamite was buried, or even to notice the earth piled under a bed. They left after chatting idly about the terrorists' cat.

The next morning was March 1. With two bombs in her lap, Sophie Perovskaya drove to her rendezvous with six other terrorists, who were armed with two more bombs. Some would be lookouts, the others throwers. They went over their signals and procedure one last time, then moved to their stations.

It was about two o'clock now, and the sky was clouded over. The wind whistled over the snowy streets, crowded with worshippers on their way home from church. The Emperor's carriage raced back to the Winter Palace by way of the Ekaterinsky Canal. Cossack guards rode beside it and ahead, while behind were two sleighs filled with policemen. When the czar's carriage came abreast of the first terrorist— Rysakov, a nineteen-year-old factory worker—he threw his bomb under it. Flames shot up, and as the sound of the explosion smashed the Sunday quiet, the back of the carriage tore apart. The frightened horses bolted ahead, dragging the royal carriage a hundred yards more before the coachman could rein them to a halt. The police rushed up and opened the door, expecting to find death. But the czar stepped out, pale, shaken, and limping slightly. The police urged him to return at once to the Winter Palace, but he wanted to go back to where the bomb had been hurled. A crowd had gathered, screaming, shouting, pushing to see the captured terrorist. On the snow lay a wounded Cossack and a dying boy. The czar walked toward them, his officers failing to restrain him. They all moved like sleepwalkers. As the czar edged his way close to the spot where the bomb had exploded, another of the terrorists, a nobleman, Grinevitsky, leaned against a wall, watching him. When the czar was two feet away, Grinevitsky flung a bomb at his feet. Stone, flesh, snow, blood, fire fountained high in the air. The bomb's roar faded, replaced by screaming. Then silence.

The czar's legs had been shattered. Blood gushed from all parts of his body. Around him lay twenty others, dying in the street, Grinevitsky among them.

The czar, still alive, was taken to the palace, where he died an hour later. Grinevitsky died soon after. Rysakov was beaten by the police but refused to give his identity. That night St. Petersburg was full of rumors that the czar had been assassinated at the order of high officials who did not want even the slightest concession made to liberalism. But the next day the People's Will issued a manifesto taking responsibility for the murder.

> Alexander II, the tormentor of the people, has been put to death by us, Socialists. He was killed because he did not care for his people, burdened them with unauthorized taxes, deprived the peasants of their land and surrendered the workers to the mercy of plunderers and exploiters. He did not give the people freedom: he did not listen to their griefs and their tears. He defended only the rich and lived himself in the utmost luxury, while the people went hungry.
>
> The Czar's servants, from the village police to the high officials, plundered the people and barbarously maltreated the peasants; and these servants of the Czar were especially protected and rewarded by the Czar. Those who stood out for the people he hanged or exiled to Silbeia.
>
> So he was killed. A Czar should be a good shepherd, ready to lay down his life for his flock: Alexander II was a ravening wolf and a terrible death has struck him. Now a new Czar, Alexander III, climbs to the throne. He must not be allowed to behave like his father. May he proceed to hold general elections in the villages and towns and in all the factories. May he recognize the sorrows and deep needs of the people, and go forward into the truth!

If measured only by the czar's death, the plot of the People's Will was a success. But from the point of view of those who sought social justice and the progress of liberty, it was an unmitigated disaster. It led only to further repression and reaction.

The public was shocked and numbed by the news. The workers did not rise up in the cities. The peasants thought Alexander had been assassinated by noblemen who wanted serfdom restored. The students did nothing but refuse to contribute to wreaths for the dead emperor.

It was a defeat for the police, but they quickly recovered, and captured the rest of the conspirators. Rysakov broke down, repented his part, and gave information. The others stood by their convictions.

The trial was swift, the verdict guilty, the sentence death by hanging. On April 3, the prisoners were dressed in black, and a placard reading

CZARICIDE fastened to their chests. They were taken in tumbrels to Semeonovsky Square, where eighty thousand people were gathered to witness the hangings.

Hardly were the trapdoors sprung when the new emperor, Alexander III, issued a manifesto announcing the end of all reforms. "The voice of God commands us to rule with faith in the power and the truth of the autocratic authority, which we are called upon to confirm and to preserve."

It was the end, too, of the People's Will. Their spirit was exhausted.

In place of a constitution, the new czar imposed what he called "the law of reinforced security." He gave dictatorial power over the citizenry to his governors. It was a Magna Carta for police terror, renewed annually for the next twenty-five years. For his chief adviser the Czar selected Konstantin Pobedonostzev, a fanatical reactionary who believed in a police state guided by the church. His slogan was "Russia for Russians."

By Russians, of course, he meant Orthodox Christians; Jews were aliens, and aliens out to rule the world. Under this man and his czar, anti-Semitism was transformed into violence against Jews. The Russian nationalist press had become openly hostile, hinting that the Jews were behind the assassination. Officials left the capital on unexplained missions to the south of Russia, where they discussed with local police chiefs a probable "outburst of the people's indignation against the Jews," implying that it would be better for the police not to thwart the people. A rumor spread of a czarist edict permitting attacks upon Jews during the coming Easter.

In mid-April, pogroms exploded all over southwestern Russia. The first attack upon the Jews was launched at Elizavetgrad on Easter Sunday. A mob ravaged and plundered the large Jewish quarter for two days under the eye of the military. The terror spread in waves as the mobs cried, "Look for the Jew!"

In the next days and weeks the bloody fever raged through 160 cities and villages in the provinces of Kiev and Chernigov and Poltava and Kherson and Ekaterinoslav. Leaders of the mobs were not local people but Russians from the north. Bands of thugs came down by train to spearhead the riots. Investigators were convinced the pogroms were organized and financed by a group of right-wing terrorists known as the

"Sacred League." Among their leaders who held high office was von Drenteln, governor general of Kiev.

As soon as one pogrom was over, the hoodlums shifted to another district to repeat their performance. Their tactics became familiar: first, placards appeared accusing the Jews of being terrorists and the assassins of the czar; then came newspaper stories repeating the charges; and finally the whispered report that the czar himself was allowing "three days to plunder the Jews."

When the mob spirit had been whipped up, a quarrel would be picked with a Jewish shopkeeper, usually a liquor merchant. A fight would break out, the liquor would be raided, and the drunken mob would rampage through the Jewish district. The police and the military, who could have ended the threatening situation with a word, almost never acted. When they did, it was against those Jews who tried to defend themselves.

What happened in the first pogrom, at Elizavetgrad, where fifteen thousand Jews lived, was reported by a government commission. Since it was never intended for publication, it's undoubtedly free of the official lies one would otherwise expect.

On the night of April 15, an attack was launched on Jewish homes, particularly taverns, in the outskirts of the city, during which one Jew was killed. About seven o'clock in the morning of April 16, the disorders were renewed, spreading through the city with enormous force. Clerks and servants of saloons and hotels, artisans, coachmen, lackeys, officers' attendants, noncombatant soldiers—all these elements joined the movement.

The city presented an unusual sight: the streets were covered with feathers and cluttered with broken furniture; doors and windows shattered; an unruly throng rampaging in all directions, yelling and shrieking, pursuing its task of destruction unhindered; and as a supplement to this scene—complete indifference on the part of the local non-Jewish residents toward the pogrom in progress.

The militia called upon to restore law and order had no definite instructions, and at each new assault of the rabble the armed force had to wait for orders from its own superiors or those of the police. Under such an attitude of the militia, the anarchical mob—smashing houses and shops in full view of the passive garrison—could only conclude that its destructive progress was not illegal, but rather authorized by the government. . . . In the evening the disorders intensified, because a mass of peasants had arrived in the city from the neighboring villages in hope of confiscating some Jewish possessions. On April 17 an infantry battalion restored law and order in Elizavetgrad.

In Kiev the initial stages were the same, except that here the police advised the Jews not to leave their shops or go outdoors on Sunday, April 26. Why, the Jews wondered, did the police urge them to hide when the city was full of troops who could easily prevent disorder? But Elizavetgrad was a lesson to be heeded, and the Jews stayed off the streets that fateful Sunday. Nevertheless, at noon in the Jewish district called Podol, according to an eyewitness account:

> The air suddenly reverberated with shrieking, whistling and whooping, and roaring laughter. A horde of youths, artisans and laborers was on the march. The destruction of Jewish houses had begun. Windows and doors were flying, and soon all sorts of objects were being hurled from dwellings and shops. The mob then attacked the synagogue and, notwithstanding the sturdy bolts and locks and shutters, it was broken into without much ado. The Scrolls of the Law were torn into scraps, trampled into the muck and destroyed. The Christian population escaped the hoodlums by displaying icons in the windows, and marking crosses on shutters and gates. In the course of the pogrom, troops, Cossacks and infantry patrolled the streets of Podol. The soldiers signalled and occasionally surrounded the rabble, and issued orders for it to disperse, but the latter grew ever more fierce in its assaults.

At night, the drunken mob attacked in the suburbs and set fire to Jewish homes. They beat some Jews to death and threw others into bonfires. The next day the troops surrounded the mob and fired into it, wounding and killing a few. The pogrom stopped at once. About a thousand Jewish homes and shops had been destroyed, several scores of Jews had been wounded or killed, and a score of women had been raped.

With Kiev setting the example, some fifty villages and towns in the same province followed through with their own pogroms. Except that when a trainload of pogromists reached Berdichev, a Jewish self-defense militia was waiting for them armed with clubs. The "visitors" took one look and decided not to get off the train. Such self-defense was rare then, and made possible only because the police chief had been bribed to permit it.

That same spring, fires swept across the Pale of Settlement, burning down thousands of Jewish homes. The torch was lit chiefly in those places where the authorities had prevented pogroms. The fires, everyone understood, were another way of delivering the same message to the Jews. Minsk was one of the places badly hit. Two thirds of its fifty thousand inhabitants were Jews. The flames destroyed a fifth of the city. In a few hours, one thousand of the wooden houses burned down, and twenty-one of the synagogues. Ten thousand men, women, and children were left homeless.

By early May the pogrom fever seemed to have subsided. The government showed little concern for the victims. It inquired instead whether the pogroms were not part of a larger revolutionary plot, directed in the first stage against the Jews as a merchant class, and to be turned next against the Russian merchants, gentry, and officials. The czar himself said the pogroms were "most likely the doing of anarchists." And added that hatred for the Jews arose from their economic "supremacy" and their "exploiting" of the Russian people. This "exploitation" theory became the official justification for the pogroms and for repressive measures taken against the Jews.

The victims of the pogroms desperately needed help, but the authorities interfered with attempts to collect funds. They went further: they began to expel by the thousands Jews who were said to be living "illegally" in Moscow, Odessa, and other cities. While most pogromists got off with nothing or with light sentences, the courts punished Jews arrested for defending themselves.

The anti-Semites took these acts as encouragement to pick up the pogroms where they had left off. In late June a second series of outrages began which lasted through the summer. At their height, the semi-official newspaper, *Novoye Vremya,* headlined an article on the violence against the Jews with a parody of Hamlet, "To Beat or Not to Beat?"— and advised its readers it was necessary to beat.

In the fall, there was another lull. But on Christmas Day the blow fell on the Jews of Warsaw. The pogrom gangs went wild in the streets. When the authorities ended it on the third day, forty-five hundred Jewish homes, shops, and synagogues had been devastated and looted.

It was the pattern seen everywhere: plunder for two days and stop on the third.

And so the year 1881 ended. It has gone down in the Jewish calendar as one of the terrible years, a year of atrocities, a year of horror, a year when barbarism again besieged Jewry.

It was a year that would radically change the course of Jewish history.

15

A Permanent Legal Pogrom

The year 1882 opened with rumors that the czar had still worse things in store for the Jews. It was easy to believe, especially when the Minister of the Interior announced to the press that the government wished to get rid of the Jews. They should use the one right they had, he said—the right to emigrate.

Protest was impossible in a police state. The Jews chose public mourning as the way to demonstrate their feelings. On January 18, fasting and prayer took place in many cities. In St. Petersburg the Jewish community gathered at the great synagogue. They chanted the hymns of martyrdom, and the rabbi spoke, describing in a trembling voice Russia's torture of the Jews. "The congregation gave way to a long, drawn-out wail," said an eyewitness; "everyone wept—the old and the young, the poor in long gaberdines and the elegantly dressed. . . . This heartbreaking wailing, this outcry of the collective misfortune, lasted some two or three minutes. . . . The rabbi could not continue his address; covering his face with his hands, he wept like a child."

As spring came on, rumors of plans for more pogroms circulated. Balta, a town in Podolia province, was said to be a prime target. The city had three times as many Jews as Christians, and the Jews made secret plans for self-defense. On March 29, during Easter Week, the violence began. The Jews forced the hoodlums to retreat at first, but when police and soldiers appeared, the mob surged back. Instead of dispersing it, the government forces began to beat the Jews with rifle butts and sabers. Then,

> The houses which were not marked with a cross were invaded by the mob. Doors were beaten in, show-windows demolished, window-frames torn out. Furniture was thrown out of windows, crockery smashed, house-linen torn up, with a joy in destruction both childlike and savage. The mob took untold delight in ripping open featherbeds and down-quilts, and sending the contents drifting in the air like a fall of snow.
>
> In several places the pleasure the mob took in sheer destruction overcame their rapacious instincts. Peasants who came from their villages with wagons to take away their share of booty were repeatedly driven away by the rioters. For in certain boroughs, after the house-gear was destroyed, the houses went—floors and roofs being carried away, and nothing left standing but the bare stone walls. Not even the synagogues and cemeteries were spared by popular fury. The tombs were desecrated and the rolls of the Torah defiled.
>
> The mob naturally made first for the taverns and taprooms. Barrels were staved in; whiskey ran down the streets; men lay down in the gutters flat on their stomachs, to gorge themselves with the stuff. In several localities, women, crazed with drink, gave pure spirits to swallow to infants two or three years old, that they might forever remember these glorious days. Others brought their small children to the ruins of Jewish homes, there to bid them "to remember the judgment they had seen overtake the Jews."

News of that savage scene was censored. Court records revealed later that 1,250 dwellings and shops had been destroyed, and fifteen thousand people had been impoverished through loss of home, property, and merchandise. Forty Jews had been murdered or seriously injured, 170 had been more lightly hurt, and twenty women had been raped. Again, the pogrom halted only on the third day, when the governor came in.

The outbreak of the pogroms was a hard blow to the enlightenment. Many *maskilim* took it as proof that all attempts to draw closer to the dominant majority were useless. Moses Leib Lilienblum, the influential

Hebrew writer who championed the rising secular generation, was thirty-eight in 1881. He wrote:

> During the pogroms, a native woman, ragged and drunk, danced in the streets, joyously shouting: "This is our country, this is our country." Can we say the same, even without dancing in the streets, without being drunk? Yes, we are aliens, not only here but in all Europe, for it is not our fatherland. Now I understand the word "anti-Semitism." This is the secret of our affliction in exile. Even in Alexandria, in the time of the Second Temple, and in all the lands of our dispersion, we were aliens, unwanted guests. . . . Yet we dream we will become children of the European nations, children with equal rights. What can be more fatuous? For we are aliens and will remain aliens. . . . Our future is fearful, without a spark of hope or a ray of light—slaves, aliens, strangers forever.

What about the response in the shtetl to pogroms? Like fires and floods, says *Life Is with People,* pogroms are treated as "acts of God," catastrophes that come from outside.

> There is usually no defense organization. If organized resistance is attempted by the prosteh or by young people who have broken away from traditional attitudes, it is criticized by the very orthodox as "un-Jewish." One pleads with God for help and mercy. Perhaps one sends a delegation to the leader of the attacking group. But to fight back is the exception rather than the rule.
> This passivity cannot be attributed simply to fear of death. There are too many instances of Jews who have accepted avoidable death rather than violate the Sabbath. . . .

That there were attempts at self-defense is evidenced by what happened at Berdichev, and again at Odessa, where students of the local university organized units that managed at times to drive the thugs away from Jewish homes.

And what of liberal Russia? Its voice was silent. There was almost no protest against the pogroms from the great Russian writers. Turgenev and Tolstoy said nothing. Like Dostoevsky, Turgenev was openly anti-Semitic. Perhaps the sole exception was M. E. Saltykov-Shchedrin, who wrote:

History has never recorded in its pages a question more difficult, more inhuman, more painful than the Jewish question . . . No history is more heartrending than the history of unending torture by one man of another.

Liberal Russia, poisoned by anti-Semitism, accepted the line taken by the government: that the pogroms were merely a "people's tribunal" over the Jews. Even worse was the radical response to the pogroms. Some of the radicals adopted the tactic of fusing class with national antagonism. Thus they hoped the violence against the "Jewish exploiters" would be the first step in the awakening of the masses, a step that would be followed by riots against landlords, aristocrats, and government officials.

On August 30, 1881, the executive committee of the People's Freedom group appealed to the Ukrainian people with a leaflet that justified and praised the pogroms.

> Good people, honest Ukrainian people! Life has become hard in the Ukraine, and it keeps getting harder. The damned police beat you, the landowners devour you, the kikes, the dirty Judases, rob you. People in the Ukraine suffer most of all from the kikes. Who has seized the land, the woodlands, the taverns? The kikes. Whom does the peasant beg with tears in his eyes to let him near his own land? The kikes. Wherever you look, whatever you touch, everywhere the kikes. The kike curses the peasant, cheats him, drinks his blood. The kikes make life unbearable. Workers, arise! Wreak your vengeance on the landowners; pillage the Jews; kill the officials!

To the Jewish socialist, Pavel Axelrod, who had fled abroad in 1874 to escape the czarist police, such a leaflet was shocking. He wrote a pamphlet to explain the disillusionment of young Jewish radicals with the revolutionary movement. But his own friends argued it would be a mistake to issue it: it would alienate the Russian masses from the revolution. So Axelrod suppressed his pamphlet.

Chaim Weizmann had something to say about the peculiar attitude of some radicals to Jewishness. It applied then and still applies today.

> They would not tolerate in the Jewish youth any expression of separate attachment to the Jewish people, or even special awareness of

the Jewish problem. Yet the Jewish youth was not essentially assimila-
tionist; its bonds with its people were genuine and strong; it was only by
doing violence to their inclinations and upbringing that these young men
and women had turned their backs, at the bidding of the revolutionary
leaders, on the peculiar bitterness of the Jewish lot. My resentment of
Lenin and Plekhanov and the arrogant Trotsky was provoked by the
contempt with which they treated any Jew who was moved by the fate of
his people and animated by a love of its history and its tradition. They
could not understand why a Russian Jew should want to be anything but
a Russian. They stamped as unworthy, as intellectually backward, as
chauvinistic and immoral, the desire of any Jew to occupy himself with
the sufferings and destiny of Jewry.

News of the Russian pogroms horrified the world outside. The facts
leaked out so slowly that it was January 1882 before the London *Times*
ran a series called "The Persecution of the Jews in Russia." The graphic
details of the mass violence rallied popular support for diplomatic action
in behalf of the Jews and for material aid to the victims. Meetings,
speeches, resolutions urged the British government to act, but its response was so mild the Russians were little concerned.

In several countries relief funds to help the Jews emigrate from Russia
were organized. Victor Hugo headed the French committee. A huge
protest rally was held in New York as the first refugees from Russia
arrived. The U.S. Congress called on the president to request the czar to
protect his Jewish subjects against violence.

The Russian Minister of the Interior, Count Ignatiev, organized
regional conferences to look into the causes of the pogroms. But at the
same time he bemoaned "the tragic situation of the Christian population" in those very areas where the Jews had been savaged. The aim was
clearly to whitewash the regime. The inquiries provided a forum for
anti-Semites to slander the Jews as thieves, swindlers, parasites, and
enemies of the state. When Jews tried to refute the charges they were
not allowed to speak.

Ignatiev's "investigation" produced what the government wanted:
accusations against the Jews and proposals for repressive measures that
would strike at the Jews more effectively than the blind rage of mobs.

The outcome was a kind of permanent legal pogrom. The form it took
was a series of regulations entitled "Temporary Orders Concerning the

Jews." The use of "temporary" was a trick, for the orders stayed in effect until the Russian Revolution of 1917. The country came to know them as the May Laws because they were published in that month of 1882.

The May Laws persecuted the Jews as an "economically harmful" people. They banned Jews from settling outside of cities and small towns, and they made it impossible for Jews to have anything to do with land or to live in agricultural districts. They even forbade the extension of existing leases on real estate. In effect, the laws set up a pale within the Pale, limiting even more the Jews' right of domicile and freedom of movement.

Before the May Laws, Jews could move from one village in the Pale to another. Now any change of residence was considered a new migration and banned. Even within the Pale, restrictions were imposed on Jews' freedom to live in four cities. Only special categories of Jews could live in Kiev, and then only within two police precincts. Similarly in the Black Sea ports of Sevastopol and Nikolayev. And the czar insisted that Yalta, the site of his summer palace, be isolated from the Jewish blight.

The May Laws were no sooner issued than more pogroms erupted. In Rostov, then in Yekaterinoslav, and in other cities and towns in that province, and finally, in Nizhni Novgorod, an ancient city outside the Pale where only a score of Jewish families lived. Of this small number nine were murdered. The government's response was to expel the survivors, capping the street pogrom with a legal pogrom.

Under an official policy of anti-Semitism, year after year the noose was drawn tighter around the Jews in regard to residence, education, and professional activity. The government's desire, it said, was "to improve the mutual relations" between the Jews and everyone else. But the effect of restriction was only to sharpen hostility. Jews were looked upon as pariahs, guilty from birth for being born Jews.

A quota system was established for Jews in the secondary schools, and soon extended to the universities and technical institutes. Two generations of Jewish children and their parents, eager for education, were anguished by the discriminatory quotas. For schools within the Pale the quota was set at 10 percent; outside the Pale it was 5 percent; and in Moscow and St. Petersburg it was 3 percent. In cities inside the Pale the Jews might number 30 to 80 percent of the total population, yet only 10 percent of them were allowed into school. At great cost, thousands of youths studied at home, with tutors or alone, until they could qualify to enter universities abroad, usually in Germany, France, or Switzerland.

Although Russian law did not prevent Jews from engaging in trade, industry, or crafts, Jewish economic activity was crippled by legal restrictions. The Pale kept the vast majority of Jews from settling in nine-tenths of the empire. Only a tiny minority were privileged to live and trade anywhere. The effect was to keep millions of Jews in poverty and prevent them from making a useful contribution to the economic growth of the country.

The doors to civil service in all branches of government were closed to Jews, nor could they teach in secondary schools. A few were allowed posts in higher education. Talented Jewish students were often promised professorships—if they would agree to be baptized.

Even those who had already managed to get a higher education saw their rights taken away. Doctors, lawyers, and technicians could engage only in private practice. State or academic posts were denied them. As emigration from Russia increased, the law imposed upon Jews collective responsibility for failure to report for conscription, and for physically unfit Jews. Other Jews had to replace them in military service. If a young Jew evaded such service, his family had to pay a fine of three hundred rubles. And "family" was interpreted to mean other relatives if the parents were unable to pay.

By 1890 there were at least 650 laws in the Russian Code which discriminated against Jews. "About 90 percent of the entire Jewish population is an insecure mass, living from day to day, in poverty and misery," said a government report. But while the czar's policy impoverished the Jews, it served to enrich the bureaucracy that administered it. From top to bottom, police and other officials took bribes offered by the persecuted as the only way to save themselves. Bribery was so common it was called the "Russian Constitution." It protected the innocent from arbitrary rule and the loss of their human rights.

Passover of 1891 began with an imperial decree taking away from Jewish artisans and army veterans the right to live in Moscow. Tens of thousands of Jews were ordered out of the city they had legally lived in for many decades. That night police raided Jewish homes, routed families out of bed, and hustled them to police stations. One witness left this account:

Whoever failed to comply with the order of the police was subject to arrest; he would be jailed, and with criminals and all sorts of riffraff await his turn for deportation under a convoy. People sought refuge in cemeteries, during freezing weather, to escape arrest; women gave birth in railroad cars; in some instances ailing persons were brought in carts and transferred to the railroad cars on stretchers. Those who were subjected to that treatment remember in particular a certain ice-cold January night (1892). Throngs of Jews and their families with their pitiful bag and baggage had filled the Brest railroad station. Threatened by deportation and imprisonment, and failing to obtain a deferment, they decided to evacuate notwithstanding the weather. Fate was destined to play a spiteful trick on the unfortunates! According to a report of the chief of police, the governor-general ordered their deportation halted until the freezing weather had subsided—but that command was issued after the expatriation. . . . About 20,000 Jews were thus forcibly banished to the Pale of Settlement.

The anti-Semitic press kept silent; the liberal editors were censored. But refugees from Moscow who reached the United States let the world know the truth. In June two men, John B. Weber, U.S. Commissioner of Immigration, and the physician Dr. Walter Kempster, reached Russia, sent by an American committee to investigate the Moscow expulsions as well as conditions in the Pale. Shocked by what they saw, they published a report which said the Jewish situation was not going to improve, and urged the United States to make immigration easier for Russian Jews.

When the artisans were shipped out, Jewish merchants who were able to pay an annual fee of a thousand rubles had been allowed to stay. Now they too were treated like criminals. The police picked up anyone spotted with a "Semitic physiogonomy" and checked his documents. If they were not in order, he was deported at once. Rewards were offered for the capture of Jews without the right of domicile. In 1899 a new series of restrictions appeared, designed to free Moscow even of those Jews who had had the right of domicile.

In the Pale, restrictions multiplied, making it difficult or impossible for Jews to take vacations in the countryside or even to get medical treatment at certain resorts.

The government, with a single decree, wiped out the occupations of a quarter of a million Jews. The liquor trade was made a state monopoly in 1894, and the Jewish dealers, inn- and tavernkeepers lost their livelihood. Many Jews would all along have preferred a better way to earn their bread, but the government never permitted it. Now, deprived of their bare livings in village taverns, the Jews had little else to turn to.

Pauperism for Jews shot up in the last half of the 1890s. From 40 to 50 percent of the entire Jewish population was destitute and had to have public assistance for the Passover.

16

Zionists and Bundists

"How comical we were, how childishly naive," wrote one young Russian Jew after the pogroms of 1881. Like so many other Jewish radicals, he had thought there was no Jewish question, only a Russian question. With the spread of education, with political and social reform, the Russian question would be solved, and all other questions too, as a matter of course. Jew, Pole, Tatar, gypsy—all would lie down together like lambs.

Then out of the blue had come Elizavetgrad, with the mob howling, "Down with the kikes." And Kiev followed, and all the other horrors. "The blood runs cold in the veins when we look at the insulted and the humiliated," the young Jew wrote. "They seem only ghosts with deathly pale faces, expecting they know not what. At all levels of society, from the university intelligentsia to the ignorant peasant, a savage attitude towards Jews can be observed."

The pogroms made a profound change in the thinking of Russian Jews. Those of the middle class who had believed in the inevitability of progress, who had expected the complete emancipation of Jews and their unification with Russians, saw their dream become a nightmare. The student youth, who preached revolutionary action, had expected the liberated Russian—worker or peasant—to embrace the Jew as his brother. Instead, the Narodniks had hailed the pogroms as a popular movement deserving their support, and the liberals had shut their eyes to the assault upon the Jewish people.

But most shocked of all, wrote Pavel Axelrod in the pamphlet he never published, were the Jewish socialists.

> The Jewish socialist intelligentsia suddenly realized that the majority of Russian society did, as a matter of fact, regard the Jews as a separate nation and that they considered all Jews—a pious Jewish worker, a petit bourgeois, a moneylender, an assimilated lawyer, a socialist prepared for prison or deportation—as kikes, harmful to Russia, whom Russia should get rid of by any and all means.

Disappointed in Russia, many Jews longed for a homeland where they could determine their own destiny. In 1882, Leo Pinsker's pamphlet, *Auto-Emancipation,* voiced their cry. First published abroad in German, it was translated rapidly into Yiddish and Russian. Pinsker, an Odessa physician, had once believed assimilation was the answer. Now he held that the Jews were a distinctive group among the nations in whose territory they lived, a separate group that could neither assimilate nor be readily absorbed. Jews should no longer let themselves be forced to wander from one exile to another, he wrote. Rather, they should direct all their energies to acquiring a productive land as a permanent refuge. He thought either some place in the Americas or in Palestine would be acceptable for Jewish colonization.

In 1882, the first small group headed for Palestine. They were twenty-five students from Kharkov, socialists convinced by the wave of pogroms that their people were not the Russians but the Jews. That July they frunded their first colony near Jaffa, naming it Rishon le Zion (The First in Zion). Others followed, as Jewish nationalism reawakened. On the theme of "Back to Zion!" Eliakum Zunser wrote poems calling on Jews to leave the poverty and despair of Eastern Europe and fashion a new life with their own hands in Israel. He helped deepen the tiny rivulet of Zionist immigration until it became a powerful flood.

Zunser typified those Jews who did not deny the gains of the Haskalah but only the blind alleys it led to: assimilation and Russification. Another who joined his voice to Pinsker's was Moses Leib Lilienblum, who now returned to the Jewish community by advocating Zionism. He and Pinsker headed a society in Odessa organized to colonize Palestine. "The pogroms taught me their lesson," Lilienblum wrote. "I am convinced that our misfortune is not the lack of a general education but that we are aliens. We will still remain aliens when we will be stuffed with education as a pomegranate is with seeds." Through the efforts of such men, several colonies were established in Judea and Galilee in the 1880s and 1890s.

The sense of national renewal was stimulated both by anti-Semitism and by the model of liberal nationalism set in the West by such leaders as Mazzini. Among the oldest Jewish traditions was the idea of one day returning to the land of Israel. The societies bent on colonizing Palestine called themselves *Hoveve Zion*—"Lovers of Zion." They became a bridge between the intellectuals once alienated from Judaism and the traditionalist masses. Under Ahad Ha-Am's leadership, the movement developed a philosophy of Jewish nationalism. Ahad Ha-Am (the pen name of Asher Ginzberg, born in Kiev province in 1856) advocated a national cultural revival. He wanted a Jewish state in Palestine to serve as the spiritual center of world Jewry. Many of the younger Jewish writers were his disciples. One of them, Bialik, said Ahad Ha-Am brought them a new way of life, teaching them how to adapt their life to the upbuilding of the Jewish nation, raising the prestige of literature in their eyes, making them feel honored to be Hebrew authors.

True nationalism, said Ahad Ha-Am, is not contrary to the universal spirit. "Nationalism is a concrete form whereby the universal spirit reveals itself in every people in conformity with that people's circumstances, special needs, and historic course." The Jewish spirit could not be preserved in a ghetto and certainly not in assimilation. It could flower only in a culturally independent Jewish community in Palestine. He called for a cultural renaissance in the Diaspora and a physical renaissance in Palestine.

The Eastern European Jews would prove to be the mainstay of the Zionist movement. Russian Jews migrated first and most eagerly, then Galician Jews, and finally the Polish. Russia held by far the greatest number of Jews. There were now about 4 million in the Pale, 1.3 million in Congress Poland, and some 900,000 in Galicia and

Bukovina. Another, much greater stream of emigration, went west, to
the United States.

But it must be remembered that the vast majority of Jews stayed in
Eastern Europe. And in the mass, they remained attached to their
traditional faith. Pogroms and poverty were God's will, as they saw it.
They had never had any illusions about the world outside the shtetl or
ever considered assimilation seriously. The changes which took place
now in Jewish thought sprang not from them but mostly from Jews no
longer satisfied with Orthodoxy's denial of the modern world. The
search for new directions came from the modernists. They wanted
neither the ghetto nor assimilation, but national self-assertion. And
while they scouted for the right path, they did not forget the signposts
put up on the ancient road of the past.

Alexander III died in this transition period and was succeeded by
Nicholas II in 1894. Nicholas was a little man in stature and character, a
spineless, scheming despot. Any liberal who dreamed that a new czar
on the throne would mean a constitution for Russia was at once
disillusioned. Nicholas announced, "I intend to safeguard the principle
of autocratic rule as steadfastly and unflinchingly as was the case with
my unforgettable father." The same reactionaries remained at the key
posts of government; the same anti-Jewish practices continued.

Russia had just moved into the age of big industry, a change that
affected the Jews too, of course. A small upper class among them had
grown wealthy through their roles as bankers, wholesalers, manufacturers, railroad builders. But the mass of Jewish workers were handicrafts-
men, unable to compete with machine production. Legal restrictions,
prejudice, or Sabbath observance made it hard for them to find factory jobs
except in Jewish enterprises. These had grown up chiefly in Poland and
Lithuania. They made but few products, and because most of them were
small-scale, wages and working conditions were bad.

In his book *The Brothers Ashkenazi*, I. J. Singer pictures the rise of
Jewish-owned textile factories in Poland. A few Jewish pioneers had
opened a path into the weaving trade of Lodz and Jewish looms became
common. Jews from the countryside around swarmed into the industry.

Fathers brought their sons in from the villages to learn the trade.
Barefoot they came on all the roads leading into Lodz. They came with

sticks in their hands to beat off the village dogs, and on the outskirts of the town they put on their boots, which they had been carrying all the way. It was the custom to apprentice the boys for three years. A sum of money, the savings and scrapings of God knew how many seasons, was paid into the hand of the master weaver. The boys would receive no pay during the apprenticeship. They would get their meals and a place to sleep in, and from morning to night they would learn.

They stood in the hundreds at their looms, their skull-caps on their heads, the ritual fringes hanging over their cheap canvas trousers, pieces of colored thread clinging to their curly hair and sprouting beards, while their hands flew swiftly over the looms, weaving from before sunrise till long after sunset the piece goods which were to be made into dresses and women's kerchiefs. As they worked they sang snatches from the synagogue services, trilling the bravura passages like real cantors, pausing with special joy on the sacred words of the high festivals. The master weavers paraded up and down the aisles, keeping an eye on the heaps of merchandise, urging the workers on, infuriated if one of them stopped to wipe the perspiration from his forehead or to roll himself a cigarette.

The chimneys of Lodz poisoned the air, and the cesspools formed near each factory poisoned the ground. Sickness was everywhere.

Children suffered from rickets, fathers from tuberculosis, mothers from the strain of frequent childbirth, all from undernourishment and malnutrition. The streets were almost as thick as the factories with the wool and cotton dust which came out of the looms, or, more heavily, from the rags which were being reconverted into thread. Medical service of a sort was, when obtainable, free; but medicines cost money; and the weavers dreaded having to go into the clean shiny apothecary's, with its picture of the Madonna and its glittering carboys. Here they could not haggle; they had to come in, hat in hand, take what was given, pay humbly, and crawl out.

Low wages jammed families into one or two rooms. Rent came first—if they didn't pay, they were put out on the street at once—then food, and last of all, clothing, which meant the weavers wore nothing but rags. And when the boss cut wages? The older weavers, beaten down over the years, took it in silence. Their wives cursed and screamed. The young workers, too, were afraid.

Nevertheless, the Jewish workers did learn to organize. Workers' circles were formed, with each member paying dues. Week by week they accumulated funds to build their movement. Organizers brought them news of how workers lived in other lands. Of the international socialist movement, of the constant struggle with bosses in other parts of Eastern Europe, and of the Marxist theories which were penetrating Russia. The workers discovered their dignity and strength and began to assert their rights. After years of struggle, as Singer points out, great changes could be seen.

> Crowds gathered everywhere fearlessly, ignoring the police and their armed attendants. The workmen's circles were well organized, and worked day and night. Their membership had grown beyond all expectation and included every class of worker: weavers, shoemakers, leather-workers, stocking-knitters, cobblers, irreligious Jews in modern clothes, religious Jews in long gaberdines, women in wigs and women who had refused to shear off their hair after marriage, but wore a red kerchief about their heads. Meetings were in progress everywhere, councils met, strikes were called, literature was distributed openly, speakers addressed the crowds in the streets.

The workers' circles had become centers of the city's life.

> Apprentices came before them to complain of ill-treatment at the hands of their employers, or denounce their employers' wives for feeding them mouldy bread and sugarless coffee; housewives reported that they had been thrown out of their homes for non-payment of rent; servant girls asked for redress when their meager wages were not paid them on time. The Unionists, as the workers' leaders were called everywhere, because of their ceaseless appeals for united action, became general advisers to the working-class population. Wives of truckdrivers came to lodge complaints against drunken husbands who did not bring home their pay, but spent it in drink; there were even couples who came with their marital difficulties and turned the workers' circles into domestic-relations courts.

The Unionists learned, and learned fast, to be effective. Day after day they did their job on the streets.

Quick decisions were rendered, strikes called, delegates elected, ulti-
matums drawn up to be delivered to recalcitrant bosses. Committees
were even sent with threats of direct action against profiteering grocery
stores. Other committees were sent out to make the rounds of all the
shops and to see to it that none of the clerks was kept after hours. Here,
too, levies were assessed, and collectors sent round to shops and employers with a demand for the sum decided on.

No one dared to fight back. The workers' circles were all-powerful at
this time. . . . There was no appeal from their decision, and there was no
way of bribing them; they listened to no arguments, and they could not
be cited before the courts for any attempt to call in the authorities would
have meant exposing oneself to the concerted vengeance of the entire
workers' movement.

Toward the end of the 1890s, this new Jewish proletariat included
over 500,000 artisans, 100,000 day laborers, and 50,000 factory workers.
In the light industries, where they were concentrated, the Jewish artisans far outnumbered the non-Jews. In 1897 several groups of Jewish
workers, meeting in Vilna, combined into a central organization called
the General Jewish Workers' Union of Lithuania, Poland, and Russia. It
became known as the Bund. It grew into a powerful force in Jewish life.
At first, its struggle was economic, for higher wages and shorter working hours. It soon became clear that the results could not be great. Most
of the Jews worked in small shops belonging to poor artisans who
themselves worked. Under the abnormal conditions of Jewish economy
in the Pale, it was a strange class struggle. The Yiddish poet Abraham
Liessin called it a war of "the poverty-stricken against the indigent."

In reality, both were being oppressed by the same regime, denied their
civil rights, denied freedom of movement and choice of employment.
The economic struggle, then, could not be separated from the political
struggle against czarist autocracy.

It was through the Bund that many alienated Jews found their way
back to their own people and culture. They experienced a double
consciousness: of themselves as exploited workers, wanting to fight
alongside their brothers for a better life, and of themselves as Jews. The
early Bundist leaders felt a special responsibility toward the working
class of their own people. But there were Jews active in the broader
Russian socialist movement—Trotsky is an example—who regardee na-

tionalism as reactionary and bourgeois. Such nationalism, they said, was against the principles of scientific socialism and would wreck working-class unity. The Marxists did, however, recognize the need for a separate organization of Jewish workers. Propaganda could reach them only in Yiddish, and they did have special political demands because of legal restrictions against them. When the Russian Social-Democratic Party was founded in 1898, the Bund became a part of it. Though the Russian party leaders opposed it, the Bund began to express the natural Jewish feelings of its members and to champion Jewish culture. It spoke to Jewish workers as Jews, in Yiddish, the tongue familiar to them. The *Workers' Voice* appeared as the first underground newspaper in Russia published in Yiddish. Gradually the Bund educated the workers who had grown up in the Pale, and broadened their cultural horizons. It organized a system of secular Jewish schools, with Yiddish as the language of instruction. The Bund ardently supported Yiddish literature, printing the work of its poets and novelists in its underground press. Its schools supported a Jewish cultural autonomy and stressed such traditional Jewish values as social justice. Trade unionism, politics, literature—all fused into a national Jewish revival.

Zionism too began to combine socialism with nationalism. Several socialist-Zionist groups emerged, appealing like the Bund to the Jewish working class. One of their leaflets in Lvov read:

> Jewish workers of all countries unite behind the banner of Poale Zion! Brothers and sisters of the workers' class! We see before us two great and powerful movements: on the one hand socialism which seeks to liberate us from economic and political slavery; and on the other hand Zionism which seeks to liberate us from the yoke of the Diaspora. Both affect us greatly. Both promise us a glorious future. Both are vital for us as life itself. . . .

The Bundists wanted the Jews to be able to control their own schools, their own press, their own arts. The Zionists insisted upon their own country. They differed, too, on the question of language. Which should it be—Yiddish or Hebrew? Bundists insisted upon Yiddish, the mother tongue of the Jewish masses, as the language in which children should be taught. Zionists wanted Hebrew and organized Hebrew-speaking circles to prepare the Jews in the Diaspora for the exodus to Palestine.

Although they quarreled over ideology and language, Bundists and socialist Zionists were alike in one important respect: both rejected the attitudes of accommodation or passive resistance that were traditional in the Diaspora. Both groups searched out and celebrated the ancient Jewish record of forceful resistance to persecution and slavery. No more of suffering in silence, they said. The Jewish heroes of old fought back. And so shall we.

17

The City of Slaughter

Kishinev . . . that had been its name for more than a hundred years. In 1903, the poet Bialik renamed it "The City of Slaughter."

It was the capital of the province of Bessarabia, in southwest Russia. Kishinev was noted for its gardens and orchards, so lush with fruit, and its wide streets, shaded by acacias. The town boasted a cathedral, a theological seminary, a college, a museum, and a public library. Adorning the squares were statues of Alexander II and the poet Pushkin. Its factories produced soap, candles, liquor, and tobacco. And its location on a river and a railroad made it a busy commercial center, trading in grain, wine, tobacco, tallow, wool, and skins.

About 125,000 lived in Kishinev, people of many nationalities: Moldavians, Wallachians, Russians, Bulgarians, Tatars, Germans, gypsies, and Jews.

The Jews were the largest single group, 40 percent of the town. On the eve of Passover, 1903, they became the victims of a massacre that outdid all other pogroms in savagery. Overnight obscure Kishinev became a name the whole world knew.

Kishinev had been free of the pogroms which bloodied Russian towns in the 1880s. But in 1897 the local tax collector, Krushevan, started an anti-Semitic newspaper called *Bessarabetz*. A government subsidy assured its success, and government officials wrote for it. In every issue the paper incited its readers against the Jews. It accused the Jews of capitalist exploitation of the Christians, while on the same pages it indicted the Jews as revolutionaries.

It was the only newspaper in Kishinev. The town's Jews appealed to von Plehve, the Minister of the Interior, for permission to publish another one, to counteract *Bessarabetz*. His reply was, "The *Bessarabetz* is good enough for Kishinev."

Von Plehve had long been identified by the Jews as their new Haman. A quarter of a century before, at the time of the pogroms which followed the assassination of Alexander II, he had been head of the empire's police. In 1902 Nicholas II named him Minister of the Interior to succeed Sipiagin, who had been shot by a terrorist. By now, revolutionary ferment had spread to wider circles. With the rise of an organized labor movement and new socialist parties, the revolutionists were no longer a handful but thousands of discontented men and women on all levels of society. When von Plehve was police chief there were never more than two underground printing presses at a time. Now there were more than twenty. Where a handful might have taken part in the rare street demonstrations of a generation before, now fifty thousand gathered in the squares of St. Petersburg to unfurl their red flags and listen to revolutionary speeches. May Day, the international holiday of labor, had become the great day for clashes between police and Cossacks on one side, and workers and students on the other.

Nicholas was shaken by the threat to the throne. The Jews, his advisers repeated endlessly, were at the center of the revolutionary danger. It was true that the Jews in the movement were greater in number than their proportion to the general population. But hounded and humiliated as they had been by czarism, it was no wonder. They had organized the Bund, of course, and they joined the Russian Social-Democratic and the Socialist Revolutionary Parties. When police publicly flogged Jews who took part in a Bund demonstration in Vilna on May Day, 1901, a Bundist shoemaker, Hirsh Lekert, shot the Vilna governor. He failed to kill him, and was executed. His act of vengeance was followed by the mass arrest of young Jews. Thousands were sent to prison or into Siberian exile.

Von Plehve tried to use the Jews as a tool to divert public dissatisfaction with the regime to attacks upon these "foreigners." He sought to destroy the freedom movement by labeling it a Jewish plot.

The ground had already been prepared. Back in 1895, Russians living in France had cooked up something called the *Protocols of the Elders of Zion*. This gross forgery presented itself as a conspiracy of Jews to seize world power which had been plotted and recorded at an imaginary assembly of Jewish leaders. The fabrication had reached the czar's court, adding its poison to the anti-Semitism long rampant there. To Nicholas II "Jew" and "enemy" became interchangeable words. He called anyone who opposed him a Jew. Plehve's plan "to drown the revolution in Jewish blood" easily won czarist approval.

The regime promoted the belief that the Jews were harmful to the state and to the people. Officials, police, military, ordinary citizens absorbed the idea that the Jews were outside the law's protection. These were "enemies" who could be abused and mistreated at will. As *Bessarabetz* whipped up anti-Jewish feeling, the police officials in Kishinev spoke openly of a coming day when the town would be rid of the Jews. Leaflets showered the streets proclaiming that a czarist edict permitted the slaughter of the Jews during Easter.

That Easter Sunday—it was April 6, 1903, and it happened to fall on the last day of Passover—the church bells rang at noon. As if by signal, gangs flooded the streets and began to beat up any Jews they encountered. The police and militia stood by, doing nothing. Their inaction convinced the pogromists that they had official approval. Crying "Kill the Jews!" the rapidly swelling mob rushed into the Jewish streets, breaking into homes and shops, smashing furniture, stealing money and goods, and beating up anyone who protested.

By late afternoon the drunken rabble armed with clubs and axes were killing Jews in their homes and on the streets. Still the authorities were silent. At 10 P.M. the pogrom halted. Some Jews rallied to defend themselves, but when they appeared on the streets with clubs, the police disarmed them.

Now the rioters controlled the town. A report described what followed:

On Monday from 3 A.M. until 8 P.M., mobs raged in the midst of the desolation and ruin which they had themselves heaped; they plundered, robbed, and destroyed Jewish property; they stole, pillaged, and spoiled; they hounded, assaulted, abused, and tortured Jewish persons. Representatives of all classes of the population participated in this frightful witches' Sabbath: soldiers and police, officials and priests, children and women, peasants, workers, tramps.

A Jewish delegation asked the governor of Bessarabia for help. He replied that the military—there were five thousand troops in the garrison—could not move without orders from St. Petersburg. Not until five o'clock that Monday afternoon did Plehve telegraph the order. The soldiers came out on the streets, and without a shot being fired, the mob melted away. But on the outskirts of town the looting and terror continued until Tuesday morning.

The toll: 45 murdered, 86 seriously injured, 500 less seriously hurt, 1,500 homes and shops plundered or destroyed, and 10,000 left homeless and penniless. The victims were chiefly the poor—artisans and small shopkeepers. The wealthy families were able to bribe the police to protect them.

Bialik was sent to Kishinev by the Jews of Odessa, who wanted to know exactly what had happened there. Instead of producing a routine report, Bialik wrote a powerful prophetic poem, "The City of Slaughter":

She saw it all, and she's a living witness,
The old gray spider spinning in the garret.
She knows a lot of stories—bid her tell them!
A story of a belly stuffed with feathers,
Of nostrils and of nails, of heads and hammers,
Of men, who, after death, were hung head downward,
Like these, along the rafter.
A story of a suckling child asleep,
A dead and cloven breast between its lips,
And of another child they tore in two,
And many, many more such fearful stories
That beat about the head and pierce thy brain,
And stab the soul within thee, does she know.

The rage felt by the Jew of Russia was in those lines, rage against those guilty of the massacre. But shame too, shame for the Jews who had given up their lives without resistance. In his poem, Bialik goes on to express that feeling:

> Can you hear? They beat their breasts, "Forgive us!"
> They call to Me I should forgive their sins!
> How sins a shadow on the wall, a dead worm?
> A broken pitcher?
> Why do they pray? Why do they lift their hands?
> Where is their fist? Where is the thunderbolt
> That would settle accounts for all the generations
> And lay the world in ruins, tear down heavens,
> and overturn My Throne! . . .
> Your unwept tear bury within you,
> Immure it in your heart, build up there
> Of hate and wrath and gall for it a fortress,
> And let it grow, a serpent in its nest,
> And you will suckle from each other,
> Yet always hungering and thirsty you will be.
> Then when the evil day comes upon you,
> Break your heart open, liberate the snake.
> And like a poisoned arrow send it
> Ravenous, with burning venom,
> Into the very heart of your own people.

The pogrom at Kishinev roused non-Jewish writers to voice their disgust with the behavior of a society that called itself Christian. Maxim Gorky said in a public letter:

> The mob, merely the hand which was guided by a corrupt conscience, driving it to murder and robbery, was led by men of cultured society. But cultivated society in Russia is really much worse than the people who are goaded by their sad life and blinded and enthralled by the artificial darkness created around them. . . . Cultivated society is not less guilty of the disgraceful and horrible deeds committed at Kishinev than the actual murders and ravishers. Its members' guilt consists in the fact that, not merely did they not protect the victim, but that they rejoiced over the murders; it consists chiefly in committing themselves for long years to be corrupted by man-haters and persons who have long enjoyed the disgusting glory of being the lackeys of power and the glorifiers of lies.

Tolstoy, who had been silent during the pogroms of the 1880s, now wrote:

> After the first reports in the newspapers, I understood the entire horror of what had occurred, and sensed simultaneously deep commiseration with the innocent victims of the ruthlessness of the population, consternation over the atrocities of so-called Christians, repugnance toward those so-called cultured people, who incited the mob and sympathized with their actions. I was dismayed in particular at the chief culprit—our government and its clergy which rouse in the people animal emotions and fanaticism, and with its gang of officials and brigands. The Kishinev crime—that is a direct result of that propaganda of falsehood and violence which our government carries on with such energy. The attitude of our government towards these events is only one more proof of the brutal egoism which does not flinch from any measures, however cruel, when it is a question of suppressing a movement which is deemed dangerous, and of their complete indifference . . . towards the most terrible outrages which do not affect government interests.

In Russia the truth of Kishinev was concealed by official censorship. The government ordered that its version be printed by the press. Plehve's story ran that the pogrom was only the chance outcome of a squabble on the street that had been started by a Jew. But the facts hurdled over the censors and found their way into the foreign press. The newspapers of Europe and America detailed the massacre and the world reacted in horror to such inhumanity. In the light of Hitler's holocaust, Kishinev may now seem minor, but Bialik's vision was true: Kishinev was a beginning whose end would be Auschwitz.

The Jews of Russia, stunned at first by the repetition of mass murder, were galvanized into action by Bialik's scathing "The City of Slaughter." Young Jews organized defense units in many towns and villages, and armed themselves against future Kishinevs. The Jewish students at the Polytechnic Institute in Kiev, recalled Nokhum Shtif, "responded with a self-defense group and with revolutionary proclamations. . . . We expanded our work, providing the region with arms. I had practically stopped studying. . . ."

One of the Kiev Polytechnic students, a socialist Zionist named Pinhas Dashevsky, tried and failed to assassinate Krushevan, the editor of *Bessarabetz,* for inciting the Kishinev pogrom. Plehve concluded the Zionists too must be suppressed. Their meetings and fund raising were banned, and the police took to hounding them.

Zalman Shazar, then fifteen, had just joined Poale Zion secretly when a group was clandestinely set up in his home town. Steibtz was full of muscular Jewish laborers, and the first thing the young party did was to organize a self-defense group. Upon hearing rumors of an impending pogrom, the Jews pitched in money and bought revolvers in Minsk. The self-defense group soon numbered a hundred trained and equipped men, divided into units of ten. Word spread that an attack on the Jews was planned Sunday after church. Shazar recalled:

> We knew that instigators had come from distant places; we saw peasant women arriving with empty wagons which, it was understood, they expected to fill with the booty robbed from the Jews. From early in the morning our members were stationed in the marketplace, lead-tipped iron bars in their hands and lead-tipped leather thongs in their pockets. The heads of our groups carried concealed revolvers and divided the watch over the marketplace among themselves.
>
> At noon an agitated and excited crowd, all ready for the attack, came pouring out of the white church above the marketplace. One of the "guests" rushed to the fore, dragging the peasants after him towards the stores. At that moment all the revolvers, scattered over the marketplace, went off at once. They shot into the air and hurt no one, but even that was enough to intimidate the crowd. Bedlam ensued. The horses were frightened, the peasant women screamed as if they were being slaughtered, and the wagons collided with each other. The peasants ran with their last breath, fleeing from the armed Jews. And the revolvers kept on shooting. In a few moments the marketplace was empty. . . .

Meanwhile, a court investigation of the Passover pogrom at Kishinev began. The official inquiry covered up all traces of government complicity. Only the common criminals caught on the scene—those who had wielded ax and torch—were tried and sentenced. Every attempt by lawyers to get at those who had given the commands was ruled out of order. The government also refused to accept civil suits by Jews to recover losses suffered in the pogrom.

The court was still sitting on the Kishinev crime when a pogrom exploded in Gomel, a town in the province of Mohilev, where 60 percent of the people were Jewish. A fight between Christians and Jews broke out in the marketplace on August 29, 1903, and a peasant was killed. The police arrested only Jews. Two days later a mob of railroad workers swarmed through the town, pillaging Jewish homes, shops, and synagogues. A detachment of hundreds of armed Jews began driving them back. But when the troops arrived they fired upon the Jews, killing three and wounding several others. Encouraged, the mob resumed its destruction, shielded by the soldiers from the Jewish self-defense unit. That night, when the pogrom ended, twelve Jews and eight Christians were dead or seriously wounded. Hundreds of homes and shops had been plundered.

A few days later the governor of Mohilev summoned leading Jews to the town council and said to them that Jews were to blame for leading all the movements against the government. That was why the Russian masses had turned upon them. He was echoing Plehve's line. The revolutionaries soon caught up with the Minister of the Interior. Sazonov, the son of a rich lumber merchant, expelled from Moscow University in a student strike and exiled to Siberia, turned terrorist and blew up Plehve with a bomb.

At the end of January 1904, the Russo-Japanese War began. The czarist government, with a population vastly outnumbering the Japanese, expected to win easily. But there was little popular enthusiasm for a war to annex Manchuria to Siberia.

In preparation for the war, the regime had expelled two thousand Jews from Port Arthur and the Far East peninsula. Refused the use of rail transport, the homeless Jews were forced to travel a thousand miles on foot in bitter winter. Nevertheless, the day after war was declared, *Voskhod,* a Jewish journal, wrote:

> This is not the time to rub salt on old wounds. Let us try—inasmuch as it is in our power—to forget, both the recent expulsion from Port Arthur and the pogroms of Kishinev and Gomel, as well as much else. Let Jewish parents not meditate now over the bitter fate of their children, who were not admitted to educational institutions. Jews will go into battle as enlisted men; but the blood of our children will be shed as profusely as that of the Russians.

Tens of thousands of Jews joined up to fight for Russian glory, even while the government continued to persecute their people. Many Jews, however, fled from military duty, and emigration to America jumped.

When the Czar's armies met defeat after defeat, the anti-Semitic press spread stories that the Jews were conniving to help the Japanese in order to avenge Kishinev. More pogroms were threatened for Easter of 1904. But in fear of internal disorders while at war, the governors were given strict orders not to allow them. None did occur that Easter—proving how easy it was for the regime to start or stop the massacres at will.

As the authorities became more brutal in their use of force, the revolutionaries became more insistent upon their demands. On the "Bloody Sunday" of January 9, 1905, the workers of St. Petersburg, led by Father Gapon, marched en masse to the Winter Palace to petition the czar for reforms. They were fired upon by the Royal Guards. The response was strikes, demonstrations, and more acts of Red terror. When the Grand Duke Sergius and others were assassinated, the czar felt he had better make some concessions. A council was appointed to draft a constitution, and recommendations were invited from the people. The Jews, divided into many political groups, hotly debated what to propose. Baron Günzburg's wealthy circle pleaded that because the Jews were useful to the state their persecution should be halted. But others would not plead: they demanded the rights due them. In April 1905 the Alliance for the Achievement of Complete Equal Rights for the Jewish People of Russia was organized. The historian Simon Dubnow, one of its founders, said that in modern times it was "the first attempt at a struggle for freedom *as a Jewish nation* rather than as a religious group."

Jews from dozens of communities followed up with petitions for equality, some adding the rights of national and cultural self-determination. The one basic reform all progressive Russians demanded was the end of autocracy and the adoption of a parliamentary constitution.

That Easter, pogroms broke out in several cities. One of them, in Zhitomir, was on the scale of a second Kishinev. It was planned by the police in conjunction with the Black Hundreds, a new organization which combined the appeals of anti-Semitism and nationalism in a way that anticipated Hitler's fascism. Crying "Attack the revolutionaries and the Jews!" a mob went into action. The police and military stood by, doing nothing to defend Jewish life or property, but interfering with the self-defense units. At the end of a two-day battle fifteen Jews and a Russian student who fought on their side were dead and sixty seriously injured. On the third day, Jews forced their way into the governor and threatened general slaughter if he did not put down the pogrom. He gave the orders and it stopped quickly.

The defeat of the Russian forces in Manchuria was followed by the Japanese victory over the Russian fleet at Tsushima in the summer of 1905. Defeated on the battlefield, the soldiers and Cossacks sought a cheap victory on the streets, killing as many as fifty Jews in Bialystok alone.

With the country torn apart by revolutionary and counterrevolutionary demonstrations, the government finally issued a draft constitution in August. There would be elections to a Duma or parliament which would have only advisory status. Jews would be allowed to vote and run for office, although they were still denied other elementary rights. Not satisfied with a token gesture, workers and students began fresh rounds of strikes that would build up to a great all-Russia general strike designed to force a truly democratic constitution upon the czar. The Black Hundreds made their plans at the same time and clashes between the two opposing forces became bloodier and more frequent. At last the government seemed ready to yield to the democratic movement. On October 17 an imperial manifesto promised full civil rights and a democratically elected Duma with legislative powers. However, the czar made no promise of equality for all citizens or for all nationalities.

The next day the Black Hundreds responded with a blood bath that protracted its horrors for a full week: large or smaller pogroms erupted in more than seven hundred cities, towns, and villages, in the Pale and even beyond it.

It was a counterrevolution—planned, systematic, ruthless. In each locality the same pattern: it began as a patriotic parade to celebrate the czar's manifesto, with marches carrying his portrait. Invariably the portrait was fired upon by persons unknown. It was shouted that Jews had done the shooting, and on this signal an anti-Jewish riot was begun. Plehve had once said, "I will choke the revolution in the blood of the Jews." It was estimated that in one week 900 Jews were murdered, leaving 325 widows and 1,350 orphans, and more than 8,000 were injured. Thousands of homes, synagogues, and shops were destroyed.

More than 200,000 Jews were in one way or another victims of the pogroms. Later, two of the Jewish deputies to the first Duma were murdered by the Black Hundreds.

The worst pogrom that week was Odessa's. It lasted four days, and left 302 dead (fifty-five of them members of the self-defense group), 5,000 wounded, 1,400 businesses ruined, 3,000 artisans reduced to beggary, and 40,000 homeless. Mendele Mocher Sforim, who lived in Odessa and was nearly seventy at the time of the pogrom, was asked by a Swiss socialist paper to write about it. He refused because he could not disguise his feelings or use Aesopian language. And if. he should say what he truly thought, it would mean exile to Siberia.

> If I should now write, my heart would flare and my blood would boil. . . . I must not do this, as I cannot remain an emigrant and I am too old for exile. . . . I, an old man, have in the days of the pogrom in Odessa hid in the janitor's pigsty. Like a pig I lay hidden! Instead of taking hold of an axe and splitting their heads—I crawled away and hid for days—like a pig! I cannot write about that! If I should sit down to write I would not be able to keep from writing something that would become my "act of accusation" to send me to exile.

Both the left and the more moderate democratic groups felt the czar had betrayed them. With one hand he had given the promise of a constitutional system, and with the other he had stabbed them in the back. His treachery brought the country to the boiling point. Assemblies, conferences, strikes took place by the hundreds. The tumult of the earlier underground days now rose to the surface of public life.

The Jewish Federation for Equal Rights met in St. Petersburg that November and made plans to direct all its efforts to organizing Russian Jewry for self-defense. The Jews would no longer beg. "We will not accept equal rights from the bloody hands of the autocracy," one young delegate cried out. "We will accept them from a free Russian parliament!" A few months later the federation met again to plan for the election of Jews to the Duma. A left-wing minority wanted to boycott the elections, but the majority decided it was better to participate in them. The goal was to elect Jewish candidates wherever possible, and in other places to vote for a non-Jew if he would promise to support the civil, political, and national rights of the Jewish people.

Of the 497 deputies elected, twelve were Jews, six of them Zionists. One of the twelve was Shmarya Levin. Born in Swislocz in 1867, he had become a Zionist in his youth. In his autobiography he describes the first meeting of the Duma in May 1906:

> I was elected almost unanimously as the representative of Vilna to the first Russian Duma. There were twelve of us in all, the representatives of between six and seven million Jews, and I wonder whether any twelve men have ever carried upon their shoulders the responsibility of so many hopes and longings. Russia was—so it seemed—about to rise out of the abyss of oppression; the Jewish people was about to rise out of an abyss below the abyss, and these twelve men were to haul it out. To make their task harder, these men had to bear in mind that they had been elected by non-Jewish as well as by Jewish voters, and frequently there was no correspondence between the work they had to do for their own people and the party needs dictated by their other constituencies. . . .
>
> Among the Jewish deputies, I occupied, in a certain sense, a special position, not for my virtues or abilities, but because of one of those fantastic anomalies which are so frequent in Russian Jewish life. I was the only one among them who had no right to stay in St. Petersburg. The others belonged, one way or another, to the class of the "privileged" Jews, either by academic association, or through their standing in the business guilds. But my degree had been taken at a foreign university, and I was no businessman. I was therefore one of the six million who could not leave the Pale. And so I walked around in St. Petersburg as the living symbol of the absurd system, as if to say: "I have no right to be living in St. Petersburg at all, and I am only here for the purpose of helping to make the country's laws." I did not neglect to point this out . . . in the Duma.

While the Duma was debating the government's role in the pogroms of 1905, a pogrom broke out in Bialystok. Soldiers joined in with the mob and shot Jews down for hours. Eighty were killed and hundreds wounded in a massacre that exceeded most others for bestiality—limbs chopped off, nails driven into heads, bellies ripped open, children's brains knocked out. When the bloody news reached St. Petersburg, Levin said:

> A tremor went through the Duma. It was not only the pogrom as such, but the hint that it contained. . . . The Duma resolved at once to

send a commission of investigation to the actual scene. . . . The Bialystok pogrom had acted like a cold shower on Jews and liberal Russians alike, and many had begun to feel that the Duma would not live much longer. Among the Jews, the depression was of course at its worst.

The commission finished its inquiry into Bialystok and returned:

> Fiery speeches were delivered in the Duma by Vinaver, Jacubson and Rodichev [Jewish deputies]. By an overwhelming majority the Duma accepted a resolution calling upon the Czar to dismiss his Cabinet, in order that the rulers of the country might dissociate themselves from the disgrace of the pogrom. The atmosphere, during the debate, was heavily charged. The deputies knew that they now stood at the parting of the ways. Two days later, when they turned up at the chamber, they found the doors locked and guarded. Outside was posted the manifesto of the Czar dissolving the Duma.

His excuse was that the Duma had gone beyond its authority in land reform and had investigated acts of the government—meaning pogroms. A Second Duma was elected, this time with only four Jewish deputies. It too had a short and fruitless life. When it was dissolved, the government arbitrarily changed the electoral law. It gave far more voting power to the landowners and the propertied city classes than was their due. The effect was to make the Third (1907–1912) and Fourth (1913–1915) Dumas the instrument of the reactionaries. The Black Hundreds were able to put through more and even worse laws against the Jews.

II

TAKING ROOT

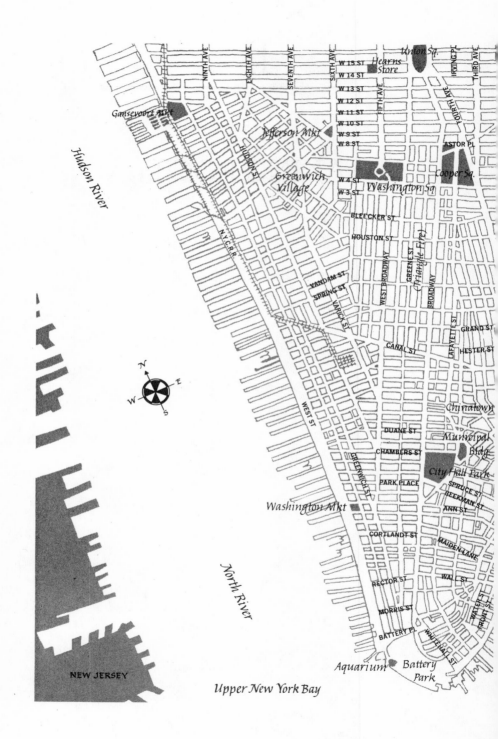

Union Sq.

Hearns
Store

NINTH AVE
EIGHTH AVE
SEVENTH AVE
SIXTH AVE
FIFTH AVE
FOURTH AVE
IRVING PL
THIRD AVE

W 15 ST
W 14 ST
W 13 ST
W 12 ST
W 11 ST
W 10 ST
W 9 ST
W 8 ST

Gansevoort Mkt

Jefferson Mkt

ASTOR PL

Cooper Sq.

HUDSON ST

Hudson River

Greenwich
Village

W 4 ST
W 3 ST

Washington Sq.

N.Y.C.R.R.

BLEECKER ST

HOUSTON ST

WEST BROADWAY

GREENE ST (Triangle Fire)

BROADWAY

VANDAM ST
SPRING ST

VARICK ST

CANAL ST

LAFAYETTE ST

GRAND ST

HESTER ST

N

W — E

S

Chinatown

WEST ST

DUANE ST

Municipal
Bldg.

CHAMBERS ST

City Hall Park

GREENWICH ST

PARK PLACE

SPRUCE ST
BEEKMAN ST

ANN ST

Washington Mkt

CORTLANDT ST

MAIDEN LANE

NEW JERSEY

North River

RECTOR ST

WALL ST

MORRIS ST

WATER ST
FRONT ST

BATTERY P.

WHITEHALL ST

Aquarium

Battery
Park

Upper New York Bay

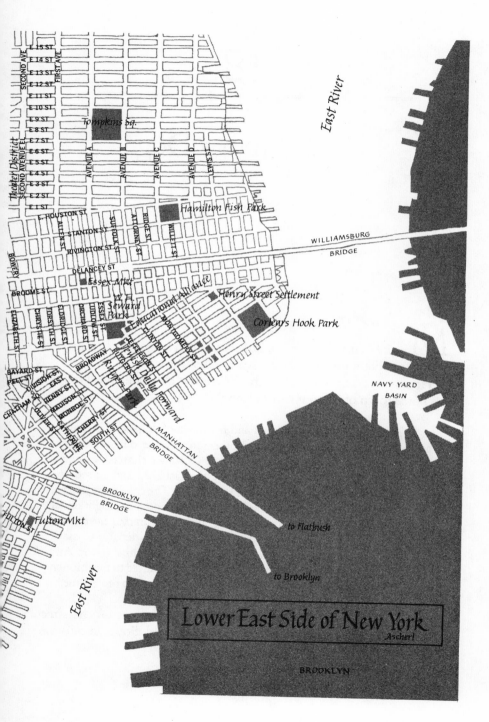

Lower East Side of New York

Ascher!

E 15 ST
E 14 ST
E 13 ST
E 12 ST
E 11 ST
E 10 ST
E 9 ST
E 8 ST
E 7 ST
E 6 ST
E 5 ST
E 4 ST
E 3 ST
E 2 ST
E 1 ST

SECOND AVE
FIRST AVE
SECOND AVE L
Theater District

AVENUE A
AVENUE B
AVENUE C
AVENUE D
LEWIS ST

Tompkins Sq.

Hamilton Fish Park

E. HOUSTON ST
STANTON ST
RIVINGTON ST
DELANCEY ST

ALLEN
SUFFOLK ST
ATTORNEY ST
RIDGE ST
WILLETT ST

BOWERY
BROOME ST
ELIZABETH ST
CHRYSTIE ST
FORSYTH ST
ELDRIDGE ST
ORCHARD ST
LUDLOW ST
ESSEX ST
CLINTON ST
MONTGOMERY ST
JEFFERSON ST

Essex Mkt

Seward Park
W H

Educational Alliance
Henry Street Settlement
Corlears Hook Park

BAYARD ST
PELL ST
CHATHAM SQ
DIVISION ST
EAST
HENRY ST
MADISON ST
MONROE ST
CHERRY ST
SOUTH ST

BROADWAY
RUTGERS ST
Rutgers Park
Daily Forward

MANHATTAN BRIDGE

WILLIAMSBURG BRIDGE

East River

NAVY YARD BASIN

BROOKLYN BRIDGE

FULTON ST
Fulton Mkt

to Flatbush

to Brooklyn

East River

BROOKLYN

18

Less Than a Dog

Maurice Sterne was only a little boy when he got his first practical lesson in what it meant to be a Jew in czarist Russia.

He was walking with his mother on a street of small Jewish shops in his home town of Libau when suddenly—

> A great noise of shouting men and horses' hoofs exploded behind us and without once looking back my mother ran with me into the shelter of a nearby doorway. A small company of Cossacks charged around a corner and into the narrow street where they laughed and cursed and swung their *nagaikas,* those infamous long whips. The crowd scattered in panic beneath their feet, and though that day no one was caught under the horses, the whips lashed out with agonizing accuracy. I have never forgotten the dreadful sound of that street, when the derisive Cossack blare mingled with the sharp, thin scream of their victims' terror. And my soul has recorded a deeper mark of the fear transmitted to me through my mother's shuddering body, which she used as a wall to protect me.

Sterne's family spoke Yiddish in the home, but not on the street. It was risky to be identified as a Jew. Raphael Soyer recalls one such incident.

My father came home one evening out of breath and upset. When my mother asked him what had happened, he told her, and I overheard, that two drunken peasants walking behind him said, "There goes a Jew, let's beat him up!" "What did you do?" asked my mother. "I made big strides." My all-powerful father sank in my estimation.

Not only Jews but all Russians of liberal or radical thought lived in the shadow of fear. The secret police were everywhere. The sound of soldiers on the street, the midnight knock on the door, made the heart race madly.

For Jews of that generation, life was a round of relentless persecution. Maurice Sterne's father died when the boy was seven; his mother got a job teaching in Moscow. Was the great city any better than little Libau? Only in the small and poverty-stricken Jewish ghetto district could the boy walk without fear of some derisive voice calling, "Jew! Jew!" At ten, Maurice entered a polytechnic school. "For the first time in my life," he said, "my classmates were not Jewish and until I was befriended by a big boy I was teased and tormented for being a Jew."

Maurice did well enough to earn a scholarship to the art academy. But only two days later the newspapers announced that all but a small number of selected Jews had to leave Moscow. The Jews were stunned. They did not know where to go, for many other parts of Russia were being closed off to them. Quickly they had to dispose of their homes, their belongings, their businesses, take any price and find ways and means of getting out. But to go where?

In St. Petersburg too, the Jews were kicked out. One of them, with desperate humor, went to Gresser, the chief of police, and said to him: "You leave the dogs in St. Petersburg. Well, I have eight children to feed, I have great difficulty in making a living. Let me remain here, and I will go on all fours like the dogs!"

"No," replied the police chief, "you are a Jew, you are less than a dog. Turn Christian."

In Warsaw the colonel commanding the g
to his troops:

Soldiers! Russia, our Little Mother, is passing through sad times. Wicked people, disturbers of the peace and Socialists, wish to divide up our country, and have even already begun to excite our brave troops, spreading their doctrine amongst the faithful servants of our Little Father, the Czar. Most of these agitators are Jews. . . .

Remember them, my brothers, who your enemies are, and exterminate them everywhere, whenever you have the opportunity. . . . Remember that we are living in a state of siege, and the more each of you exterminates his enemies, the greater will be his reward.

That evening a company commander came into the barracks and spoke to his men, piling more fuel on the fire his colonel had lit:

All the misfortunes which have befallen our country come exclusively from the Jews, who drink our blood, and yet pass for friends of the moujik and the Russian working man. But do not believe it! Mochka [he pointed to a Jewish soldier], he is your enemy, and I, a Russian and Orthodox gentleman, I warn you. Do not believe Mochka! Spit in his face!

The soldiers surrounded the Jew and carried out literally the order of their commander. When Mochka could stand it no longer, he struck back, was court-martialed, and sent to military prison.

Such anti-Semitism was easily transformed into pogroms. These violent outbreaks against the Jews were ancient history in Russia. One of the earliest recorded goes back to the year 1113, when the Jews of Kiev were attacked and pillaged. In the sixteenth century Ivan the Terrible ordered thousands of Jews to be drowned when they refused to abandon their faith and accept Christianity. In 1871 the Jews of Odessa suffered a pogrom, supposedly caused by some Jew breaking a cross in a Greek Orthodox church. A similar legend was the excuse for a Warsaw pogrom in the same period.

But it was in the 1880s that pogroms by the hundreds overwhelmed the Jewish population of Russia. This time the authorities invented a new explanation: it seems that the peasants and workers had been enslaved by the Jews, and were rising up against their exploiters. The truth, of course, was that the economic misery of the Russian people was only the inevitable result of the brutal serfdom in which Russia's rulers had held them for centuries, long after the rest of Europe was moving into modern times. To divert the blame for oppression from themselves, the Czar, the nobility, and the landlords made the Jews the scapegoat.

Russian radicals, driven to terrorism by their failure to make any progress in winning basic reforms, killed the czar with a bomb in 1881. The result was only to make things worse. Six weeks after the assassination the authorities unleashed a pogrom in Elisavetgrad, where 15,000 Jews lived. The police and the military stood by, watching, while drunken mobs burned down homes, looted shops, raped women, and mutilated and murdered Jews regardless of age or sex. The rage to kill Jews, incited by the government-supported press, swept through 160 cities and villages in the next few weeks.

As the news of the pogroms reached communities at some distance from the scenes of horror, the effect upon the Jews was terrible. It became clear to them that the Jewish people had been virtually outlawed, and that no one would dare raise a hand in their defense. Shmarya Levin describes the mood in his town of Swislowitz.

No pogrom occurred in Swislowitz, but the terror of the pogrom was suspended almost visibly over our heads. There were times when we envied the cities that had already suffered the pogrom. "Better an end with terror than a terror without end." The fear that would not be abjured, the uncertainty that haunted us in the home and in the streets, the momentary expectation of the storm that did not break—this is a species of mental torment that cannot be described. The Jews of Swislowitz went around, as I remember, like shadows of themselves. They could not lie down and die; there was their daily bread to earn for themselves and their families, and pitifully small as their needs were, they could not satisfy them without maintaining their usual contact with the Gentiles. The contact was traditional, intimate. True, these Gentiles were our own village folk; but all that belonged to yesterday. Who could tell what deadly thoughts were theirs today? The volcano, too, is peaceful just one moment before it breaks out.

The sight of mobs clubbing down Jews in the streets forced a great change in the attitude of many Russian Jews. The government, they saw, had openly encouraged the pogromists. And every sector of society had applauded, or remained silent. The Jewish liberals and radicals, who had thought progress inevitable, that education would lead to reform, that Jews would win emancipation and equality, suddenly recognized that to most Russians the Jew was a despised outsider, an enemy to be gotten rid of by any means.

In Kiev, where the Jewish quarter had been devastated by a pogrom, a day of fasting and prayer was proclaimed by the rabbis. The synagogues were filled with weeping victims. Suddenly a group of young men entered one of them, and the crowd fell silent. The newcomers, all Jews, were students of the University of St. Vladimir, rarely seen at worship. Their leader spoke:

> Brethren, we are a committee of the Jewish students of the university, sent to clasp hands with you and to mingle our tears with your tears. We are here to say to you, "We are your brothers; Jews like yourselves, like our fathers!" We have striven to adopt the language and manners of our Christian fellow countrymen, we have brought ourselves up to an ardent love of their literature, of their culture, of their progress. We have tried to persuade ourselves that we are children of Mother Russia. Alas! we have been in error. The terrible events which have called forth this fast and these tears have aroused us from our dream. The voice of the blood of our outraged brothers and sisters cries unto us that we are only strangers in the land which we have been used to call our home; that we are only stepchildren here, waifs to be trampled upon and dishonored.
>
> There is no hope for Israel in Russia. The salvation of the downtrodden people lies in other parts—in a land beyond the seas, which knows no distinction of race or faith, which is a mother to Jew and Gentile alike. In the great republic is our redemption from the brutalities and ignominies to which we are subjected in our birthplace. In America we shall find rest; the stars and stripes will wave over the true home of our people.
>
> To America, brethren! To America!

To America they went. At first in a trickle, then in a torrent. Four million Jews left Eastern Europe between 1880 and 1924. Over three million of them came to the United States. Because of that heavy immigration, the Jewish population of the United States increased at a more rapid rate in that period than the population as a whole. The vast majority of Americans of Jewish descent today stem from that immigration.

That they suffered from pogroms is only part of the truth. They knew less violent forms of persecution too. Tens of thousands of Jews were injured or killed in the pogroms of the early 1880s, and many more in the waves of pogroms that broke in 1903, in 1905, in 1919–1920. Millions of others were the victims of a "cold" pogrom. This was the ever-growing body of restrictive laws directed against the Jews. Long before, they had been penned up in the provinces of western and southwestern Russia, in an area called the Pale of Settlement. Not content with isolating 95 percent of the Jews in this huge ghetto, the Czars humiliated and hounded them with hundreds of restrictions. One of the heaviest burdens was military conscription for a term of twenty-five years or more, with no chance to rise above private. Quotas barred all but a few Jews from the schools and universities. In 1886 Jews had little choice not only where they could live but in how they could earn a living. A small number managed to achieve wealth, but the vast mass of Jews starved in the villages (the shtetls) or the city slums. By the 1880s the four million Jews of Russia were a desperate, driven people. Across the Russian border, in the Austr-Hungarian provinces of Galicia and Bukovina, the Jews were almost as badly off. They too suffered great poverty, although their political and civil disabilities were lighter.

So they left home: one out of every three Jews in Eastern Europe emigrated. Of course, they were not the only ones to pick up and go. The whole continent of Europe was on the move in that century. The Jews were a part of that wandering. Between 1830 and 1930, forty million Europeans came to the New World. Thirty million of them arrived after 1880, and most of these were Slavs, Italians, and Jews out of Southern and Eastern Europe.

It is hard to grasp the vast scale of that migration. It was the biggest movement of peoples in world history. It followed the paths of promise, which led westward. They came—no matter from where—for similar reasons. They wanted to climb out of poverty, to break free of political oppression, to crack the mold of class, to worship as they pleased.

It was the people of the more advanced countries of Eastern and Central Europe who moved first. Then came the less developed Eastern and Southern countries, especially when cheaper rail and ship passage made flight easier. By the early 1900s, 1.5 million people were leaving Eastern and Southern Europe each year.

This was the mass migration that the Jews joined.

19

To Go—or Not to Go

What is it like to pull up roots in your native land and seek a home in a strange place? What kind of person can do it?

Not everyone: that's clear. If one out of every three Jews in Eastern Europe migrated to America, it means two out of every three stayed where they were. Twice as many, then, decided not to leave, or never even thought of going.

What was the difference between the two groups? All, or nearly all, shared the same problems, felt the same pressures of poverty and persecution. How then do we account for the decision to go or not to go?

A look at the nature and condition of the Jews in Eastern Europe may help explain why. In 1800 the region held half the Jews of the world. Expelled from Western Europe in the centuries roughly between 1500 and 1800, the majority of Jews had moved east of the Rhine, chiefly to Polish territory. When that kingdom was dismembered by its warring neighbors, the Jews fell under Russian, Prussian, or Austro-Hungarian rule.

Most Jews were Orthodox then. They gloried in their separateness, writes Moses Rischin.

Rendered conspicuous by their dress, language and customs, and confined in their occupations and habitat, they knew they were Jews, anchored in religious traditions by their needs, their convictions, their communal life, and the state of the surrounding peasantry.

Adversity fashioned an inner existence that flamed up in direct proportion to the bleakness of an outer world that was shaped by rumors and realities of forced conversions and persecutions. Everyday life was transcended and embellished by a rich heritage of learning, liturgy, custom, and special observance. . . . Religious learning, the only kind of learning comprehensible to Jews, disciplined all. . . .

Much was tolerable on this earth, since this world was only an anteroom to the Hereafter and all Israel had a portion in the world to come. Whatever the strains between the well-to-do and the poor, all Jews shared in the pervasive personal and familial ties of the small towns. They were sustained by their sense of community, by a belief in a common destiny, and by a feeling of moral superiority to the surrounding world of lords and peasants.

But fresh social forces and the new ideas they gave rise to disrupted that self-contained Jewish world. The movement for Jewish enlightenment, called the Haskalah, which began in the eighteenth century, spread from the West to Poland and Russia. If Jewish customs and thought were modernized, argued its leaders, the Jews would be treated equally with non-Jews, and political emancipation would follow. The Western influence reached the larger cities first, then penetrated to smaller towns where Jewish youngsters from throughout Russia were schooled in renowned yeshivas. Unsettled youth were open to Haskalah teachings and the values of Russian and Western culture. When they found higher education and professional careers closed to them, many turned to radicalism. Socialist teachings reached not only the students but the emerging Jewish working class of the cities. The Bund was formed 8n 1897 to organize Jewish workers and to participate in independent political action. The Pale of Settlement, once lamented by the enlighteners as a stagnant pool where Jewish life had decayed, became "the hotbed of revolutionary work." Jewish nationalism, long dormant, was ignited by the torch of the pogromists. As Bundists demanded national cultural autonomy for Jews, the Zionists proposed plans to establish a homeland for the oppressed.

Jewish life in Eastern Europe had been in ferment, then, long before the wave of pogroms began in the 1880s. The inertia and immobility which characterized the community life of the Orthodox had begun to give way. Eastern European Jews, though only a handful, had made the long journey to North America as far back as the colonial period. With the beginning of Haskalah, with the introduction of military conscription, with the uprooting of Jews by edicts of expulsion, larger numbers began to flee abroad.

What made the early emigrants think of America? Many learned about it in the 1840s from *Zofnath Paaneach,* a Yiddish translation of J. H. Campe's German book about the discovery of America. "The Columbus," as they referred to it, became so popular "that almost all Jews read it," recalls A. B. Gotlober in his memoirs. There were penny booklets too that circulated the legend of an America whose streets were paved with gold.

Little of practical use was learned from such books, but they stirred a hunger for more knowledge about America, and brought it closer to mind. By the 1840s Jews near the western borders were crossing over into Germany and some moved on from there to America. One Jewish writer of that time, Dr. S. Ettinger, fictionalized the adventures of Polish and Galician Jews who went to America and sometimes returned, usually to marry a hometown girl. Soon after, there was a book by the enormously popular Yiddish novelist of Vilna, I. M. Dick; he told the story of a forgotten relative who made a fortune in America and bequeathed it to the village teacher, Reb Khaykel Yente of Tsyusk, the hero of the tale.

The shipping agents drummed up business by distributing handbills on the wonders of life in the Golden Land. The slogan *"Auf zu Amerika!"* was heard in Austria-Hungary now. Before the American Civil War the records show Eastern European Jews living in such places as Utica, Rochester, New Orleans, Chicago, San Francisco, Los Angeles. By 1860 there were perhaps 15,000 of them in New York City.

The numbers swelled in the 1860s and 1870s. Alexander II, who began his reign (1855–1881) as a liberal, lifted some of the restrictions on the Jews and freed the peasants from bondage. The economic development of Russia was stimulated. But denied enough land or capital to stand on their own, the peasants stayed poor. It was a dismal prospect for the Jewish tradesmen and artisans in the towns and villages who depended upon the peasants as customers. The peasants who gave up on the land moved to the cities, where they competed with the Jews for jobs. Epidemics of cholera, and famine caused by bad harvests, made life even worse. In 1869 an Odessa newspaper reported that "the situation of the hungry Jews is beyond imagination. Masses of them leave our fatherland and go to foreign countries to look for means to alleviate their hunger." From that year until 1881, about 3,000 Jews annually left Eastern Europe to seek new homes in America. Their mood is captured in the public appeal a group of Russian Jews made in 1880 to the Jews of America for help in emigrating:

> Give us a chance in your great and glorious land of liberty, whose broad and trackless acres offer an asylum and a place for weary hearts but courageous souls, willing to toil and by the sweat of the brow earn our daily bread. Come, Brothers of Israel in America, come to our help.
> Give us the means to migrate to your shores. Let us touch with our feet the sacred soil of Washington, and with our freedom we shall become new-created for the great struggle of life.
> We do not fear work. We ask you but to land us on your free territory and send us to your Western lands, and we will answer for the rest.

That open letter, printed in the press and in the *Congressional Record,* foreshadowed the enormous upheaval which began a year later, after the pogroms of 1881–1882. A million and a half Russian Jews came to the United States in the span of the next thirty years.

Was it the result of the pogroms? It is too facile an answer to let it go at that. For in the same period more than 300,000 Jews came to America from Austria-Hungary, especially from its Galician province. And there were *no* pogroms or oppressive decrees in that region. Further, the same period saw a huge rise in the emigration of *non*-Jews from Eastern Europe. The Jewish and the non-Jewish emigrants shared two social conditions: a large rise in their population and a great worsening of their economic position. The Eastern European Jews experienced a five-fold increase in their population in the nineteenth century. The economy, failing to keep pace with such growth, left the masses worse off than before.

For some Jews the pogroms—hot and cold—may have been the final push to the decision to emigrate. But we are still left with the question: why did a third of them go, and the other two thirds stay? The historian Solomon Grayzel says many of those who stayed led "a spiritually satisfying life." Those were the Orthodox Jews who in the early years regarded America as profane. Later, when some did go, it was in large measure because their children went. The Orthodox were never a major part of the emigrants.

Another group who stayed, and openly disapproved of those who emigrated, were the enlightened, the assimilated, the affluent. They were distressed at the depth of the despair for the future which many Eastern European Jews felt. They urged the people to stay at home and improve themselves. They expected vocational training and diversification to win the Jews a stronger position in the economy. They believed modernized dress and the learning of Russian would bring social acceptance and cause anti-Semitism to disappear. (How wrong they were, history would soon demonstrate.)

Poverty, persecution—these economic and social facts conditioned the environment of the Eastern European Jews. But of themselves they did not oblige people to change their relationship to that environment, in this case, to make the grave decision to emigrate. The influence of environment upon each individual is indirect, mediated through his own temperament and ideas. Behind the decision of the Jews who emigrated were personal motives. And it is these which psychologists study in the hope of finding the link between social necessity and personal initiative. One researcher, Moses Kligsberg, himself an emigrant from Poland, analyzed a major source for the Jewish immigrant's own view of himself. He examined more than three hundred autobiographies written by Jewish immigrants in 1942 for the Yivo Institute for Jewish Research on the theme "Why I Left the Old Country, and What I Have Achieved in America." Most of the life stories represented the first mass immigration of the 1880s and 1890s. He concluded from the evidence that "the Jewish immigrant community in the United States is by and large a concentration of one social-psychological type, that is, the enterprising, activistic person with a strong individualistic attitude."

Not all of them, of course. There were many women and children who came to join husbands or fathers. And young men and women (some only teenagers) who came alone, and later brought over their parents, brothers, sisters. But Kligsberg felt certain that in America this type was "much more strongly represented than in any normal, settled Jewish community of Europe."

What moved this type of personality to emigrate? As adults, he said, they had a living ethnic heritage. Like all other immigrants, they came to America with personalities formed by a particular social and ethnic environment. Their Jewishness, the folkways and mores transmitted down the generations, was engrained in them. This Kligsberg calls the "passive" part of the immigrant's spiritual baggage. In addition, says Kligsberg, "he brought with him an active set of goals and aspirations: the Jewish immigrant came to America not merely to live with greater ease. He arrived with a powerful urge to achieve a goal, and with the dynamism appropriate to such an urge."

The Jewish immigrant may not have been aware of this; he may have voiced other reasons for leaving home, especially the standard explanation—hunger and pogroms. But the statistics show that Jewish emigration rose steadily during the relatively quiet years between the major pogrom periods of 1881–1882 and 1903–1904. More likely it was the superior economic conditions in the United States which attracted immigrants. For the trend of Jewish emigration to America paralleled the general flow of emigration by other ethnic groups.

Poverty does not fully account for the vast emigration any more than pogroms. The number who suffered from hunger was much greater than the number who emigrated. And there is evidence to show that not the poorest, but those a little better off, were the ones who emigrated.

What, then, explains the emigration of the Jews? Kligsberg attributes it, quite convincingly, to a unique guiding principle of Eastern European Jewish life. From earliest childhood, he says, Jews were confronted with one word: *takhlis*. The Hebrew word meant to them an end goal: "What will the *takhlis* be?" That was always the important question.

A man realizes his full significance only in having achieved something, in having advanced in his environment, or at least in having maintained a high standard already achieved by his milieu. There can be neither meaning nor satisfaction in simply living one's life: one must achieve something, get somewhere. This, it can be said, is the core of the Jewish outlook for the individual.

Traditionally, Eastern European Jews sought *takhlis* in the spheres of learning, status, and financial security. The highest ideal parents held up to their children was to be a rabbi, a position that achieved all three goals. But when Jewish community life was breached by the rise of modern secular movements, and enlightened Jews began to look over the ghetto walls, they saw new paths to *takhlis* in the world beyond. It was then that the barriers to achievement which law and social custom had set up became more difficult to bear. For generations such restrictions had not mattered much in the daily life of the traditional Jew. He could aspire to become a rabbi or a merchant-scholar in spite of the wicked Gentiles. Now, however, when the modern Jew wanted to become a doctor, lawyer, engineer, professor, businessman, the denial of equal rights was felt as an intolerable insult to his self-respect.

For large numbers of the younger generation, this Eastern European life came to have no *takhlis*. They looked to America, a land where they heard you could achieve *takhlis*. America promised the freedom to work your way up, to realize your own possibilities, and espeeially to school your children so that they could make their mark in the world.

It is this concept which enables us to understand the extraordinary "dynamism and zeal which the greatest number of Jewish immigrants manifested in America . . . the patience with which they bore the immensely difficult conditions of life—the sweatshops and tenements—and the fact that so small a number returned to the old country."

20

Crossing in Steerage

The lure of America drew Jews from the most remote corners of Eastern Europe. In 1886, someone in Shavl, a village in the province of Kovno, sent this report to a Hebrew newspaper published in St. Petersburg:

> In the last ten years all local inhabitants were blinded and dreamt only about America with the gold and silver that is found there on the streets. This has increased the number of migrants. This year, in particular, a greater number of steamship tickets [*shifskarten*] were sold by salesmen. During the past week a substantial group of people, including fifty young persons, left for America and more were expected to go during the following week. Those who accompanied the immigrants wept on the way because they feared that their dear ones may not return or might encounter mishaps, or that some of their material support will be missing at home.

That vision of a golden America was satirized by Sholem Aleichem, the best-known Yiddish writer of modern times, who himself left the Old World for the New. Berl-Isaac, a character who is always letting his imagination run away with him, returns to Kasrilevka after a long stay in America. He tells the open-mouthed villagers of the wonders he has seen:

> To begin with, the country itself, a land flowing with milk and honey. People make plenty of money; you dig into money with both hands, you pick up gold by the shovelful! And as for "business," as they call it in America, there is so much of it that it just makes your head spin! You can do anything you like. You want a factory—so you have a factory; you want to, you push a pushcart; and if you don't, you peddle or go to work in a shop—it's a free country! You may starve or drop dead of hunger right in the street—there is nothing to prevent you, nobody will object.
>
> Then, the size of the cities! The width of the streets! The height of the buildings! They have a building there, they call it the Woolworth—so the top of its chimneypot reaches into the clouds and even higher; it is said that this house has several hundred floors. You want to know, how do they climb up to the attic? By a ladder which they call an elevator. If you want somebody on the top floor, you sit down in the elevator early in the morning, so you get there towards sunset, just in time for your evening prayers. . . .
>
> Now take their life—it's all a rushing, a running, and a hustling. "Urry-hop" they call it there. Everything is in a hurry, and even when it comes to eating it is also done heels over head. You rush into a restaurant, order a schnapps, and as for the meal, I myself once saw a fellow being served something on a plate, something fresh, alive, and kicking, and when he cut it in two, one half of it flew to one side and the other half to the other side, and the fellow was through with his lunch. . . .
>
> Now, take their language. It's all turned upside down, as if for spite. If we call somebody a meat-merchant, they call him a butcher; if we say a houseowner, they say a landlord; a neighbor is a next-door-man or a next-door-woman; a hen is a chicken. Everything topsy-turvy. Once I asked the missus to buy a cock to kill for the Day of Atonement. So I couldn't explain to her what I wanted until I hit on the idea of telling her: "Buy me the gentleman of the chickens." This she understood and only then did she deliver herself of that fine word, "Alright," which means almost the same as when we say, "Be it so, why not? Sure, with the greatest of pleasure!"

No wonder, as Maurice Hindus put it, the villagers "out of sheer envy or incredulity might have been swung to support of Ivan the Fool, who

had proclaimed the existence of America an invention and a fraud."
Hindus, born in Russia in 1891, came to America at the age of fourteen
and found it no fraud. In *Green Worlds* he describes the fantastic material
abundance he saw. "The more meager the information of those who
came," he said, "the more overwhelming was their joy in its discovery."
And thinking of where they had come from:

> Only then, in the light of this opulence of America, could they
> envisage the real destitution of the old village, of the whole world out of
> which they had come. What destitution! No socks, no handkerchiefs, no
> underwear, seldom enough soap, generations behind the New World,
> and with no visible hope of putting itself in a position to reach out for the
> knowledge, the energy, the ambition to transform itself to anything
> similar. How could it, steeped as it was in "the deep and horrible mud," as
> my mother would say, and all that it implied in daily living? It was hard
> enough to pull cows and horses and wagons and sometimes our own feet
> out of that black muck. To lift the whole scheme of living out of it would
> have required a power that was nowhere in sight, a power that could
> blow the mud off the face of the earth.

They did not transform their village, but many found the power in
themselves to shake its mud from their feet and venture to America.
Mary Antin, who was born in Polotzk, saw her father go off alone,
without means, to a strange world where he had no friends, pioneering
the way for his family. As they read together his first letter home, she
sensed in it "more than the words seemed to say. There was an elation, a
hint of triumph, such as had never been in my father's letters before. I
cannot tell how I knew it. I felt a stirring, a straining. . . . My father was
inspired by a vision. He saw something—he promised us something. It
was this 'America.' "

His next letters told them that in America it was no disgrace to work
at a trade. Cobbler and teacher alike were addressed as "Mister." And *all*
the children—Jews and Gentiles, girls and boys—went to school. One
day a letter arrived with a third-class steamer ticket for the family. Mary
describes the effect upon the town.

> Before sunset the news was all over Polotzk that Hannah Hayye had
> received a steamer ticket for America. Then they began to come. Friends

and foes, distant relatives and new acquaintances, young and old, wise and foolish, debtors and creditors, and mere neighbors—from every quarter of the city, from both sides of the Dvina, from over the Polota, from nowhere—a steady stream of them poured into our street, both day and night, till the hour of our departure. And my mother gave audience. Her faded kerchief halfway off her head, her black ringlets straying, her apron often at her eyes, she received her guests in a rainbow of smiles and tears. She was the heroine of Polotzk, and she conducted herself appropriately. She gave her heart's thanks for the congratulations and blessings that poured in on her; ready tears for condolences; patient answers to monotonous questions; and handshakes and kisses and hugs she gave gratis.

What did they not ask, the eager, foolish, friendly people? They wanted to handle the ticket, and mother must read them what is written on it. How much did it cost? Was it all paid for? Were we going to have a foreign passport or did we intend to steal across the border? Were we not all going to have new dresses to travel in? Was it sure that we could get kosher food on the ship? And with the questions poured in suggestions and solid chunks of advice.

Planning for a trip today is infinitely easier than for those emigrants of a hundred years ago. Almost every inch of the earth's surface has been explored, mapped, and reported to the rest of the world by the instantaneous means of communications we now enjoy. Travel bureaus, public and private, advise us on transportation by car, rail, ship, or plane, inform us of schedules and costs, describe accommodations and make reservations, whether in the next county or on the far side of the globe. (All you need is cash or a credit card.)

It was altogether different back in the 1880s. There were no automobiles or airplanes. Passage across land was by foot, horse and wagon, carriage, or train. Across the ocean it was by sailing or steam vessel. Steam was beginning to take over from sail, although it would be another thirty years before sailing ships would almost disappear from the seas. The telegraph was the rapid communications link. There was neither radio nor television nor motion pictures. The telephone was just being installed in a handful of homes and the typewriter was almost as new.

Think of what it was like for a Jew in Eastern Europe back in that time. Finding everything going wrong, you make a great resolve to begin life all over again. The way to do that, you decide, is to start on new soil. You determine to emigrate to America. But how will you go from the Old World to the New? What route should you take? What season is it best to travel in? How will you get out of the country when the government restricts passports? What will it all cost? And where will you get the money? You mean to go alone, to prepare the way for your family to follow. How will they live while you are gone?

One of the young men who struggled with such decisions wrote:

> On a day in August I left Znamenka for America. Gershon, my father's partner, brought the horse and wagon to drive me to the station. When I began to say goodbye, I saw tears in my father's eyes and my mother fainted. My brothers and sisters were crying loudly. I was almost ready to stay at home. When my mother was brought to, I said that if she wished it, I would not go.
>
> "No," she said, "I shall faint again when they take you away to be a soldier—and, maybe, to war, and then you won't be able to stay."
>
> My father, Gershon and I climbed on the wagon and drove off. Gershon was begging me not to go. "I served as a soldier," he said, "and am I not alive?"
>
> I hurried into the train not to be seen. My father bought me a ticket to Kremenchug and gave me money. The bell rang for the third time, we kissed each other, and in another minute or two the train was leaving.

At Kremenchug he had to change for the train to Romny, and from there go to Vilna to meet the agent of those who were to smuggle him across the border into Germany. After paying the agent fifty-five rubles, he spent the night hidden in a garret. The next day, with twenty others gathered for the same purpose, he was taken by train to Shavli, where they went to the home of a driver who was to bring them over the border.

> That evening we were crowded into a covered wagon. The driver went as fast as he could and we were well shaken and bounced about. Every three hours they changed the horses. In the morning we stopped at a house in Tovrick. The man in charge put some of us in the garret, some in the cellar, the women in the only room, and me and another, perhaps because we had complained least, into the privy in the yard.
>
> In two hours we were ordered back into the wagon and told not to worry—the coast was clear. "Each of you will get a passport and when

the soldier asks for it, just give it to him." I read mine: my name was Bassie Baila Hendler, female, sixty-seven years old, grey-haired, and so forth. I could not help laughing at what had become of me.

We came to a little bridge. A soldier shouted, "Halt!" and said to the man sitting beside the driver, "How many have you there?"

"Twenty-one."

"Have all passports?"

"As always."

"Let me have them." The soldier climbed into the wagon and counted the passengers, took away their passports, counted them, and said, "Right. Twenty-one rubles." The agent gave him the money, the driver whipped the horses, and in two minutes we were in Germany. The passengers began to joke and laugh at what they had been through. At the railway station, I sent this telegram to my parents and uncle: "Merchandise arrived comhlete and satisfactory."

From the border he went by train to Memel, then Stettin, and finally Hamburg, where he boarded a steamer for America.

The father of Morris R. Cohen left his family in Neshwies, a town in White Russia, and journeyed to America. Morris and his mother followed later. They too paid an agent to get them across the border illegally. "So many people went to America that way that the enterprise was quite standardized," he said. Russian law at that time prohibited emigration. The majority had to pass the border secretly or by bribery. Later, happy to get rid of Jews, the government changed its policy.

The first wave of the mass emigration came immediately after the pogroms of 1881. As committees formed outside Russia to appeal for aid to the victims, Jews began making their way to the Austrian border town of Brody. Jewish leaders of Western Europe were anxious to help, but when the number of emigrants mounted daily, they feared the wave would engulf their own countries. They began urging the emigrants to head for America, "that vast, free and rich country where all who want to work can and will find a place."

Jewish leaders in New York were not eager to welcome the Eastern Europeans. They protested the attempts to direct the people in Brody to America. Then the Austrian government changed its liberal policy, and some 8,000 fugitives were forced to return to Russia.

Large-scale emigration was renewed in the early 1890s when anti-Jewish restrictions—the cold pogrom—were rapidly intensified. This time Jewish philanthropists abroad were better prepared to help. Again, however, they tried to turn the tide away from their own countries. Significant numbers did go to Canada, South Africa, Germany, England, Latin America, and Palestine. But most of the emigrants had their eyes fixed on the United States. The graph of Jewish immigration began with about 6,000 in 1881, doubled in the next year, rose to 32,000 by 1887, and 50,000 in 1891. In the decade before World War I (1904–1914) the annual number went over the 100,000 mark. It peaked at almost 150,000 in 1906, 1907, and 1914. The number of arrivals totaled two million by 1914.

The hardships of the Atlantic crossing came on top of the risks taken in trying to cross the border illegally in order to reach the bewildering ports of Western Europe. Ahead lay the terrors of the unknown Atlantic and the miserable conditions imposed upon steerage passengers by greedy shipowners. By the time of the great Eastern European emigration, steamships had shortened the length of the voyage. But it took a long time for the human needs of space, air, food, sleep, and privacy to be recognized in law. The immigrants were so much freight to the shipping lines, nothing more.

Sleeping quarters in steerage were compartments holding three hundred or more persons. Berths, six feet two inches long, were in two tiers, with two and a half feet of space above each berth. Only an iron pipe separated the berths. Think of each berth space as an oblong box: that was the immigrant's territory. The iron framework held a mattress and a pillow (stuffed with straw or seaweed) and often a life preserver was the substitute for a pillow. The blanket was usually so flimsy passengers had to sleep in their clothing to keep warm. Stewards never changed or cleaned the berths, even when voyages lasted sixteen days or more. There was no room for hand baggage. As almost everyone came with a few household belongings—pots and pans, the family samovar, a prized pillow—these had to be kept in the berth space. (The floor was forbidden.) There were no closets or hooks for clothing; it had to be piled someplace on the berth. Some lines handed out eating utensils, which the passengers used throughout the voyage, and these too must be placed somewhere in the berth, as well as any personal towels or toilet necessities.

The shippers allowed limited open deck space to steerage and often provided no dining rooms. The immigrants lined up for their food and ate it in their berths. Since no waste barrels or sick cans were supplied, the steerage floor was always damp and filthy and the air stank beyond endurance.

Samuel H. Cohen recalls some details of his trip across the Atlantic, made in the early 1880s.

On the first day I went to the mess counter for food, and was handed a chunk of white bread and herring which I took to my bunk. (Of course meat or soup, which was *treife,* I would not take.) I bit into the bread. It tasted like chalk. The herring stunk. I threw it all away. . . . We dug out of Joseph's pack some of the hard tack and rock-like farmer cheese that one of our relations had supplied. We munched on that. The following day we did not need food. In fact we seemed to have plenty to give up. It was stormy. The boat rocked and shook. The portholes had to be closed to prevent flood. The smell of disinfectant stifled me. I kept tossing about. I stuck my head out of the bunk a little. A shower of vomit came down from the upper bunk on my face. . . .

There was no privacy. Men, women and children were all mixed together. . . . Our greatest suffering was due to a scarcity of water. We all provided ourselves with a tin can to hold the water distributed every evening. It was all you could get until the following evening. After a few days out, the quantity that each one received was cut down, but it soon became generally known that for money, more water could be procured. That day I ate a piece of herring. Soon after, I drank all the water I had. The same evening I was burning up with thirst.

Some ships built the bunks in three tiers. Morris R. Cohen crossed on one such, the *Darmstadt,* which took fourteen days from Bremen to New York.

We were huddled together in the steerage literally like cattle—my mother, my sister and I sleeping in the middle tier, people being above us and below us as well as on the same level. Naturally we could not eat the food of the ship since it was not kosher. We only asked for hot water into which my mother used to put a bit of brandy and sugar to give it a taste. Towards the end of the trip when our bread was beginning to give out we applied to the ship's steward for bread, but the kind he gave us was unbearably soggy. The hardships of the trip began to tell on my mother, so that she took sick and developed a fever.

To diminish the discomforts and indignity of the crossing, the U.S. Immigration Commission of 1908–1911 investigated steerage-class conditions. The investigators were disguised as travelers and sent to Europe. Then they made the return trip in steerage. Anna Herkner crossed the ocean three times in steerage in 1908. In her report she describes the conditions she observed. What struck her above all was the entire lack of privacy for steerage passengers. People were herded together in hundreds. They had to spend every hour of the twenty-four, many days running, in the presence of so many others.

> The sleeping quarters were always a dismal, damp, dirty and most unwholesome place. The air was heavy, foul, and deadening to the spirit and the mind. Those confined to these beds by reason of sickness soon lost all energy, spirit, and ambition. . . . They continued to lie in their bunks as though in a stupor.

The washing and toilet rooms were quite as inadequate as the sleeping and eating accommodations, she said. There were eight toilets and eight washbasins for over two hundred women and children and the same ratio for the men. The toilet seats were always wet and water often stood inches deep on the floor. The immigrants had to rise at five or earlier if they hoped to get into a washroom before breakfast at seven. "It really was no wonder to me when some finally gave up trying to keep clean." A thorough washing of the body or even part of it was out of the question; there were no bathtubs and to monopolize a basin for more than a few moments was impossible. All the human needs were miserably provided for, or else entirely ignored, she said. It meant the steerage passenger would "arrive at the journey's end with a mind unfit for healthy, wholesome impressions and with a body weakened and unfit for the hardships that are involved in the beginning of life in a new land."

Just before docking, each woman was given a piece of candy and each man a pipe and tobacco. The intention was to sweeten the last memory of steerage. . . .

21

The Green Ones Arrive

One of the first Eastern European Jews to arrive in the early 1880s was young Abraham Cahan. Long after, when he was the famous editor of the Yiddish daily, the *Forward,* he recalled how it felt to sail into New York Harbor.

The immigrant's arrival in his new home is like a second birth to him. Imagine a new-born babe in possession of a fullh-developed intellect. Would it ever forget its entry into the world? Neither does the immigrant ever forget his entry into a country which is, to him, a new world in the profoundest sense of the term and in which he expects to spend the rest of his life. I conjure up the gorgeousness of the spectacle as it appeared to me on that clear June morning: the magnificent verdure of Staten Island, the tender blue of sea and sky, the dignified bustle of passing craft—above all, those floating, squatting, multitudinously windowed palaces which I subsequently learned to call ferries. It was all so utterly unlike anything I had ever seen or dreamed of before. It unfolded itself like a divine revelation. I was in a trance. . . .

"This, then, is America!" I exclaimed, mutely. The notion of something enchanted which the name had always evoked in me now seemed to be fully borne out.

The immigrants were ferried over to Castle Garden, originally a fort built just before the War of 1812 at the foot of Manhattan Island in Battery Park. Renamed Castle Garden ten years later, the great rotunda was used as a concert hall. In 1855 it became the country's first receiving station for immigrants. By the time Cahan arrived, nearly half a million immigrants were passing through it each year.

Until 1882 almost anyone could enter the country. Government policy had been "hands off." Immigrants could come as they pleased. Nothing was done to encourage or discourage them. That year Congress adopted the first national immigration law. Inspection of immigrants was to be carried out by state boards under uniform rules at all ports of entry. Undesirables were to be kept out. This meant prostitutes, Chinese "coolies," or "any convicts, lunatics, idiots, or any person unable to take care of himself without becoming a public charge." Shipping lines were taxed fifty cents per immigrant to cover the costs of running the landing depots and attached hospitals. (Seven out of every ten immigrants came through the port of New York; the others entered at Portland, Boston, Philadelphia, Baltimore, Key West, New Orleans, Galveston, and San Francisco.)

Castle Garden would survive as a landing depot only another ten years, when it was replaced by Ellis Island. But in its last decade it processed over five million immigrants, far too many for its facilities. One of those millions was I. Kopeloff, a young Russian Jew. His first impression:

> Castle Garden, a large circular, rotunda-shaped building, had the appearance, to my eyes, of the arsenal in the castle of Boberisk, or of its tower, and struck me with gloom. . . . The main hall was huge and barren, and gave off an uncanny coldness which produced in its inhabitants an involuntary oppression. One after another sighed and sighed . . . [It] was often so crowded, so jammed, that there was simply nowhere to sit by day, or any place to lie down at night—not even on the bare floor.
>
> The filth was unendurable, so many packages, pillows, feather beds and foul clothing (often just plain rags) that each immigrant had dragged with him over the seas and clung to as if they were precious—all of this provided great opportunity for vermin, those filthy little beasts, that crawled about freely and openly over the clutter and made life disagreeable.

The constant scratching and the distress of the little children touched one
to the quick.

Failure to anticipate the tidal wave of immigration accounted for the
overcrowding. But greed and inhumanity were responsible for many
other abuses. It started back in the old country when unsuspecting
immigrants paid secondclass fares for subsequent steerage passage. On
this side of the ocean, transfer agents demanded double the normal price
to ship the immigrants' baggage, the railroads extracted gross profits
from the sale of tickets, money changers chopped down the going
market rate, the telegraph charged for messages that were never sent.
Complaints piled up until the federal government decided to dispense
with state control, take over the immigration process, and build a new
center for New York.

To replace Castle Garden, the government chose a tiny blob of
mud and sand lying in a shallow of New York Harbor. Workers had to
double the three acres of Ellis Island with landfill in order to provide
space for a substantial building. The two-story station constructed of
wood was about 400 by 150 feet, and looked like a seaside hotel.
Opened in 1892, the firetrap burned down in 1897 (no one was injured,
luckily); it was replaced in 1900 by a new brick building. Again the
planners guessed wrong, for they never expected the half-million annual immigration rate of the recent past would ever climb higher. It did.
And for the next fifteen years, the newcomers had to fight fiercely for
room, even though the island was eventually filled in to an area of
twenty-one acres.

Surrounding the main building on Ellis Island were medical facilities,
bathhouse, laundry, kitchens, dining room, and an electric power plant.
With the new facilities came new regulations. The 1882 law was
replaced with a more comprehensive one in 1891. Federal control was
placed in the hands of a new Bureau of Immigration whose Superintendent reported to the Treasury Department. The stricter set of rules added
new categories of "undesirables"—polygamists, people guilty of "moral
turpitude," and people suffering from "a loathsome or contagious
disease." A law of 1885, intended to keep out workers brought over
under contract to employers, was toughened. Aliens who came in
illegally or who became public charges within a year of arrival were to

be deported. (In 1904, over 8,000 aliens were deported.) The 1891 law was stiffened two years later by amendments.

In a single day Ellis Island sometimes handled as many as 7,000 immigrants. How did it manage it? Jacob Riis, a reporter, watched the newcomers in 1903 and told what he saw in *Century* magazine.

By the time the lighters are tied up at the Ellis Island wharf their human cargo is numbered and lettered in groups that correspond with like entries in the manifest, and so are marshaled upon and over the bridge that leads straight into the United States to the man with the pen who asks questions. When the crowd is great and pressing, they camp by squads in little stalls bearing their proprietary stamp, as it were, finding one another and being found when astray by the mystic letter that brings together in the close companionship of a common peril—the pen, one stroke of which can shut the gate against them—men and women who in another hour go their way, very likely never to meet or hear of one another again on earth. The sense of the impending trial sits visibly upon the waiting crowd. Here and there a masterful spirit strides boldly on; the mass huddle close, with more or less anxious look. Five minutes after it is over, eating their dinner in the big waiting-room, they present an entirely different appearance. Signs and numbers have disappeared. The groups are recasting themselves on lines of nationality and personal preference. . . .

Behind carefully guarded doors wait the "outs," the detained immigrants, for the word that will let down the bars or fix them in place immovably. The guard is for a double purpose: that no one shall enter or leave the detention room. . . . Here are the old, the stricken, waiting for friends able to keep them; the pitiful colony of women without the shield of a man's name in the hour of their greatest need; the young and pretty and thoughtless, for whom one sends up a silent prayer of thanksgiving at the thought of the mob at that other gate, yonder in Battery Park, beyond which Uncle Sam's strong hand reaches not to guide or guard. And the hopelessly bewildered are there, often enough exasperated at the restraint, which they cannot understand.

Harsh and discomforting as the inspection system at Ellis Island seemed to the immigrants, still, it was relatively efficient. The other major immigration ports—Boston, Philadelphia, Baltimore—were undermanned and chaotic.

Once accepted for entry, the immigrants heading out of New York were ticketed with the name of the route that was to carry them to their new homes. But even on this last leg of the long journey the immigrants were marked as prey for the greedy. Anna Herkner, the Immigration Commission's investigator, reported what happened in the room where she and the other immigrants were sorted according to the railroad by which they were to continue their journey.

A rough guard pushed me to the pen into which I belonged. A commissary clerk met me, led me to a spot where my baggage could be deposited, then to a counter, saying "Show your money." I was about to obey, as a steerage passenger obeys these commands given at so many points of his journey, when I concluded that this was the attempt to compel one to buy a box of provisions for his further journey. Many of the passengers had told me of it and warned me. I refused to show my money, saying I was going only to Baltimore and did not need provisions for so short a journey. The man continued shouting, thinking to force me into buying, until he spied someone else entering. Then he dropped me and ran for the new victim. . . . The immigrants are practically forced to buy these boxes, regardless of the length of their journey or their desires. . . .

Finally we were taken from here to our respective stations. We who were going on the _____ Line crossed in a ferry to a dingy, dirty, unventilated waiting room next to the _____ station in Jersey City. Here we waited from 6 o'clock in the evening until after 9. About 8 o'clock the attendant signaled us to go downstairs, showing our tickets as we went. We all expected we were to board the train, so anxiously hurried along, dragging our heavy and numerous hand baggage. The poor, travel-tired women and the sleepy little children were pitiful sights. Arrived at the bottom of the long stairs, we waited and waited, but there was no train.

At last they boarded a train and arrived in Philadelphia, halting in the middle of the yards because they had to change trains.

We piled out in the middle of the night, all laden down with baggage, the women having, in addition, sleeping and sleepy little children. A trainman guided this weary and dejected party along the car tracks through the sleet and snow over an endless distance, it seemed, to the station . . . to what evidently was a lounging room for section hands. We were locked in there for an hour and a half, when we were again led to the station to be put on a train. They assigned us to the smoker—women, children and all—and refused even to open the women's toilet for us, compelling us to use the men's. . . . What those immigrants who had to travel longer distances suffered can well be imagined from the experiences of this short journey.

The alien had little or no protection. Ignorant of the devices of fraud, he responded to friendly overtures, thinking everyone in this wonderful America was eager to help. Countless thousands were cheated at docks and on trains and boats, risked health and safety in wretched traveling conditions, and suffered painful losses at the hands of dishonest travel agents, lawyers, bankers, notaries, interpreters. The U.S. government only admitted the immigrant; he was on his own in everything else.

Take Maurice Hindus, who came to America in the autumn of 1905.

I arrived in New York wearing my best clothes—my Russian school uniform, black belted tunic, long trousers, and military cap with a black shiny visor. I must have been an outlandish sight, especially to children. They stared and laughed at me, and overnight my eldest brother, who had come ahead of us and had paid for our ship tickets, changed me into an American outfit: knee pants, jacket, black stockings, and a soft cap. Proudly I walked the streets, but inwardly I felt bewilderingly alien, for no two worlds could have been more stupendously unlike than the mud-sodden village from which I had been uprooted and the towering New York into which I was flung. . . .

The overpowering surprises of New York—the tall buildings, incredibly tall, the gas and electric lights that banished night from the streets, the horsecars and trolleys that carried one wherever one chose to go and, marvel of marvels, the elevated trains thundering right over one's head. Least of all did rural or town Russia prepare me for the newsstands which sold enormous-sized dailies at a penny each—an unbelievably low price for so much paper. . . .

The streets lured me irresistibly. They were my first American school. It was in the streets that I saw for the first time Negroes, Chinese, Italians, Hungarians, Irish, others of the multitude of nationalities that made up New York. I had read of these people and now I saw them in the flesh. I yearned to speak to them, to learn all I could about them: how they lived, what foods they ate, what books they read, what they talked about when they were by themselves, what they thought of the peoples among whom they lived, and how they differed from the muzhiks, the Jews, the intellectuals I had known in the Old World. But language was a barrier I couldn't hurdle—not yet. I contented myself with watching and wondering about them—the Chinese in the laundries, the Negroes as day laborers, the Irish as truck drivers, policemen, and saloonkeepers, the Italians as shoe-shiners, ice and coal carriers, peanut venders, and organ-grinders.

Abraham Cahan tells of the immigrant who rushes from Ellis Island to the heart of the Jewish East Side. Unlike Hindus, he wants first of all to see and be with other Jews.

The streets swarmed with Yiddish-speaking immigrants. The signboards were in English and Yiddish, some of them in Russian. The scurry and hustle of the people were not merely overwhelmingly greater, both in volume and intensity, than in my native town. It was of another sort. The swing and step of the pedestrians, the voices and manner of the street peddlers, and a hundred and one other things seemed to testify to far more self-confidence and energy, to larger ambitions and wider scopes, than did the appearance of the crowds in my birthplace.

The great thing was that these people were better dressed than the inhabitants of my town. The poorest looking man wore a hat (instead of a cap), a stiff collar and a necktie, and the poorest woman wore a hat or a bonnet. . . .

Many of the passersby paused to look at me with wistful smiles of curiosity.

"There goes a green one!" some of them exclaimed. . . .

I understood the phrase at once. And as a contemptuous quizzical appellation for a newly arrived, inexperienced immigrant, it stung me cruelly. As I went along I heard it again and again. "Poor fellow! He is a green one," these people seemed to say. "We are not, of course. We are Americanized."

22

Sheeny!

The Jews flooding in from Eastern Europe arrived at a time when America was transforming itself into the foremost industrial nation of the world. Mechanization, which had begun in the 1850s, was given a tremendous boost by the Civil War. The agricultural society of the prewar era was changing beyond belief.

Take the year 1900—the midpoint of the new immigration wave and the beginning of another century—as a marker. The people first: their number stood at 76 million. It was a population in great flux. Although the free land of the frontier was gone, a continuous stream of people kept pouring into Texas, the Plains states, and the Pacific Coast. Even more people, however, were deserting the countryside and the small towns for the rising cities. Many were jobless farmhands, forced off the land by the new labor-saving machines.

Add to these changes the tidal wave of the new immigration from Southern and Eastern Europe. It was not only a huge addition to the American population in numbers but a spectacular shift in source. Fewer than before meant to settle on the land. They too saw the promise of a more abundant life in the great urban centers. (In the dime novels of the day the boys who made good did it in the cities.) In just one decade,

1880–1890, the urban population soared from 14 to 22 million. By 1900 one out of every three Americans was a city dweller. In 1920 they would be the majority of the population.

Many of the immigrants who entered at the port of New York simply stayed there. The city rapidly doubled in size, reaching 3.5 million. The furious pace of urban growth created a need for the immigrants' labor. By 1900 over a third of all New Yorkers were foreign-born. Chicago experienced the same dizzying rise, reaching half New York's population, but with three fourths of its people foreign-born.

The older Americans saw in the newcomers a threat to the country's basic institutions. The coming of so many millions of strangers and in so short a period of time alarmed them. It was not the first time that immigrants were made to feel unwelcome. Nativism—distrust of newcomers—had taken root early in colonial times. Even the revolutionary Founding Fathers—Franklin, Jefferson, Hamilton—had argued against free immigration for fear that "foreign elements" would disrupt the new nation's life.

Sharp increases in immigration had begun with the arrival of the Irish in the pre-Civil War decades. It triggered an anti-Catholic hysteria. Cries went up of a "foreign conspiracy" engineered by the Pope to seize the United States. The Irish, who came poor, were treated with open contempt, called brutish, clannish, vicious. That did not prevent the young industrialism from making use of the cheap, plentiful labor the Irish provided, which could not be found easily among the older American stocks. For a generation or more the Irish did the dirtiest and hardest work. As they climbed the social scale, they were replaced by the much larger immigration which began in the 1880s.

With the huge numbers pouring in from Eastern and Southern Europe came a renewal of nativism. Now it was not one but a dozen different ethnic groups arriving. Their strange languages, religions (mostly Greek Orthodox, Roman Catholic, and Jewish), social customs, and political backgrounds again made the dominant white Anglo-Saxon Protestants fearful and hostile. Some believed the era of American expansion had ended and that there would be no place for the newcomers. Then, disappointed and hungry, they would overturn the country by revolution. Another argument ran that these immigrants were different from the earlier ones and inferior, incapable of adjusting to

American life. Even the reformer Henry George saw the new immigration as a process of "dumping garbage" on American shores. And Emma Lazarus, the Jewish poet, though a friend to the immigrants, in her famous sonnet spoke of them as "wretched refuse."

Racial theories, which had recently sprung into virulent life in Europe, spread rapidly in America. The new pseudoscience held the "Nordic" or "Aryan" stock to be superior, and the Southern and Eastern European peoples fit only to serve the master races. On the one hand, it was charged that the newcomers could never be absorbed into the mainstream. And on the other, that if they were, by intermarriage, it would destroy the character of the nation and bring chaos and ruin.

A harsh selfishness marked the treatment of all minorities in that age. The Indians, ruthlessly exploited from the beginning, were now herded onto reservations. The limited gains the emancipated blacks had made during the brief Reconstruction era were steadily eroded. The Mexicans laboring in the West were dismissed as "dirty greasers." The Chinese, "those yellow rascals" who had been sweated in the mines and in the building of the railroads, were suddenly shut out of America completely by the Chinese Exclusion Act of 1882.

When hard times came—the depressions of 1873 and 1893—many citizens, frantic with fear of losing what they had, made scapegoats of the foreign and the weak. The new middle class especially was prone to hysteria under the erratic pressures of rapid industrialization and urbanization. The popular culture of the period illustrates their insecurity. The Currier & Ives lithographs and the small colored trade cards given away to promote consumer products made the Irish, the blacks, and the Chinese the targets of a racist put-down humor.

The merchants, professionals, white-collar workers, and skilled mechanics felt the rising tide of immigration threatened their hard-won status. Practically all these newcomers were job seekers, over 60 percent were males, and the same percentage were young (between fifteen and forty). Worse in the eyes of the established wage earners was the fact that most of the immigrants were poor and unskilled. Eager for jobs and experience, the newcomers would "work for almost nothing and seem to be able to live on wind—something which I cannot do," as one worker put it. Union men therefore objected to unlimited immigration. Their leaders thought it would be almost impossible to organize people who spoke so many different tongues. The immigrants did prove hard to organize in some cases, and occasionally they were used to scab. But the trade unions themselves shared the blame so long as they refused to recruit the masses of unskilled workers.

It was during these years that American Jews began to encounter greater social anti-Semitism. It was part of the general rise in anti-foreign feeling. Many immigrant groups were attacked, some worse than the Jews. Catholics as a whole were the target of an organized opposition which the anti-Semites never developed to the same degree. And Italians were the victims of far more violence. Still, Jews were not safe from fist or rock. William Zorach recalls the treatment his family received on the streets of Cleveland.

> When one of my brothers came home from work, he was attacked and beaten up by a bunch of rowdies. He said nothing, but when this began happening every night, he became more and more miserable and finally told my father. My father and a couple of my older brothers went out that night. They took crowbars and went after this gang. We heard the crowbars flying and clanking around the street. After that my brother had no more trouble.
>
> My father used to be harassed and attacked and stoned. Boys yelled "Sheeny" at him on the streets. I remember some kids getting him into their yard to buy a sack of junk. It was supposed to be iron, but when he looked in, it was only rocks. When he wouldn't fall for it, they began pelting him with the rocks. He ran down the street yelling, with the kids after him. . . . I was miserable for my father and myself.

In the Brownsville neighborhood of Brooklyn, Morris Cohen ran up against anti-Semitism as he walked to school.

> Beyond Dean Street I passed a number of houses inhabited by Germans who delighted to set their young children on me, yelling "Sheeny" and running after me as if they were going to attack me from the rear. When I turned around they would retreat, but as soon as I resumed my walk they would return to their annoying pastime. One day I became so irritated that I ran after one of the youngsters and slapped his face. At once, his older brother came out of the house and gave me a good thrashing for hitting someone below my size. But the total result was satisfactory for the youngsters thereafter left me alone.

Until the Civil War, anti-Semitism in the United States had been only sporadic. There were but 150,000 Jews in America in 1860. Most Americans never saw and probably never thought about them. Attacks upon Jews were usually directed against individuals, often by those who envied or competed with them. Jews who earned prominence in any field were the more likely to be attacked for their origins or faith. Nevertheless, Jews were capable of winning public support, as evidenced by the election of a number to public office of both high and low degree.

America's Jewry was different from other Jewries, younger by far (except now for Israel), and with a history that began without the problem of Emancipation that faced other Jewries in modern times. From the founding of the United States the Jews were guaranteed freedom of religion and equal rights. It was a status they never had seriously to contest. The question of Emancipation of the Jews has therefore never become an issue dividing the American people. Anti-Semitism may be found in every class and in every political persuasion, from right to left. But no one has built a political movement upon it (as in France, Germany, Poland, Russia) with demands that Jews be made second-class citizens, expelled, or exterminated. Anti-Semitism has been more of a social or cultural phenomenon, casual, impulsive, lacking any long-range radical goals.

The dormant prejudice is likely to be awakened by vast national upheavals, such as the Civil War. In both North and South, Jews were made the scapegoats for hurts suffered during the long agony of the struggle over slavery. And for the first and only time in American history, the Jews as a *people* were punished by anti-Semitism. The notorious episode revolved around the action of General U. S. Grant in expelling the Jews as a class from an occupied Southern region where speculators were profiteering on cotton. Far more non-Jews than Jews were guilty of the corruption, but Grant closed his eyes to the others. President Lincoln revoked the unjust order when Jews bombarded the White House with protests.

Jewish stereotypes that originated abroad and in much earlier times found their way to America. They were basically of two kinds, the religious and the economic, and as is often true of stereotypes, they expressed mixed feelings. In the religious stereotype the Jews were seen as God's Chosen People, miraculously preserved to carry out His divine purpose. But at the same time they were held to be the deserving victims of His wrath as the "betrayers" of Christ.

In the economic stereotype the Jews were held to be of keen and resourceful intelligence, a constructive and enterprising force in the development of the economy. But again, at the same time, they were portrayed as grasping, greedy, and unscrupulous (the Shylock image). The religious stereotype faded to a degree in America, but the negative side of the economic stereotype gained ground rapidly after the Civil War. For it was now that the German Jews, who had made the first mass migration of Jews to America beginning in the 1830s, became conspicuous. In less than one generation many had risen from rags to riches. Starting often as peddlers, they became leading retail merchants, bankers, manufacturers. Perhaps no other immigrant group had made good so fast. Their ambition and their success made them easy targets. The common ethnic stereotypes stress inferiority, but the Jews left an opposite impression, of superior capacity. Anti-Semites soon twisted this into "the overbearing ability of Jews to gain advantage in American life."

The middle- and upper-class Gentiles, themselves scrambling for place and power among the nouveaux riches of the Gilded Age, began to exclude the Jews from summer resorts, neighborhoods, clubs, private school. In 1881 Nina Morais, a Philadelphia Jew, described what was happening.

> The provident hotel-keeper avoids the contact of the Hebrew purse; the little child in school finds no room for the Jew in the game at recess; the man of business, whose relations with an Israelite have been close and honorable, gives vent to a passing feeling of displeasure in the reproach of "Jews." In social and professional clubs, the "Jew" is blackballed. "Jew" is the text of the political opposition orator. The liberal-minded host tells his guests, with an apologetic air, that the stranger among them "is a Jew, but quite a cultured man." An agreeable companion is spoken of as "a good fellow, if he is a Jew." The merchant who cheats his creditors, the criminal in the prisoner's dock, is a civil offender if he belongs to the Baptist or Episcopal denomination, but if he comes of Hebrew blood, Judaism is made responsible for fraud and theft. Jew, Jew, Jew is the one all-comprehensive charge.

One magazine, *The Journalist,* always referred to Joseph Pulitzer, the innovative publisher of the New York *World,* as "Jewseph Pulitzer." The editor remarked that Pulitzer "is a smart businessman because he is a Jew and has the commercial instincts of his race very sharply developed within him."

At first the plight of the Jews in Czarist Russia evoked sympathy among Americans. When news of the tens of thousands of Jews injured or killed in the pogroms of 1881–1882 appeared in the press, seventy-five non-Jewish groups held a protest meeting in New York City. But only a couple of months later the influential magazine *Century* ran an article by a Russian which sought to justify the pogroms. The nasty Jews, it seemed, had brought the pogroms upon themselves. Although Emma Lazarus replied to the slander in the next issue, the original article was a sign that the intellectuals too were infected with anti-Semitism.

Emma Lazarus stood apart from the many German-American Jews who were hostile to the Eastern European Jews. The German Jews felt they had barely established themselves and here was a mass migration of "outlandish foreigners" threatening to wreck everything they had created. The Yiddish of the newcomers they ridiculed as a "piggish jargon." The business competition that rapidly developed between the two groups sharpened the antagonism. The Germans spoke contemptuously of their Russian rivals, many of whose names ended in "ki," as kikes.

It was for such reasons that the established Jewry—the "uptown Jews"—proposed limits on the immigration of the Eastern Europeans. They also feared a huge financial burden would be imposed upon them for the care of the immigrants. The United Hebrew Charities, formed in 1874 for the relief of needy Jews, returned to Europe all immigrant Jews incapable of earning a living here. Needy immigrants who stayed looked to the charities for help, but there were not enough funds to take care of all. By the 1890s, however, there was a readier acceptance of the newcomers, partly because of a deepening sense of obligation to the less fortunate members of the faith. In 1884 the Hebrew Sheltering House Association was founded on the Lower East Side to befriend the Jews on arrival. It provided shelter and food, helped locate relatives and friends, and got jobs. In 1909 it merged with the Hebrew Immigrant

Aid Society. The Jewish welfare program expanded to national and international scope. The earlier arrivals joined in with manpower and money, believing it their duty to help the next ones to get started. Wherever they found themselves, religious, cultural, and historical ties bound Jews together.

23

Tenements and Strangers

One square mile on the Lower East Side of New York became the America of the Eastern European Jews—the "downtown Jews." It was to New York that most of the immigrants came, and in New York that they stayed. Before the 1870s there was no truly distinct Jewish neighborhood in the city. It began when the German Jews set up their wholesale and retail enterprises in lower Manhattan. Both Grand Street and Canal Street were packed with their garment shops. Many of the Polish Jews, who were among the first Eastern Europeans to come, were skilled tailors. They secured work from the German Jews and found it convenient to settle nearby, at the foot of Canal Street. Here, at Rutgers Square, four major arteries met—Canal, East Broadway, Rutgers, and Essex. When the Russian Jews began arriving in 1882, they were drawn to the same neighborhood. It became the heart of the Jewish quarter.

There were many such immigrant enclaves in New York; it was natural for the newcomers to collect in neighborhoods where they could feel at home with their own. There were a dozen different ethnic colonies—Irish and German, Austrian and Hungarian, Bohemian and Italian, French and English. By the 1890s, the Lower East Side had become largely Eastern European Jewish. Older New Yorkers, crowded

by the newer, left for less congested corners of Greater New York. The
city stretched its limits beyond Manhattan, and by 1898 embraced the
Bronx, Brooklyn, Queens, and Richmond, completing the metropolis
we know today.

One of the immigrant boys whose family settled on the Lower East
Side was Samuel Chotzinoff. He gives us the view from Rutgers Square.

> East Broadway was a wide thoroughfare. Our apartment on the third
> floor of a house on the corner of Rutgers Street overlooked a large square,
> or rather oblong, adorned by a large black marble fountain rising in
> several tiers. I could sense the possibilities of the neighborhood. For,
> besides the fountain, all the buildings on the west side of East Broadway,
> extending from Essex to Jefferson streets, had been razed for the eventual
> construction of a park, and the debris offered the very terrain for possible
> war games, with rival armies marching and counter-marching and striv-
> ing to gain certain desirable heights. . . .
>
> Looking up Rutgers Street toward the east, there was the river in the
> distance, with boats of every description plying up and down. Huge
> warehouses near the water's edge were forever discharging crates and
> barrels with mysterious contents, and at night one could sit on the large
> empty trucks parked on the wharves and watch the river and the lights
> from Brooklyn across it. Within walking distance were splendors like
> Brooklyn Bridge, the City Hall, and the Post Office. The mysterious
> alleys of Chinatown were no more than half a mile away. Certainly East
> Broadway, at its meeting with Rutgers Square, was the center of
> the universe.

The Jews clustered in neighborhoods according to the parts of Eastern Europe they had come from. Moses Rischin mapped a cultural
geography of the Lower East Side, street by street.

> Hungarians were settled in the northernmost portion above Houston
> Street, along the numbered streets between Avenue B and the East River,
> once indisputably *Kleindeutschland.* Galicians lived to the south, between
> Houston and Broome, east of Clinton, on Attorney, Ridge, Pitt, Willett,
> and the cross streets. To the west lay the most congested Rumanian
> quarter, "in the very thick of the battle for breath," on Chrystie, Forsyth,
> Eldridge, and Allen streets, flanked by Houston Street to the north and

Grand Street to the south, with the Bowery gridironed by the overhead elevated to the west.

After 1907 Levantines, last on the scene and even stranger than the rest, for they were alien to Yiddish, settled between Allen and Chrystie streets among the Rumanians with whom they seemed to have closest affinity. The remainder of the great Jewish quarter, from Grand Streee reaching south to Monroe, was the preserve of the Russians—those from Russian Poland, Lithuania, Byelorussia, and the Ukraine—the most numerous and heterogeneous of the Jewries of Eastern Europe.

The immigrants sailing into the port of New York in the early 1880s saw nothing like the skyline of today. The Statue of Liberty would not be erected until 1886, Ellis Island was nothing but a blob of mud, and the biggest building in town was only ten stories tall. North of Battery Park, church spires pierced the sky, and beyond them were visible the treetops of rural Manhattan. Off to the right soared the towers of the new Brooklyn Bridge, spanning the East River. The city was just about to enter its most explosive era of expansion. The upward thrust of the skyline began in 1882 with the erection of the Washington Building at No. 1 Broadway, "the first skyscraper." In the 1890s the profile of downtown New York changed enormously, as one after another new steel-skeleton buildings competed for the title of "the tallest building in the world."

The Lower East Side could lay claim to a different distinction: the most crowded slum district in the city, and probably in the world. The young Maurice Hindus, fresh from rural Russia, was enthralled by it.

I loved to wander the streets of the Lower East Side and get lost in the adventure. The noisy bustling crowds fascinated me, everyone so feverishly busy. Immigrants mostly, they seemed like a new race in the world, different in manners and behavior from the people I had known on the other side of the ocean. Energetic and purposeful, they were astonishingly informal: well-to-do shopkeepers walked around without coats, sometimes with shirt sleeves rolled up as no member of their profession would deign to do in the scruffy little city where I had gone to school. Overalled janitors, icemen, peddlers tipped their caps to nobody— the very custom was unknown, and so was hand-kissing.

Several blocks from where we lived was roaring, bustling Hester Street. The pavement was lined with stalls and pushcarts, and men with cribs or baskets suspended on leather straps from their necks pushed their way along, crying their wares—needles, thread, shoelaces, soap, socks—like hawkers in a Russian bazaar. The filthiest section of the neighborhood, it was also the busiest and most exciting. Customers haggled over prices as violently and abusively as muzhiks. Shopkeepers grabbed the arms of passers-by and with torrents of cajolery endeavored to pull them inside their stores, cursing those who had escaped their clutching hands. Russian or Polish women, obviously peasants, struggled through the crowds calling for someone to rescue them from clinging Hungarian or Romanian peddlers or shopkeepers whose language they didn't understand. All was bedlam, a cacophony of voices, the Yiddish dialects of Eastern Europe rising above all others. Here the Old World strove loudly against the New with all its undisciplined brashness, a product of the ruthless century-old struggle for survival.

New York was growing too fast for its inhabitants to either understand or control it. The Tenth Ward, the center of the factory district on the Lower East Side, was the most crowded in the city, with 523.6 inhabitants per acre. (Manhattan as a whole averaged 114 per acre, and the entire city sixty per acre.) The health officers called it the "typhus ward" and to the Bureau of Vital Statistics it was the "suicide ward." People were jammed more densely into its tenements than anywhere else in the world, including the notorious slums of London, India, and China.

Looking at Rivington Street, the English novelist Arnold Bennett said, "The architecture seemed to sweat humanity at every window and door." By 1914 the streets below Fourteenth held a sixth of the city's population—this on one eighty-second of New York's total land area.

The heavy influx of immigrants created a similar mosaic of crowded ethnic neighborhoods in many cities. But compare New York's density with other places. The Baltimore slums of 1890 held 7.71 persons per dwelling; Philadelphia held 7.34; Chicago 15.51; and New York—36.79! Plague-ridden Bombay was the only other place in the world to come close to New York's slums for congestion. And not really that close, for it held a third less people per acre.

From steerage quarters aboard ship, the immigrants came to slum tenements ashore. In 1881 Manhattan's 22,000 slum tenements held 500,000 people. By 1895 the number of tenements had almost doubled, to 40,000, but the population they contained had risen far higher proportionately—to 1,300,000. And more than 95 percent of those slum dwellers were immigrants and their children.

Living on the Lower East Side meant living in a tenement. New York had divided its building lots into rectangles 25 feet wide by 100 feet long. Twice that space was needed for proper light and air, but profits didn't lie that way. The "dumbbell" tenement became the standard by the time the mass immigration began. Six to seven stories tall, the tenements were arranged in the shape of a dumbbell, four apartments on a floor, two at each end of a narrow separating corridor. The front apartments were usually four rooms; the rear, three. But only one room in each apartment got direct light from the street in front or a yard in the rear. An air shaft less than five feet wide separated the tenement buildings. The common toilet was in the hallway.

A reporter took a look at dumbbell tenements on the Lower East Side and summed up his impressions.

> They are great prison-like structures of brick, with narrow doors and windows, cramped passages and steep rickety stairs. . . . The narrow courtyard . . . in the middle is a damp foul-smelling place, supposed to do duty as an airshaft; had the foul fiend designed these great barracks they could not have been more villainously arranged to avoid any chance of ventilation. . . . In case of fire they would be perfect death-traps, for it would be impossible for the occupants of the crowded rooms to escape by the narrow stairways, and the flimsy fire escapes which the owners of the tenements were compelled to put up a few years ago are so laden with broken furniture bales and boxes that they would be worse than useless. In the hot summer months . . . these fire-escape balconies are used as sleeping-rooms by the poor wretches who are fortunate enough to have windows opening upon them. The drainage is horrible, and even the Croton as it flows from the tap in the noisome courtyard seemed to be contaminated by its surroundings and have a fetid smell.

Summertime on Orchard Street is recalled by J. R. Schwartz, who reached the East Side in 1899.

> There hasn't been any breeze or rain to speak of. The sun beats down mercilessly. The only shade is indoors and indoors it's stifling. People are listless from the energy-sapping heat. The street-cleaner turns on the

street hydrant to flush the pavement and let the little kids splash in the gushing stream. The water isn't cold. . . .

You walk along the street. . . . The flies and mosquitoes add to the discomfort. The smells from the uncollected garbage are nauseating. The rivulets in the gutter, sweeping along the slops from the wash-pail water dumped by the storekeepers, are black and the smells are putrid. Little boys, unabashed, urinate into the flow of bilge and add to the stench.

A pushcart peddler, either too lazy to seek out some toilet or uncon-cerned about proprieties, urinates against a wagon wheel regardless of the women pedestrians. . . . At another spot you see a middle-aged woman looking for vermin or insects crawling between her breasts while another is sitting in front of a stoop openly suckling her infant. In the middle of the street a wagon stops and the horse lets go a gusher of urine and drops a load of manure.

You look up at the fire escapes and see them filled with the young and the old seeking an elusive breeze. Thinking that here they have privacy, they are clad in flimsy underwear or shirts as token coverages and signs of their modesty.

The worst place in the tenement was a basement or cellar apartment. Lower Manhattan was flat and without enough sewers for the rain and waste to reach the rivers underground. Terrible stinks came up from the street openings and assaulted the basement dwellers. Chicago's slum basements were no better. Lucy Robbins Lang, who came from Russia at nine, remembers hers.

For $4.50 a month Aunt Yente Chave rented rooms for us in the basement of the house on Morgan Street in which she lived, and she also found for us an unsteady table, some lame chairs, a rusty bed, and an ancient sofa.

The basement was divided in two, and we lived in the part toward the street. The front room had a barred window, through which we could see only the feet of passers-by and the rats that thronged under the wooden sidewalk. The second room was the kitchen, and in it was a smoky stove. Then there was a half room, like a cave dug into a black cliff, and the bed was placed there, near the windowless wall. The other half of the basement contained the toilet and the coal bins, which were infested with rats as big as cats. When the tenants came to get coal, they had to fight the rats, which fled towards our apartment. Mother, who was very unwell, lived in fear of the rats.

Privacy in such homes was practically unknown. The average three-room flat had a kitchen, a parlor, and a bedroom. The parlor was converted into sleeping quarters at night, and so was the kitchen when families were large—and they often were. Gussie Kimball recalls that much of social life took place on the other side of the apartment door.

Twenty-four families occupied our tenement, six families on each floor. The halls were very busy places, mostly because the toilets and running water were community services in the halls. If you went to the sink to fetch water, you were bound to meet a neighbor or two. Someone would have a pitcher to fill with drinking water. Someone else would have a cooking pot to fill. And usually a mother would be waiting to fill a tub for her youngsters' baths.

Getting the water was important, but just as important was the chance to talk—or listen. Papa called the halls our "talking newspapers." Here was where the gossip was passed around about who was getting married, or expecting a baby, who was ill or dying, who was having a *bris* (circumcision), or who was being *bar mitzva* (confirmed).

"Privacy," said Samuel Chotzinoff, "could be had only in public. The streets in the evening were thick with promenading couples, and the benches around the fountain and in Jackson Street Park, and the empty trucks lined up at the river front were filled with lovers who had no other place to meet."

How the mass of Eastern European Jews felt about living under such conditions we do not know. No scientific surveys of public opinion were made in that time. The nearest we come to it are the impressions set down in autobiographies, stories, poems, plays, and in interviews recorded long after the event.

Writing of a tenement house on Suffolk Street, Leon Kobrin, who immigrated from Russia in 1892, conveys the variety of human life within its walls.

Jewish immigrants live here—most of them working-men and working-women, most of them not working people in the old country . . . on every floor, behind every door, a different past, a separate present, a different life-experience, an isolated existence—one sorrowful, beaten, wounded, hopeless and another cheerful, sunny, triumphant, filled with hope and expectation. . . . Refined folk and coarse, scholars and ignoramuses, parents of children who are a source of joy, and of children who might better not have been born. . . . Children who had left their parents in the old homes, and yearned for them, and parents whose American children had deserted them. . . . Parents who are ashamed of their offspring and children who are ashamed of their parents. . . . The dreamy eyes of the young, illumined by thought, and dull eyes of exhausted workers in which thought has been quenched for a long time. The impudent animalism in the face of a young gangster and the refined meditative face of a college man—all these are hidden in the high, gray, stone walls of the tenement house.

Some felt lost and lonely in the crowded slums. Maurice Hindus said that he wept with anguish the day he had to leave the muddy Russian village of his birth.

My ancestors had lived there for centuries, had become intimately intertwined with the life and culture of our lowly, talkative, hospitable muzhik neighbors. Now I was leaving it, the only home I had known. Though my mother, brother, and sisters were with me, I felt the desolation of the uprooted. Despite poverty, mud, bribe-extorting Czarist officials, I had loved the old home with a fierce primitive emotion, and leaving it was like tearing something out of my very soul.

The tenement flat his family moved into on the Lower East Side, poor as it was, had many conveniences they had never known at home. But nothing compensated for what he had lost.

You couldn't get to love a tenement flat; it was not home. We never stayed long enough in one flat anyway. That was the way it was in the big city. People moved from house to house from one neighborhood to another, never missing the old place, glad perhaps never to have to see it again.

In the big city people were as rootless as tumbleweeds, as flitting as birds. Today's friend might vanish overnight and be gone forever. You felt a sudden void within yourself but there was nothing you could do about it. You were one of a crowd you rubbed shoulders with, strangers about whom you wondered but who vanished as suddenly as they appeared.

You yearned for an attachment to something outside of yourself and the yearning remained unsatisfied. You were an alien, belonging nowhere, attached to nothing, alone. Even though you lived with your family, there was no fireside at which to warm the cold inner emptiness.

You lived with your family—and often with many strangers. Samuel Cohen's parents, for instance, had a two-room flat on Bayard Street for which they paid ten dollars a month in rent. They took in four boarders, all dry-goods peddlers, at seventy-five cents a week each, which included morning coffee and his mother's doing their laundry. Yuri Suhl writes of a widow who earned her living by running a "private restaurant" in the kitchen of her flat. She usually had eight or ten boarders crowded around the table, most of them from her own Rumanian village. It was necessary to take in boarders to make ends meet.

The boarder soon became a standard character in Yiddish folklore, the *griner cuzine* of fiction and the stage. In Yiddish humor he figured as the clumsy greenhorn, the fool who tenanted every flat. He suited any fantasy, committing good or evil deeds. But usually, remembers Harry Roskolenko, he was "lonely and bereft, a totally alien individual . . . a boarder living with a family in some kind of lackluster, ego-suffering relationship. He was tolerated, as a rule, merely for the money he paid out. . . ."

The Lower East Side was the beachhead from which many Jews moved further inland. Some were drawn west by friends and others were urged out of New York by immigrant-aid societies who raised the hope of better opportunities in less crowded places. Everywhere they went the immigrants looked for the cheapest rents in tenements close by a place of work. By the early 1900s the Jews had established a ghetto in Chicago centering on Maxwell Street. Louis Wirth, who taught sociology at the University of Chicago, describes it.

Maxwell Street, the ghetto's great outdoor market, is full of color, action, shouts, odors, and dirt. It resembles a medieval European fair more than the market of a great city of today. . . . Buying is an adventure in which one matches his wits against those of an opponent, a Jew. The Jews are versatile; they speak Yiddish among themselves, and Polish, Russian, Lithuanian, Hungarian, Bohemian, and what not, to their customers. They know their tastes and their prejudices. They have on hand ginghams in loud, gay colors for one group, and for one occasion; and drab and black mourning wear for others.

The noises of crowing roosters and geese, the cooing of pigeons, the barking of dogs, the twittering of canary birds, the smell of garlic and of cheeses, the aroma of onions, apples and oranges, and the shouts and curses of sellers and buyers fill the air. Anything can be bought and sold on Maxwell Street. On one stand, piled high, are odd sizes of shoes long out of style; on another are copper kettles for brewing beer; on a third are secondhand pants; and one merchant even sells odd, broken pieces of spectacles, watches and jewelry, together with pocket knives and household tools salvaged from the collections of junk peddlers.

Everything has value on Maxwell Street, but the price is not fixed. It is the fixing of the price around which turns the whole plot of the drama enacted daily at the perpetual bazaar. . . . The sellers know how to ask ten times the amount that their wares will eventually sell for, and buyers know how to offer a twentieth.

Just as in the Pale of Settlement in the old country, where women did the selling while men studied the Talmud, here many Jewish women had become the best merchants on Maxwell Street.

They almost monopolize the fish, herring, and poultry stands. All the stands are on wheels, and are moved nightly. At five-thirty every morning a mob of men, women and children may be seen flocking into an empty lot . . . where an old man rents pushcarts for twentyfive cents per day. He knows each of his carts individually, and when anyone hastens away with one of his 300-odd vehicles without paying, the owner of the pushcarts comes to the market later and collects. . . . By six o'clock in the morning the best and largest pushcarts have been hauled away. Everyone tries to maneuver for the most favorable position on the street. A corner location, especially on Maxwell and Halstead streets, is worth fighting for. Frequently the policeman who patrols the street has to decide who came first and is entitled to squatter rights for the day. After "Charlie the Policeman" has settled all the quarrels, fraternization ensues.

The Jewish immigrants outside New York lived in neighborhoods whose conditions were not much different from those on the Lower East Side. Whether it was Philadelphia, Boston, Baltimore, or a dozen other cities, it was a slum. The housing in Chicago's Jewish ghetto, said

Charles Zeublin in 1895, was of the same three types that cursed most Chicago working people.

> . . . the small, low, one or two story "pioneer" wooden shanty, erected probably before the street was graded, and hence several feet below the street level; the brick tenement of three or four stories, with insufficient light, bad drainage, no bath, built to obtain the highest possible rent for the smallest possible cubic space; and the third type, the deadly rear tenement, with no light in front, and with the frightful odors of the dirty alley in the rear, too often the workshop of the "sweater" as well as the home of an excessive population. On the narrow pavement of the narrow street in front is found the omnipresent garbage-box, with full measure, pressed down and running over. In all but the severest weather the streets swarm with children, day and night.

24

Cheese It—the Cops!

Grim as the East Side tenements were, the streets that separated them provided youngsters with soul-satisfying pleasure and perils. Every street had its gang, frowned on by police and parents, but often harmless. The kids talked tough because it was the smart thing to do, and they shot craps in the yards with a lookout stationed for cops. The gangs of the really tough, however, extorted money from weaker boys, stole anything in sight, and fought rival gangs for blood.

The milder kind of gang was formed to play games, especially ball. These had little organization except for a leader who was the strongest or played ball best. Based on a well-defined territory, such gangs detested others on their borders and threw down challenges to combat. Fists, sticks, and stones were the weapons in battles that began after school and broke up around suppertime when family scouts collared the combatants and hurried them home.

In the 1890s asphalt began to replace the stone that had paved the East Side streets. Asphalt was easier to clean and it dried quickly after rain. It made a much better playing surface than the muddy, slippery, jagged stone. The new surface was great for marbles, rolling hoops, prisoner's base, and the variety of ball games developed to suit the tenement canyons.

One o' cat, a favorite of Jewish boys, was really a form of baseball, reduced in scale and dispensing with the usual equipment of bats, balls, gloves, and uniforms. Instead of a ball, a chunk of wood was whittled to about a four-inch length and an inch in diameter at the center, tapering to dull points at each end. There were sides, as in baseball, the number of players depending on who was around at the moment. There was no pitcher. The piece of wood was put on the ground, the batter whacked an end lightly with a stick, sending the "ball" two or three feet in the air, and then he struck it as hard as he could with his stick. Sometimes the blow sent it half a block. The batter ran bases (their number varied) as the fielders tried to grab the "ball" and make an out by flinging it to a baseman or tagging the runner. (We played the same game in Worcester, Massachusetts, when I was a child, but we called it "peggy," our name for the wooden "ball.")

In the summertime there was swimming to enjoy. The Rutgers Square fountain played all day and boys stripped and dove into its lowest basin. The law banned it, so one boy would stand guard over the heap of clothing and holler, "Cheese it—the cops!" when he spied one coming. The lookout would grab the clothes and rush off in one direction while the swimmers would jump out of the basin and scatter in other directions to confuse the cop. They would meet their sentry at some rendezvous, dress, and stroll away innocently.

It was no crime to swim in the East River a few blocks off, so long as you kept your underwear on. But the fountain was better; it was riskier. Still, you didn't really have to play ball or swim or do anything to get fun out of living on the Lower East Side. There was satisfaction in just being an onlooker, as Samuel Chotzinoff said.

There were gang wars to be fought, police to annoy and outwit, and sentimental couples to be teased and ridiculed. Standing unobserved at one's window, one could focus a burning-glass on the face of a person resting on the stone bench of the fountain and relish his annoyance and anger as he tried helplessly to locate his tormentor. From the same vantage point, one could let down a weight attached to a long string, conk the head of a passerby, and draw up the missile before the victim could look around for the offender; or, with the aid of an accomplice stationed on the curb, stretch a string head-high across the sidewalk, which, unseen by some unsuspecting pedestrian, would lift his straw hat or derby from his head and send it rolling down the street. . . . There were ambulances to be run after and horse-cars to hang on to—unobserved by the conductor. If one was on intimate terms with a currier in a livery stable, one could sit bareback astride a horse and ride through the streets.

Something was constantly happening which one had to repair to the spot to see at first hand. People were being knocked down by horse-cars. There were altercations on every street, often ending in blows. The changing of streetcar horses at certain termini was a spectacle well worth a walk of a mile. One could run after an ambulance with a view to being in a position to give an eyewitness account of an accident to one's comrades. There were parades to be followed, also organ-grinders, bums, and itinerant sellers of cure-alls, who would assemble a crowd in a moment, deliver a stream of seemingly sensible, yet strangely incomprehensible, oratory, quickly dispose of some wares, and suddenly move on. . . .

On election nights, there were bonfires to watch and perhaps assist in making. Fires broke out constantly in all seasons, and the air was seldom free from the clang of fire engines, the shrieks of the siren, and the clatter of the horses on the cobblestones. Following the fire engines could conceivably occupy all one's leisure time. . . .

Diversions were also available closer to home. One could spend a profitable afternoon in one's own back yard. The poles for clotheslines soared five stories in the air. To shinny up a pole was a feat in itself, and the exhilaration felt on reaching the top had a quality of its own. . . . A restaurant in the adjoining house kept its milk cans in our yard. These served for games of leapfrog and also offered a means of revenge on the proprietor of the restaurant, a man insensitive to the need of children to play and make noise. Every time he chased us out of the yard, we would return at night, pry open his milk cans, and drop sand and pebbles in them. . . .

Tenement roofs offered a series of connected playgrounds. The element of danger in playing tag on roofs was considerable enough to heighten the ordinary excitement of the game. Cornices were only knee-high. They could hardly be a barrier to destruction should one, in running to escape the tagger, fail to have the presence of mind to veer quickly to right or left. Some buildings were taller than others, this necessitating a thrilling drop of ten or twelve feet, and on returning, an equally exciting scrambling up skylights and chimneys. A breath-taking hazard was the open air shafts that separated houses otherwise contig-uous. To miss, even by an inch, a jump over an airshaft meant death, but death did not really matter. For death was only an academic concept, a word without reality, at worst something that could happen only to others.

Evenings the candy store became the social center. It served as an informal clubhouse where schoolchildren could meet old friends and make new ones. In 1900 a *Tribune* reporter counted at least fifty in the Tenth Ward, all of which had a young clientele. Some were used as meeting places for clubs. The newsman described the typical candy store.

A counter along the length of the store decked with cheap candles and perhaps with cigar and cigarette boxes, and invariably a soda water fountain make up the entire furniture of the store, if we except a few cigarette pictures on the wall. Usually the proprietor lives with his family in the rear of the store. Some stores, making a pretense of stylishness, have partitioned off a little room from the store to which they give the elegant name of "ice cream parlor," a sign over the door apprising you of its existence. One or two bare tables and a few chairs furnish the "ice cream parlor." But this little room is very useful as a meeting place for a small club for boys or as a general lounging room. Occasionally a dozen or more youngsters are entertained here by a team of aspiring amateur comedians of the ages of sixteen or seventeen, whose sole ambition is to shine on the stage of some Bowery theater. The comedian or comedians will try their new "hits" on their critical audiences (and a more critical one cannot be found), dance, jig, and tell the jokes heard by them in the continuous performances at vaudeville theaters.

Of course, the candy-store owner didn't welcome the boys out of the goodness of his heart. He charged them a small fee if they borrowed his playing cards, and if they played for money, as they usually did, he took his cut. He took his chances too, for he had to guard against vandalism and thievery.

Was it all fun? And what about the girls? Lincoln Steffens, who covered the Jewish quarter in the 1890s, observed how quickly children, especially the girls, took on the burdens of adults.

The children, acquiring English quickly, with the adaptability of tender years, often assume the responsibilities that would rightfully belong to their elders. One girl of eleven habitually signs the checks and does all the writing necessary in transactions with certain charitable bureaus that help her mother, and during her mother's illness undertook the cooking, washing, and general superintendence of five younger children, one of whom was an infant. When the baby had croup she doctored him herself, and on another occasion kept a paid position for her mother, proving an admirable substitute until she could be relieved. . . .

Another little girl is the real, although her mother is the ostensible janitress of a big tenement house, the child conducting all the interviews with Board of Health officials, the streetcleaners and other authorities, and personally conducting interviews regarding the renting of rooms, collecting, etc. She undertakes to make her bay-lodgers behave well and to enforce proper attention to the contracted area dignified by the term of "yard," generally coming off victor in the pitched battles in which she has to engage.

25

Peddlers and Pushcarts

"The Jewish needle," said reporter Jacob Riis in 1890, "made America the best-dressed nation in the world." It also came close to enslaving the immigrant generation in the sweatshops where that needle was plied. A majority of the newcomers entered the garment industry, but they could be found in many other trades, for none was barred to them. A report of their occupations made in 1910 showed a rich variety. They were not only in clothing but in the building trades, they were cabinetmakers, tinsmiths and house painters, metalworkers and mechanics, blacksmiths and plumbers, tobacco workers and watchmakers, roofers, masons, locksmiths, electricians, furriers, jewelers, leatherworkers, bookbinders, printers . . .

In the old country, the proletarian occupations—work you did with your hands—had been looked down upon. The unschooled people, the laborers and artisans who did the dirty work, these were the prosteh, the lower class of Jews. They were the great mass of Jews in Eastern Europe. A small minority of Jews did not work with their hands, but lived by trading on some scale—merchants, dealers, shopkeepers. These were the sheyneh, the fine Jews. It was more respectable to be your own boss, even in a losing enterprise, than to work for someone else. Part of the distinction between the sheyneh and the prosteh had to do with using your head. To make your living with your brains rather than your brawn was somehow better. It meant therefore that the more learned too (whether they earned anything or not), such as rabbi, teacher, cantor, or student, fell into the superior class.

America upset the old distinctions. Here it was no disgrace to work with your hands. Workers were not held in contempt. A carpenter or a house painter was as good an American as anyone else. The immigrant Jews soon found that to have your son become a rabbi no longer brought prestige. Instead, parents pointed their sons to the secular professions—medicine, law, pharmacy, dentistry.

As for women, only the lower class (but they were by far the majority) worked in the old country. Before marriage, they might be domestics or seamstresses. After marriage, if the husband devoted himself to the study of the Talmud, the wife became the breadwinner. Women ran shops, kept stalls in the marketplace, baked knishes and rolls at home or baked matzos in factories, raised vegetables, tended cattle, labored endlessly at anything that would keep the family going.

In America, Jewish parents tried to keep their daughters out of the factories. Better to have them stay in public school, if they could get by without their wages, and then send them on to a business course so that they could get jobs as office workers. The girl who was able to become a bookkeeper or a teacher had reached the top of the ladder.

The bottom of the ladder for many immigrants was peddling. It was the simplest way to enter the world of commerce. In the old country, Jews in the shtetl had made goods available to the peasants in the countryside. Here the peddler found his first market among other immigrants. They were poor, they would rather trade with people like themselves, they could not afford the new and the best, they were willing to use the secondhand, the castoffs, the misfits.

The peddler's store was his pack. It took little capital to start, only the will to work hard for small profit. Arriving in the 1880s, Samuel H. Cohen began peddling tinware utensils. They were widely used in the tenements—pails, dishpans, cups, plates, wash boilers, baby rattles. The smaller articles you stowed in a big basket, slung by a strap on your back. In front, hanging by another strap, you carried a wash boiler filled with miscellaneous dishpans and other articles the basket couldn't hold. When fully loaded, only your head and arms could be seen.

On Sam's first day out—he was going on sixteen—the tinware dealer helped him pack front and rear expertly, and told him what block across the Bowery to start working.

At my first port of call my heart was in my mouth. I hesitated. Taking a long breath I climbed up a stoop and yanked the bell. I was in suspense. The door opened. A red-headed young giant appeared. He looked at me and my outfit without a word. He was not a bit rough. He merely laid his hand very gently on the boiler in front of me and gave me a good shove. I descended backwards rapidly, finally landing in a sitting position in the middle of the street, my stock strewn about me in all directions. With great effort I managed to readjust my basket and wash boiler. Now what? I thought I couldn't pull another bell if I tried. I turned back to Elizabeth Street. Entering a yard I saw an open door—a woman near it. I made my first sale—a cup for ten cents—the profit was not bad! It was now near noontime. I saw girls eating on the first floor near the window. One of them motioned that I come nearer. I did. I was soon pelted with all the egg pancake they had left.

He went back to the dealer, dropped his load, and quit.

Early the next morning he tried selling fans—it was hot weather—and by nine at night had made five dollars. Then it turned cool. No sales. For one week he huckstered hairpins. Matches were next; they were needed to start the kerosene lamps.

With several packs in a bag, some loose packages in my hand, I started out. It was a case of running up and down stairways the whole day long. I kept a record of a day's work. I climbed the stairs of fifty houses, with an average of four flights to each. It made two hundred flights of stairs per day. Sales averaged about $2. Net profit was seventy-five cents.

But up and down two hundred flights of stairs daily was too much for him to endure. For a while he peddled dusters and whisk brooms office to office in the financial district. That didn't produce enough to live on either. He quit, this time for good.

Many came to the same dead end. Others did better. While the economy was expanding, they made their way from pack or pushcart to

chromium and plate-glass store. And some to department-store bar-
onies. If you weren't tough enough, you caved in fast. Nathan Kuskin
bought $1.47 worth of cotton, pins, shoelaces, matches, and other
notions, put them in a basket, then walked past block after block of
Philadelphia's houses, trying to get up enough nerve to ring the first
doorbell. When at last he rang a bell, a woman came to the door. He
stood there dumbly: he didn't know the right English words to offer his
wares. He uncovered his basket, and the woman took a package of pins
and gave him a nickel. He thanked her and walked away. He knew she
didn't need the pins. She had given him the money as charity. He was
through. No push, no nerve, no success, not in this trade.

The West, where other greenhorns had gone before you, might be a
greener pasture. Bernard Horwich described the peddlers he saw on the
West Side of Chicago, a filthy place where crime was rampant and Jews
were beaten on the streets. Most peddlers went from house to house,
carrying packs of notions and light dry goods, or junk and vegetables.
Every streetcar bore Jewish peddlers riding to and from their routes.
While many peddlers had no other trade, some were skilled workers
who were obliged in dull seasons to do anything because work in the
busy season had not paid enough to carry the family over. They took up
basket or pushcart to bring in a few pennies.

The pushcarts sold a fantastic variety of merchandise. "It ran,"
according to J. R. Schwartz's alliterative threnody, "from knishes to
knick-knacks, from vegetables to vests, from lamps to leeks, and from
pickles to pants." There were even peddlers selling packages of dirt, the
genuine mother earth from Jerusalem. If you paid a peddler's asking
price, you were considered an easy mark. A good shopper mastered the
fine art of haggling. Schwartz, who was a medical student in 1910, was
told to buy Weisse's *Dissection of the Human Body.* Its price was $6.50. He
didn't have the money, and had to share a classmate's copy. One day,
strolling along the seven blocks of stores and pushcarts that made up
Orchard Street, he came across a cart piled high with books. And there
was a copy of Weisse! His heart skipped a beat.

> I looked at the vendor, an elderly Jew, and wondered how much he
> knew about the books he was selling. Without displaying any interest or
> enthusiasm I casually asked him what he wanted for this book. He took it

from me, looked it over in a sort of knowing manner, hefted it for weight and said:

"*Far dem buch vill ich haben finif und sibetzik cent.*" (For this book I want seventy-five cents.)

I put on a look of indifference and told him I thought it was too much money.

"*Aber zey nor, zindele, es hat a sach bilder.*" (But look, sonny, it has a lot of pictures.)

I offered him twenty-five cents. He looked at me with compassion and said, "*Wie azoi ken ich machen a leben as ich beit bei dir finif und sibetzik cent und die gibst mir nor finif und tzwantzik. Nu, freg ich dich, is das a geschaft?*" (How can I make a living when I ask you seventy-five cents and you offer me only twenty-five cents? Is this a business?)

But right away he came down to sixty cents. I offered him thirty and he came down to fifty, with the final upshot that I got it for forty cents.

There were peddlers who sold the sacred as well as the profane. In Boston, E. E. Lisitzky's father peddled rags and bottles during the day and in the evening peddled Hebrew lessons to Jewish boys preparing for bar mitzvah. During the month between Purim and Passover he also walked the streets selling Passover necessities (matzo, wine, etc.) on the installment plan. The son's memory of the way his father eked out a livelihood conveys the miseries of peddling.

Every morning, after the services and breakfast, he would stick on his hat a brass badge marked with black letters and numbers against a glossy background—the badge which the Boston authorities had ordered every rag peddler to wear—shoulder his sack, and leave for work. He walked his route through the city, crying "R-r-rags and bot-tles!" He looked up at the tenement houses, looking at the windows for a sign that one of the tenants wanted to bargain over their discards and rags. Sometimes young rowdies threw stones at him, and in the winter snowballs with pieces of coal inside, sometimes hoodlums pulled his beard, sometimes he'd be attacked in dark hallways and his pockets emptied. "Rags and bottles!" he would call again after such a mishap, his voice ringing with pain and grief, but not with bitterness or protest. He was inured to suffering and submitted to it.

The boys he peddled bar mitzvah lessons to much preferred playing ball to reading in the Hebrew prayer book. The lessons were forced upon them by their parents; the boys made life hard for the man who sold them pieces of his learning for pennies.

His customers lived far apart, but the pennies he earned through so much toil were too precious to be spent on streetcar travel, so he half-ran, half-walked from lesson to lesson. Late at night he dragged his weary feet home. After prayers he sat down to an appetiteless supper—work had killed his hunger.

Orchard Street lured crowds not only from the surrounding East Side but from far-off Brooklyn and the Bronx. The bargains were said to be the best in America, so why not? Everything was for sale cheap and in a hurry because there was no place to store unsold goods. If you bought in the stores lining Orchard Street, you were sure to pay more. It was the pushcarts (1,500 of them, one newspaper estimated) which offered the best bargains. The peddlers paid twenty-five dollars a year for their licenses and rented their carts for a dime a day.

Harry Roskolenko was raised near Orchard Street's universal market and never forgot what he saw.

The pushcarts came small, came large, came bigger than large—and in double or triple tiers. . . . These conglomerate street bargains had a variety of prices—depending on the age, the smell, the look, and certainly the taste, for you were offered a taste of everything edible and not edible. Milk sold for two cents a quart, with your own pitcher. It was ladled out of 40-quart cans that were not too clean. It was done in a splash by the husband or the wife, depending on who was nearest to the huge milk cans. . . . Butter, smelling a bit rancid, sold for five cents a pound—smell and all. Bread, a cent a pound; but if you wanted a half of a pound it was cut for you from a huge round bread weighing over twenty pounds.

Potatoes, sacked, were bought to make the winter viable. Nobody bothered to buy a pound of potatoes. Potatoes came in sacks weighing fifty pounds—and off we went, father and sons, carrying the sack ten blocks to home. Prunes, plums, tangerines—all of our fruits—came in round crates, and similarly were hauled off home. The difference between prices when buying in bulk and buying in small amounts was something that made bankers of all of us on Orchard Street—the earliest street of bulk and container packaging done in a hurry. As for grapefruits, nobody trusted them yet. They were a bastard fruit, as tomatoes once had been. My mother called tomatoes "love apples"—whatever that must have meant to her. I thought tomatoes were invented to throw at the rich or the street-corner politicians around Election Day.

Making cigars and cigarettes was a trade which many immigrants entered in those early years before mass production of tobacco products. Two of Sam Chotzinoff's sisters made cigarettes in their Lower East Side home. Their combined weekly piecework earnings ran to four or five dollars. At the age of ten, Lucy Robbins Lang went to work as a tobacco stripper in a cigar shop in Chicago. Because the owners had known her grandfather in Kiev, they paid the beginner a dollar a week; most children were paid nothing while learning the trade and some even paid tuition for the privilege. Lucy worked from 7 A.M. to 6 P.M., and since carfare would have eaten up her weekly dollar, she walked to work, an hour each way. Maurice Sterne's first job in New York was like Lucy's: at eleven he stripped tobacco in the rear of a cigar store on Eighth Avenue.

To learn many of the trades you had to pay a sizable fee, twenty-five to fifty dollars, and work at least one to three months for nothing. Unable to raise that amount, Samuel Cohen went into a cigarette factory on Water Street in New York. The hours were as long as Lucy's in Chicago, the tobacco stuck in your throat and nose, but, he was told, the labor wasn't as killing as in the garment trade: "You just use your fingers." The process seemed intricate and difficult to the beginner, but he saw other workers could roll 500 cigarettes in one hour. Sam's first week's earnings were $2.42. The second week he made 4,000 cigarettes, at eighty cents per thousand, less shortages and poor work, and received $3.10 in his pay envelope. "It was a thrill," he said. "I could almost eat."

26

Sweatshop

If the immigrant didn't turn to peddling as the way to make a living in "the golden country," the chances are he found work in the clothing industry. Either one meant hard work for low pay. The clothing shops were usually overcrowded, dirty, badly lit, poorly ventilated rooms where men, women, and children labored in a speed-up system for fifteen or even eighteen hours a day. At least 60 percent of the newcomers entered the needle trades. Many had never done manual labor in the old country, where they might have been yeshiva students, teachers, clerks, insurance agents, bookkeepers, storekeepers. Here they were harnessed to machines which hurried them to the last breath.

The documents of those days contain few happy accounts of life in the garment trades. They are full of frustration and anger. One immigrant wrote, "There was no one who liked his work. All hated it and all sought a way of being free of it. All looked upon the boss as upon their enemy, the exploiter who fattens upon the marrow of his workers and gets rich on their account." The disappointments they met made them curse Columbus for having discovered the country. (A klog tzu Columbus!)

The garment industry was expanding rapidly in the late nineteenth century. And like earlier immigrants of whatever nationality, the Jews turned to wherever the work was. It had nothing to do with a talent for the needle or previous training. (Only about 10 percent had been tailors in Europe.) Here was an industry clamoring for cheap labor and here was a mass of people who had to take any kind of work to stay alive. Most of the early garment makers were German Jews. In Germany, Jews had often dealt in new and secondhand clothing. Arriving here in midcentury, they began as peddlers or retail merchants and moved up to manufacturing. By 1880 there were over 500 shops employing 25,000 workers. As the immigration tide rolled in, the German Jews gave work to large numbers of the newcomers. The sewing machine, the cutting knife, the shears, and flatiron became the tools by which thousands earned their living in Chicago, Boston, Philadelphia, Baltimore, and most of all in New York, the heart of the needle trades. By 1890, some 13,000 Jews were on the great East Side treadmill. Ten years later, over 150,000 Jewish immigrants and their families were making their living in the garment industry.

The development of the sewing machine made it possible. It revolutionized the production of clothing of all kinds. Before its invention, tailor-made suits and dresses, cut and fitted by skilled craftsmen, could be afforded only by the rich. Now immigrant workers could be swiftly taught the modest skills needed to operate machines that could mass-produce ready-made clothing from standard patterns. Long and costly apprenticeships were no longer necessary. Each step of production was broken down into smaller and simpler processes. What was demanded of the worker was speed, dexterity, and willingness to submit to the endless round of dull and repetitive tasks. This piece-work system brought new and fashionable clothing within the reach of the millions for the first time.

But it was done at great cost to the garment worker. The production system which rapidly came to dominate the industry trapped men, women, and children in the infamous "sweatshop." Bernard Weinstein describes one.

> The boss of the shop lived there with his entire family. The front room and kitchen were used as workrooms. The whole family would sleep in one dark bedroom. The sewing-machines for the operators were located near the windows of the front room. The basters would sit on stools near the walls, and in the center of the room, midst the dirt and the dust, were

heaped great piles of materials. There, on top of the soft piles, several finishers would be sitting. . . . Old people . . . using gaslight for illumination, would stand and keep the irons hot and press the finished coats, jackets, pants and other clothes on special boards.

Baxter Street on the Lower East Side housed many sweatshop workers. There was nothing romantic or noble about the way they lived. Outsiders coming down to look for local color found only dark and ugly tones. One visitor, Edward W. Townsend, sketched his realistic impression of Baxter Street in 1895.

The people, from the younghst to the oldest, were speechless and grave and hopeless-looking. Men staggered past, their bodies bent almost double under what seemed impossible loads of clothing they were carrying to and from the sweaters' and the workshop-homes; women carrying similar bundles on their heads, or perhaps a bundle of wood from some builder's waste, not speaking to those they passed; none of the children seen was much more than a baby in years, and they were silent, too, and had no games: they were in the street because while the sweaters' work went on there was no room for them in their homes. In the dress of none was any bright color, and the only sounds were the occasional cry of a hurt child, the snarling of the low-browed men who solicited trade for the clothing stores, quarrelling for the possession of a chance victim; and always, as the grinding ocean surf mutters an accompaniment to all other shore sounds—always, always, always—was heard the whirring monotone of the sewing-machine.

Tenement-house manufacture spread rapidly in Chicago too, entering many industries besides the garment trade. Wherever the system went, the trade became a sweated one, carried on in the worst conditions. Only full exposure of the harsh facts of human suffering could hope to effect change. Florence Kelley described in a state-sponsored report the Chicago garment sweatshops which investigators visited in 1894.

Shops over sheds or stables, in basements or on upper floors of tenement houses, are not fit working places for men, women, and children.

Most of the places designated in this report as basements are low-ceiled, ill-lighted, unventilated rooms, below the street level; damp and cold in winter, hot and close in summer; foul at all times by reason of adjacent vaults or defective sewer connections. The term cellar would more accurately describe these shops. Their dampness entails rheumatism and their darkness injures the sight of the people who work in them. They never afford proper accommodation for the pressers, the fumes of whose gasoline stoves and charcoal heaters mingle with the mouldy smell of the walls and the stuffiness always found where a number of the very poor are crowded together.

In shops over sheds or stables the operatives receive from below the stench from the vaults or the accumulated stable refuse; from the rear, the effluvia of the garbage boxes and manure bins in the filthy, unpaved alleys; and from the front, the varied stenches of the tenement house yard, the dumping ground for all the families residing on the premises.

Shops on upper floors have no proper ventilation; are reached by narrow and filthy halls and unlighted wooden stairways; are cold in winter unless all fresh air is shut out, and hot in summer. If in old houses, they afford no sanitary arrangements beyond the vaults used by all tenants; if in modern tenements the drains are out of order, water for the closets does not rise to upper floors, and poisonous gases fill the shops. This defective water supply, the absence of fire escapes and the presence of the pressers' stove greatly aggravate the danger of death by fire.

Shops on the middle floors are ill-lighted, ill-ventilated, and share the smells from the kitchens and drains of surrounding living rooms.

As "greeners" came off the boat, their relatives already here steered them into the sweatshops. Or the newly arrived immigrant would go to the "Pig Market," a sort of labor exchange which grew up around Hester and Essex streets. There he would stand and wait for a contractor in need of "green hands" to offer him a job. Both workers and employers often came from the same towns in Eastern Europe. One *landsmann* hired another or taught another. S. L. Blumenson recalls the early 1900s when about 80 percent of the bosses and workers in the section of the industry which made children's coats (called "reefers") were *landsleit* or relatives.

They all came from a small district in Lithuania, the *uyezd* or county of Hooman, in the province of Minsk—from such villages as Schmilovits, Dukor, Puchovitch, Hooman, Bobroisk, Berezin. . . .

Most of the manufacturers were graduates of a pioneer shop established in a loft on alley-like Pelham Street, near Pike. . . . This shop was opened in the year 1889 by an immigrant from Dukor, his two sons, and his son-in-law. The father was a tailor by trade, as was the son-in-law. The two sons, however, were ex-yeshiva *bochurim,* and excellent Hebrew scholars. When they opened their own shop, after working in various sweatshops, the father did the cutting and finishing and pressing, and the other three operated the sewing machines. The business grew and prospered, and it soon became a beehive of new immigrants from the county of Hooman. Older men, small town *baalabaatim* (householders), became pressers; younger men became *araushelfers* (helpers to operators), and the young women, mostly teenage, became finishers.

In one of his stories Sholem Asch depicts such a *landsmann* operation on the East Side, where a whole village from the old country became faithful slaves to the "pharaoh" of the sweatshop, Uncle Moses.

> Kuzmin sat at work, sewing coats, trousers and vests for persons whom they would never see. The whole village of Kuzmin worked upstairs in Uncle Moses' shop. There was Reb Joel Chayim, the head of the synagogue, and Itshe the cobbler's boy, and Junder the ladies' tailor— the dandy of Kuzmin, who once had woven a spell around the hearts of Kuzmin's beauties. . . . All Kuzmin sat there sewing for Uncle Moses; he had reduced the entire population to the same level. There were no more leading citizens, synagogue dignitaries and humble artisans—no more Talmudic experts and coarse fellows. No more cobblers, foremen, men who applied bleeding-cups to women . . . and men who tickled the women while they fitted on their dresses. All now served a single idol; all performed the same rite—they sewed trousers.

To be part of that substantially segregated economy was like being part of the shtetl. Jews worked for Jews and the relations between them (often bitter class conflict) were carried on within the framework of a ghetto. Yiddish, the mother tongue, was everyone's language, boss or worker. The Jewish immigrant who entered such an environment immediately on arrival might have no need for the English language so long as he stayed within this small world.

The fact that Jewish workers labored for Jewish bosses created a unique situation other ethnic groups did not share. The non-Jewish immigrant's job was rarely inside his own ethnic neighborhood. He never encountered the owner of the mine or mill or railroad where he worked. His foreman probably spoke only English. The mark of the worker's foreignness brought down upon him derision and contempt. But Jewish workers and employers shared roots, religion, culture, history. Which was why in the beginning, and for some time after, Jewish workers organized into Jewish unions.

The garment industry became the typical trade of the tenements. No other in the city or state of New York employed so many workers. The thousands of shops jammed into the streets below Fourteenth produced over half of America's ready-made clothing. It grew so fast because of the enormous demand both here and abroad for its products, but also because the unit of industrial production was small. What better chance was there to set up your own shop, and move up from worker to boss? S. L. Blumenson shows how the reefer makers from Hooman did it.

In time, some . . . opened places of their own, two or three pooling their skills and their few dollars. It did not require much capital to start a small factory. A dark hole of a loft, more often than not over a smelly stable, at a monthly rental of ten or twelve dollars, a few wooden horses and boards for a cutting table, a few chairs, a long cutting knife, and a gas or wood stove for the solid press irons—these made up a shop. Every operator had to supply his own sewing machine.

The "capitalists" bought a few bolts of very cheap cloth, cheap even for those days, and manufactured children's wearing apparel ranging in price from 90 cents to $2 a piece wholesale, and women's and misses' finery from $1.50 to $3.75. Despite these low prices, and to compensate for the cheapness of the cloth, these garments had to have "style." Yards and yards of soutache, braid, and gimp were sewed onto them in all manner of geometric design, and some were trimmed with innumerable ornamental buttons. It does not require a cost accountant to determine that little was left over for the payroll.

And that little the boss whittled down to even less by a system of extortionate fines. If a worker was late five minutes, half a day's pay forfeit. If he left work too early, half a day's pay more. If he fainted from the heat on the job, a day's pay lost. If he didn't return an empty spool, fifty cents fine; if he lost a "number" ticket, twenty-five cents fine.

The Yiddish labor poet Morris Rosenfeld, who sweated in a garment factory, cried out against the cost to the human spirit:

The Clock in the workshop—it rests not a moment;
It points on, and ticks on: eternity—time;
Once someone told me the clock had a meaning,—
In pointing and ticking had reason and rhyme . . .
At times, when I listen, I hear the clock plainly;—
The reason of old—the old meaning—is gone!
The maddening pendulum urges me forward
To labor and still labor on.
The tick of the clock is the boss in his anger.
The face of the clock has the eyes of the foe.
The clock—I shudder—Dost hear how it draws me?
It calls me "Machine" and it cries [to] me "Sew!"

Sam Liptzin tells of bosses he worked under who were like Haman, that tyrant of tyrants. An especially bad one was Levy & Son on Chrystie Street.

> There was no clock in the shop. Wages were paid every three or four weeks and even then, in "part payments." Worst of all, however, was the sadistic nature of Mr. Levy. He once caught an operator smoking at a machine. He crept up in back of the man, snatched the cigarette out of his hand and choked it out against his arm. In the washroom he removed the door from the stall, to prevent anyone smoking there or taking a few moments' rest.

Another boss named Strickman liked to pull "practical jokes."

> One of the workers, Lazer the finisher, had been complaining that the thread was rotten and falling apart in his hands. Strickman pretended to stage an experiment to test the strength of the thread. He pulled and pulled on a length of thread until it broke and his fist struck Lazer, standing nearby, in the eye. Lazer's vision was irreparably damaged by this "accidental" blow. But this was not enough for Mr. Strickman. He made up a "clever joke." Afterward, whenever Lazer had trouble threading a needle, he would say, "Here, Lazer, take this chalk and put a mark on the needle, so you'll know where the hole is!"

In the sweatshop system manufacturers distributed material to contractors. They in turn subcontracted it to people who did the tasks in their homes. The system began here early in the nineteenth century, when immigrant English tailors and then Irish tailors brought into their homes the work handed out by the contractors.

When the sewing machine arrived and introduced division of labor, the older tailors, reluctant to adopt the new methods, were replaced by the Jewish immigrants. Around 1900 the "sweating district"—bounded by Eighth Street, the Bowery, Catherine Street, and the East River—enclosed some 450,000 people living and working in the tenements. The most intense competition was fostered by the sweating system. Competing manufacturers farmed out the material for garments to competing contractors, who in turn distributed it to men and women competing for the work of making up the garments. There were usually several stages in the process. Wholesale manufacturers cut and bunched garments, distributing them in job lots to smaller contractors. Each of these specialized, one taking coats, another trousers, still another dresses, and so on. These smaller shops might do some of the work in their own place, and subdivide the rest among the "sweaters"—men who operated in their own tenement homes. The sweater's family lived in one of the few rooms, the others occupied by ten or twenty sewers and pressers employed by him. But he too might subcontract some of the work given him, handing the material on to other families in the neighborhood who would make up the finished garments and deliver them to him. At each step downward profit was sweated out of the next in line, with the tiniest compensation left for the super-exploited worker at the bottom.

The contractor was more than a mere middleman. He had to know tailoring in order to organize the labor called for. The tasks were broken down into various grades and forms of skill—baster, machinist, presser, and then their subdivisions, such as fitter, busheler, finisher, buttonhole maker, feller, bagging puller, and so on. The economist John R. Commons discussed the attributes of a contractor or sweater in a 1901 report of the U.S. Industrial Commission.

The man best fitted to be a contractor is the man who is well acquainted with his neighbors, who is able to speak the language of several classes of immigrants, who can easily persuade his neighbors or their wives and children to work for him, and in this way can obtain the cheapest help. The contractor can increase the number of people

employed in the trade at very short notice. During the busy season, when
the work doubles, the number of people employed increases in the same
proportion. All of the contractors are agents and go around among the
people. Housewives, who formerly worked at the trade and abandoned it
after marriage, are called into service for an increased price of a dollar or
two a week. Men who have engaged in other occupations, such as small
business, peddling, etc., and are out of the business most of the year, are
marshaled into service by the contractor, who knows all of them, and can
easily look them up and put them in as competitors, by offering them a
dollar or two a week more than they are getting elsewhere.

The sweating system prolonged a primitive mode of production.
Power for the sewing machines came from the foot, and the shops were
in homes, alleys, attics, over stables. Low rent and low wages enabled
small shops to compete successfully with the large factories powered by
steam or electricity. Ironically, a relatively liberal labor law (compared
with earlier conditions) in New York State gave sweaters a competitive
edge. The law limited working hours to ten per day, required a forty-
five-minute lunch break, a closing time of 9 P.M., and curbed child labor.
But the law applied only to work done in the factory. The *home*—that
was different, a man's private affair. So the home sweatshops could
recruit immigrant workers fresh from the old country and pay them
piece rates so low they had to work fifteen to eighteen hours a day, and
often seven days a week, for enough to stay alive.

An outsider's view of the sweatshop comes from Ernest Poole, the
novelist. In 1903 he went down into the Lower East Side on a magazine
assignment. He wanted to see how the small coat shops were operated.
It was nine at night, and the lights were burning everywhere.

> The room is low and crowded. The air is close, impure, and alive with
> the ceaseless whir of machines. The operator bends close over his
> machine—his foot on the treadle in swift, ceaseless motion; the baster
> stands just behind, at the table; the finisher works close between them.
> On the table is a pile of twenty coats. This is their "task"—the day's
> work, which most teams never accomplish. Of the three teams here, the
> swiftest can finish their task in fourteen hours' labor. The other two
> seem forever behind and striving to catch up. Five tasks a week is their
> average. They need no overseer, no rules, no regular hours. They drive

themselves. This is the secret of the system, for three men seldom feel sick or dull or exhausted at the same moment. If the operator slackens his pace, the baster calls for more coats. If at six o'clock the baster gives out, the finisher spurs him on through the evening.

The positions are tense, their eyes strained, their movements quick and nervous. Most of them smoke cigarettes while they work; beer and cheap whiskey are brought in several times a day by a peddler. Some sing Yiddish songs—while they race. The women chat and laugh sometimes—while they race. For these are not yet dumb slaves, but intensely human beings—young, and straining every nerve of youth's vitality. Among operators twenty years is an active lifetime. Forty-five is old age. They make but half a living.

By this time the small shops had lost much ground to the large factories. About 70 percent of the coats, for instance, were now factory-made. How did it happen? And was it better for the worker? Ernest Poole answers:

Endless saving, dividing, narrowing labor—this is the factory. Down either side of the long factory table forty operators bend over machines, and each one sews the twentieth part of a coat. One man makes hundreds of pockets. On sewing pockets his whole working life is narrowed. To this intensity he is helped and forced and stimulated at every possible point. His strength is no longer wasted on pushing a treadle; the machine is run by power. The coat passes down the long bench, then through the hands of a dozen pressers and basters and finishers—each doing one minute part swiftly, with exact precision. Through thirty hands it comes out at last fourteen minutes quicker, four cents cheaper; the factory has beaten the task shop.

And the human cost—is it, too, reduced? Is the worker better off here than he was in the sweatshop? To consider this fairly we must compare the nonunion factory with the nonunion sweatshop. Wages by the week for the most skilled workers are slightly higher in the factory than they were in the sweatshop. They are lower for the unskilled majority. This majority must slowly increase, for the factory system progresses by transferring skill to machinery. Hours are shorter; work is less irregular; the shop is sanitary; the air is more wholesome—but the pocket maker is often as exhausted at 6 P.M. as the coat maker was at 10 P.M., for his work is more minute, more intense, more monotonous. This concentration, too, is growing.

27

Where Children Slowly Roast

The pleasures and opportunities of childhood were denied to millions of immigrant boys and girls who supplied cheap and unskilled labor to the employers. If adults were exploited unfeelingly, the lot of children was even worse. Some sewed coats in sweatshops, some made paper lanterns, artificial flowers, paper boxes, some sold papers, shined shoes, minded pushcarts, some labored in printing plants or woodyards or ran messages for the telegraph company.

A physician who treated people on the Lower East Side said that wherever she found working children their wages made up the greater part of the family income. An example was a woman whose husband was under treatment for tuberculosis. The wife went out to do washing whenever she could get the work. Their three children, eleven, seven, and five, worked at home covering wooden buttons with silk at four cents for every twelve dozen. The oldest went to school, but worked with the others evenings and weekends. The family's combined wages were three to six dollars per week, with children earning two thirds of it.

Child labor was nothing new, of course. As early as 1832, two out of five workers in the factories of New England were children under sixteen. Employers preached that idleness was bad for children. In 1870 over 700,000 children aged ten to fifteen were at work. In 1880 the number had risen to over 1,000,000, and in 1900 to 1,750,000. Nearly one of every five children in the country was working for wages.

Maurice Sterne, as an immigrant boy of twelve, went to work in a flag factory on the Lower West Side of New York. The year was 1892; Grover Cleveland was running for President and there was a big demand for small flags to carry in election parades.

> The factory was on the third floor of a four-story loft building. The only light came from gas jets burning overhead, the heat in summer was stifling, and there was the sickening odor of fish glue at the boiling point. To add to the discomfort, the whole building vibrated from a machine shop on the lower two floors. I could hardly wait for the 6 P.M. siren. The sticker boys—there were about a dozen of us—worked under the stern and often bloodshot eye of a foreman named Meyer, a former sergeant in the German Army. . . . He called [us] "Verfluchter Hund," "Schweinhund," and "Lausbub" (cursed dog, pig-dog and louse-brat). I was almost always a "Lausbub."
>
> The flags, each about the size of a postcard, were printed twelve dozen to a sheet, and Herr Meyer's job was to cut them apart, using a heavy, brass-edged ruler, and then to arrange them in gross lots for the sticker boys. It was tedious work. . . . Almost invariably, when he was angry, he would shuffle across the floor and hit one of us sticker boys on the head with his brass ruler.

Street trades drew a great number of immigrant children. William Zorach was eight when he started as a wage earner, selling papers and shining shoes on the streets of Cleveland. He used to get up at 6 A.M. to go on his paper route. That career ended one stormy winter morning when his mother said, "You can't go out on a day like this." Later, at twelve, he wandered the town looking for "Boy Wanted" signs. The jobs he got, nobody else wanted.

> They never lasted more than a few days or a week. . . . I got a machine shop job; a boy told me, "Watch yourself. The last kid working that punch machine lost all his fingers on one hand." I stuck a bar into the machine and broke it. I was fired. I had a job in a hat factory and got bored to death dusting hats. There was a job in a brass factory working with buffing wheels in an atmosphere dense with metal dust, which filled the

lungs and eyes and left one coated from head to foot with brass. My job
was to dip the hot brass in benzine and roll it in sawdust. It was so painful
to the hands that I was in agony. I quit.

The pain young Zorach felt was hidden from public sight. Yet this
was the social reality: children degraded and destroyed by conditions of
production which no human being should have to bear. Florence Kelley,
the daughter of a Pennsylvania congressman who served the interests of
his state's iron and steel masters, grew up to defend industry's victims.
After an education at Cornell and in Europe, she moved into Chicago's
Hull-House settlement. The surrounding conditions of slum life horrified her. When Governor Altgeld appointed her chief factory inspector
for Illinois in 1893, she exposed the effects of factory labor upon the
health of children.

> It is a lamentable fact . . . that children are found in greater number
> where the conditions of labor are most dangerous to life and health. Among
> the occupations in which children are employed in Chicago, and which
> most endanger the health, are: the tobacco trade, nicotine poisoning
> finding as many victims among factory children as among the boys who
> are voluntary devotees of the weed, consumers of the daily cigarette
> included; frame gilding, in which work a child's fingers are stiffened and
> throat disease is contracted; button-holing, machine-stitching and hand-
> work in tailor or sweat shops, the machine work producing spinal curva-
> ture, and for girls pelvic disorders also, while the unsanitary condition of
> the shops makes even hand-sewing dangerous; bakeries, where children
> slowly roast before the ovens; binderies, paper-box and paint factories,
> where arsenical paper, rotting paste, and the poison of the paints are
> injurious; boiler-plate works, cutlery works, and metal-stamping works,
> where the dust produces lung disease; the handling of hot metal, accidents;
> the hammering of plate, deafness. In addition to the diseases incidental to
> trades, there are the conditions of bad sanitation and long hours, almost
> universal in the factories where children are employed.

The Kelley report went on to detail many examples of the reckless
injury done to children in the shops. Joseph Poderovsky, fourteen, was
one of them. Running a heavy buttonhole machine by foot power, he
came down with double lateral curvature of the spine. Or there was
Bennie Kelman, a young Russian Jewish immigrant who had been put

to work in a boiler factory at thirteen. Lifting heavy masses of iron had given him a severe rupture, but nothing had been done for him. He could read only Yiddish. His parents knew no English either, nor where to turn for help until Kelley's inspectors came across Bennie and hospitalized him.

Many children worked in the sweatshops, often alongside their parents. To quit school and go to work, a boy or girl had to be sixteen and obtain working papers. The law was no barrier, said Sam Liptzin.

All the immigrants had plenty of old-country experience in faking the age of their children, either up or down. So it was that many 12- and 14-year-old children, of both sexes, were "accelerated" into the sweatshops. There was a saying among the immigrants, "If I only had ten or twelve children I could open up my own little shop . . ."

Mr. Bobrich was one of these lucky ones with a houseful of nine children. There was only seven years difference between the oldest and the youngest. (Two sets of twins.) All the children worked in the shop with their father, even the one with the crippled hand, who earned a few pennies a day by running errands for the men in the shop.

Mr. Bobrich kept the door to his establishment locked at all times, in order to keep out truant officers. He was constantly paying graft to one official or another on this account. But the best preventive was, of course, not to get caught red-handed violating the law, hence the locked door. At least it gave him a fighting chance to "hide the evidence."

Jane Addams, the Chicago social worker, was bitter about parents "who hold their children in a stern bondage which requires a surrender of all their wages and concedes no time or money for pleasures." But what choice did poor families have? At the wages they worked for, they could not afford to send their children to school. Women and children too had to work to keep the household going. The whole family was sacrificed to the greed of the manufacturers.

Jacob Riis, a Danish immigrant who arrived penniless in New York in 1870 and made himself into a crusading reporter, found poverty and child labor yoked together on the Lower East Side, as everywhere. Whether Jewish, Italian, or Slavic, the sweatshop workers were exploited in the same way. Riis tells of what he discovered when he dropped in on a sweatshop employing Jews.

From among 140 hands in two big lofts in a Suffolk Street factory we picked 17 boys and 10 girls who were patently under 14 years of age, but who all had certificates, sworn to by their parents, to the effect they were 16. One of them whom we judged to be between 9 and 10, and whose teeth confirmed our diagnosis—the second bicuspids in the lower jaw were just coming out—said that he had worked there "by the year." The boss, deeming his case hopeless, explained that he only "made sleeves and went for the beer." Two of the smallest girls represented themselves as sisters, respectively 16 and 17, but when we came to inquire which was the oldest, it turned out that she was the 16-year one. Several boys scooted as we came up the stairs. When stopped, they claimed to be visitors. . . .

In an Attorney Street pants factory we counted 13 boys and girls who could not have been of age, and on a top floor in Ludlow Street, among others, two brothers, sewing coats, who said that they were 13 and 14, but, when told to stand up, looked so ridiculously small as to make even their employer laugh. Neither could read, but the oldest could sign his name. . . . He was one of the many Jewish children we came across who could neither read nor write. Most of them answered that they had never gone to school. . . . They were mostly the children of the poorest and most ignorant immigrants, whose work is imperatively needed to make both ends meet at home.

There were numerous restrictions on the hiring of minors; the issue of child labor was not ignored in the late nineteenth century. But policing of the law was not effective. Employers avoided giving out accurate data on the age of their workers. In the sweatshops as well as the mines, children were often classified not as workers but as "helpers" to their parents. Contrary to popular belief was the fact that most children who worked were not in the factories. They were in the street trades, occupations not regulated by law. Newsboys, bootblacks, peddlers were considered "independent contractors," not employees.

Critics of child labor who investigated conditions were convinced that putting your children to work meant sentencing them to a lifetime of drudgery. Instead of acquiring knowledge and skills at school, they wore themselves out at dull and repetitive tasks. In 1901 about half of New York State's 1,500,000 children aged five to eighteen did not go to school. Ten percent of these children were factory workers. The others were in street trades. "It is a popular fallacy that bootblacks and newsboys grow up to be major generals and millionaires," said one newspaper. "The majority of them, on the contrary, become porters and barkeepers."

Millionaires?

A study of 160 families on the Lower East Side, made by the doctor who treated them all, showed the average *total* waae—the earnings of parents and children combined—was $5.99 per week. The highest family wage was $19, earned by three persons. The lowest was $1.50, earned by a woman in the needle trades.

The cheap labor offered by women and children depressed the general wage scale. The tendency was for the real income of a *family* to approach what an *individual* had earned previously. The old saw "Heaven will protect the working girl" must have meant that no one else would. In New York in the 1880s, women's pay averaged only half as much as men's.

Few Jewish women worked in factories before the 1880s. A decade later about 20,000 of them, mostly American-born, were employed in stores, offices, and schools. The immigrant women now arriving usually worked in tenement sweatshops. As legislation restricted the sweatshops, production of women's clothing in factories expanded and drew young Jewish women in rapidly growing numbers. Their wages in 1890 ran from $2 to $4.50 a week, a level frequently reduced by heavy fines for trivial offenses. But there were girls earning as little as 30 cents a day to pull threads. One sweatshop operator paid women 20 cents to make a dozen flannel shirts. They worked eleven hours in the shop and another four at home, supplying their own thread and paying for their machines out of their wages. Women were paid $1.50 to make a dozen calico wrappers, 25 cents to make a dozen neckties. A dozen was about all you could do in one day.

In his New York *World*, Joseph Pulitzer tried to help the immigrant women in the shops by telling their story to the public. One of his reporters in 1885 noted what women earned and how they tried to manage on those wages.

The general average [for shirtmakers] is from $5.50 to $6 per week, when work is steady and a girl is at her machine ten hours a day.

Cloakmakers average a little higher—from $6 to $7 per week. Fur-sewers about the same. . . . Tailoresses, whose work is hardest and heaviest of all machine sewing, earn from $6 to $7 per week. . . .

Bindery girls average $6 to $7 per week. Paperbox makers do not average more than $6. . . . Milliners earn higher wages than any of the other trades of this class, averaging from $12 to $18 per week. But it must be remembered that theirs is what is known as a "season trade," and their work is good only for three months each in the spring and fall.

By these figures the average pay of working women is shown to be $7 per week. . . . The usual price of a clean hall bedroom in a respectable house, with reasonably good and sufficient food, is $5 per week. . . . Washing at the lowest estimate is 50 cents per week; fire, a necessity in winter, 50 cents more. If lunch is not furnished that will be 60 cents per week, at the very least. And if a girl is obliged to ride to and from her work, there is 60 cents more for carfare.

How could you manage a budget on such wages?

As the new century began, garment workers were putting in a fifty-six- to sixty-hour week. Annual earnings ranged from $500 a year for the less skilled to $900 for the cutters, the aristocrats of the trade. A study of living standards made by the Russell Sage Foundation concluded that $800 a year was the minimum needed for a decent way of life in New York City. It found, however, that incomes went above $700 only when a family took in boarders or had the wife and children work too.

The investigators also looked at the way immigrants of different ethnic origins spent the same range of income. Italians were compared with Jews. Jews, they reported, spent more on fuel and light, on doctoring, and on charity. Italians spent more on food, especially on fruit, vegetables, cereals, and wine for the table, but less than Jews for meat and fish.

One Jewish family studied had four children between six months and six years of age. A week's groceries, bought at a ground-floor store or from pushcarts, included 6 quarts of milk, 2 pounds of butter, one dozen eggs, 3½ pounds of sugar, 6 pounds of potatoes, bread and rolls, beef and fish, ¼ pound of coffee, 2 ounces of tea, tiny amounts of cheese, dried fruit, and Sabbath wine. They spent one dollar a month for lamplighting gas in summer and two dollars in winter.

Economists hold that during this immigration period real wages rose about one third, meaning the standard of living went up. But immigrants got less than their share of the benefits. They worked for the lowest pay, and at jobs afflicted by short or irregular working seasons. Garment work especially was highly seasonal. And unemployment caused by depression (1893–97) struck hardest at these workers who were the last to arrive, came with the least skill, and teetered on the edge of subsistence.

One Jewish researcher named A. Schalit decided around 1910 to find out how Eastern European Jews were getting along in America. He gathered economic data in New York, Philadelphia, Boston, and Chicago. His figures showed the average wage of Jewish working women was $6.50 a week. Allowing for dull seasons, he estimated their annual average earnings at $240. Jewish men were earning $12 a week. Their annual income he put at $450.

He then asked what this meant in the light of the Russell Sage figure of $800 a year required for minimum reasonable comfort. He concluded that beyond doubt the average income of the Jewish immigrant family was barely half that. "But," he added, "ideas of Americans and East European Jews on minimum necessities are *not* the same. The poor," he said, "are not on charity, except for hospitalization; they save money, and they send great sums to relatives in Europe each year."

A charge frequently heard was that the Jewish workers had lowered the standard of living. Burton Hendrick, a reporter who investigated the accusation, called it "ridiculous." The Jews, he said, were not pulling the rest of the population down to their level. The truth was "they constantly seek to raise their own." When describing the immigrants, the press always focused on the Lower East Side. But that district, by the early 1900s, was the home of the newly arrived. The ambition of most Jews living there was to leave it. "In this the children are especially persistent. They quickly outgrow the three- and four-room flat. Their parents may have worked in the sweatshop but they eschew it. The increase of Italian workmen in the clothing trades, and the gradual decrease of the Jews . . . is one of the most striking evidences of economic improvement. Under the pressure of the second generation the old folks pack their goods and leave Hester, Suffolk and Essex Streets for more sanitary and pretentious quarters. The prosperous . . . find their way to Lexington, Madison, Park and Fifth Avenues and the adjoining streets. The great Jewish bourgeoisie, however, lives in Harlem." By 1907 it was made up almost entirely of former Lower East Siders. At least 70,000 had migrated northward in the preceding five years. Even more had crossed into Brooklyn's Brownsville district.

Many Jewish workers, of course, did not climb into the middle class. They were not alone in failing to earn enough to provide a family with the vaunted American standard of living. The Catholic economist John A. Ryan estimated in 1906 that at least 60 percent of adult male wage earners received less than $600 a year. Father Ryan went beyond bread and butter in his progressive thinking. He contended that families deserved more than just enough food, clothing, and shelter to survive. They should be able to obtain sufficient physical necessities to enjoy good health and maintain self-respect. They should have enough put by for savings and insurance. And they should be able to spend for "mental and spiritual culture"—education, books, sports and recreation, membership in church, labor union, club. Finally, he urged, all the good things of life should be paid for from the father's earnings. Wife and children should not have to work to make ends meet.

28

Run, Do, Work!

Few Eastern European Jews found a living on American farms. In the old country nearly all of them had been town dwellers because the czar's law prevented them from owning farmland. Some were able to rent orchards and sell their crops to dealers. The law did not keep them from owning cattle, and dairymen were common in the *shtetl.* But the only way for other Jews to farm was to lease land from absentee owners. The desire to have their own piece of land when it had been so long denied them was therefore strong among some of the immigrants.

Jewish projects for colonizing on American soil had been launched well before the Civil War. A few actually materialized, such as Shalom begun in the 1930s by Moses Cohen in Ulster County, New York. They lasted briefly. B'nai B'rith organized a Hebrew Agricultural Society in the 1850s to encourage Jews to take up farming as a vocation. But not until the mass exodus of Eastern European Jews began was agriculture suggested as a solution for the Jewish emigrants.

Soon after the first pogroms of 1881 a movement in Russia called Am Olam (Eternal People) dedicated itself to redemption by tilling of the soil. Understandably, a people exiled for millennia from their homeland tended to idealize the land. One of the aims of Am Olam was to refute anti-Semitic propaganda that the Jewish people were "unfitted by habit, nature and sentiment for honest toil." The young hero of Abraham Cahan's novel *The Rise of David Levinsky* is inspired by Am Olam's vision: "I saw a fantastic picture of agricultural communes in far-away America, a life which does not know of mine and thine, where all are brothers and all are happy. Previously I had thought that this could be reached only in the future. Now it was going to be realized in the present. And I would be a participant." But neither David nor Cahan himself took part in Am Olam's mission. Nor were there many among the million Jews arriving in America in the last two decades of the nineteenth century who were willing to stray beyond the familiar immigrant quarters. After all, in the old country they had been town folk. And what kind of life would it be if you left relatives and friends? Still, young idealists were induced to join communes at Sicily Island in Louisiana, New Odessa in Oregon, and Cremieux and Bethlehem Judea in South Dakota. All of them failed, despite the ardor of their founders. Their lack of training and practical experience, as well as soils not suited for agriculture, ruined their chances. In Louisiana the Mississippi flooded their land and carried away all they had. In South Dakota there was first the "wheat bug" and then a drought that lasted two hundred days.

Other sponsors stepped in, placing some hundreds of families in New Jersey farm colonies at Alliance, Carmel, and Rosenhayn. These settlements persisted, although with great difficulty. Their nearness to large cities simplified the problem of marketing their products. More important, the colonists began to supplement their income by combining agriculture with the manufacture of clothing. The best example was launched at Woodbine, New Jersey, in 1891 by the Baron de Hirsch Fund. It grew into an industrial Jewish township circled by satellite farms.

In the early 1900s, the Jewish Colonization Association tried to relieve the crowding of Jews in the ghettos of the large Eastern cities by directing immigrants inland. Working with the Jewish Agricultural Society, it managed to settle over 3,000 Jewish families on farms in New England, New York, New Jersey, and regions farther west. More might have been done to select suitable families with care and give them farm training. But any large-scale success was impossible. The time was wrong. How could the new immigrants be expected to settle on the land when the children of native Americans were deserting the farms for the cities? With the general trend away from agriculture, it was a mistake to believe the Jews—or any other immigrant group—would move in the opposite direction. Agricultural colonization would indeed exert great influence on Jewish life. But in Palestine, not in America.

Jewish philanthropy then sought to find nonfarm jobs for Jews outside the ghettos. An Industrial Removal Office was set up. Once the immigrants' fear of the unknown America beyond New York was dispelled and the small Jewish communities scattered over the country were aroused to a sense of their obligation to welcome the newcomers, resettlement began. By the time the Removal operation was shut down in 1922, it had distributed over 100,000 Jews to more than a thousand places in every state of the Union. Many times more than that number were drawn to those communities when they heard of the satisfactory life of the pioneering immigrants. The presence today of perhaps a million American Jews in so many small towns and villages throughout the country can in part be traced to that program.

Nevertheless, by far the larger part of the Jewish immigrants lived out their lives in the great urban centers. Ever since 1890, at least two out of every three American Jews have lived in the largest cities—New York, Chicago, Philadelphia, Los Angeles, Boston. Today New York City alone contains about one third of America's six million Jews.

Whatever occupation the immigrant Jews turned to, at least it was of their own choice. Here in America the Eastern European Jews found the freedom to make a living, a freedom they never enjoyed in the autocratic regimes of the czar's Russia, the Emperor's Austria-Hungary, or the King's Rumania. The streets of New York did not prove to be paved with gold, but a Jew was not told he could work only at this or that, or only in this place or that. He could try to make a living wherever he chose. But, points out the historian Lucy Dawidowicz, "the freedom to make money became an obsession" for some. It was an end in itself. It began with a good purpose—to raise the children decently, to keep them out of the sweatshops if possible, to lay aside funds for their education and for old age. But in the process of scrambling for money, "family life was neglected, community was disregarded, tradition abandoned."

By 1890 the path to financial success was already clear. A guidebook put out for immigrant Jews gave this advice:

Hold fast, this is most necessary in America. Forget your past, your customs, and your ideals. Select a goal and pursue it with all your might. No matter what happens to you, hold on. You will experience a bad time but sooner or later you will achieve your goal. If you are neglectful, beware for the wheel of fortune turns quickly. You will lose your grip and be lost. A bit of advice for you: Do not take a moment's rest. Run, do, work and keep your own good in mind.

And no wonder. What America did, said a writer of that period, was to substitute for "the ancient tradition of hospitality a system of heartless exploitation and of neglect. . . . The determining factor in our hospitality has been the necessity for laborers—slaves if you will."

For the rank and file of workers in the mass-production industries there was little chance to advance. Those who came unskilled were almost invariably kept at that level. How many of the untrained could develop skills or accumulate the capital to climb the ladder into management or ownership?

But for the Eastern European Jews who entered commerce or the garment trades, the chance proved somewhat better. The sweatshop system of production which centered in the tenements gave the enterprising operator his opening. In the minute division of labor, subcontracting became the key. It was only a step from journeyman to contractor, and another step from contractor to manufacturer. The man with reckless ambition to get ahead needed very little capital and just a few simple machines to get started. For cheap labor he turned to his own people, whose habits and desires he knew well enough to exploit. Out of their skins he sweated his pennies of profit.

Early in 1907 the muckraking journalist Burton J. Hendrick took a look at what the Eastern European Jews had achieved in the business world of New York. "No people," he wrote in *McClure's*, "have had a more inadequate preparation, educational and economic, for American citizenship. . . . Their only capital stock is an intellect which has not been stunted by centuries of privation, and an industry that falters at no task, however poorly paid. In spite of all these drawbacks, the Russian Jew has advanced in practically every direction. His economic improvement is paralleled by that of no other immigrating race."

Hendrick gave some examples of Jews who had climbed from East Side slums to mansions on Fifth Avenue.

Harry Fischel: a Vilna carpenter who arrived in 1884 with 60 cents in his pocket. His first job paid $3, then $6 a week, part of which he sent home to his starving parents. In eighteen months he had saved $250. On that capital he set up as a builder and in a year had piled up $300,000. Now worth $800,000, he had built a home next to Andrew Carnegie.

Harris Mandelbaum: fled the pogroms of the early 1880s, started as a calico peddler, then sold clothes to the poor on the installment plan (50 cents a week), saving enough to buy a tenement house. Now he owned twenty parcels of real estate and was worth a million.

Herman Adelstein: a tinsmith, arrived in 1892, found work in a metal shop, became the owner of an iron foundry. Now he was worth $400,000.

Nathan Hutkoff: a forty-year-old glazier when he came, put in glass lights on the East Side for a pittance, then opened a little glass store on Canal Street. Now he was one of the largest plate-glass merchants in New York, with a fortune of $400,000.

Bernard Galewski: a cobbler, began repairing shoes in an alley off Orchard Street twenty-five years ago at 5 to 25 cents a pair, then went into real estate. Now he was worth several hundred thousand.

Israel Lebowitz: started as a peddler twenty years ago, then opened a gents' furnishing store on Orchard Street. Now one of the largest shirt manufacturers in the city, he had half a million invested in real estate.

Samuel Silverman: once a sweatshop worker, he was now a cloak manufacturer, with a fortune estimated at $500,000.

S. Friedlander: millinery merchant on Division Street, he made $500,000 in twenty-five years.

Etc., etc., etc. . . .

How did it happen?

Hendrick attributed it to two marked characteristics in the Russian Jew.

He is a remorseless pace-maker. He allows himself no rest or recreation, and works all hours of the day and night. He saves every penny, will constantly deny himself and his family nutritious food, and until he has made his mark will live in the most loathsome surroundings. Whether a child in the primary schools, the bent stitcher in the sweatshops, the

manufacturer, the merchant, the professional man: constant industry, the
determination to succeed—that is his only law. Again, he is an individual-
ist. . . . There is tremendous energy, but it is expressed individually and
not collectively. The Jew constantly strives to get ahead; to him the
competitive system is the industrial ideal.

Only a comparatively few of the Jews who began with packs on their
backs or standing behind pushcarts were still at those "traditionally
Jewish" trades, Hendrick said.

> The great mass have been living refutations of a popular anti-Semitic
> libel—that the Jew is congenitally a money-changer, a trader, and not a
> workman, a manufacturer, an actual producer of wealth. New York's
> great Jewish community has always supported itself by the labor of its
> own hands. It is the city's largest productive force and the greatest
> contributor to its manufacturing wealth. The Russian Jew had not been
> here many years before he had worked himself up, in large numbers, into
> all the productive industries. By thousands he took to rolling cigars,
> making paper boxes, manufacturing surgical instruments, wrought-iron
> articles, lamps, hardware, cut-glass, practically all the ready-made wood-
> work used in the building trades, proprietary medicines, drugs, leather
> goods, cutlery, furniture, upholstery, wagons, harness—indeed, it would
> be hard to find a manufacturing field in which he has not succeeded. His
> greatest triumph, of course, has been his absolute control of the clothing
> industry. It is the largest industry of New York. It employs 175,000
> craftsmen, who annually turn out a product valued at $300,000,000. It
> manufactures more than half of all the wearing apparel—men's and
> women's suits, cloaks, overcoats, underwear, hosiery, neckties, collars
> and cuffs, shoes, slippers, etc.—used in the United States. Its predominant
> factors are now the Russian Jews.

The profits made in manufacture or commerce were often invested in
real estate. "The East Side," Hendrick observed, "is possessed of an
unending earth hunger. Wherever you see a Russian Jew, however
insignificant his station, you see a prospective landlord." Prestige came
from acquiring wealth; the form of wealth most esteemed was real
estate. On the East Side, tenement properties ranged from $35,000 to
$50,000 each in the early 1900s. Yet thousands of immigrant Jews
managed to acquire them. How? Hendrick traces the process.

First they became lessees. By constant saving the East Sider gets together $200 or $300 with which, as security, he gets a four or five years' lease of a house. He moves his own family into the least expensive apartment. He himself acts as janitor; his wife and daughters as scrubwomen and housekeepers. He is his own agent, his own painter, carpenter, plumber, and general repair man. Thus he reduces expenses to the minimum. He lets out apartments by the week, always calling promptly himself for the rent. By thus giving constant attention to his work, he has, perhaps, a few hundred dollars every year as a profit. By the time his lease expires, this has swollen to a few thousand. With this he buys a tenement outright. He puts down from $3,000 to $5,000 on a $45,000 building, giving one, two, three, sometimes four mortgages in payment · of the rest. Then he repeats his old operation: moves into the cheapest flat, presses his family into service, cuts down all possible expenses, and gives the property his own immediate supervision. When the third or fourth mortgage comes due, he has invariably made enough out of the building to pay it off. He keeps on hard at work and likewise pays off the third and second. Then, as his rents still come in, he invests them in more tenements; until, as a monument to a life spent in the hardest sacrificial toil, he may own a string scattered all over the town.

Jews who could not scrape together the few hundred dollars for a start often combined their smaller savings in a syndicate to acquire a property. Eventually, as it earned profits, each associate might become a prosperous landholder. Jews who had ventured into other fields often speculated on the side in real estate. With as little as twenty-five dollars, men and women took a hand in the game. As new subways, tunnels, and bridges linked the central city with the outlying districts, thousands of hitherto unreachable acres became habitable. Jews bought up old estates, parceled them out, and reaped the profits. Jewish builders put up block after block of apartments. Immigrants moving on up left the Lower East Side for Harlem, Washington Heights, Brownsville, Williamsburg, and the Bronx. The construction business, once controlled by old native stock, and then by the Irish and the Germans, was coming almost entirely into the hands of the Jews. They built not only housing but hotels, factories, and office buildings. The contractors drew their fellow immigrants in as workmen. The Harry Fischel who could afford to build a home on Fifth Avenue and make himself neighbor to Andrew

Carnegie encouraged Jews to enter the building trades by giving them the Sabbath holiday at half pay.

In scarcely twenty-five years Eastern European Jews acquired holdings valued in the hundreds of millions. In the Jewish quarter of the Lower East Side, "the former starving subjects of the Czar now hold 70 percent of all the land," Hendrick reported in 1907. It was land once owned largely by the great estates—Astor, Stuyvesant, Whitney. The sixty blocks of Harlem real estate bounded by 110th and 125th streets and Seventh and Lenox avenues were controlled mostly by Jews. It happened this way, said Hendrick, because the Jews "have shown themselves the fittest to survive." Others interpreted this to mean the Jews were bloodsucking landlords, squeezing higher rents out of their tenants than other landlords and giving them worse quarters to live in. But in Hendrick's opinion the Jews were not responsible for the city's slum problem. The tenements were terrible, yes, but they had been there decades before the Jewish immigration began. Housing conditions were as bad or worse in the 1850s and 1860s, when non-Jews owned everything. No landlords were more neglectful of their tenants than Trinity Church, the heart of a huge real-estate empire.

Nor, for that matter, were any of the immigrant businessmen in the same financial league as the vestrymen of Trinity Church. Most of the Eastern European Jews who became capitalists were only "crumb-gatherers on the periphery of the American economy," as Judd Teller put it. Some played not insignificant roles in their corner of the stage, but taken as a whole, they were secondary figures. In no way could they be compared with the robber barons who dominated the headlines: Morgan, Rockefeller, Fisk, Gould, Harriman, Astor, Mellon, Hill, Carnegie—non-Jews all, whose wealth and power were enormous.

The precarious position of many of the Jewish newly rich crumbled when the Great Depression of thr 1930s set in.

29

From Greenhorn to American

What went into the making of an American?

Young William Zorach's mother and father came to this country from Russia in their forties. Although they could speak five languages, they had no schooling and could neither read nor write. Stubbornly persisting in being what he was, a Russian Jew, Mr. Zorach never mastered the English language, kept his beard, wore felt boots, and in winter wrapped himself in a huge black overcoat he tied round his waist with a rope.

A few years after settling in Cleveland, the Zorachs sent for their cousins in Russia. "When they arrived," William recalled, "they were dressed in the clothes that children wore in Russia—long pants, boots and gay overshirts with belts. My aunt was scandalized and ashamed of such greenhorns. She immediately stripped them of their clothing and dressed them in all new clothes from the store—Americanized them right away."

Mary Antin's father, like William Zorach's aunt, couldn't bear to be thought a greenhorn. He had come to the United States ahead of his family. Now he wrote back to his wife urging her to leave in Polotzk the wig which religion required married Jewish women to wear. Reluctantly she took the first step toward Americanization, starting off for the New World in her own hair.

As soon as she and the children joined Mr. Anrin in Boston, they were led to a department store uptown. There, Mary said, they shed their "hateful" homemade European clothes for "real American machine-made garments." They could no longer be pointed out on the streets as greenhorns.

Names were changed as readily as clothes. From Yacov (Hebrew) or Yankel (Yiddish) to Jacob and finally to Jack. From Hyman to Howard, Leybel to Lester or Leon, Berel to Barnett or Barry, Chai-Sura to Sarah, Breina to Beatrice, Simcha to Seymour, Chatzkel to Haskell, Meyer to Max, Moishe to Morris, Aaron to Allan.

Mary Antin tells how it was done in her family.

> With our despised immigrant clothing we shed our impossible Hebrew names. A committee of our friends, several years ahead of us in American experience, put their heads together and concocted American names for us all. Those of our real names that had no pleasing American equivalents they ruthlessly discarded, content if they retained the initials. My mother, possessing a name that was not easily translatable, was punished with the undignified nickname of Annie. Fetchke, Joseph, and Deborah issued as Frieda, Joseph, and Dora, respectively. As for poor me, I was simply cheated. The name they gave me was hardly new. My Hebrew name being Maryashe in full, Mashke for short, Russianized into Marya, my friends said that it would hold good in English as Mary; which was very disappointing, as I longed to possess a strange sounding American name like the others.

Everything that typified the old country, in family names as well as first names, had to go. The Russian -skis and -vitches were dropped. Levinsky became Levin, Michaelowitch, Michaels. Russian and Polish names were Anglicized: Bochlowitz to Buckley, Stepinsky to Stevens, Shidlowsky to Sheldon, Horowitz to Herrick, Willinsky to Wilson. Davidowitz became Davidson, Jacobson became Jackson. The Germanic names too were readily translated into English: Weiss-White, Preiss-Price, Reiss-Rice, Rothenberg-Redmont.

Sometimes the decision to change names was not the immigrant's own. Immigration officials at the ports of entry refused to be bothered with exact transcriptions of a new arrival's difficult name. Down on the forms went totally new and easy names—Smith, Jones, Johnson, Robinson, Taylor, Brown, Black, White, Green. And then there were Jews who named themselves after the old streets on the Lower East Side—Clinton, Rivington, Delancey, Rutgers, Stanton, Ludlow. Or when children went to school, teachers who found a name unpronounceable put down on the records something close enough but easier to say. After a time the parents would accept the new name the children brought home.

It was not only a national desire "to be American" like everybody else which accounts for changes in name. Many firms refused to hire people whose names ended in "ski" or "sky." That was "too foreign" for their patrons, was the excuse. If the elite would not trade with or hire people with certain names, then the names were changed. The old folks especially minded the loss of the family name under such conditions. But if it was necessary to make a living . . . And as one East Side patriarch said to a New York *Tribune* reporter in 1898: "We honor our fathers just as much, even if we drop their names. Nothing good ever came to us while we bore them; possibly we'll have more luck with the new names."

In America, the way to success seemed to be the way out of the ghetto. The newcomers were in the minority. They were attracted by the ways of the old and settled majority. "As in a teacup one sees the little bubbles drawn to the larger ones and merging instantly when once in contact, so the larger life tends to absorb the smaller group," wrote one observer, Emily Greene Balch. "Indeed, the prestige of America, and the almost hypnotic influence of this prestige on the poorer class of immigrants, is often both pathetic and absurd. They cannot throw away fast enough good things and ways that they have brought with them, to replace them by sometimes inferior American substitutes."

In thinking back upon his childhood the novelist Saul Bellow regretted the way in which the newcomers imitated what they found here.

It was common in that generation and the next to tailor one's appearance and style to what were, after all, journalistic, publicity creations, and products of caricature. The queer hunger of immigrants and their immediate descendants for true Americanism has yet to be described. It may be made to sound like fun, but I find it hard to think of anyone who underwent the process with joy. Those incompetents who lacked mimetic talent and were pure buffoons were better off—I remember a cousin, Arkady, from the old country who declared that his new name was now, and henceforth, Lake Erie. A most poetic name, he thought.

Eventually, Cousin Arkady simply became Archie and "made no further effort to prove himself a real American." Others did not give up so easily. A greater obstacle to overcome than name or clothing was language. The tongue he spoke singled out the "greener." Yiddish was the badge of an alien culture; English was the proper language for an American. The place to learn it was in school, obviously, but not everyone could go. Walking the streets of Philadelphia in search of a job, Nathan Kuskin tried to learn English by reading the signs and billboards.

> I was puzzled by the many words spelled differently from their pronunciations. In Russian every consonant and vowel is pronounced as written, but in this strange language I found wide variations. . . . The reading of signs on stores gave me wrong impressions about many things. For instance, I had an idea that "Mr. Ice Cream" was a multimillionaire chainstore owner because I had seen so many stores with his name on them. To accelerate my learning, on Sunday mornings . . . I would walk over to any church on Broad Street, not to pray, but to listen to the sermon and thus add a few words to my vocabulary. If I did not understand a word I would memorize it and later look it up in my pocket Russian-English dictionary.

Kuskin entered a night school for workers, paying five dollars for a year's course in English. Working hard all day in a cigar shop and studying every night proved too much. He joined with several other immigrants to hire a private tutor. They met once a week to read a book together and discuss it in English.

The impatient Abraham Cahan started even earlier, on the way to America. He picked up a German-English dictionary before boarding ship and on the thirteen-day voyage used it to help the immigrants explain their needs to the ship's officers. For a while he struggled alone with English grammar, then decided he needed a more solid grounding. He went to an East Side elementary school and for several months sat with a class of twelve-year-olds. A year later this immigrant knew enough English to be able to tutor other immigrants.

This zest for education had ancient roots. The Jews were probably the first people to aspire to total literacy—at least for the males. It rose out of the religious obligation to study the Bible and Talmud as the pathway to God. The greatest prestige went to religious scholars. If a man stayed illiterate and ignorant his religious piety was questioned. So universal education for males was a critical goal of Jewish society. The hope was to educate each man to the limit of his ability. And when formal education ended, it was his obligation to continue study on his own. The more learning, the more life. Study made you into a human being.

Of course, the learning to be sought was Jewish learning, religious learning. To acquire knowledge of the secular world was a personal choice. But once the Enlightenment took hold, secular learning began to undermine Jewish learning. The secular scholars said you couldn't understand the world unless you went beyond the mastery of Jewish culture. And well before the mass migration of Eastern European Jews began in the 1880s, secular education had begun to change the lives of many. The fervent dedication to religious study was transposed to worldly study. So explosive was the effect upon intellectuals of Jewish origin that Jews were making enormous contributions to science and scholarship well before World War I.

The millions of Eastern European Jews who migrated to the United States seized upon the freedom to go to school as a right to be cherished as passionately as the freedom to make a living. And the two became linked, for secular education was seen as the door to success in the New World. In Russia, Jews were denied equal opportunity in the schools. Here the public schools were open to all. You did not have to bribe an official or convert to Christianity to get into school.

The economic rewards of education were not a paramount consideration in the old country. Here, for many, success became synonymous with prosperity. The American commitment to education, initiated by the Protestant culture, was strengthened by the great influx of Jews. Family status was held to be dependent upon it. Not only by the first generation to come, but by their American-born children, who in this respect did not rebel against a powerful family value. Other immigrant groups might permit or encourage their children to evade compulsory schooling. But not the Jews. As a group they made an almost super-human effort to acquire the education and culture America offered.

Mary Antin was one of about a hundred "green" children who started school in Boston's Chelsea neighborhood in 1894. Her proud father himself brought his four children the first day, "as if it were an act of consecration." He had written his family repeatedly that his chief hope for his children was free education, "the essence of American opportunities, the treasure that no thief could touch, not even misfortune or poverty." As for Mary's feelings, she was, she said, "carried along by a tremendous desire to learn, and had my family to cheer me on." She was put in the second grade, under Miss Nixon.

> There were about half a dozen of us beginners in English, in age from six to fifteen. Miss Nixon made a special class of us, and aided us so skillfully and earnestly in our endeavors to "see-a-cat," and "hear-a-dog-bark," and "look-at-the-hen," that we turned over page after page of the ravishing history, eager to find out how the common world looked, smelled, and tasted in the strange speech. The teacher knew just when to let us help each other out with a word in our own tongue—it happened that we were all Jews—and so, working all together, we actually covered more ground in a lesson than the native classes, composed entirely of the little tots.

Like Mary Antin, Samuel Chotzinoff started school in the second grade, but on the Lower East Side. His mother fitted him out with an oblong pencil box (ten cents), four writing pads (a penny each), and a set of colored blotters (a nickel). The graying, middle-aged Miss Murphy had fifty boys to teach.

> She was severely distant, and her impersonal attitude, added to the formality of being called by our last names, cast a chill on the classroom. Soon one began to long for the sound of one's first name as for an endearment that would, at a stroke, establish a human relationship between oneself and Miss Murphy. But it was not to be. . . . Notwithstanding Miss Murphy's frigidity, she soon commanded our interest and respect, and we made good progress in reading and spelling. . . .
>
> Miss Murphy, who read aloud to us, appeared neither interested in nor moved by the McGuffey stories. She read without nuances and exhibited no emotion. Completely indifferent to the music of poetry, she would

recite a line like the exquisite, "How would I like to go up in a swing, up in the air so blue!" in a cold, earth-bound voice, look up from her book, and say, "Plotkin, spell swing." Yet she was an excellent disciplinarian, and our class speedily gained a reputation for good spelling.

Public School No. 1 at the corner of Catherine and Henry streets was a big whhte building trying to educate what one reporter described as "the miserably poor polyglot population" of the East Side district. Among the twenty-five-odd ethnic groups sending their children to it were the Swedes, Austrians, Greeks, Armenians, Irish, Welsh, Italians, Poles, Germans, Chinese, Russians. The Jewish children predominated.

To teach such classes must have been a great challenge. What Harry Roskolenko remembers of P.S. 31 is the discipline invoked.

> Schooling in my time, at P.S. 31, was very stern. The teacher, though not a cop, was nevertheless a ruler-wielding teacher. We knew the ruler because it was often applied to our asses by both teacher and principal. We would get slapped, and they were right. I was never right at any time—said my parents, who were immediately told of each incident by a note from the teachers or the principal. They sided with the teachers, and my report card proved that I was sleeping when I should have been studying. I was *left back*—a phrase that became quite familiar around our house. . . . Nevertheless, all of us learned quickly. There was no easy route to high school and college.

P.S. 79 was the grammar school J. R. Schwartz attended on the Lower East Side. Long after the red brick building on First Street had been turned into a warehouse, he could still recall almost every teacher he had, beginning at the top.

> I still remember Mr. Phripp, the principal, a tall rangy individual, with a pointed, sandy-colored Van Dyke beard and a bulbous, gigantic nose. Every morning with all classes at assembly he read a portion of the Bible in his benign voice. At first blush he gave the impression of utter goodness, a goodness that was a mask for a vindictive nature. Woe unto him who was unfortunate enough to be sent by his teacher to his office with a note for some infraction of school discipline. . . . Mr. Phripp was harsh, unrelenting and satanically lavish in doling out punishment.
>
> My first teacher at P.S. 79 was Miss Reilly. In the succeeding term I had a Miss Keilly. Then as the grades advanced and we changed to the

departmental form, I had Miss Donovan, she with the strabismic eyes, as my regular class teacher. She was nicknamed "Cockeye" Donovan. Miss Keilly was blessed with a satanic smirk. Mr. Collins, who taught American literature, must have been afflicted with adenoids. He talked with a nasal twang. Mr. Patsy Beamer taught algebra and Mr. Krampner arithmetic and English. Mr. Ruskin had charge of the elementary physics class and Mrs. Devereaux, the first-year French. Then there was a Mr. Fish, a little man with a large, sandy-haired head and red face who substituted for any teacher who would be absent from class. And finally, Mr. Foster, who taught shop work. Mr. Foster was never known to crack a smile. He was a little pompous man who took himself very seriously. . . . Mr. Telluson, who also taught English, was a kindly man who seemed to understand us and went out of his way to make us see the beauty in poetry.

Mr. Krampner was the only Jewish teacher on the staff until Mr. Ruskin showed up, from Russia via London, where he must have adopted the respected name of the British art of critic.

> He endeared himself to the pupils because on Saturdays he would invite different groups to his home where we all sat around on the floor and he expounded to us the wonders of nature and science. When the weather was clement he would take us to the various parks of the city "to hold communion with nature in her visible forms."

Teachers, the immigrant children learned, were not all of a piece. When Morris R. Cohen started school in Brooklyn his first teacher was a Mrs. Phinney. She opened the day by asking all the boys to recite with her the Lord's Prayer. He didn't like it, but he didn't dare protest. And when she scolded a classmate and said to him, "Don't walk like a sheeny," young Morris was depressed. It was bad enough that the boys called the few Jews in the class by that name. But before long he and Mrs. Phinney became very good friends: she proved to be an imaginative and caring teacher who brought out the best in her pupils. He could overlook her prejudices.

His last year of high school (it was 1894–1895) was one of "great intellectual as well as physical awakening" for fifteen-year-old Morris Cohen. He met the masterpieces of English and American literature, discovering that not only novels but essays and history and poetry were revelations of marvelous new worlds. By the year's end he was thrilled to be reading Plato. Benjamin Franklin's *Autobiography* gave him the happy and practical notion of keeping a record of his intellectual progress by jotting down the day's thoughts in a diary. When he won a gold medal for the highest mark scored on a college entrance examination, his mother cried. Not because of the medal, but because it meant her son could go to college. When one of his aunts remonstrated, "You can't afford to send your son to college," she replied, "If need be I'll go out as a washerwoman and scrub floors so that my Morris can have a college education."

For Maurice Hindus the first "truly American world" that opened to him was Stuyvesant High School. It educated boys from all the boroughs, rich and poor. There was at that time only a sprinkling of immigrants like himself. The boys were clean and well dressed, and excited by sports in a way he couldn't understand. Unlike most of them, Maurice worked long hours in a shop after classes and on Saturdays. He tells why the school was an adventure for him.

> It was not the students as much as the teachers who stirred my imagination. There was nothing of the stiffness and severity of Russian teachers about them. The manual training teachers did not mind soiling their hands with greasy tools or with paint. They showed no feudal disdain of menial work. They never made students aware of a social gulf between them, which made the school a lively and happy community, though not untouched by the petty rivalries, the exuberant roughness, the guileful rogueries that now and then seize teenage boys. . . .
>
> I soon discovered that in my relationship with teachers my immigrant origin instead of being a liability was a real asset. English was my favorite subject and I couldn't have had more helpful and generous-spirited instructors. . . . If I wrote a composition that pleased them, they were lavish with praise in their written comments and often spoke to me after class, advising me what books to read and encouraging me to write.

Hindus won first prize in the annual short-story contest for sophomores. From reading so much English literature he became, he said, "passionately Anglophile."

The training of future citizens, everyone agreed, was the first duty of the public schools. And to speak and write English well was the primary path to that goal. The children of the Jewish immigrants heard Yiddish at home, a mixture of many languages on the street, plus the latest American slang, and "proper" English for only five hours of the day in school. But the result of training after only five or six years in school was "wonderful," reported the New York *Evening Post* in 1903. Not only for the pupils, it went on, but for their parents, who learned daily the rudiments of English through the medium of their children. The method used at school was constant drill in enunciation and pronunciation. The best pupils were chosen to speak at assemblies; they set models of good English for the others, while competing for medals for excellence.

Just as important as learning English, said the *Post*, was learning the absolute necessity of cleanliness for good health in children. A major task of the teacher was to insist upon clean hands and faces, combed hair, and shined shoes or boots. Monitors stood at assembly doors to see that the pupils passed inspection.

The study of civics and American history was foremost for citizenship education. Besides the class work, the training called for the recitation of patriotic pieces at the morning assembly, the singing of patriotic songs, and the daily salute to the flag. Special exercises to honor national holidays were red-letter days in school life. Army generals were brought in to fire up assemblies with their memories of Civil War days.

The largest public school in the world—P.S. 188—was located on the Lower East Side. Five thousand boys and girls jammed its ninety-six classrooms. When a *Tribune* reporter visited the school in 1906, he asked a class of thirty-eight boys (average age fourteen, and the majority Jewish) what they wanted to be when they grew up. Eleven said, go into business; nine intended to be lawyers; six, civil engineers; three, doctors; three, dentists; two, teachers; and one each, electrical engineer, mechanic, clothing designer, and engraver.

Special classes were provided for children just off the boat. One such class the reporter looked in on held thirty-three girls, all Jewish and about thirteen years old. Twenty had been born in Russia, seven in Hungary, and six in Austria. Half had arrived in New York in the last six months, fleeing the recent pogroms. "Do they appreciate the opportunities of this country?" asked the reporter. The teacher put the question to Rosie in Yiddish. Her answer, translated, was: "I love sweet America. They are kind to me here."

30

The Melting Pot Leaks

"They are kind to me here."

They tried to be, many of them. But did they know how? They—the older Americans, the ones who had come here earlier and who had acquired wealth and position and power—they determined public policy. They shaped the schools. And they were white Protestants. Naturally their success made them believe they were the best. Whatever they had become in their American existence was to be the model for the new-comers pouring into the Golden Land.

So when the public schools dedicated themselves to "Americanizing" the masses of immigrants from Eastern and Southern Europe, they had in mind the manners, the style, the culture, the morals, the values of the solidly entrenched white Protestant elite, chiefly the New England Yankees. One of the leading educators of the time said the major task of the schools was "to break up those [immigrant] groups of settlements, to assimilate and amalgamate these people as part of our American race, and to implant in their children, so far as can be done, the Anglo-Saxon conception of righteousness, law and order, and popular government."

You can make it here, he was saying, if you will only become "real" Americans. Drop what makes you different. Forget where your parents came from, what they brought with them, their own feelings and experience, their own beliefs and values.

As the immigrants continued to pour in, the magazine *Scientific American* urged them to "assimilate" quickly or face "a quiet but sure extermination." If you keep your alien ways, it warned, you "will share the fate of the native Indian."

How wrong this attitude was, only a few understood. Jane Addams, the founder of Hull-House in the Chicago slums, was one of them. She wrote:

> The public school too often separates the child from his parents and widens the old gulf between fathers and sons which is never so cruel and so wide as it is between the immigrants who come to this country and their children who have gone to the public school and feel that there they have learned it all. The parents are thereafter subjected to certain judgment, the judgment of the young which is always harsh and in this instance founded upon the most superficial standard of Americanism.

As far back as 1908, Jane Addams urged the schools:

> . . . to do more to connect these children with the best things of the past, to make them realize something of the beauty and charm of the language, the history and the traditions which their parents represent. . . . It is the business of the school to give to each child the beginnings of a culture so wide and deep and universal that he can interpret his own parents and countrymen by a standard which is worldwide and not provincial.

I know what she meant. For as the son of immigrants I can see now what I missed in the schools I went to. My parents had come from Eastern Europe just before the turn of the century. Many of the children I went to school with in Massachusetts were the first American-born generation. My parents, like those of most of my schoolmates, had only the most rudimentary schooling in the old country. They were in a grand rush to become Americans. My mother had come here at fourteen, my father at eighteen. They did not want to be ridiculed as greenhorns, and as Yiddish was the badge of foreignness, they spoke so little of their own tongue that I learned scarcely a word of it. They told me nothing of their own years in Eastern Europe. Was it because they wanted to forget the world they had left behind? Or because they thought I had no interest in their culture?

Whatever the reason, I learned little about my people's past in my home. And nothing at all in my school. The schools stripped the immigrant children of their Old World heritage. We felt embarrassed by the language of our ancestors. Their history, their traditions, were not thought worthy of study. America was the land of the Anglo-Saxon Protestant elite. Our own ethnic identity was swept under the rug. I felt myself an outsider. What happened to me was not unique. What child without an Anglo-Saxon name or skin has not felt himself an outsider? We were given nothing to make us sure of ourselves and proud of what we were.

For the goal of the schools was to Americanize the newcomers. That meant to shape us into loyal and patriotic citizens. But it was an uncritical Americanization. We were not taught to ask questions about this country and its institutions. Julia Richman thought that was wrong. The first woman to be made a district superintendent of schools in New York City, she chose to work on the Lower East Side. How can we demand uncritical Americanization of these children, she said, when all around them is a "general corruption of municipal government" and a "general unethical basis of the commercial world"? She too, like Jane Addams, believed that an Americanization which blanked out the history of immigrant children was wrong.

In popular thought America has been glorified as a melting pot of different peoples. But apart from whether or to what degree this happened, was it a good idea, when it meant melting diversity into conformity with Anglo-Saxon characteristics? If you were unable to do it or didn't want to go along, then you were abused or shut out because middle-class America accepted only those who conformed to their super-culture. Everyone else was but a "spick," "mick," "dago," "greaseball," "hunkie," "Polack," "nigger," "Yid." Their race, their religion, their people's culture made them unworthy of America in the Nordic eyes of the "old Americans." The effect? Michael Novak puts it this way:

> Under the whiplash of such attitudes, many descendants of immi-
> grants for many years withered into silence about their identity. Many

suppressed the instincts of their flesh, the impulses of their sensibilities, and perhaps even the signals from their genes. (Teachers made Italian boys sit on their hands all morning long, to make them stop gesticulating.) A great many try desperately to *be all alike,* to look the way Americans do in the magazines, and movies and streets: to make it, to pass.

Among many of the immigrants total assimilation seemed contrary to the spirit of democracy. To them democracy meant freedom to make choices, freedom to be oneself, and they stubbornly resisted attempts to force them into the melting pot. The wiping out of their own culture was too high a price to pay.

But even back then the melting-pot theory did not go unopposed. Some thinkers pointed out that if the ethnic groups were not robbed of their cultural differences these special qualities would enhance American life. More, they challenged the notion that the immigrant groups which had come before the 1880s had already lost their identity. Some or even many individuals, yes, but never the group as a whole. (Today historians and sociologists agree that Americanization did not rub out the distinctive traits of the ethnic groups and create a new American.)

The idea of cultural pluralism was put forth to stress the desirability of maintaining ethnic variety. Its proponents argued that to demand cultural homogeneity was as oppressive as to deny the right to freedom of speech or freedom of religion. The immigrant of whatever ethnic origin is no outsider, they said. The culture of any ethnic group is rightly part of the ever-changing pattern of culture that makes up America. Horace M. Kallen, a Jew and a philosopher who was one of the earliest spokesmen for cultural pluralism, said, "Since people have to live together, plurality is a basic condition of existence. The need is to bring differences together to make a union, not unity."

Jews particularly, but by no means exclusively, have been aware of their individuality as a people. For how many centuries have they shown how unwilling they are to surrender it? The Poles too, and the Bohemians, the Pennsylvania Germans, the Irish, the Slavs, the Italians, to name only some. All intensely nationalist, even when they rose from proletarian status to prosperity. As they freed themselves from the stigma of "greenhorn," they developed group self-respect and pride.

They clung to their language and their religion, maintaining out of worker's wages schools and a press in their national tongue.

Putting aside, for the moment, the failure of the schools to teach the immigrant children something of their heritage, how effective was the education they did try to impart? Much is said today of the decline of the public schools, implying that they were excellent in the "good old days." But "the truth is," writes Colin Greer, "that our public schools have always failed the lower classes—both white and black." In his study *The Great School Legend*, he concludes it is simply not true that the schools took the poor immigrants who crowded into the cities and molded them into the homogeneous productive middle class we claim as America's strength and pride. On the contrary:

> In virtually every school effectiveness study since the one made in Chicago in 1898, more children have failed in urban public schools than have succeeded, both in absolute and in relative numbers. Among the school systems which had large numbers of immigrants and poor pupils, in Boston, Chicago, Detroit, Philadelphia, Pittsburgh, New York and Minneapolis, failure rates were so high that in no one of these systems did the so-called "normal" group exceed 60 percent, while in several instances it fell even lower.

Only a small number of young people got as far as high school in the first place. Scarcely 8 percent aged fourteen to seventeen were high-schoolers in 1900. And of these, only about 12 percent finished and graduated. But the immigrants' children did as well—or as badly—as the children of native-born whites, says the educational historian Edwin A. Krug.

The Jews are often given as the example of immigrant success in the schools. They were one of the ethnic groups who did better than some others. But by no means did all Jews do well. Otherwise, asks Colin Greer, "why the remedial classes and dropout panic in several of the schools on New York's Lower East Side with as much as 99 percent 'Hebrew' registration? Where the family was poor enough to take in boarders to cover rental costs, and desperate enough to join the city's welfare rolls, delinquency and criminality were then, as they are now in some urban neighborhoods, the burden of Jewish families too." The Jews too had their prostitutes, pimps, con men, gangsters, and killers.

As with other ethnic groups, school performance seemed to be tied to the socioeconomic position of the pupil's family. The better off the parents were, the better the child did in the classroom. Greer concludes that those who succeeded rarely did so because of the public schools.

The white working class never climbed upward as rapidly or as surely as it has become traditional to believe, Greer says. The school dropout rates for all groups, including blacks, were tied to "the terrifying vulnerability" of the unskilled labor the parents did. When adult employment fell off, the children dropped out in direct proportion.

Only a few hard facts about the schools of that era are enough to show what the children were up against. City schools were under the control of political bosses who looted education funds. As a result, books and supplies were short and buildings overcrowded. Schools built for a thousand pupils often held double that number. In 1893 one Brooklyn classroom packed in 153 students; many classes had 90 or 100 students. Lighting and ventilation were usually poor. Physical punishment with stick or fist was legal and common. The pupils were force-fed information. Not thinking, but memorization was the accepted path to knowledge. And repetition—endless, deadening repetition—was the way to mastery of the three Rs. Every pupil was considered to be exactly like every other one—a receptacle into which unrelated and meaningless information was mechanically dumped like so much garbage. Spontaneity was suppressed, imagination ridiculed. The pupil could have nothing worthwhile to say; the teacher was the fount of all wisdom.

For the poor there was the added handicap of hunger. A 1905 survey of schoolchildren in four major cities showed one out of every three came to school having had no breakfast or a very poor one. Huge numbers could not learn because they were listless and apathetic; many others could not learn because they were exhausted from long hours of work they had to do outside school hours to help support their families.

And what of the quality of the teachers? Before 1900, teaching was not a true profession. Someone who wanted a teaching job needed only the most brief and casual training or simply political pull. The "normal schools," the forerunners of the teachers colleges, gave better preparation, but many didn't even require high-school diplomas of their students. Of course, there were still teachers with natural talent who cared for the boys and girls entrusted to them. But the patronage, graft, and favoritism which riddled the school system, and the low pay and slow promotion which rewarded their efforts, could discourage even the ablest and most devoted.

If people like Morris R. Cohen have given us happier memoirs of their schooling than this picture suggests, it was because they were extraordinary. The great mass made no mark in the world and have left us no record. We have only the statistics of success and failure to go by, the facts the historians of education have unearthed. The one exception, Colin Greer reports, was the Jews. They were more able than other white ethnic groups to use public education as a way up. But by no means all Jews, he adds, were successful.

The public school was the most powerful force for Americanization. It was compulsory, and in some big cities such as New York, it was free from kindergarten right through college. There were two other forces, however, which helped mold the immigrants and their children into the forms of New World life. One was the settlement house and the other the library.

On the Lower East Side the librarians found the appetite of the immigrants for knowledge to be insatiable. Self-education was the most persistent work of the newcomers. A report investigating these "foreign book-worms" in 1913 uncovered this story:

> A stout, deep-eyed, dark-complexioned Russian came to the librarian of the Seward Park Branch several years ago and asked her for books on advanced chemistry. He had read all those available through the library, but lacked enough money to buy the more expensive and technical volumes. His request was similar to those she had frequently heard and she as often had been compelled to refuse. She knew the young man, however, and in a few days interested a chemist from one of the large manufacturing concerns of the city.
>
> In the spirit of adventure this man climbed the stairs of a narrow Canal Street tenement and knocked at the door of an attic room. When the Russian admitted him the visitor stood at the threshold dumbfounded. He thought he was calling at the "bunk" of an immigrant. Instead he walked into a shabby but fully equipped chemical laboratory, hidden under the rafters of a five-story building.
>
> Here was a young man who had been banished from Odessa because he was a Jew. He had sought political and religious freedom in the United

States and did his first work in a sweatshop. From there he went to a clothing store, and in the evening tutored himself with public books. The few dollars he could save he spent for instruments.

Not many days after this meeting he was supplied with the latest books. He then passed the Regents' examinations and now is professor of chemistry in a Brooklyn institute.

At the branch libraries serving the East Side non-fiction was reported to be most in demand. Readers asked for economics, philosophy, history, politics. The fiction requested included the works of Dickens, Scott, Thackeray, Dumas, Tolstoy. In one library a hundred copies of *David Copperfield* were not enough to meet the demand. In 1903 the *Evening Post* sent a reporter to the Chatham Square branch to see how the immigrant children were using it. He found that as soon as school closed at 3 P.M. lines of children formed at the library, reaching down two flights of stairs and into the street.

The children are drawing books in English at the rate of 1,000 a day. Opened four years ago, the branch has 15,000 members. It stands third in the number of its circulation and since its opening has ranked first in the proportion of history and science taken out. It is almost wholly used by Jews. A few Italians from Mulberry Street, a handful of Chinese from Mott and Doyers, and a scanty representation from other races come here occasionally.

Probably the most popular book in the whole library is a history for young people entitled *The Story of the Chosen People,* the many copies of which are always traveling raggedly to the bindery. Rivaling it, however, is *Uncle Tom's Cabin.* As the story of an oppressed race it strikes a responsive chord in the Jewish child. Sue's *The Wandering Jew* is another prime favorite.

The librarians are a constant source of astonishment to the children. A peculiarly cordial spirit pervades the building. Every assistant is interested in her work, for those who are not interested do not stay. In return the children love them all, write them fervid letters of adoration, make them presents, and run their errands. And that the objects of so much sincere admiration should be Christians puzzles their small heads. . . .

The letters written to the librarians by the children display all the luxuriance of an Oriental imagination. "My dear Miss Sheerin, only God knows how much I love you. I send you as many kisses as there are pennies in the world," wrote one fanatical little adorer.

The Jewish child has more than an eagerness for mental food; it is an intellectual mania. He wants to learn everything in the library and everything the librarians know. He is interested not only in knowledge that will be of practical benefit, but in knowledge for its own sake. Girls and boys under twelve will stand before the library shelves so much absorbed in looking up a new book that they do not hear when spoken to. No people reads so large a proportion of solid reading.

In Boston, Mary Antin discovered the public library in the summertime when school was closed.

The library did not open till one in the afternoon, and each reader was allowed to take out only one book at a time. Long before one o'clock I was to be seen on the library steps, waiting for the door of paradise to open. I spent hours in the reading-room, pleased with the atmosphere of books, with the order and quiet of the place, so unlike anything on Arlington Street. The sense of these things permeated my consciousness even when I was absorbed in a book, just as the rustle of pages turned and the tiptoe tread of the librarian reached my ear, without distracting my attention. Anything so wonderful as a library had never been in my life. It was even better than school in some ways. One could read and read, and learn and learn, as fast as one knew how. . . . When I went home from the library I had a book under my arm; and I would finish it before the library opened next day, no matter till what hours of the night I burned my little lamp.

Mary read nearly everything that came to hand. Louisa May Alcott's stories first of all, but boys' books of adventure too. Anything in print, even the stained old newspapers that enclosed fish brought home from the market. She enjoyed the Yiddish newspapers her father subscribed to and the library's many-volumed encyclopedia, especially for its sketches of famous people and her favorite authors. Visiting the main library on Copley Square was a special treat. She felt it was "my palace—mine!" even though she was born in Russia and lived in a slum. She spent her longest hours in the vast reading room.

Here is where I liked to remind myself of Polotzk, the better to bring out the wonder of my life. That I who was born in the prison of the Pale should roam at will in the land of freedom was a marvel that it did me good to realize. That I who was brought up to my teens almost without a book should be set down in the midst of all the books that ever were written was a miracle as great as any on record. That an outcast should become a privileged citizen, that a beggar should dwell in a palace—this was a romance more thrilling than poet ever sang. Surely I was rocked in an enchanted cradle.

31

Settlements in the Slums

Uptown Jewry took an early hand in Americanizing the immigrants downtown. As the flood of newcomers rose, the German Jews realized they had better help the Eastern Europeans. If these "raw and unciv-ilized" Jews were not assimilated rapidly, non-Jews would identify them with *all* Jews. So the German Jews set out to "uplift, refine, and Americanize" the new arrivals. They backed experimental ventures in kindergartens, in vocational training, in the teaching of English. For many years their major effort would be centered in a new settle-ment house designed to "dissolve the ghetto" around it. Enough funds were raised by 1891 to open the Educational Alliance, housed in a five-story building at East Broadway and Jefferson Street. Through educa-tional, religious, and civic training, moral and physical culture, the trained staff aimed to better the condition of the Jews on the Lower East Side. From 9 A.M. to 10 P.M. the settlement was open to all who wanted to use its auditorium, gymnasium, shower baths, library, and roof garden.

The Educational Alliance was soon reaching 6,000 Jewish immi-grants, two thirds of them children, every weekday. On weekends more than sixty clubs held meetings in the building. The children were given intensive lessons which succeeded, within six months of their landing, in passing them on to the public schools (which would not accept them until they were able to use English).

In its early years the Alliance banned the use of Yiddish within its walls. It gave no encouragement to the expression of the immigrants' own culture. The newcomers were bathed in an artificial atmosphere of Anglo-Saxon culture. There were classes in English, in civics, in American history, in the literature of America and England. Bryant, Longfellow, Lowell, and Emerson were the favorite poets. The students delved into the ancient worlds of Greece and Rome, but not the history of the Jew. And like the public schools, the Alliance waved the flag and preached patriotism on the national holidays.

It took over a decade before the Alliance found links between the traditional life of ghetto and shtetl from which the immigrants fled and the urban life of modern New York into which they plunged. The use of Yiddish in classroom teaching became the bridge between the two. The Alliance prepared a guidebook in Yiddish (*Sholem Aleichem tsu immigranten*) for the newcomers and translated the Declaration of Independence into Yiddish. To the immigrants the Declaration, Franklin's *Autobiography*, and the Constitution became basic scripture. But "we must not forget," warned one settlement librarian, "that these are the children for whose parents were written such distinctly non-Anglo-Saxon books as *Anna Karenina, Crime and Punishment*, and *Taras Bulba.*" She did not want to see her young Russian-Jewish patrons denied their heritage.

The many other settlement houses which sprang up in New York took the same nonsectarian position as the Alliance. Their intent was to bring the multi-ethnic New Yorkers together, not stress what they feared (mistakenly) might keep them apart. By the end of the century there was a string of new settlement houses running up the East Side: the University Settlement, the Henry Street Settlement, the College Settlement, Madison House, Clark House, Christadora House . . .

As early as the age of seven, the Educational Alliance became for Harry Roskolenko the place where he learned to become a junior carpenter, remaking his Russian-Jewish home with bookcases, stool, chinning bar, and towel rack. In the crowded Alliance classes he studied subjects he couldn't get, at his young age, in public school.

Carpenter, about-to-be-mariner, Boy Scout, I knew about birds, flowers, tides, rocks—and how to repair a broken head, with bandages. For the Educational Alliance taught a sullen or a happy boy to be less violently errant, more decently dutiful, and almost properly American—with our East Side local combinations. It was an alliance of American hope plus universal scope. All a boy student had to do was go there, try not to beat up the then-tough teachers—and he was due to become a doctor in twenty years, so well trained that he would never be sued for malpractice.

If you were a sickly, pale, underweight, bronchial boy and your mother was a talking *baleboosteh,* she quickly convinced one of the Alliance's many extraterritorial departments that her son, about to die from every known form of undernourishment, must have a two-week free vacation at Surprise Lake Camp, some miles from New York, in middling mountains, with natural cows, and a lake to swim in. . . .   .

There was a Mother's Department at the Alliance, hoping to teach young mothers to become older mothers, and another department for girls interweaving between the alerted mothers. There were sewing classes, homemaking studies, dance socials, and gymnasiums—but nothing about sex. It was a taboo subject. . . .

There was music at the Alliance, with fiddlers, pianists, and quartets; and there were children's study halls, men's reading rooms, a religious education department, for Torah studies, as well as Yiddish, Hebrew, Russian—and accented Litvak. One day a boy running between his house and the Alliance's many cultural departments would cease to run, and become the man his father was not—a cultured American.

Out of the Alliance's art classes came such distinguished painters and sculptors as Ben Shahn, Leonard Baskin, Peter Blume, Adolph Gottlieb, Jacob Epstein, Jo Davidson, Chaim Gross, Abraham Walkowitz. There John Garfield began his acting career, Nat Holman coached basketball teams, Arthur Murray learned to dance, David Sarnoff studied English, and Sholem Aleichem discussed Yiddish literature.

The Alliance taught adult immigrants English with the aid of Yiddish-speaking instructors. Some five hundred students attended (while a thousand waited for space), the day workers going at night, the night workers going during the day. The immigrants of whatever age were saturated with the English language, so that in a short time the Yiddish brought from Eastern Europe was liberally sprinkled with English words and phrases.

The Friday-evening forums conducted at the Alliance were famous for the quality of the speakers and the liveliness of the discussion. One winter, for instance, the series dealt almost entirely with labor issues— trade unions, strikes, arbitration, cooperation versus competition.

One of the favorite teachers at the Alliance was a non-Jew, Edward King. Born in Massachusetts in 1848, King started as a reporter and editor and then poured his talents and energy into the labor movement and the fight for civil liberties. Deeply sympathetic with the ghetto Jews, he wrote one of the best novels on Lower East Side life (*Joseph Zalmonah*). He taught history at the Alliance and exerted a strong influence on the intellectual growth of the newcomers. Abraham Cahan, his close friend, said that King "became a kind of patriarchal uncle in our little world of Russian-Jewish immigrants."

How a man like King could affect the immigrants whose lives he touched is depicted in the memoirs of Maurice Hindus. As a youngster, Hindus wandered by chance into one of King's evening lectures. He left this impression of the man:

> On a small platform beside a stand piled with books, some of them open, stood a short stocky man with a rolling abdomen and a lofty forehead. He wore glasses, and his eyes were overhung by brows as massive and gray as his mustache. He spoke with a fluency, a fervor that held his audience entranced. So many were the learned words he used that I understood only a small part of what he was saying. Yet I too found myself immersed in the lecture. The warmth of the man, the melodiousness of his voice, the magnificence of his diction stirred me. Sweat shone on his brow, and he frequently wiped it with a handkerchief. On and on he spoke, earnestly, thoughtfully, and neither he nor his audience showed the least fatigue. The thrill of hearing him was all the greater because of my identification of words that I had learned from the dictionary and my study book, but that I had never used and never had heard anyone else use.

When the lecture was over, Hindus stayed for the discussion and was noticed by King after most of the audience had left. "Reaching out his hand, he greeted me with a hearty handshake and a word of welcome. Then I knew that, so far as he was concerned, my knee pants did not matter." He asked the boy a few questions about himself. Hindus said his hardest job was to master English. King suggested the better way was not to memorize words out of a dictionary and textbook but to start reading a novel that would be easier to understand and more interesting to follow. He advised Hindus to jot down words he didn't know and after finishing a page look them up in a dictionary, write out their definitions, and memorize them. Then he was to reread the page, and if he knew all the words, go on in the same way to the next page and the next till he finished the book.

Hindus came back the next week and King gave him George Eliot's *Adam Bede* to start with. Hindus followed his advice, and to his immense joy his knowledge of the language grew very rapidly. Visiting King in his small apartment on the Lower East Side, Hindus found it overflowing with books. They cluttered the rooms and hallway and when King's pupils dropped by he would pull some out and talk fascinatingly about the joy of collecting them and reading them. It was a life centered on his books and his students, a life that gave life to generations of immigrants.

Every city the immigrants poured into had its version of an Educational Alliance. In Boston it was Hale House, located on Garland Street in the center of the slum where Mary Antin lived. In her *Promised Land* she tells how Hale House molded the children on the street corners into "noble men and women." To her the settlement was the lighthouse which guided the immigrants through "the perilous torrents of tenement life." Its Natural History Club, through its meetings and frequent field trips to woods and shore, made her into an enthusiastic amateur naturalist.

Hull-House on Chicago's Halsted Street, founded in 1889, became perhaps the best known example of the settlement movement in America. The settlement workers—Jane Addams, Ellen Starr, Florence Kelley, Alice Hamilton—wanted more meaningful lives for those who lived in the city's poverty. Instead of doing traditional charity work from a safe distance, they went to live among the poor. They soon realized they could never transform the slums without reforming the city, the state, the nation—in fact, the whole social and political fabric of America. In spite of their intense commitment, they often failed to make large or lasting improvement in immigrant life. But they did point to a dynamic current of change, and they succeeded in helping many individual immigrants, especially those ambitious to break free of slum and sweatshop.

One of those who came to Hull-House was Philip Davis, a Jewish immigrant from Russia. He called the settlement his "university of good will, good English, good citizenship." After study at the University of Chicago and Harvard, he became himself a settlement worker and an author. In his autobiography he said this of the settlement's leader:

> Jane Addams had the happy faculty of liking people of diverse back-grounds. Unlike critics of the immigrants of that day, she encouraged us to build proudly on what was most valuable in our heritage. I remember her listening sympathetically to the account of my boyhood in Motol, of my aunt Weizmann, my little village, and the wedding ceremony. Through such personal conversations with her neighbors on Halsted Street (with Greeks, Italians, Poles, Russians, and many others) she acquired an impressive knowledge of old-world cultures transplanted in part to this nation.

To encourage pride in national heritage, Hull-House created a theater where the immigrants could present plays in their native tongues. Greeks, Poles, Lithuanians, Russians took great pleasure in this opportunity to educate the ignorant Americans. By 1900 the settlement had its own theater group, the Hull-House Players, which earned national recognition for its professional quality. Typical of its achievement was the production of plays written by immigrants. Hilda Satt, who came from the Warsaw ghetto to Chicago in the 1890s, began working in a factory at thirteen, and had her first play, dealing with working-class life, presented at Hull-House.

The settlement houses were but one example of Jews helping Jews in a time of need. The mitzvah—the doing of a good deed—was carried out in dozens of different ways. The old charitable societies, founded in the mid-nineteenth century, multiplied their clients. But many new organizations were formed under the pressure of the mass influx. They tended to become more specialized, more sophisticated. At first they helped the immigrants with food, lodging, medical services, and jobs, following no general plan, overlapping in function and control, sometimes confused and inefficient. Until, in the early 1900s, the Hebrew Immigrant Aid

Society integrated and centralized the work of receiving the newcomers and offering them assistance.

Special responsibility for immigrant women was assumed by the National Council of Jewish Women. It began with a small refuge on Orchard Street "to keep single girls from the hands of the white slavers." Located near a district where prostitution flourished, the refuge helped the young women find jobs and housed them until they could support themselves.

Gradually the immigrant-aid groups learned to unite their fund raising, to substitute professionals for volunteer help, and to plan and spend by "scientific" design. But the immigrants didn't wait to be helped. They resented having nothing to say about the policy of institutions trying to help them. They were angry when their customs, their habits, even their religion, were put down by the kind ladies and gentlemen doing the volunteer work. They feared the wedge being driven between themselves and their children. Falling back upon their own resources, they turned first to their hometown groups—*landsmanshaft* made up of Jews from the same village or neighborhood in the old country. They aided each other through medical, unemployment, and strike insurance. They provided interest-free loans, sick benefits and disability payments, funeral costs and burial plots. This was better, they felt—taking part in the mutual aid of your own group rather than accepting charitable patronage. Just as important was the deep need to join with your friends in maintaining some connection with the old country, with the life of the past. They were trying to make the *landsmanshaft* take the place of the shtetl.

In the Old World the shul, the synagogue, had been the center of Jewish communal life. But in America the synagogues multiplied in chaotic fashion. Religion was no longer so important in bonding Jews together. The divisive pressures of big-city living led the immigrants to seek outside the synagogue for the satisfaction of social needs. So the religious societies that had once provided social benefits too gave way to a variety of groups, large and small, such as the *landsmanshaft*. Hundreds of them in New York and other cities reached into almost every immigrant home. In nearly every household was the *pushke,* the little collection box to hold the pennies destined for scores of charitable causes.

The self-help groups founded their own orphanages, hospitals, and homes for the elderly. Only this way could they be sure of a kosher diet and the warm Jewish atmosphere they desired. They organized societies for helping widows, children, prisoners, unwed mothers, the deaf, the blind, the tubercular, the retarded, the crippled.

It didn't take long to see how much better it would be if these random efforts were pulled together. The Federation of Jewish Philanthropies became the means for coordinating all such agencies. The American Jewish Committee was formed in defense of Jewish interests here and overseas. When World War I broke out, the American Jewish Joint Distribution Committee was shaped out of existing organizations to carry on relief work in Europe. As the war came to an end, the American Jewish Congress was organized to work for the establishment of a Jewish national home in Palestine and for the defense of the civil rights of Jews everywhere.

32

My Parents Don't Understand

In the passage from the culture of Eastern Europe to the broader stream of American modernity, much that was Jewish was often thrown overboard. The major centers of Jewish life—the home, the synagogue, and the school—were gradually deserted.

"I want to forget," said Mary Antin, "sometimes I long to forget. . . . It is painful to be consciously of two worlds. The Wandering Jew in me seeks forgetfulness." It was easy to Americanize her name and her clothes, harder to drop Yiddish and master English, but she managed to do that and quickly too, proud that she even learned "to think in English without an accent."

But what could she do about her father? That middle-aged man from Polotzk—he was too obviously Eastern European and Jewish to keep up with his Mashke-called-Mary. In spite of how he tried, he would always, she said, be "hindered by a natural inability to acquire the English language." He was tied to the monumental past, but not Mary. "I am the youngest of America's children," she said. Polotzk was gone forever.

For the freedom to be an individual, the Jewish immigrants risked the dissolution of their group. Everything which America might find foreign they must decide whether to discard. Mary Antin moved speedily to adopt the American way of life. But no one forced her to. In America the process of making your way into the broader community was as fast or as slow as you chose to move. If you liked, you could remain in the ghetto until you died. This was a big country, with room for Lower East Sides in whatever city you picked to live.

Inevitably the movement toward assimilation led to conflict between the immigrants and their American-born children. When the older generation tried to keep elements of their native culture it often made the children ashamed of their parents. Children need a sense of security and a feeling of acceptance if they are to enjoy healthy emotional growth. The transplanted immigrant parents had a degree of both security and acceptance in their relations with immigrants of their own kind among whom they usually lived in the new country. But their children grew up with bilingual and bicultural conflicts at home, in the school, and on the playground. They lacked their parents' memories of the old country to give them rootedness and security and a sense of their own value. And if they turned to their parents with questions about the new country, the answer was often, "I don't know."

Worse, whatever marked the child's parents as foreign labeled them as inferior. To win acceptance the child had to make himself into an "American." It meant rebellion against parental authority; and often too it meant contempt for one's own ethnic identity. Everything that was Jewish (or Italian or Polish or Armenian or Greek or . . .) was rejected. Evelyn W. Hersey, who studied the American-born children of immigrant parents, concluded, "I have come to believe that this pervasive feeling of rejection of 'foreignness' is felt by all second-generation young people no matter how secure and adequate they seem."

The influence of everything American was irresistible. The immigrants found themselves suddenly the parents of *American* children. They felt astonishment, shock, pride, regret, but what could they do about it? They were helpless in the face of the glorification of America and the passionate desire of children to be exactly like their schoolmates.

Jim was the sixteen-year-old son of Jewish immigrants who lived in a California neighborhood mostly of non-Jews. Interviewed in *Survey* magazine, he talked of his conflicts with his parents.

I don't like to bring my American friends around. They were born here and so were their parents. My mother speaks "English" to them, and they make fun of her. When I ask her to leave them alone she says: "They are only goyim [Gentiles], ain't I good enough to entertain them?" Sure, she "entertains" them—at my expense. My father won't allow us to play ball on the lot. He says it's a waste of time and a disgrace to make such a lot of noise over nothing. He was raised in Poland. But then he don't believe in sweatshops either, but has never been anything but a cutter in a sweatshop. It's awfully embarrassing to bring any American friends to the house. . . .

My parents don't believe in beaches and never go swimming. I don't like to stay home, and my parents don't understand what boys need, and they expect me to be old-fashioned and go to *shul.*

I have never taken very much stock in religion. I don't see any sense in it. Our Sabbath begins Friday at sunset, but my father works in the shop all day Saturday. Oh, he sighs and hopes to be in the land of the "faithful" before he dies, but that don't help him any. I don't see why a faithful people should suffer and be laughed at like we are. My parents nag me to go to *shul* on holidays. They make many sacrifices to keep their traditions, but they don't mean anything much in my life. . . . That's just why I don't like to stay home. I don't want to hurt my parents and I can't follow their advice.

Few of the Jewish (or other) immigrants escaped the clash of cultures. Some parents bitterly fought off any change which might weaken the values they brought with them. Others, seeing it was a losing battle, resigned themselves to maintaining their culture for themselves while tolerating their children's adoption of new beliefs and behavior. A third group, determined to keep close bonds with their children, gave up their own culture and plunged into Americanization themselves. ("If you can't lick 'em, join 'em.")

The Jewish education centers—the cheder and the Hebrew school— were another source of conflict between parents and children. The immigrant generation started them, but the American-born generation turned away from them. While the parents gave wholehearted support to the public schools, they wanted their children to get a Jewish education as well. That meant schooling in the Torah and the Talmud. Here it had to be confined to hours outside the public-school sessions.

All over the Lower East Side, cheders sprang up to offer Jewish tutoring. They were schools privately owned and operated by individual rebbes (teachers), many of them ill prepared. It was learning by slapping. The pupils were crowded into a single small room, often in a cellar. Fees were fifty cents to a dollar a month.

Teachers and cheder are sketched by Henry Roth in his novel of East Side childhood, *Call It Sleep*.

> He was not at all like the teachers at school. . . . He appeared old and was certainly untidy. He wore soft leather shoes like house-slippers, that had no place for either laces or buttons. His trousers were baggy and stained, a great area of striped and crumpled shirt intervened between his belt and his bulging vest. The knot of his tie, which was nearer one ear than the other, hung away from his soiled collar. What features were visible were large and had an oily gleam. Beneath his skull-cap, his black hair was closely cropped. Though full of misgivings about his future relations with the rabbi, David felt that he must accept his fate. Was it not his father's decree that he attend a cheder? . . .
>
> David sat down, and the rabbi walked back to his seat beside the window. Instead of sitting down, however, he reached under his chair, and bringing out a short-thonged cat-o'-nine-tails, struck the table loudly with the butt-end and pronounced in a menacing voice: "Let there be a hush among you!" And a scared silence instantly locking all mouths, he seated himself. He then picked up a little stick lying on the table and pointed to the book, whereupon a boy sitting next to him began droning out sounds in a strange and secret tongue.

Other schools—the Talmud Torahs—were supported by the community. They were designed to give an elementary Jewish education to both boys and girls, rich or poor. There were a variety of kinds, arising from the different religious and social trends struggling for supremacy within the Jewish community. But they diminished in numbers as parents and children alike grew unwilling to see so much time given to what seemed to matter less and less. The schools did not produce students really at home in the Hebrew language and familiar with its scriptures and literature. And what use was Jewish education in an American society where religion played no central role?

Rather than require children to attend two separate schools—the public and the Jewish—some parents organized all-day schools in which the curriculum was divided between Jewish studies and general studies.

These ran from kindergarten through high school and were supported by tuition fees and contributions.

The Jewish religious schools failed to attract or keep more than a fraction of the immigrants' children. "Jewishness, Hebrew learning, and tradition," as Azriel Eisenberg pointed out, "were equated with foreignness, squalor, and boredom, and thus came to be regarded with contempt and antagonism."

It was the same with youthful attendance at the synagogue. These multiplied rapidly as the Eastern European immigration rose. In 1880 there were 270 in New York. By 1916 the number was 1,900. But most of the congregations were small. Only ten Jews are needed to form a congregation and they are free to worship as they desire. Jews from one shtetl or neighborhood in the old country (*landsleit* they were called) converted stores or tenement flats into their own tiny houses of worship. The religion that had governed their lives from birth was still vital to them. But much less so to their children.

Trying to explain this to a New York *Tribune* reporter in 1903, the head of the Educational Alliance, Dr. David Blaustein, underscored the enormous difference between the role of the synagogue in czarist Russia and its role in the United States.

The Jew [in the old country] is never interfered with in his religious observances. He simply loses, on account of them, all civic and economic rights. He pays for his religious liberty with the latter. His church has infinitely greater power and importance in Russia than in America. The rabbi keeps all the vital statistics. The rabbi marries and divorces. The rabbi has charge of all education. He also acts as a court in both civil and criminal cases. . . . At every turn of the road the Jew's religion is recognized. He is taxed as a Jew, enlisted as a Jew. . . . You can imagine the confusion in the immigrant's mind when he reaches America. He finds his church of no account whatever. No one cares what church he belongs to or whether he belongs to any church or not. The state delegates no rights or powers to the church. All that is asked is whether he is an American or not. . . . In place of finding the congregation all powerful and all embracing, he finds when he joins a congregation that he has simply joined a liberal society . . . a mutual benefit society . . . a club-room where the men meet to talk over old times, read letters from home, discuss politics . . . or study the Talmud. . . . Religious services are also

held, with one of their number, not necessarily an ordained rabbi, acting
as leader.

Still, there was a loyalty to modern Jewish spiritual values which
many immigrants did not want to give up. Resisting the American
pressure for total assimilation, they wanted to see Jewish group life
strengthened. They opposed the early Jewish socialists who envisioned
a society in which all national differences would be erased. They
believed nationalism could be a creative force for spiritual and cultural
betterment. Intellectuals like Chaim Zhitlowsky (1865–1943) exerted a
powerful influence campaigning for the opening of Jewish secular
schools to teach modern Jewish culture centered on the Yiddish language. This, they believed, would help bind Jews together so that they
could continue creatively as a people.

The Labor Zionists were the first to open such a school, in 1910.
Within a few years there were two other programs following the
secularist trend in Jewish education—the Workmen's Circle schools and
the Sholem Aleichem schools. Eventually it was realized that teaching
the Jewish religion "from a cultural historical standpoint" was necessary to explain to children why Jews are what they are. All three types
of schools came to recognize Bar Mitzvah and to celebrate Jewish
holidays in both their childhood and adult-education programs.

With the stress shifting from religious to secular learning, the model
for the young to pattern their lives upon was no longer the rabbi or the
Talmudist but the professional or the scholar.

But before the flight from the ghetto turned into a stampede, there
was an extraordinary time when a secular Jewish culture flourished
in America.

33

Cahan and the Cafés

After generations of censorship, what must it feel like to know sudden freedom to speak, write, assemble, organize, think as you please? How different America was from the czarist prison house! The immigrant Jews rushed to exercise their new-found right of expression. Liberated journalists, pamphleteers, orators, poets, novelists, dramatists, actors exploded with an energy and intelligence that astounded the outside world.

One of the newcomers who landed at the beginning of the mass immigration was Abraham Cahan. When he arrived in 1882, the Yiddish-speaking population was about a quarter million. The shul was their only institution. There was no Jewish press, no literature, no theater, no labor movement, no political party. Cahan's would be the most powerful hand in the shaping of the cultural life of the immigrant community.

Cahan was born in 1860 in a Lithuanian shtetl, the only child of a poor family which moved to Vilna before he was six. He studied at a yeshiva, went to a government school, began reading Russian writers, and lost his faith in Judaism. While working as a Jewish teacher he joined the revolutionary underground plotting to overthrow czarism.

When Alexander II was assassinated in 1881 he escaped arrest and fled to the United States. He learned English quickly and began teaching it to immigrants. Plunging into New York's radical movement, he became a noted speaker, giving the first lectures in Yiddish on socialism. Soon he was reporting in English for the New York newspapers while editing and writing for the Yiddish socialist press at the same time. In 1897 he helped found the Jewish socialist daily, the *Forward* (*Forverts*), but soon left it to work in English as a reporter for the New York daily press. He published short stories and novels in English which dealt with immigrant life in the tenements and sweatshops of the Lower East Side. He became the friend of men like the muckraking reporter Lincoln Steffens and the novelist William Dean Howells. In 1902 he returned to the *Forward,* which he edited with absolute control for almost fifty years.

His plan was to put out a paper for the Jewish immigrant masses, not just for the small group of socialists at whom the Yiddish press usually aimed. His target was an audience unfamiliar with a daily paper. (There had been no Yiddish daily in Russia.) To arouse interest he adapted the methods of the big New York papers—sensational news stories topped by screaming headlines, reader contests, features on love and sex. But at the same time he meant to hang on to the Jewish workers who were passionately involved in labor and socialist activity. For them he published articles by the leading European socialists, novels by such men as Sholem Asch and I. J. Singer, and poems by dozens of Yiddish writers.

If numbers are proof, Cahan succeeded. He built the *Forward* from a circulation of 6,000 in 1902 to a peak of 250,000 in the late 1920s. During the earlier years the *Forward* was a great force for organizing the Jewish trade unions and the Socialist Party. The paper wrote about the need to organize, to fight for higher wages and lower hours, for decent treatment by the bosses, for a new and better social system. At the same time Cahan led the paper in a campaign to speed the Americanization of his readers. He taught the largely uneducated masses of the pre-1905 migration their cultural ABCs. But, his critics said, he never carried them beyond. He kept to the elementary level of Anglo-Saxon manners and mores, with editorials on how to use a handkerchief instead of the sleeve or how to set a table properly. He showed a great talent for popularization, making the contents of the *Forward* appealing to the nonsocialist immigrants he was trying to bring closer to the movement.

One of his best-read innovations was "Das Bintel Brief" ("A Sheaf of Letters"), a daily feature started in 1906. It gave readers a chance to express themselves through letters to the paper. A flood of mail began to come in daily, readers opening their hearts to others, describing their personal problems, seeking advice, approval, consolation. It was a timely outlet for a mass of immigrants deeply troubled by the tensions of a new life, so vastly different in custom and code from what they had lived by in the old country. There they could take their troubles to the rabbi. Here they could seek help from the editor. They wrote about poverty, hunger, sickness, about love and divorce, about joblessness, intermarriage, loss of faith in Judaism, or on socialism, about parents versus children. . . . Often the questions raised were thrown open for public discussion and readers sent in their opinions. Women became the closest followers of "Das Bintel Brief" and the most frequent contributors.

As editor, Cahan insisted on getting a "Yiddish Yiddish" from his writers. He rejected the stilted form of Germanized Yiddish in favor of a plain Yiddish the ordinary Jews spoke at home and at work. He encouraged his writers to follow the general custom of incorporating incorrectly pronounced English words into their Yiddish articles, thus opening himself to the charge of corrupting the language. Yiddish writers who loved their language attacked Cahan for spitting on it. He was promoting *shund,* they said, meaning he was serving up a cheap mixture of vulgarity and sentimentality. Cahan's defense was that it worked: his readers liked the penny paper—circulation, advertising, and profits kept rising. One of his colleagues, Melech Epstein, said that while Cahan built the *Forward* into a powerful medium, he learned too much from William Randolph Hearst.

The *Forward,* while the leading Yiddish daily, was only one of nearly a hundred Jewish papers born between 1885 and 1900. In New York alone, about twenty Yiddish dailies came to life in the great immigration period. "The Yiddish press," says one of its critics, Lucy Dawidowicz, "had a violent and extremist tone, whether politically conservative and Orthodox or radical and antireligious. The irresponsible tone, with slashing accusations directed against government, capital, Jewish institutions, or competing papers, was due partly to the license spawned by American freedom, and partly to the lessons learned from the yellow journalism that William Randolph Hearst was then cultivating."

Whatever its weaknesses, this was the press that nourished the migrating Jewish millions in their own language. And that language? Harry Roskolenko defines it.

> Yiddish was a language of journalism that was indeed new to America but old, for those who could read, in Eastern Europe. There it had come into its own as a wanderer's speech, picking up, after its basic "German," words in Russian, Polish, Romanian, Hungarian—and the related words and sounds that came with the borrowings of many tongues. Each country had added special words or words had been altered by accents, to merge with the Jewish created during the Middle Ages—and to add confusion as well as cohesion to East Broadway's variegated readers of Yiddish. On the wide streets were editors, satirists, playwrights, novelists—and working journalists, often the same people. A poet, too, was always a journalist—in order to make some sort of living, when he was not, too often, working in a factory. . . . No matter what a man did, it was done with accents, flavors, and gusto in his speech. It was a Yiddish of many variations and humor that one Jew spoke to another, and what they said dealt with what they did.

Among the other prominent Jewish papers was *The Day,* directed to a more literary and scholarly audience, and with an English section to help integration along. It was Democratic and Zionist, and purist in its approach to Yiddish. The *Morning Journal* was both Republican and Orthodox. For the anarchists there was *Der Freie Arbeiter Stimme (The Free Worker's Voice),* which was still going in the early 1970s, eighty years after its birth. And for the Communists there was the *Freiheit,* founded in 1922. Assessing them as a group, Judd Teller concluded, "The caliber of their serious material surpassed anything that the metropolitan press has ever offered. . . ." Morris R. Cohen, too, thought the Yiddish press did more than the English press for the education of its readers. "It tried to give its readers something of enduring and substantial value. . . . The Yiddish press has prepared millions of Jewish people to take a worthy part in American civilization while also promoting the natural self-respect to which Jews are entitled because of their character and history."

East Broadway was where most of the Yiddish papers were published in those years. The journalists met in the lunchrooms and over herring, bread, and tea damned one another's pieces, politics, and papers. Their work was often sentimental and primitive, its main impulse to evoke tears. But when Yiddish was not crying, said Roskolenko, who used to peddle the papers, it could reach the level of the best world press.

The one-block triangle where East Broadway, Canal, and Division streets met was called Rutgers Square. At the turn of the century it became for the Lower East Side what the Piazza San Marco was for Venice or St. Stephen's Platz for Vienna. S. L. Blumenson, who knew it in those years, recalls what it was like.

> During the day Rutgers Square was a quiet business district, but with the coming of darkness it erupted "kultur" like an active volcano: religion and atheism, free love and vegetarianism, politics and ideologies. But in peace. The presence of our neighbor, Thomas Mulvaney, and the "billy" in his belt, gave *kapuler untzuherenes* (tactful hints) that culture would not be disturbed.

Nearby in a basement was the café called Zum Essex, whose owner (and cook) was Sigmund Manilescu, a dignified Rumanian Jew. There the feuding factionalists of the worlds of politics and art adjourned from the street corners or theaters to continue their disputes.

> The Zum Essex was famous for its lavish cuisine. Sigmund served a five-course dinner (supper) consisting of soup, meat, potato, stewed prunes, and all the pumpernickel one could eat, for the price of twelve cents. (To Litvaks he made a concession: he served herring and onion instead of soup.) In addition, any steady customer could come in any time for a free glass of seltzer. On Friday night, the Sabbath meal, he added generous portions of gefilte fish, with strong horseradish flavored with beet juice. Sigmund was as proud of his horseradish as a French chef is of his special salad dressing. A moment's pause for soda water. It was fizzing seltzer flavored with a dollop of syrup, and in those days it cost a penny a glass. The favorite flavors were vanilla, chocolate, strawberry, raspberry, lemon and mint, shelved in colored bottles to tempt the eye. For two cents the glass was a bit bigger and the syrup a bit richer. But who had two cents?

On the south side of East Broadway was the meeting place of the Brotherly Beneficial and Kultur Society.

Its purpose was to help needy brothers in distress and to spread Kultur through lectures (pronounced "lektzyes"), discussions and *forlezungen* (readings). During the business part of the meetings the members addressed each other with the title of *bruder* (brother); during political discussions as *genosse* (comrade); during cultural debate as *kolege* (colleague), with the hard "g." It was considered an insult to be called *bruder* or *genosse* when engaged in cultural pursuits. . . .

Once a week, on Friday nights, there were popular lectures by members of the unemployed pool of lecturers. The persecutions in Russia had driven many writers, intellectuals, and students into exile, and some by way of Germany and Paris and London came to the East Side seeking employment. Among these were names like Feigenbaum, Zametkin, Winchevsky, Girizansky, Kats, Selivokits, Philip Krantz, Jacob Magidoff, Hermalin, Kobrin, Zevin, and later Chaim Zhitlowsky and many others who were to become well-known journalists and authors.

An actor and artist called Kolege Lebel, a member of the Kultur committee, had a special contribution to make. Blumenson, his second cousin, describes what it was.

Lebel was an exponent of the Little Theater movement and directed a little theater group made up of some of the members of the Society and their girl friends. He favored such plays as *Der Yiddisher Kenig Lear, Der Yiddisher Hamlet, Der Yiddisher Rober fun Schiller, Di Yiddishe Medea, Di Yiddishe Veber fun Hauptmann, Di Yiddishe Verzunkene Glocke, Got, Mensh un Teufel* by Jacob Gordin, and most of all, *The Bells* by Emile Erekmann. Nice *light* plays, as you can see. Lebel's whole spare time was devoted to the theater. . . .

Lebel was also in great demand by many East Side radical organizations for staging *"lebedige pikches,"* dramatic clusters of living statues, at their annual balls. . . . At all these joyous occasions half the space was usually occupied with the posturrngs of Kolege Lebel's groups. In one corner five or six miners were dying of silicosis, and their wives and small children, faces full of talcum powder, were starving to death. Another group featured consumptive garment workers coughing away over their sewing machines, while a boss with an artificially bloated stomach stood over them with a whip. Lebel's artistic groupings were greatly enjoyed by everyone and were praised in the radical press.

On the north side of East Broadway was the meeting place of the Kolege's hated rivals, the youthful anarchists of the Pioneers of Freedom. "Most of them were in their teens," said Blumenson, "newly arrived from the small towns and villages of Russia and Galicia and Poland, where they had been compelled to follow small-town *derech eretz* (conventions) and the strict rules of Orthodoxy. Now they were behaving like young colts let out to pasture for the first time." They loved to sing and dance, and to welcome arriving exiles with banquets. The feasts, prepared by the Zum Essex for nine cents a guest, were topped off by fizzing seltzer toasts to the honored guest and hymns to the coming revolution. To spite God, the anarchists sometimes held their celebrations in their own clubrooms, where "they served ham sandwiches, smearing loads of sharp mustard to kill the taste, and tea *with milk*." It shocked the Orthodox on the East Side, who called such outrageous affairs *chazer* (pig) parties.

The real intellectual comrades, says Blumenson, met on Norfolk Street in Sachs' Café.

There the "cream" of the *radikalen* gathered nightly, and over Mrs. Sachs's fine coffee and famous cheesecake discussed the problems and philosophies of the day. Unlike the *genessen* in Herrick's Café, there was no gesticulation or noisy argument. These were mannerly, *gemuetliche* intellectuals, exiles and martyrs of world revolution, graduates of many famous universities.

At one table would be Comrade Solataroff, well-known lecturer and exponent of world revolution. Beside him Comrade Kats, editor of *Die Freie Gezelshaft*, the Yiddish anarchist weekly opposing the policies of editor Yanofsky of the *Freie Arbeiter Stimme*. . . . At Comrade Yanofsky's table sat the "Poet of Revolt," Edelstadt, the "Yiddisher François Villon," reciting his latest epic to a fascinated audience. There was "Grandpa" Netter, a bearded patriarch, a great Talmudist, who in his old age repudiated Orthodoxy and joined the Comrades. With him was his daughter, Chaverte (fem: *chaver,* comrade) Netter, young and good-looking and devoted to the holy cause. At other tables were slummers, members of the English-language press looking for local color, and occasionally members of the Bomb Squad, in very evident disguise.

There were cafés of all kinds, some of them only smelly saloons in damp and dirty cellars where the beer, the kvass, and the schnapps tasted sour. There were cafés for domino players where the game was everything and cafés for newspaper readers where men hid behind the pages and slurped tea from saucers while they groaned over the news from the old country. Above all, the cafés were forums for argumentative Jews, and there was never a shortage of these. Harry Roskolenko heard them all as he peddled his papers inside.

> The talkers were men of extraordinary abilities—as talkers. Talk was the major art of the cafés with these aristocrats of rhetoric, the bringers of useless data, as they competed with their compote-quotes about all things of value. In this free arena, the circus without measure, it was the claque that each man had that denoted the worth of the speaker-orator-lecturer-statesman-*schnorrer.* It was private meandering, public pontificating—and no decisions; for the talk went on for weeks or until one speaker suddenly decided that the dead end was truly dead. Running out of his audience, he moved to another café. There he built another circus with newer spectators, philosophers—and kibitzers, for they could not always be told apart easily. . . .
>
> Ideas about God, the synagogue, the union, intermeshed. It was difficult, then, for me to see how men could be two things—like Zionist-anarchists; or Zionists who were also atheists; or socialists who were Zionists and atheists. It was like a chess game—with no rules. . . . Who was not at least two or three separate spiritual and physical entities on the Lower East Side? My father managed socialism, Orthodoxy and Zionism, quite easily, and so did the kibitzers and the serious.

34

Actors and Poets

The Yiddish theater rivaled the Yiddish press in popular appeal. The actors were even greater folk heroes than the journalists. For cold print could hardly match the living stage in evoking an electric response from the Jewish immigrants. The origins of the Yiddish theater are traced back to the traditional Purim play, which dramatized annually the Book of Esther. The religious occasion was the only time that Eastern European Jews could enjoy public entertainment. In the mid-nineteenth century the rigid ban on secular drama relaxed in Rumania, where Yiddish singers and instrumentalists of Hasidic background began to entertain in the cafés of the cities. Hasidic folk material was gradually worked up into skits which framed the songs.

The first playwright was Abraham Goldfaden, a Russian Jew who became a teacher and wrote poems and songs in Hrbrew and Yiddish. Unable to support his family, he went into business, failed, and then tried journalism, moving to Rumania to edit a paper. Encouraged by a Yiddish café entertainer who sang his songs, he began in 1876 to write musical plays for his own traveling theatrical troupe. Other companies arose, sustained by a Jewish audience hungry for this kind of entertainment. In 1879 Goldfaden took his troupe touring in southern Russia, recruiting new actors on the road. Many of them were to achieve stardom later on East Side stages.

The few Yiddish playwrights limited themselves at first to domestic comedy. Then they turned to Jewish folk material and Biblical sources, converting them into historical operettas. Their next step was to adapt plays on Jewish themes written by Gentiles, putting them into Yiddish. In 1883 the growth of the infant art was suddenly choked off by the czar; he issued a ban on all Yiddish theater in Russia. The fledgling dramatists and actors had to go abroad to start new theaters. Some went to Germany, to England, to Rumania; one group, with Joseph Lateiner as playwright, headed for America. In 1884 the company gave its first performance in New York, on East Fourth Street, and later established the Oriental Theater on the Bowery. (Two years earlier a group of amateurs, composed chiefly of the Thomashefsky family from Kiev, had performed briefly on the Bowery.)

By the turn of the century there were three major Yiddish theaters flourishing on the Bowery, employing some eighty professional actors who performed the works of about a dozen prolific playwrights. (The combined output of three of them ran to over three hundred plays.) Goldfaden's charming folk operas—*Shmendrik* and *The Two Kuni-Lemels*— remained a staple of the repertory, but other writers had taken over the creation of new material. Two of them, Lateiner and Moshe Horowitz, "together brought Yiddish theater to a new low," as Ronald Sanders put it. Horowitz, who dominated the Windsor Theater, wrote more than 160 plays, largely romantic and inaccurate adaptations of Jewish history. They were clumsy, conventional melodramas, "full of historical plunder," as one critic charged. One reason for the superabundance and low quality was the short run most plays had. They rarely went over twelve performances and often had only three or four. The dramatists sold their rights for as little as $25 to $85. The audience, which had never seen professional theater in the old country, was an easy victim of trash.

The most favored playwright of the Yiddish audiences for some time was Joseph Lateiner. As feverish a writer as Horowitz, he ground out over one hundred plays, "no one of which," commented Hutchins Hapgood, "has form or ideas." They were a mishmash of melodrama and vaudeville—exactly what, Lateiner insisted, his audience wanted. Hapgood, who went to see them, said they were "the very spirit of formlessness—burlesque, popularly vulgar jokes, flat heroism combining about the flimsiest dramatic structure." To intellectual critics Lateiner was a businessman, not an artist. He often wrote directly for the star of his company at the Thalia—Boris Thomashefsky (1868–1939). Boris, "young, fat, with curling black hair, languorous eyes . . . was thought very beautiful by the girls of the ghetto," said Hapgood. With Jacob P. Adler (1855–1926) and David Kessler (1860–1920) Boris shared the heights of popularity in that era.

The three Yiddish theaters they performed in expressed the world of the Lower East Side. The performances drew the entire community, wrote Hapgood.

> Into these three buildings crowd the Jews of all the ghetto classes, the sweatshop woman with her baby, the day laborer, the small Hester Street shopkeeper, the Russian-Jewish anarchist and socialist, the ghetto rabbi and scholar, the poet, the journalist. The poor and ignorant are in the great majority, but the learned, the intellectual, and the progressive are also represented, and here, as elsewhere, exert a more than numerically proportionate influence on the character of the theatrical productions, which, nevertheless, remain essentially popular. The socialists and the literati create the demand that forces into the mass of vaudeville, light opera and historical and melodramatic plays a more serious art element, a simple transcript from life or the theatric presentation of a ghetto problem. But this more serious element is so saturated with the simple manners, humor, and pathos of the life of the poor Jews that it is seldom above the heartfelt understanding of the crowd.

On the first four weekdays the theaters were sold out to clubs, lodges, and unions for benefit performances. It was the beginning of the theater-party system. On weekends—Friday, Saturday, and Sunday nights—the tickets were bought directly by playgoers at twenty-five cents to a dollar.

> On these nights the theater presents a peculiarly picturesque sight. Poor workingmen and women with their babies of all ages fill the theater. Great enthusiasm is manifested, sincere laughter and tears accompany the sincere acting on the stage. Peddlers of soda water, candy, of fantastic gewgaws of many kinds, mix freely with the audience between the acts. Conversation during the play is received with strenuous hisses, but the

falling of the curtain is the signal for groups of friends to get together and gossip about the play or the affairs of the week.

The break with the Horowitz-Lateiner brand of theater came through Jacob Gordin. Gordin, born in the Ukraine in 1853, rejected both Orthodoxy and Jewish nationalism when a youth. He married and became editor of a small Russian paper seeking to bring "light, education, and hope" to the Jewish people. In 1891 he came to New York with his wife and eight children. He wrote his first literary sketches in Yiddish for the press, using much dialogue. A meeting with the actor Jacob Adler spurred him to try his hand at playwriting. His first effort, *Siberia,* was in the tragic vein of Russian realism which the East Side intellectuals so admired. Abraham Cahan praised the play as a departure from the secondhand melodrama and predicted it would "bring about a complete revolution on the Yiddish stage." Gordin's next play was *The Pogrom.* He went on to write problem plays about ghetto life, voicing the rebellion against poverty and injustice which brought passionate applause from the socialists in the audience. His play *The Beggar of Odessa* pitted rich villains against the noble poor. In *Vogele* the poor Jews satirized the rich Jews. *Mirele Efros* portrayed Jewish life in old Russia. *Minna* was a drama about a Yiddish Nora in an East Side Doll's House. Gordin's *Jewish King Lear,* adapting Shakespeare to the ghetto, dramatized the painful break between immigrant parents and Americanized children. It was a great success and led Gordin to write more plays based upon the themes and plots of masterpieces of world drama. The note he sounded most frequently was the cry for women's emancipation.

Gordin wrote more than sixty plays, many for Adler, who was the most ardent promoter of serious Yiddish drama. But Kessler and Thomashefsky, too, often performed in Gordin's plays. Sadly, straight realism had a hard time on the Bowery. Even from the actors. They loved to ad-lib dialogue and to improvise whatever action the spirit moved them to try. Gordin had to struggle against them to preserve the integrity of his text. Even so, to win and keep audiences, he sometimes inserted clownish or operatic moments in his work. By the early 1900s he and Adler grew pessimistic about the future of Yiddish drama. They felt commercialism would kill it even before the Americanization of their audiences turned them away from the Yiddish language. But though *shund* persisted, the Yiddish theater experienced a revival during World War I which extended through the 1930s. In 1918 the actor Maurice Schwartz launched the Yiddish Art Theater with a company that included Paul Muni and Jacob Ben-Ami. Plays by Sholem Aleichem, Peretz, Hirschbein, David Pinski, Osip Dimov, Z. Libin, and Leon Kobrin won new audiences for their superior quality. Gordin died in 1909, but his plays, translated into many European languages, are still performed here and abroad.

Was the American theater in any better condition than the Yiddish? Lincoln Steffens thought it worse. He wrote in his autobiography that in those years the best theater in New York City was the Yiddish. Professors of drama used to take their students to see Gordin's plays, likening him to Ibsen (a comparison which hardly stands up today). Still, how many American dramatists were trying to lend aesthetic universality to the daily life around them? In any event, serious Yiddish theater lost ground rapidly when ten-cent vaudeville and the ten-cent movie flooded the East Side.

If Jacob Gordin was considered the great monument of the drama in that pre-World War I era, Morris Rosenfeld is often held up as the peak of Yiddish poetry. "But upon closer examination," says Lucy Dawidowicz, "they appear like Hollywood foam-rubber boulders, an illusion created by distance and accepted as real because of condescending and indulgent literary standards. The Yiddish theater and Yiddish poets like Rosenfeld fascinated outsiders who were captured by the energy and intelligence of the Jewish immigrants. No doubt they felt much like Samuel Johnson about a woman preaching—not that it was done well, but surprised that it was done at all, like a dog walking on its hind legs."

What can be said for that early East Side literature, she goes on, is that "it testifies to the powerful persistence of folk poetry" among the Yiddish-speaking immigrants.

The tradition of writing for the people goes back to the early nineteenth century. Not art for art's sake, but writing for the ordinary reader was the foundation of authentic Yiddish literature. Out of the Haskalah came a new Jewish literature that functioned in two languages— Hebrew and Yiddish. The early Haskalists scorned Yiddish as the jargon of the ignorant masses, the brand of an exiled people. Yet, when two-thirds of the world's Jews spoke not Hebrew but Yiddish, how else could they reach the unenlightened? They were driven to the use of Yiddish.

As the wave of assimilation swept many young people away from Jewish identity, and anti-Semitism peaked in widespread pogroms, Jewish writers began to change their views. The Haskalah "failed to provide us with a philosophy we could live by," said I. L. Peretz. Yiddish writers continued their efforts to modernize Jewish life, but they also fought hard against anti-Semitism and for equal rights for Jews. Jewish nationalism mounted in Eastern Europe. The poet Chaim Nachman Bialik (1873–1934) created a powerful modern idiom in Hebrew but it was through Yiddish, the language of the shtetl, that he and others found their greatest audience. Their goal was to be accessible to the everyday reader. Yes, they wanted to appear in the best literary journals, but they did not cut and trim their work to suit the limited, cultivated audience. They also sought publication in the mass-circulation press.

By the 1890s Yiddish literature had found new soil to grow in. The Jewish masses were moving into the cities and entering the working class. They joined trade unions, went on strike, plunged into socialism, Zionism, Yiddishism, reached out for education and culture. Writers responded to the awakening, and through Yiddish fiction and poetry helped plant new ideas in their readers' minds. Eliakum Zunser (1836–1913) was among the earliest. A Vilna writer, his satires and poems were read and recited, sung and chanted everywhere in the Pale.

Mendele Mocher Sforim (pen name of Sholem Jacob Abramowitz, 1836–1917) earned his living as principal of a Jewish school in Odessa. He began his literary career in Hebrew but soon asked himself what good was this work if his writings were of no use to his people. He turned to Yiddish to depict the tragicomic characters of the Pale, writing bitter novels which cried out to the Jews to struggle for a better life.

One of his great followers was Solomon Rabinowitz (1859–1916), who wrote as Sholem Aleichem. He began in Hebrew too but at twenty-four published the first of those Yiddish stories which would win him universal recognition as the voice of the Jewish people. He was at once a popular entertainer and a major artist.

Another founding father of Jewish literature was Isaac Leib Peretz (1852–1915). He began publishing in Yiddish while still a teenager, practiced law, and then served as a functionary in the Warsaw Jewish

Civic Center. He developed a pithy idiomatic Yiddish that drew upon folk tales to illuminate the Jewish renaissance. Around him flourished Warsaw's Jewish literary life, and to him many young writers came for guidance.

Thus what is called *Yiddishkeit* blossomed. The word means Yiddishness, a Jewish culture linked to the Yiddish language. There was still resistance to its use. The early Jewish socialists, hostile to both Judaism and Jewish culture, rejected Yiddish. Even the Bund, the pioneer Jewish socialist movement in Eastern Europe, at first used Yiddish reluctantly, out of necessity, as the only way to reach the working class. Later the Bundists realized the enormous value of sustaining Jewish culture while building an economic and political movement. And Yiddish became the beloved tongue, the core of their strength. The Zionists, too, in their infant years despised Yiddish and folk culture because they were part of the millennia of exile. It took a while to overcome this negation of everything creative which had emerged in the Diaspora. Eventually all came to find in the culture of *Yiddishkeit* the foundation they could build on.

A major dilemma is the very ground of the existence of *Yiddishkeit*, as Irving Howe and Eliezer Greenberg point out.

> For insofar as the Yiddish writers continued in the path of their own tradition, they could not open themselves sufficiently to the surrounding cultures of Europe and America, nor engage themselves sufficiently with the styles and values of modernity to which they now and again aspired. Yet insofar as they accepted the secular cultures of their time, they risked the loss of historical identity, a rupture with that sacred past which could still stir the skeptics quite as much as the believers. . . . It [*Yiddishkeit*] had always to accept the burden of being at home neither entirely with its past nor entirely with the surrounding nations. Out of its marginality it made a premise for humaneness and out of its strivings to elevate Yiddish into a literary language, an experience of intellectual beauty.

The energy of *Yiddishkeit* generated by Eastern Europe's Jews was carried by the immigrants to America. Of the founding masters, only Sholem Aleichem reached New York, and very late in life. But many younger Yiddish writers came over with the mass migration. The first group, who arrived in the last two decades of the nineteenth century, were called the "sweatshop poets." Their poems grew out of the experiences they shared with the immigrant workers.

The major influence on the early immigrant poets was Morris Winchevsky (1856–1932). He learned about socialism in Russia and Germany, and by twenty-one had published satires and poems in both Hebrew and Yiddish. Expelled from Germany as a revolutionary, he moved to London, where he spent fifteen years as an editor and writer in the Jewish labor movement. In the 1880s he published the first socialist pamphlets to appear in Yiddish. But he was a poet above all, writing fresh Yiddish lyrics about working-class life which won wide readership on both sides of the Atlantic.

When he moved to New York in 1894 he was welcomed as the *zeide* (grandfather) of the Jewish socialist movement. He was, says Melech Epstein, "practically the sole socialist veteran whose internationalism did not contradict his Jewishness." In his role as the great awakener he reached and moved the younger poets.

One of these was David Edelstadt (1866–1892), a childhood witness of the Kiev pogrom of 1881. At sixteen he fled Russia for America and for three long years made buttonholes in a Cincinnati garment factory. He began writing passionate protest poems in the Yiddish he learned from his shopmates, then moved to New York to edit *Die Freie Arbeiter Stimme.* Stricken with tuberculosis, the sweatshop disease, he died at twenty-six. Like Winchevsky's poems, Edelstadt's were set to music and as hymns and marching songs were sung by Jewish workers everywhere.

The revolutionary lyricist Joseph Bovshover (1872–1915) burned out too by the same age, though he lived on much longer. He had a Jewish schooling in Russia and knew Yiddish well when he arrived in New York in 1891. The next year, upon the death of Edelstadt, he wrote an elegy which brought his gift to public attention. Emotionally unstable, he drifted about, living on odd jobs and aid from friends or family. His translation into Yiddish of *The Merchant of Venice* and his lyrics brought him acclaim. But by the age of twenty-six he had sunk into a deep depression and he lived out the rest of his years in a mental institution.

It was Morris Rosenfeld (1862–1923) who received the greatest attention from the non-Jewish world. He was born into a family of fishermen in Poland and given a Jewish education in Warsaw. At eighteen he married, apprenticed briefly in Holland as a diamond cutter, then moved to London, where he worked in sweatshops for three years, writing his poems at night and circulating them among the workers. Poor and sick, he migrated to America in 1886, hearing that the tailors had won a strike which shortened their hours. But in New York it was again the drudgery of fifteen-hour days in the sweatshops, living on stale bread to save the pennies for bringing his wife and children over.

Somehow he managed to study the poetry of great writers, especially Heine, and to attempt the first Yiddish lyrics to abide by the rules of prosody. His best work boiled up out of his hatred for the sweatshop. The poems indicted the system which encouraged the brutal exploitation of man by man. His personal suffering and his anger were powerfully expressed in a simple and idiomatic Yiddish. His was the true voice of the worker. When the first volume of his Yiddish verse appeared, it was highly praised by Professor Leo Wiener of Harvard in *The Nation*. Wiener then edited a prose translation of the poems under the title *Songs of the Ghetto*. Other critics joined in hailing Rosenfeld as an authentic and important poet. Yiddish was coming into its own as a respectable literary medium.

Pleased by this response, wealthy German-American Jews tried to rescue Rosenfeld from the sweatshop by setting him up in a candy-store business. He detested that too and quit to make his living in journalism and on public platforms, reading his poems. His later verse dropped in quality. He was overpraised simply because he was among the first Yiddish poets; he had the painful experience of seeing his reputation grow dimmer and dimmer. But his satiric journalism was always pointed and pungent. His prose, said Joseph Opatoshu, "is as significant as his poetry; perhaps even more so for the historian seeking to familiarize himself with the Jewish life of that period."

It was the immigrants arriving after the failure of the 1905 Revolution in Russia who birthed a new kind of Yiddish writing. They never considered going back to the old country. They struck new roots here which flowered in a new literature. Called "Die Yunge" (The Young), this group rejected the social preaching of the sweatshop poets in favor of an artistic self-sufficiency. They spurned the traditional sentimentalism of the older writers and would not accept the notion that Yiddish was only a tool destined for the junk heap. Another group soon formed, called the Introspectivists. They worked toward modernism and free verse. Neither group was a school or cult, but rather a force protesting mediocrity and struggling for a Yiddish literature whose justification would no longer be as a means of enlightenment but as an artistic end in itself.

Joseph Opatoshu (1886–1954), a Polish Jew who came to New York in 1907 at the age of twenty-one, saw America as a new center of the Diaspora. He cut leather soles in a shoe factory, sewed shirts in a sweatshop, delivered newspapers, and mastered civil engineering. His short stories and novels began to appear in 1910, earning him a major place in Yiddish literature. He had this to say about the Yiddish writers of that time:

> Every people creates spiritual resources; folk resources are created haphazardly. Out of these folk resources artists who can see and listen, with alert senses, create order. Mendele was the greatest among these artists. But there are artists who do not depend upon the resources of the folk. These are insufficient for them. Such artists seek to fathom the power that creates a people, they want to discover if that power is also within them as artists. I know the universe to which Mendele and Rosenfeld belong. Peretz's universe, however, as it seeks to discover and liberate itself, is not that easy to grasp. This spirit which strives to liberate itself was always present among Jews; whether in Judah Halevi or Peretz, poets of genius sought and found their justification in Jewish life. The American Yiddish writers of whom I am speaking—Yehoash, Liessin, Pinski, Halpern, Rolnik, Mani Leib, I. J. Schwartz, Leivick, Boraisho, Leyeles, Glatstein, Siegel—all sought and found those depths of Judah Halevi and Peretz. . . . Yiddish literature in America is still a multi-branched tree that sheds its withered leaves and grows new ones, fresh ones.

35

To Shake the World

In her eightieth year Pauline Newman could still remember what it was like to help bring the labor movement to birth on the Lower East Side. She was barely eight when she got her first job in a garment shop. She had arrived from a Lithuanian shtetl in 1901, settling in New York with her family. That same year she went to work at the Triangle Shirtwaist Company.

We were kids. When the operator was finished with the machine, we had scissors to cut off the threads that were left over when they pulled out the shirtwaists. We worked from 7:30 in the morning until 8 or 9 at night. No overtime, no supper money. Seven days, but on Sunday you might work only until noon or 2, and that was a half day. There were signs that warned, "If you don't come in Sunday, don't come in Monday."

The two people who ran Triangle were damnable, the worst of the lot, and I worked for a number of bosses. But these wouldn't even talk to you. You were not allowed to sing. On Saturday they handed you an envelope with $1.50, your salary for the week. By the end of eight years there, in 1909, I had worked up to $6. I was promoted to cut threads from the embroidery that had been inserted into the shirtwaist.

Get another job somewhere else? But the alternatives weren't any better. Pay and working conditions were bad throughout the industry. In the early 1880s the Knights of Labor had tried to help the women's garment workers to organize. With no lasting success, for labor had no rights in law and the public was indifferent. The long-suffering Jewish workers would flare up in despair every once in a while, strike for a raise in the busy season, get a few pennies and return to work, only to see their wages slashed in the slack season. "Seasonal union!" snorted the professional organizers; they thought these immigrants were hopeless union material. They did not understand that the strike was often the workers' only way to protest against a mass society trying to transform them into zeros. They were the nobodies, demanding recognition from the somebodies.

In 1887 there were thirty such futile strikes in New York, and many more elsewhere. The next year a few socialists decided it was time to educate the Jews in trade unionism. Men like Abraham Cahan and Morris Hillquit, intellectual radicals, knew you couldn't leave change to spontaneity. They helped form the United Hebrew Trades in New York. All they could find alive were two infant Jewish unions—the typesetters and the chorus singers—with a grand total of forty members. The UHT's first forays were made among the Jewish actors, the knee-pants makers, and the bakery workers.

Among the Eastern European Jews arriving in those decades were revolutionaries with creeds and programs they were sure would shake the world, America included. Some were orthodox socialists, followers of Marx and Engels; some were violent anarcho-syndicalists of the Bakunin school; some were believers in Kropotkin's peaceful, philosophical anarchism. And while many were well educated, others were half baked. Most of the radical intellectuals were young, passionate, and devoted to "uplifting the masses." They were the levers needed for that gigantic task.

The trouble was, there were so many ideas about how to do it. No movement can be free of theories. It takes ideas to give a movement meaning and direction. But the labor and radical movements of the late nineteenth and the early twentieth century were torn by bitter factional feuds and contradictory dogmas. Some people believed in one big union for all workers; they were against political action and distrusted all government. Then there were the anarcho-syndicalist ideas which animated both the Knights of Labor (founded in 1869) and then the Industrial Workers of the World, founded a generation later. The American Federation of Labor, started by the Jewish cigar maker Samuel Gompers in 1886, believed in "pure and simple" unionism. But as industry grew bigger and bigger and monopolies took control of huge sections of the country's economy, labor had to move from purely economic action to political action if it was to survive. The Knights and the IWW failed to adjust to the changing America and died.

When it was clear the AFL was winning out over the Knights, the socialists among the garment workers began to orient themselves toward its more effective unionism. During the early 1890s the New York cloak makers struck against the sweatshops but this time sought help from the United Hebrew Trades. Joseph Barondess was sent in to lead the union to victory. In Chicago, Boston, Baltimore, Philadelphia, the same shift from seasonal to permanent labor unions took place. The New York cloak makers struck again, this time welcoming support from the AFL, and won new gains. The fledgling union tried to extend itself nationwide in the trade but collapsed under factional pressures. Rival unions tossed by political storms appeared and disappeared. Where most of the workers were women and girls, the infant unions died fast, chiefly because the top organizers were men grossly indifferent to the needs of women. But everywhere the idea of unionism caught fire and many branches of the garment trade began to organize.

By the turn of the century the Socialist Party had formed out of earlier radical groups, under the leadership of Eugene V. Debs and Victor Berger, and the *Jewish Daily Forward* was launched with Cahan at the helm. Both forces opposed dual unions and helped organize the garment workers. By now almost a third of the industry's labor force was made up of women and girls. They worked in the dress, shirtwaist, and white-goods branches. "We didn't know much about trade unions or organization," Pauline Newman recalls, "but we had the spirit and fortitude. We believed that things had to get better." Like it or not, the labor chiefs realized they had to organize the women if the unions were to survive.

A national union was badly needed for an industry which now ranked among the major makers of consumer goods. By 1900 there were over 80,000 workers employed in some 2,700 shops. That June delegates from several cities and locals met in New York to form an

industrial union of all crafts in the women's garment trades. They
named it the International Ladies' Garment Workers' Union. A few
weeks later the AFL issued a charter to the new ILGWU. It grew fast,
climbing to 51 locals with 10,000 members by 1903. Half the members
worked outside New York and a third were women. For several years a
long depression and raids by the IWW set the union back badly. But as
the depression began to lift in 1909, the union made a comeback. "The
girls took the lead," said Pauline Newman. "In those days the men
didn't believe that women would stick to a union. Our union was one of
the first not to differentiate between men and women." About 80
percent of the shirtwaist makers were women, most of them between
sixteen and twenty-five. Almost half of them arrived not long ago from
Eastern Europe, radicalized by the Bund and the Russian revolutionary
movement. Although the tenement sweatshops had almost disappeared,
merciless exploitation continued in the new factory lofts. As business
improved, the workers began to rebel openly against conditions and
their leaders started talking up a general strike to build the union and
win recognition from the manufacturers.

But the International was cold to such a daring proposal. The women
found encouragement only from the Women's Trade Union League.
The League was a new part of the progressive movement, sponsored by
middle-class and professional women, among them the muckraking
journalist Ida Tarbell and the settlement-house leader Lillian Wald. The
only working-class woman among them was Rose Schneiderman.
They were in the feminist stream, concerned to help women win equal
rights by working for labor legislation and union organization. Taking
heart from the ardent support of the League, the shirtwaist makers
tested their strength with shop disputes and walkouts.

On November 22 they held a mass meeting at Cooper Union. For
two hours the platform speakers droned on, until suddenly a teenager
asked for the floor. It was Clara Lemlich, a fiery unionist who had been
beaten by cops on the picket lines. She exploded into Yiddish:

> I am a working girl, one of those who are on strike against intolerable
> conditions. I am tired of listening to speakers who talk in general terms.
> What we are here for is to decide whether we shall or shall not strike. I
> offer a resolution that a general strike shall be declared—NOW!

Instantly the audience rose to its feet, shouting, waving arms and hats and handkerchiefs. For five minutes the uproar continued until the chairman, B. Feigenbaum, asked if anyone seconded Clara's motion. Again the big audience leaped up, everyone yelling, "Second!" Carried away, the chairman summoned up the power of old religious ritual. "Do you mean faith? Will you take the old Jewish oath?" he asked. And up came two thousand hands as the two thousand voices chanted in Yiddish, "If I turn traitor to the cause I now pledge, may my right hand wither from this arm I now raise!"

And the historic Uprising of the Twenty Thousand, as it has come to be known, began. Five hundred shops closed down as the shirtmakers and dressmakers, most of them young women, took to the picket line. The Triangle Shirtwaist factory, where Pauline Newman worked, was one of them. Two months before, a hundred of its workers had gone to a secret meeting to organize a union, but the names leaked out and many workers were fired. The United Hebrew Trades, the Socialist Party, the Women's Trade Union League, all rallied their members to help the strikers. There was frequent fighting on the picket lines between the workers and goons hired to break the strike. The police and the judges took the side of the employers and flooded the courts and the cells with arrested picketers. Sentencing one striker, a judge said, "You are on strike against God and nature, whose firm law is that man shall earn his bread in the sweat of his brow. You are on strike against God!" But the girls did not frighten. Hundreds bloomed overnight as leaders, speakers, organizers. They raced from hall to hall to address strikers, they battled cops and scabs on the streets, they raised money for relief, they sought support before community groups, they went round the clock without food or sleep. Arrested almost daily, they would be bailed out and hurry back to the battle. Only fourteen, Pauline Newman was sent upstate by the union to raise money for the strikers. It was her first trip out of New York, but she came home from Buffalo with $250 from unionists there.

The newspapers and the public were swept into strike support by the electric energy, the courage and devotion of these young women. Appalled by the exposure of shop conditions, thousands jammed a huge mass meeting the union held in the Hippodrome. The strike soon spread to Philadelphia. But finally, on February 15, it came to an official end. The results, though marking an important advance, were scattered.

Many of the smaller shops had settled earlier, thereby weakening the effort to win a general settlement. The big firms had managed to hold out and in the end gave no recognition to the union. But in the older branches of the industry, where men predominated on the job, the spark had been ignited. Now the cloak makers, too, were calling for a general strike. The union leaders had learned the lesson that women counted, and could be counted on. And valuable ties between the middle-class reform movement and labor had been made. It was an alliance that would grow over the next decades into a strong influence on political life.

Five months later the New York cloak makers voted overwhelmingly for a general strike. The strike had been prepared systematically and brought out 60,000 workers. It was "a gigantic uprising of a whole people against their oppressors." The demands made included not only improvements in wages, hours, and working conditions but union recognition and a closed shop. More than three hundred of the smaller shops settled soon, but the employers refused to begin bargaining unless the closed-shop demand was dropped in advance. Jewish leaders were angered by their inhuman stubbornness and pressured them to negotiate before they ruined the good name of the Jewish community. Movement began when a board of arbitration, made up of such powerful Jewish leaders as Louis Marshall, Jacob Schiff, and Louis D. Brandeis, stepped in. Brandeis (who would later serve on the Supreme Court) was a distinguished lawyer from Boston who had counseled business and labor in the past. Together with Samuel Gompers he was able to get both sides to agree in September on a settlement called the Protocol of Peace.

The agreement set better standards for wages, hours, and working conditions, and gave the union official recognition. But in place of the closed shop, a Brandeis formula for the "preferential shop" was accepted. It meant that if competing job applicants were otherwise equal, the union man would get preference. It was a favorable end for labor to the nine-week "Great Revolt of 1910" and the greatest victory New York workers had yet won. For in establishing the principle of collective bargaining it helped the whole labor movement in its struggle for justice.

If anything else was needed to make labor and the public alike realize how important unions were, the shock was provided seven months later. It began at 4:45 on the afternoon on March 25, 1911. The 850 employees in the city's biggest shirtwaist factory, Triangle, had one hour to go before quitting time. Most of them were young girls. (Pauline Newman was not among them; she had gone to work for the union after the strike.) The company occupied the seventh, eighth, and ninth floors of a ten-story building at Washington Place and Greene Street, close by Washington Square. A man going to the toilet lit a cigarette on the way and dropped his match to the floor. The tiny flame touched scraps from the cutting table and a fire blazed up. The cutters and designers working at the tables ran into the hallway and yanked the fire hose from its stand. They raced back to the flames, but the hose, rotted at the folds, broke into pieces. The fire reached highly inflammable cleaning fluids and in seconds huge tongues of flame were darting out of the windows.

Some of the panic-stricken girls rushed for the rear exit, forgetting the bosses locked it every afternoon to force the workers to stand inspection for pilferage at the front door as they left work. The heavy iron door would not give way to pounding fists and battering bodies. Some workers thought of the fire escape and ran for it. It was a lone ladder going down to a narrow rear court and up to the roof. Only one small door gave access to it. The girls struggled to get through, breathing fire and choking on smoke. About seventy made it to the roof or the street that way. Many others reached the elevators, and were rushed to safety by the elevator men, who risked the ascent and descent a score of times until, twenty minutes later, fire streaming into the shaft and licking at the cables made them stop.

Ten minutes after the first alarm had been given, the firemen reached the building. Their ladders climbed only to the sixth floor and their hoses jetted only to the seventh. They spread nets on the street below; above, at the blazing windows, women and men could be seen leaning far out, mouths screaming wide.

Morris Rosenfeld, the sweatshop poet, told *Forward* readers what happened, building his account from eyewitness reports.

One girl after another fell, like shot birds, from above, from the burning floors. The men held out a longer time, enveloped in flames. And when they could hold out no longer, they jumped, too.

Below, horrified and weeping, stood thousands of workers from the surrounding factories. They watched moving, terrible, unforgettable scenes. At one window on the eighth floor appeared a young man with a girl. He was holding her tightly by the hand. Behind them the red flames could be seen. The young man lovingly wrapped his arms around the girl and held her to him a moment, kissed her, and then let her go. She leaped, and fell to the sidewalk with great impact. A moment later he leaped after her, and his body landed next to hers. Both were dead. . . .

It took a whole hour before the firemen could enter the burning building, and by then it was all over. The sidewalks were full of dead and wounded, and no one could be seen at the windows any longer. The poor girls who had remained inside the building lay all about burnt or smothered to death by fire and smoke. The ambulances and patrol wagons that arrived were not sufficient for the job. Grocers, butchers, and peddlers contributed their wagons and pushcarts. Dozens of stores were transformed into hospitals or morgues.

The catapult force of the long plunges made the nets useless. The bodies tore the nets from the firemen's grasp or ripped right through the cords to the pavement. By 8 P.M. the supply of coffins had given out and the morgue sent back many already used once. Now bodies were being taken out of the building at the rate of one per minute and sometimes four or six coffins were loaded together on the waiting wagons. The crews of police and morgue attendants were so overcome by the appalling task they had to be replaced three times before the work was done.

On April 7 a mass funeral took place in the rain. Fifty thousand people marched silently through the Lower East Side in remembrance of the dead. But more than the lost lives were remembered. The conditions immigrants were forced to work under had been glaringly illuminated by the flames. The mourning was mixed with rage. Harris and Blanck, the Triangle partners, were tried for manslaughter, and acquitted. Still, the social meaning of the disaster was not lost. Humane middle- and upper-class Americans already concerned with urban reform now saw that infinitely more had to be done for justice and equality. Not "the inscrutable decrees of Divine Providence," but the greed of unscrupulous men accounted for these preventable disasters.

A Factory Investigating Commission was appointed by New York State. For three years it examined industrial working conditions, heard testimony on proposals to deal with them, and prepared reports for the legislature to consider. The lawmakers overhauled the state's industrial code with thirty-five new measures.

Out of the Triangle tragedy came a revolution in laws for protection of the workers in factories—fire prevention, factory inspection, liability insurance, workmen's compensation. The garment workers' own organization, the ILGWU, became a spearhead of reform and ultimately one of the leading labor unions in America. The trades the Jewish immigrants had taken to were one after another unionized: the Cap Makers in 1901, the Fur Workers in 1904, the Amalgamated Clothing Workers in 1914. By 1918 over a quarter of a million Jewish workers were affiliated through their unions with the United Hebrew Trades.

Despite the hopes of the Protocol of Peace, the unions enjoyed no lasting security. In the cities beyond the Hudson the employers stuck to the open shop. It took a long time for the unions to defeat the hire-and-fire policy. Not until the New Deal of the 1930s did collective bargaining become a legally enforced right. One of the labor leaders who helped bring about that enormous change was Sidney Hillman.

Born in an Eastern European village in 1887, Hillman had gone to the famous yeshiva of Slobodka. Turning radical, he left to join the Bund. He was arrested in the 1905 revolutionary year and served six months in prison. In 1907 he became one of the many refugees from the Russian Revolution and settled in Chicago. From cutter's apprentice in a men's clothing factory he rose through labor's ranks to president of the new Amalgamated Clothing Workers—the equivalent in the men's garment industry of the ILGWU.

Hillman came to see the strike as a desperate weapon in jungle warfare. While the young radical Jews and Italians in the shops talked class warfare, his pragmatic mind sought ways to convince employers that acceptance of the union was to their advantage as well as the workers'. Like other Jewish labor leaders, he turned his energy toward the democratization of industry. He stimulated joint union-management activities. He was the first garment union leader to encourage technological progress in production, and to set up a research department to plan for scientific management. His union led the way in providing unemployment benefits, establishing the only successful labor bank, and building low-cost cooperative housing.

It was the Jewish socialists who deserve credit for organizing the Jewish immigrant workers. No one else was capable of carrying out that task, says C. Belzalel Sherman.

Their great achievement was that they transformed these degraded Jewish immigrants into a social force which not only altered the course of Jewish history in the United States but left its mark on the country's entire labor movement. The remarkable thing was that these beaten-down laborers, who worked under such abominable conditions, who were not part of a tradition of independent trade union action, who were worlds away from a proletarian psychology, and who were, perhaps in their majority, Orthodox in religion, founded their first trade unions as socialist organizations. The socialist ideology of the leaders found a warm response in the sense of social justice that lived in the soul of the ordinary Jew—a sense that derived from a combination of the prophetic vision and his unjust treatment at the hands of the non-Jewish world.

36

The Door Closes

With the coming of World War I in 1914 there was a vast upheaval in Jewish life. The major battlegrounds of the Eastern Front were the homelands of the Jews. Hunger, disease, and massacre became the common fate. In 1917, Messianic hopes were rekindled when czarism was overthrown, the Russian Jews emancipated, and the Balfour Declaration issued by Britain favoring the establishment in Palestine of a national homeland for the Jewish people.

The immigrant Jews in America saw in these grand events salvation for their kindred. But it did not come about. Eastern Europe fell into bloody chaos, with civil war drowning Jewish hopes in waves of pogroms. And here at home, a nativist outburst against aliens was triggered by the trauma of the war. When President Woodrow Wilson preached "a crusade to save the world for democracy," it had the paradoxical effect of causing repression at home. Wilson himself said, "Once lead this people into war and they'll forget that there was ever such a thing as tolerance." As American troops joined the battle, a reign of terror was launched against those who opposed the war on pacifist or radical grounds or because of ethnic sympathies. Dissenters were whipped, tarred and feathered, and a few even lynched. Volunteer

informers made antiwar talk dangerous and new Espionage and Sedition laws powered the crusade for conformity. Over 1,500 radicals were
arrested, the IWW was suppressed, and many of the left-wing and
ethnic newspapers were muzzled.

The nativists were especially rabid against Jews and Catholics and
Americans of German origin. Immigrants hoping to become Americans
were pressed even harder than before to slough off every trace of Old
World custom and culture. Many states adopted laws banning the use of
foreign languages in school instruction.

Two years later one of the unhappiest episodes in nativist hysteria
erupted. Attorney General A. Mitchell Palmer, an ambitious Democrat
seeking the Presidency, ordered federal agents to conduct a mass roundup
of "Reds." In one night his men raided thirty-three cities and netted over
4,000 "suspected" radicals, most of them immigrants. The victims were
held for days, weeks, months, to be deported "back to where they came
from" or jailed for twenty-year sentences. In that Red Scare period intense
suffering was inflicted upon thousands of people who, radical or not, had
a right to their beliefs. The weak and fragmented radical movement was
no threat to anyone. Yet the federal government brushed aside the Bill of
Rights to carry out ruthless suppression.

Dislike for the Jew, as in any time of social crisis, had begun to rise
with the onset of the war. Everything "foreign" and "radical" was
under suspicion. Politicians like Palmer, intent on advancing their political careers, saw that fending off these internal devils promised special
rewards. By riding popular fears they might reach high office. Tom
Watson, a Southern populist who had long attacked the blacks, turned
against the Catholics, and then began baiting the Jews on the platform
and in the press. In 1915, Leo Frank, a young Jew from the North, was
accused of murdering a girl in the Atlanta factory where he worked, and
convicted on the flimsiest evidence. Watson ranted that the way to get
rid of Jewish interference in Georgia was to execute Frank. A brave
governor commuted Frank's death sentence. Watson's inflamed followers abducted Frank from jail and lynched him.

It was during these years that many books were written voicing fears
about the new immigration. One of the most influential was Madison
Grant's *The Passing of the Great Race* (1916). Grant, anthropologist at the
American Museum of Natural History, repeated the supposed proofs of

Jewish inferiority which the British anti-Semite Houston Stewart Chamberlain was promoting. Both argued that human inequality was a fact, and that if inferior peoples (this "wretched, submerged, human-flotsam of the Polish ghettos") were not segregated, the superior people (Nordics) would be in danger. (Hitler became one of Chamberlain's passionate disciples.) As popular a book was Lothrop Stoddard's *The Rising Tide of Color* (1920).

But it was not only from conservatives that racist appeals came. Historians, sociologists, and economists who were progressive by the standards of the day wrote such books too. The scholars John R. Commons, Edward A. Ross, and Henry Pratt Fairchild all held that the superiority of democracy was due to the superiority of Anglo-Saxons. They looked upon the Southern and Eastern European immigrants as ignorant, filthy, coarse breeds, whose mixture with the old American stocks would mean national degeneration. The rising sentiment against the blacks is recorded in the many race riots and lynchings, North and South, which bloody the calendar of that generation. As for the Jew, "the time has come," said the leader of the St. Petersburg, Florida, Chamber of Commerce, "to make this a hundred percent American and gentile city as free from foreigners as from slums."

In 1916, when President Wilson nominated Brandeis of Boston for the Supreme Court, a bitter struggle broke out in the Senate and the country over his confirmation. A petition signed by over fifty promi-nent Massachusetts men, headed by President Lowell of Harvard and studded with the "best" family names, protested that Brandeis was not fit for the Bench. But everyone knew the underlying reason was that the nominee was a Jew. Another protest signed by seven men who had held the presidency of the American Bar Association struck the same blow against Brandeis. The anti-Semitic campaign made the stereotyped accusations that Brandeis was a trickster and always had a mercenary motive for his actions. Wilson was nominating him only as "bait for the Hebrew vote" in the next election. A number of wealthy and conserva-tive Jews suggested quietly that Wilson withdraw the nomination because they feared the uproar it was causing would upset their plans for gaining status gradually and peacefully. The counsel of the timid was ignored; Brandeis won (by a very close margin) and became one of the most distinguished jurists in the Court's history.

The Russian Revolution of 1917 provided another occasion for anti-Semitic propaganda. It was widely charged that the Jews had plotted the Communist take-over of power and now controlled it. The accusation fed neatly into the notorious *Protocols of the Elders of Zion,* an anti-Semitic concoction of a Jewish plot to rule the world. Henry Ford, the auto magnate, spent millions on his weekly newspaper, the *Dearborn Independent,* reprinting the *Protocols* and adding "evidence" of how the plot was going in the United States.

In the 1920s the Ku Klux Klan, a secret society founded in the South after the Civil War to persecute the emancipated blacks, was revived as the bulwark of 100 percent Americanism. Now it declared itself the foe not only of blacks but of Catholics and Jews as well. The KKK's *Fiery Cross* warned that "the Jews dominated the economic life of the nation while the Catholics are determined to dominate the political and religious life." Its appeal to racism rallied over five million members, chiefly in the small towns and rural regions of the South and Midwest.

Those millions were susceptible to racist ideas because, says the historian George E. Mowry:

> The Klan represented a deeply troubled group of Americans, recruited mainly from the countryside, conscious of their growing inferiority, and deeply sensitive to the destruction of their traditional values by the new mass-producing, mass-consuming culture of the burgeoning cities. . . . They readily accepted the technology and the financial and selling techniques upon which the new mass culture rested, but they assailed its social results. Needing a villain, they turned to the convenient Catholic, Negro, and Jew, who together had probably far less to do with the destruction of the ancient rural heritage than their fellow Protestant Americans caught up with the glittering material promises of the great boom.

These fellow Protestant Americans included a select group in the Northeast, remote from the "hicks and rubes and drivers of second-hand Fords," which is how Imperial Wizard Hiram Evans described his KKK followers. But the Boston Brahmins looked upon the new immigrants in much the same way. To Senator Henry Cabot Lodge, the powerful Republican, these "inferior" people were invaders as dangerous to America as the Goths and Vandals who trampled over Rome. He pushed a bill in Congress to require all European immigrants to prove their ability to read and write for admission. It was the best legal device to keep out undesirables.

Nathaniel Shaler, dean of Harvard's Graduate School of Science, was another spokesman from polite and educated circles who gave respectability to the notion that Southern and Eastern Europeans were radically inferior. Less "scientific" but equally poisonous were the views of the historian Henry Adams, friend of Lodge, who recoiled in horror when he encountered a "furtive Jacob or Ysaac still reeking of the Ghetto, snarling a weird Yiddish." "The Jew," he wrote, "makes me creep."

The old established families of Boston and New York resented the incursion of prosperous Jews into their society. Nearly all of them were anti-Semitic. The novelist Henry James, returning home for a visit in 1904, after a long sojourn abroad, was repelled by the new America but disgusted especially by the "swarming" Jews he saw on a tour of the Lower East Side. They reminded him of "small, strange animals . . . snakes or worms. . . ." It was the same dehumanized response as Hitler's view of the Jews as bacilli or vermin. Neither could see a Jew as an individual, only as a stereotype.

What joined Boston Brahmin, university professor, and KKK'er in a common belief? They were frightened by the tumultuous growth of industry and cities. They blamed the newcomers for depressing wages, lowering living standards, creating slums, committing crime, spreading disease. "There emerged a sense," says the historian John J. Appel, "that the American people must define what was American, what alien. Many older Americans were uneasy, even fearful over what appeared to be the breakdown of ethnic homogeneity and the loss of old values. . . . Unlike those liberals who by the 1900s had begun to accept the necessity for regulation but insisted on the continued ability of American society to assimilate the newcomers, those favoring their exclusion on racist and nativist grounds saw themselves as the true defenders of traditional ideals of the United States as the most perfect society on earth, its customs and values fixed, to be protected from alien assault and perversion."

The president of the AFL, too, added his voice to the chorus calling for restriction of immigration. When the U.S. Immigration Commission issued a massive report in 1911, paving the way for racist quota laws,

Gompers gave organized labor's official support to it. Most of the American craft unions had long tried to exclude strangers. And now Gompers found himself teamed up with Senator Lodge in seeking to curb the new immigration.

In 1917, after several attempts, Congress passed a bill, over Wilson's veto, which limited immigration through the literacy test Lodge had urged. When immigrants began coming in again after the war, the nativists decided the literacy barrier was not enough. In 1921, Congress passed a temporary law introducing the principle of numerical restriction based upon nationality. It was a stopgap until 1924 when the Johnson-Reed Act slammed the door on mass immigration. It set a ceiling of 150,000 a year. A quota formula was adopted that would remain in effect for forty-one years. The law fixed the quota of each nation at 2 percent of the number of its immigrants here in 1890. After 1929 a permanent ceiling of 150,000 persons a year was set, with quotas based on the 1920 census. With more than two-thirds of the Americans in 1920 of Northern European ancestry, the goal was clear: to keep Nordics *über alles*. The much larger numbers of people in Southern and Eastern Europe who desired to immigrate sat on long waiting lists. They could not enter because their small quotas were always filled. (Not until 1965 did Congress end the national origins quotas.) The effect of the 1924 law upon the Jews is one example of the way the new measure worked. In that year, the last year of mass immigration, 50,000 Jews entered the country. In the next, 10,000. The flood of Jewish immigration had been dammed. And the great century of migration was over.

It was in these years that American Jews became the targets of an extended system of exclusion. In the Gilded Age, entrenched wealth had begun to shut Jews out from society. The fashionable resorts and hotels made known they did not welcome Jews as guests. By the end of the century the pattern had spread to the clubs and even the philanthropic organizations of the cities. High society set the tone, and the middle class aped it. Jews began to find they could not move into any neighborhood they wished. Informal understandings, "gentlemen's agreements," and restrictive covenants in deeds of sale did the job. By 1910, fields of employment were also being closed off to the outsider. Many of the Jews had been concentrated in a relatively few trades or industries. But as some Jews acquired the training or education to enter different callings, they met discrimination. Many companies had a flat policy against hiring any Jews. Employment agencies helped by never referring Jews to openings. The public press carried ads reading "No Jews Need Apply" or "White Protestants Only." The demand for manpower created by World War I lowered the barriers somewhat, but up they went again, and even higher, in the 1920s. By now many of the biggest businesses in the land—even those which were public utilities or required chartering by the state—considered exclusion of the Jews their private privilege.

The professions proved especially attractive to Jews, particularly the first American-born generation. In medicine, law, teaching, engineering, it would seem you need only have the talent and the training to qualify for admission to the free callings. The proper family or financial connections seemed irrelevant. The Jew whose parents had left the *shtetl* only yesterday had just as much right to practice a profession as the son of a Lowell or a Stuyvesant.

But did he? Respectable law and engineering firms would not hire qualified Jews. Colleges and universities between 1870 and 1930 gave professorships to only a handful of Jews. Even the lower rungs of the academic ladder were hard to get hold of. But the worst discrimination occurred in medicine. Membership in medical societies and hospitals, often vital to successful practice, was denied to qualified Jewish physicians. And that restrictive policy soon reached down into medical education itself. As the number of medical schools declined, under pressure to eliminate poor schools and badly trained doctors, Jews were the first to be refused admission.

With all the professions the reasons were pretty much the same. The non-Jews feared competition. They also believed association with Jews would lower their professional and social status. And why risk tainting the profession with these odious outsiders? A major device for exclusion was introduced: the quota system. All medical schools used it to reduce the number of Jewish students.

The same system, sometimes called the *numerus clausus,* was picked up by many private schools and liberal-arts colleges. Jewish students, if not refused altogether, were limited to a tiny fixed quota.

Only gradually did the Jews wake up to what was happening. The immigrants confined to ethnic trades and neighborhoods were unaware of the threat outside. It was the more prosperous Jews who felt it first. Their initial response was defensive. We deserve equal treatment, they argued, because we Jews have been in America since the founding of the colonies, we have served loyally in every American war, we've worked as hard as anyone to build this country.

The discrimination not only persisted, it increased. Argument, no matter how strong, fell on the deaf ear of the prejudiced. Bolder and more practical measures were called for. The B'nai B'rith created its Anti-Defamation League in 1914 to fight against prejudice and discrimination. And the American Jewish Congress and American Jewish Committee joined in. They organized protests, spoke up when public issues such as the immigration quota bill concerned Jews, used the influence of leading Jews to exert personal pressure at strategic points.

But it was hard to prevail against the growing hostility. How prove, for instance, that the conspiracy charged in the *Protocols* was a fiction? Legal action forced Henry Ford to apologize publicly and retract his accusations. But false charges influenced the popular mind through countless pieces of propaganda. The courts ruled that an individual could not be injured by libel against his group. It was almost useless to try to beat out the flames ignited by emotional mass movements.

What the defense organizations could do was to prevent anti-Semitism from turning into law, or influencing government action. The Constitution did protect religious freedom. And luckily, the Klan and other such groups had no practical political program. Their major success in the 1920s was the passage of the immigration quota laws.

Two lessons did emerge from that troubled time. One was that the security of Jews could best be assured by a struggle for the rights of *all* Americans. Jews join in the defense of every minority; the survival of each depends upon the survival of all. The second lesson was that the fate of the Jews is linked to the condition of American democracy. When it is healthy and growing, when it is liberal and progressive, the climate is favorable. Where reaction sets in, Jews are in danger. Serious social and economic problems which go ignored (as soon they would in Germany) prepare the way for demagogues to rise to power, for totalitarianism to crush democracy and wipe out liberty and life. Any society that fears change and suppresses dissent will be hostile to Jews.

Bibliography

I came to this work severely handicapped by my inability to read Hebrew and Yiddish. Much of the source materials on the antecedents of American Jewry are to be found only in those languages. I owe thanks all the more, therefore, to the Yivo Institute for Jewish Research and to its librarian, Dina Abramowicz, for guiding me to what was available in English in that incomparable collection.

Among the many scholars to whom I am indebted, three especially must be singled out: Mark Zborowski and Elizabeth Herzog for their pioneering study of the shtetl, *Life Is with People,* and Lucy S. Dawidowicz for her book, *The Golden Tradition: Jewish Life and Thought in Eastern Europe.* I mined both works mercilessly, and must give extra thanks to Ms. Dawidowicz for her translations of many Yiddish texts. My grateful appreciation at the same time to all the other translators from the Yiddish and the Hebrew whose work is too often ill-paid and unacknowledged.

The best way for a reader to go deeper into the world of East European Jewry is to read its liierature—the short stories, sketches, novels, plays, memoirs, letters, poems, essays, speeches. It was to such original sources that I went to discover how it felt to be a Jew in the Eastern Europe my mother and father came from. These eyewitness accounts give us a human passage to the past, and I have used them liberally in my narrative.

For one unfamiliar with the literature, there are good guides to follow: Maurice Samuel's *The World of Sholem Aleichem,* his book about I. L. Peretz, *Prince of the Ghetto,* and the two collections of Yiddish material made by Irving Howe and Eliezer Greenberg, illuminated by their superb historical introductions.

The sources listed below are a selection of the books and articles I referred to in my research. I also made frequent use of the files of contemporary newspapers and periodicals, and of historical journals found either at Yivo or in the Judaica collection of the New York Public Library.

I should like to mention at least the most important journals and yearbooks whose articles I found especially helpful: *American Hebrew, American Jewish Archives, American Jewish Historical Quarterly, American Jewish Year Book, Commentary, Ethnicity, Jewish Social Studies, Labor History, Publications of the American Jewish Historical Society, Yivo Annual of Jewish Social Science.*

The edition of a book given in the following list is the one I used; sometimes it is a later edition than the first. A number of the titles are now available in paperback.

Abrahams, Israel. *Jewish Life in the Middle Ages.* London: Goldston, 1932.

Abramovitch, Hirsch. "Rural Jewish Occupations in Lithuania." *Yivo Annual of Jewish Social Sciences,* vols. II–III (1947–1948), pp. 205–221. New York: Yiddish Scientific Institute-Yivo.

Ain, Abraham. "Swislocz. Portrait of a Jewish Community in Eastern Europe." *Yivo Annual of Jewish Social Sciences,* vol. IV (1949), pp. 86–114. New York: Yiddish Scientific Institute-Yivo.

Antin, Mary. *The Promised Land.* Boston: Houghton Mifflin, 1969.

Appel, John J., ed. *The New Immigration.* New York: Pitman, 1971.

Baron, Salo W. *A Social and Religious History of the Jews.* 3 vols. New York: Columbia University Press, 1937.

Ben-Sasson, H. H., and Ettinger, S., eds. *Jewish Society Through the Ages.* New York: Schocken, 1971.

Bernheimer, Charles S., ed. *The Russian Jew in the United States.* New York: Ozer, 1971.

Billington, James H. *The Icon and the Axe, an Interpretive History of Russian Culture.* New York: Knopf, 1966.

Bookbinder, Hyman H. *To Promote the General Welfare: The Story of the Amalgamated Clothing Workers.* New York: Amalgamated Clothing Workers, 1950.

Bremner, Robert H. *From the Depths: The Discovery of Poverty in the United States.* New York: New York University Press, 1956.

Bross, Jacob. "The Beginning of the Jewish Labor Movement in Galicia." *Yivo Annual of Jewish Social Sciences,* vol. V (1950), pp. 55–84. New York: Yiddish Scientific Institute-Yivo.

Buber, Martin. *Origin and Meaning of Hasidism.* New York: Horizon, 1960.

Cahan, Abraham. *The Education of Abraham Cahan.* Philadelphia: Jewish Publication Society, 1969.

——. "Jewish Massacres and the Revolutionary Movement in Russia." *North American Review,* vol. 77 (July 1903), pp. 49–62.

——. *The Rise of David Levinsky.* New York: Harper Colophon, 1966.

Charnofsky, Michael. *Jewish Life in the Ukraine.* New York: Exposition, 1965.

Chotzinoff, Samuel. *A Lost Paradise.* New York: Knopf, 1955.

Chyet, Stanley F., ed. *Lives and Voices.* Philadelphia: Jewish Publication Society, 1972.

Cohen, Morris R. *A Dreamer's Journey.* New York: Free Press, 1949.

Cohen, Samuel H. *Transplanted.* New York, 1937.

Davidson, Gabriel. *Our Jewish Farmers: The Story of the Jewish Agricultural Society.* New York: Fischer, 1943.

Davis, Allen F. *Spearheads for Reform: The Social Settlements and the Progressive Movement, 1890–1914.* New York: Oxford, 1967.

Davis, Allen F., and McGree, Mary L. *Eighty Years at Hull-House.* Chicago: Quadrangle, 1969.

Davitt, Michael. *Within the Pale.* Philadelphia: Jewish Publication Society, 1903.

Dawidowicz, Lucy S., ed. *The Golden Tradition: Jewish Life and Thought in Eastern Europe.* New York: Holt, Rinehart and Winston, 1967.

Dimont, Max I. *Indestructible Jews.* New York: New American Library, 1971.

——. *Jews, God and History.* New York: New American Library, 1962.

Dinnerstein, Leonard. *Anti-Semitism in the U.S.* New York: Holt, 1971.

Dinnerstein, Leonard, and Jaher, Frederic C., eds. *The Aliens: A History of Ethnic Minorities in America.* New York: Appleton-Century-Crofts, 1970.

Dubnow, Simon. *History of the Jews: From the Congress of Vienna to the Emergence of Hitler,* Vol. 5. New York: Thomas Yoseloff, 1973.

——. *History of the Jews in Russia and Poland.* Philadelphia: Jewish Publication Society, 1916–1920.

Dunne, Thomas. *Ellis Island.* New York: Norton, 1971.

Eisenberg, Azriel, ed. *The Golden Land.* New York: Yoseloff, 1964.

Elbogen, Ismar. *A Century of Jewish Life, 1840–1940.* Philadelphia: Jewish Publication Society, 1944.

Epstein, Melech. *Profiles of Eleven.* Detroit: Wayne State University Press, 1965.

——. *Jewish Labor in the U.S.A.* New York: Ktav, 1969.

Feldstein, Stanley, and Costello, Laurence, eds. *The Ordeal of Assimilation.* New York: Doubleday Anchor, 1974.

Finkelstein, Louis, ed. *The Jews.* 3 vols. New York: Schocken, 1971.

Fishman, William J. *Jewish Radicals: From Czarist Stetl to London Ghetto.* New York: Pantheon, 1975.

Flannery, Edward H. *The Anguish of the Jews: Twenty-three Centuries of Anti-Semitism.* New York: Macmillan, 1965.

Frumkin, Jacob, Aronson, Gregor, and Goldenwieser, Alexis. *Russian Jewry, 1860–1917.* New York: Thomas Yoseloff, 1966.

Glazer, Nathan. *American Judaism.* Chicago: University of Chicago Press, 1957.

Glazer, Nathan, and Moynihan, Daniel Patrick. *Beyond the Melting Pot.* Cambridge: M.I.T. Press, 1963.

Goodman, Henry, ed. *The New Country.* New York: YKUF Publishers, 1961.

Gordon, Benjamin Lee. *Between Two Worlds.* New York: Bookman, 1952.

Grayzel, Solomon. *A History of the Jews.* Philadelphia: Jewish Publication Society, 1962.

——. *A History of the Contemporary Jews: From 1900 to the Present.* New York: Atheneum, 1972.

Greer, Colin. *The Great School Legend.* New York: Basic Books, 1973.

Handlin, Oscar. *The Uprooted.* Boston: Little, Brown, 1956.

——, ed. *Immigration as a Factor in American History.* Englewood Cliffs, NJ: Prentice-Hall, 1959.

Hapgood, Norman. *The Spirit of the Ghetto.* New York: Schocken, 1966.

Harap, Louis. *The Image of the Jew in American Literature.* Philadelphia: Jewish Publication Society, 1974.

Harcave, Sidney. *Years of the Golden Cockerel: The Last Romanov Tsars, 1814–1917.* New York: Macmillan, 1968.

Hartmann, Edward. *The Movement to Americanize the Immigrant.* New York: AMC Press, 1948.

Heschel, Abraham J. *The Earth Is the Lord's: The Inner World of the Jew in East Europe.* New York: Schuman, 1950.

Higham, John. *Strangers in the Land: Patterns of American Nativism, 1860–1925.* New York: Atheneum, 1972.

——. *Send These to Me: Jews and Other Immigrants in Urban America.* New York: Atheneum, 1975.

Hillquit, Morris. *Loose Leaves from a Busy Life.* New York: Macmillan, 1934.

Hindus, Maurice. *Green Worlds.* New York: Doubleday, 1938.

——. *A Traveler in Two Worlds.* New York: Doubleday, 1971.

Hindus, Milton, ed. *The Old East Side.* Philadelphia: Jewish Publication Society, 1971.

Howe, Irving, and Greenberg, Eliezer, eds. *A Treasury of Yiddish Stories.* New York: Meridian, 1958.

——, eds. *Voices from the Yiddish.* Ann Arbor: University of Michigan Press, 1972.

Jacob, H. E. *World of Emma Lazarus.* New York: Schocken, 1949.

Janowsky, Oscar, ed. *The American Jew.* New York, 1942.

Jones, Maldwyn. *American Immigration.* Chicago: University of Chicago Press, 1960.

Joseph, Samuel. *Jewish Immigration to the United States.* New York: Columbia University Press, 1914.

Juergens, George. *Joseph Pulitzer and the New York World.* Princeton: Princeton University Press, 1966.

Kallen, Horace M. *Culture and Democracy in the United States.* New York: Arno, 1970.

Kaplan, Simon. *Once a Rebel.* New York: Farrar & Rinehart, 1941.

Karp, A. J., ed. *The Jewish Experience in America.* 5 vols. New York: Ktav, 1969.

Krug, Edwin A. *The Shaping of the American High School: 1880–1920.* Madison: University of Wisconsin Press, 1969.

Lang, Lucy Robbins. *Tomorrow Is Beautiful.* New York: Macmillan, 1948.

Laqueur, Walter. *A History of Zionism.* New York: Holt, Rinehart and Winston, 1972.

Levine, Louis. *The Women's Garment Workers.* New York: B. W. Huebsch.

Lifson, David S. *The Yiddish Theater in America.* New York: Yoseloff, 1965.

Liptzin, Samuel. *Tales of a Tailor.* New York, 1965.

Liptzin, Sol. *Eliakum Zunser: Poet of His People.* New York: Behrman, 1950.

Lisitzky, E. E. *In the Grip of Cross-Currents.* New York: Exposition Press, 1959.

Madison, Charles. *Yiddish Literature: Its Scope and Major Writers.* New York: Schocken, 1971.

Marcus, Jacob R., ed. *The Jew in the Medieval World: A Source Book, 315–1791.* New York: Atheneum, 1969.

Margolis, Max L., and Marx, Alexander. *A History of the Jewish People.* Philadelphia: Jewish Publication Society, 1927.

Metzker, Isaac, ed. *A Bintel Brief.* New York: Ballantine, 1972.

Monas, Sidney. *The Third Section, Police and Society in Russia Under Nicholas I.* Cambridge: Harvard University Press, 1961.

Novak, Michael. *The Rise of the Unmeltable Ethnics.* New York: Macmillan, 1971.

Novotny, Ann. *Strangers at the Door.* New York: Chatham, 1972.

Palmer, Francis H. E. *Russian Life in Town and Country.* New York: G. P. Putnam's Sons, 1901.

Payne, Robert. *The Terrorists.* New York: Funk & Wagnalls, 1957.

Peretz, I. L. *My Memoirs.* New York: Citadel, 1964.

Pinson, Koppel S., ed. *Simon Dubnow, Nationalism and History.* Philadelphia: Jewish Publication Society, 1958.

Plotkin, Abraham L. *Struggle for Justice.* New York: Exposition, 1960.

Raisin, Jacob S. *The Haskala Movement in Russia.* Westport: Greenwood, 1972.

Ravitch, Diane. *The Great School Wars: New York 1805–1973.* New York: Basic Books, 1974.

Report of the United States Immigration Commission, 61st Cong., 3d sess. 41 vols. Washington, D.C.: U.S. Government Printing Office, 1911.

Reznikoff, Charles. *Family Chronicle.* New York: Universal Books, 1972.

Ribalow, Menachem. *The Flowering of Modern Hebrew Literature.* New York: Twayne, 1959.

Riis, Jacob A. *How the Other Half Lives.* New York: Scribners, 1890.

———. *Jacob Riis Revisited.* New York: Doubleday Anchor, 1968.

Rischin, Moses. *The Promised City: New York's Jews, 1870–1914.* New York: Harper Torchbook, 1970.

Rosenblum, Gerald. *Immigrant Workers: Their Impact on American Labor Radicalism.* New York: Basic Books, 1973.

Roskolenko, Harry. *The Time That Was Then.* New York: Dial, 1971.

Sachar, Howard M. *The Course of Modern Jewish History.* New York: World, 1958.

Samuel, Maurice. *Little Did I Know.* New York: Knopf, 1963.

———. *Prince of the Ghetto.* New York: Schocken, 1973.

———. *The World of Sholem Aleichem.* New York: Knopf, 1943.

Sanders, Ronald. *The Downtown Jews.* New York: Harper, 1969.

Schneour, Zalman. *Noah Pandre's Village.* London: Chatto & Windus, 1938.

Schoener, Allon, ed. *Portal to America: The Lower East Side, 1870–1925.* New York: Holt, 1967.

Schwartz, J. R. *Orchard Street.* New York: Comet Press, 1960.

Schwartz, Leo W., ed. *Great Ages and Ideas of the Jewish People.* New York: Random, 1956.

Schwartz, Samuel. *Tell the Children.* New York: Exposition, 1959.

Schweitzer, Frederick M. *A History of the Jews: Since the First Century A.D.* New York: Macmillan, 1971.

Scott, Franklin D. *The Peopling of America: Perspectives on Immigration.* Washington: American Historical Association, 1972.

Selzer, Michael, ed. *Kike: Anthology of Anti-Semitism.* New York: World, 1972.

Selzer, Michael. *Wineskin and Wizard.* New York: Macmillan, 1970.

Seton-Watson, Hugh. *The Russian Empire, 1801–1917.* New York: Oxford, 1967.

Shazar, Zalman. *Morning Stars.* Philadelphia: Jewish Publication Society, 1967.

Sherman, C. Belzalel. *The Jew within American Society.* Detroit: Wayne State University Press, 1965.

Singer, I. J. *The Brothers Ashkenazi.* New York: Knopf, 1936.

———. *Of a World That Is No More.* New York: Vanguard, 1970.

Sklare, Marshall, ed. *The Jew in American Society.* New York: Behrman, 1974.

Solomon, Barbara M. *Ancestors and Immigrants.* Chicago: University of Chicago Press, 1956.

Soyer, Raphael. *Self-Revealment: A Memoir.* New York: Random House, 1969.

Spargo, John. *The Bitter Cry of the Children*. Chicago: Quadrangle, 1968.

Stein, Leon. *The Triangle Fire*. Philadelphia: Lippincott, 1962.

Stephenson, Graham. *Russia from 1812 to 1945*. New York: Praeger, 1970.

Sterne, Maurice. *Shadow and Light*. New York: Harcourt, 1965.

Stiles, W. C. *Out of Kishinev*. New York: Dillingham, 1903.

Taylor, Philip. *The Distant Magnet: European Emigration to the U.S.A.* New York: Harper Torchbook, 1972.

Teller, Judd L. *Strangers and Natives*. New York: Delta, 1968.

Thaden, Edward C. *Russia Since 1801*. New York: John Wiley & Sons, 1971.

Todd, A. L. *Justice on Trial: The Case of Louis D. Brandeis*. New York: McGraw-Hill, 1964.

Vorspan, Albert. *Giants of Justice*. New York: Union of American Hebrew Congregations, 1960.

Waksman, Selman. *My Life with the Microbes*. New York: Simon & Schuster, 1954.

Weizmann, Chaim. *Trial and Error: An Autobiography*. Philadelphia: Jewish Publication Society, 1949.

Wirth, Louis. *The Ghetto*. Chicago: University of Chicago Press, 1956.

Wischnitzer, Mark. *To Dwell in Freedom: History of Jewish Emigration Since 1800*. Philadelphia: Jewish Publication Society, 1948.

Wolwolff, Israel. *I Yield to Destiny*. New York: 1938.

Zborowski, Mark, and Herzog, Elizabeth. *Life Is with People: The Jewish Little-Town of Eastern Europe*. New York: International Universities Press, 1952.

Zorach, William. *Art Is My Life*. New York: World, 1967.

Acknowledgments

Acknowledgment is made for permission to quote from the following works: *A Dreamer's Journey* by Morris R. Cohen, Copyright 1949 by the Free Press; *My Memoirs* by I. L. Peretz, Copyright © by Fred Goldberg 1964, by permission of Citadel Press, Secaucus, NJ; *Morning Stars* by Zalman Shazar, by permission of The Jewish Publication Society of America; "The City of Slaughter" by Chaim Nachman Bialik, translated by Joseph Leftwich, by permission of Thomas Yoseloff, A. S. Barnes & Co.; *Life Is with People* by Zborowski and Herzog, by permission of International Universities Press, Inc.; *Jewish Life in the Ukraine* by Michael Charnofsky, © 1965 by Michael Charnofsky, and *Tell the Children* by Samuel Schwartz, © 1959 by Samuel Schwartz, by permission of Exposition Press, Inc., Jericho, NY; *Trial and Error* by Chaim Weizmann, by permission of Harper & Row, Inc.; "The Eastern European Era in Jewish History" by Abraham Joshua Heschel, from *Voices from the Yiddish*, edited by Howe and Greenberg, by permission of the University of Michigan Press; *Promised Land* by Mary Antin, by permission of Houghton Mifflin Company; *My Life with the Microbes* by Selman Waksman, copyright 1954 by Selman Waksman, M.D., by permission of Simon and Schuster, Inc.; *Eliakum Zunser* by Sol Liptzin, by permission of Behrman House, Inc.; *The Brothers Ashkenazi* by I. J. Singer, copyright 1936, renewed 1964, by Alfred A. Knopf, Inc., and *The World of Sholem Aleichem* by Maurice Samuel, copyright 1943 by

Maurice Samuel, by permission of Alfred A. Knopf, Inc.; *Noah Pandre's Village* by Zalman Schneour, translated by J. Leftwich, by permission of Chatto & Windus, Ltd., London; *A Treasury of Yiddish Stories* by Irving Howe and Eliezer Greenberg, copyright 1954 by The Viking Press, Inc., by permission of The Viking Press, Inc.; *Of a World That Is No More* by I. J. Singer, copyright © 1970, by permission of Vanguard Press, Inc.; *The Golden Tradition: Jewish Life and Thought in Eastern Europe,* edited by Lucy S. Dawidowicz, copyright © 1967 by Lucy S. Dawidowicz, by permission of Holt, Rinehart and Winston, Inc.; *The Time That Was Then,* by Harry Roskolenko, copyright © 1971 by Harry Roskolenko, by permission of The Dial Press; *The Promised Land,* by Mary Antin, copyright 1912 by Houghton Mifflin Company, copyright 1940 by Mary Antin, by permission of Houghton Mifflin Company; *A Lost Paradise,* by. Samuel Chotzinoff, copyright 1953, © 1955 by Samuel Chotzinoff, by permission of Alfred A. Knopf, Inc.; *Green Worlds,* copyright 1938 by Maurice Hindus and *A Traveler in Two Worlds* by Maurice Hindus, copyright 1971 by Frances McClernan Hindus, both reprinted by permission of Doubleday & Company, Inc.; *The Ghetto,* by Louis Wirth, © 1928 and 1956 by The University of Chicago Press, by permission of the University of Chicago Press; *The Spirit of the Ghetto,* by Hutchins Hapgood, © 1966, by permission of Funk & Wagnalls; *Art Is My Life,* by William Zorach, © 1967, by permission of Thomas Y. Crowell Company, Inc.; "Revolt of the Reefer-Makers," by S. L. Blumenson, copyright © 1949 by The American Jewish Committee, and "Rutgers Square," by S. L. Blumenson, copyright © 1950 by The American Jewish Committee, both reprinted by permission of *Commentary; The Rise of David Levinsky,* by Abraham Cahan, © 1917 and 1945, by permission of Harper & Row; *A Dreamer's Journey,* by Morris R. Cohen, copyright 1949 by The Free Press, by permission of Macmillan Publishing Company, Inc.; *Shadow and Light,* by Maurice Sterne, © 1965, by permission of Harcourt Brace Jovanovich.

Index

Abramovitz, Sholem Jacob (Mendele Mocher Sforim), 74, 101–102, 153, 294
Actors, 289–293
Adams, Henry, 313
Addams, Jane, 233, 258, 271
Adler, Jacob P., 291
Agriculture
  Jews in, 4
  shtetl life, 63–64
  United States, 239–241
Ain, Abraham, 66, 67, 72
Aleichem, Sholem, 49, 75, 83–84, 97, 173, 269, 293, 294, 295
Aleichem, Sholem (Sholem Rabinowitz), 101, 103–104
Alexander I (c. of Russia), 25
Alexander II (c. of Russia), 39–43, 68, 91, 107, 116–119, 144, 168, 282

Alexander III (c. of Russia), 120, 137
Altgeld, John Peter, 232
American Federation of Labor, 301, 313
Americanization
  melting pot ideology, 257–266
  process of, 247–256
American Jewish Committee, 274, 316
American Jewish Congress, 274, 316
Anarcho–syndicalism, 300–301
Anti–Defamation League, 316
Antin, Mary, 28, 31, 175, 247, 252, 265, 271, 275, 276
Anti–Semitism
  Crusades, 6–7
  emigration motivation, 169
  immigration restrictions, 312–316
  Jewish persecution, 160–164
  Kishinev slaughter, 143–155

Anti–Semitism *(continued)*
   Poland, 10–11
   Protestantism and, 8
   Russia, 99, 110–112, 120–124,
      125–133
   Russian Revolution, 312
   United States, 192–196
   World War I, 309–310, 311
   Zionism and, 136
Antokolsky, Mark, 65
Appel, John J., 313
Aramaic, Yiddish and, 97
Artisans, shtetl social division, 67
Asch, Sholem, 224, 282
Ashkenazim; *see also* Eastern Europe
   origins of, 3–8
   Poland and, 9–18
   populations of, 3
   Zionism and, 136–137
Assimilation
   Americanization, 247–256
   generational conflict, 275–280
   Haskalah and, 167
   melting pot ideology, 257–266
Austria
   Jews in, 23–24
   Polish partition, 19–20
   revolution in, 39
Axelrod, Pavel, 128, 135

Baal Shem Tov, Hasidism and, 15–16,
      21
Babylonia, *Ashkenazi* Jews, 4
Bakunin, Mikhail Aleksandrovich,
      113, 300
Balch, Emily Greene, 249
Baron, Zelda, 52
Barondess, Joseph, 301
Baskin, Leonard, 269
Bellow, Saul, 249

Ben–Ami, Jacob, 293
Berger, Victor, 301
Bialik, Chaim Nachman, 100, 136,
      143, 146–147, 148, 294
Blaustein, David, 279
Blume, Peter, 269
Blumenson, S. L., 223, 225, 285,
      287
B'nai B'rith, 316
Bovshover, Joseph, 296
Brandeis, Louis D., 304, 311
Branfman, Joel, 110
Buber, Martin, 17
Bund, labor movement and, 140–141

Cabala, study of, 15
Cahan, Abraham, 182, 188, 240,
      281–283, 292, 300, 301
Campe, J. H., 168
Carnegie, Andrew, 245–246
Castle Garden (N.Y.C.), 183–184
Catherine the Great (c. of Russia), 19,
      20
Catholic Church. *See* Christians;
      Roman Catholic Church
Censorship, Russia, 36–37
Chamberlain, Houston Stewart, 311
Charnofsky, Michael, 45–46, 51–52,
      79, 80–81
Cheder
   shtetl life, 71–79
   United States, 277–278
Chernishevsky, Nikolai G., 109
Chicago
   Hull–House settlement, 232, 258,
      271–272
   immigrant life in, 216, 232–233
   immigrant populations of, 190
   sweatshops in, 222
Children

labor of, 230–238
shtetl life, 80–82
tenement life, 208–212
Chinese Exclusion Act of 1882, 191
Chmielnitsky, Bogdan, 13
Chotzinoff, Samuel, 198, 203, 209, 219, 252
Christadora House, 268
Christians, Moslems and, 4–5; see also Roman Catholic Church
Citron, Samuel Leib, 98
Clark House, 268
Cleveland, Grover, 231
Cohen, Morris R., 33, 46–47, 71–72, 178, 180, 192, 254, 263, 284
Cohen, Moses, 239
Cohen, Samuel H., 180, 205, 214, 219
College Settlement, 268
Commerce. See Economic factors
Commons, John R., 227, 311
Conscription, Russia and, 26–35
Cossacks, revolt of, 13–14
Craftsmen, shtetl life, 63
Crimean War, 39–40
Crusades, Jews and, 6–7
Cultural life
actors and poets, 289–298
newspapers and cafés, 281–288

Dashevsky, Pinhas, 148
Davidson, Jo, 269
Davis, Philip, 272
Dawidowicz, Lucy, 283, 293
The Day, 284
Debs, Eugene V., 301
Dick, Isaac Meir, 101, 168
Diet, shtetl life, 64
Dimov, Osip, 293

Discrimination, anti–Semitism, 314–316
Dostoevsky, Fyodor, 113, 127
Dubnow, Simon, 111, 151

Eastern Europe; see also Ashkenazim; Russia; Shtetl; Western Europe
commercial development of, 6
feudalism in, 22
geography of, 3
shtetl life in, 44–50
World War I, 309
Economic factors
discrimination, 314–316
education and, 262
immigration restriction and, 191
Poland, 10, 11–12
shtetl life, 51–61
United States
child labor, 230–238
mobility, 239–246
occupations, 213–219
sweatshops, 220–229
Edelstadt, David, 296
Education
melting pot ideology, 257–266
Russia, 37–38
United States, 251–256
Educational Alliance, 267–271
Eisenberg, Azriel, 279
Eliot, George, 271
Ellis Island (N.Y.C.), 184–185
Emigration; see also Immigration
motivation for, 166, 168, 169–172
from Russia, 164–165
Engels, F., 300
Epstein, Jacob, 269
Epstein, Melech, 283, 296
Espionage and Sedition laws, 310

Ettinger, S., 168
Evans, Hiram, 312

Fairchild, Henry Pratt, 311
Family names
  Americanization, 248–249
  Russia, 24–25
Federation of Jewish Philanthropies,
    274
Feigenbaum, B., 303
Fischel, Harry, 243
Ford, Henry, 312, 316
Forward, 282–283, 305
Frank, Leo, 310
Franklin, Benjamin, 255, 268
Frederick II (e. of Prussia), 19
The Free Worker's Voice (Der Freie Arbeiter
    Stimme), 284
Der Freie Arbeiter Stimme (The Free
    Worker's Voice), 284
Freiheit, 284
French Revolution, 21
Friedlander, S., 243

Galewski, Bernard, 243
Galicia, Hasidism and, 91
Gaon of Vilna, 17, 21
Gapon, Father, 151
Garfield, John, 269
Garment industry, sweatshops,
    220–229
Generational conflict, United States,
    275–280
George, Henry, 191
German immigrants, to Poland, 10
German language, Yiddish and, 97
Ginsburg, Mordecai Aaron, 93
Ginzberg, Asher (Ahad–Ha–Am),
    136
Gogol, Nikolay Vasilyevich, 113

Goldenberg, Gregory, 115
Goldfaden, Abraham, 94, 101, 289
Gompers, Samuel, 301, 304, 313–314
Gordin, Jacob, 292, 293
Gordon, Benjamin Lee, 24–25
Gordon, Judah Leib, 98
Gorky, Maxim, 147
Gotlober, A. B., 168
Gottlieb, Adolph, 269
Grant, Madison, 310
Grant, U. S., 193
Grayzel, Solomon, 170
Greenberg, Eliezer, 103, 295
Greer, Colin, 261
Grinevitsky, Aleksandr, 118
Gross, Chaim, 269
Guilds, Jewish, 11–12
Gunzberg, David, 69, 70
Gunzberg, Horace, 70, 101, 151
Gunzberg, Joseph, 69
Gunzberg, Sophie, 69, 70

Hamilton, Alice, 271
Hannover, Nathan, 13–14
Hapgood, Hutchins, 290
Harkavy, V. O., 41
Hasidism
  Baal Shem Tov and, 15–16
  Haskalah versus, 87–95
  language and, 96
Haskalah
  assimilation and, 167
  Hasidism versus, 87–95
  language and, 96, 98
  poetry and, 293
Hearst, William Randolph, 283
Hebrew; see also Language; Yiddish
  Haskalah and, 96
  Yiddish and, 96–106, 97
Hebrew Agricultural Society, 239

Hebrew Immigrant Aid Society, 195, 272–273
Hebrew Sheltering House Association, 195
Heine, Heinrich, 297
Hendrick, Burton J., 237, 242–243, 244, 246
Henry Street Settlement, 268
Herkner, Anna, 181, 186
Hersey, Evelyn W., 276
Herzen, Alexander, 29–30, 113
Herzog, Elizabeth, 49
Heschel, Abraham Joshua, 73
Hillman, Sidney, 307
Hillquit, Morris, 300
Hindus, Maurice, 174–175, 187, 199, 204, 255, 270, 271
Hingley, Ronald, 25
Hirschbein, 293
Hitler, Adolf, 3
Holidays, shtetl life, 80–86
Holman, Nat, 269
Horowitz, Moshe, 290
Horwich, Bernard, 216
Howe, Irving, 103, 295
Howells, William Dean, 282
Hugo, Victor, 129
Hull–House settlement, 232, 258, 271–272
Hutkoff, Nathan, 243

Ignatiev, Count, 129
Immigration; see also Emigration
  Americanization, 247–256
  arrival conditions, 182–188
  child labor, 230–238
  children, 208–212
  cultural life
    actors and poets, 289–298
    newspapers and cafés, 281–288
  economic life, 213–219
  economic mobility, 239–246
  education, 251–256
  generational conflict, 275–280
  labor movement and, 299–308
  living conditions, 197–207
  melting pot ideology, 257–266
  nativism and, 190–191
  opposition to, 178–179
  population statistics, 189–190
  process of, 173–181
  racial theories and, 191
  restrictions on, 312–316
  self–help efforts, 267–274
  sweatshop conditions, 220–229
Industrialization, Russia, 137–139
Industrial Workers of the World, 301, 302, 310
International Ladies' Garment Workers' Union, 302, 307
Irish immigration, nativism and, 190
James, Henry, 313
Jewish Colonization Association, 240
Jewish education
  shtetl life, 71–79
  United States, 277–279
Jewish identity, loyalty to, 88
Jewish survival, language and, 99
Jews, trade and, 4–5
Johnson–Reed Act of 1924, 314

Kahal
  conscription and, 27–28, 33
  functions of, 11, 88
Kallen, Horace M., 260
Karakozov, Dmitri, 107, 108
Katzenelenbogen, Yaakov Shalom, 31–32
Kelley, Florence, 222, 232, 271

Kelman, Bennie, 232
Kempster, Walter, 132
King, Edward, 270, 271
Kishinev slaughter, 143–155
Kligsberg, Moses, 170, 171
Knights of Labor, 300, 301
Kobrin, Leon, 203, 293
Kochel, Motke, 65
Kopeloff, I., 183
Korchmal, Nachman, 97
Kosciusko, Thaddeus, 19
Krochmal, Nachman, 91
Kropotkin, Dimitri, 115, 300
Kropotkin, Peter, 39
Krug, Edwin A., 261
Krushevan, 148–149
Ku Klux Klan, 312, 316
Kuskin, Nathan, 216, 250

Labor movement
    immigration restriction and,
        313–314
    Russia, 139–141
    United States, 191–192, 299–308
Lang, Lucy Robbins, 202, 219
Language; see also Hebrew; Yiddish
    Haskalah and, 96
    melting pot ideology, 258–259
    United States, 255–256
Lateiner, Joseph, 290, 291
Lazarus, Emma, 191, 195
Lebensohn, Abraham Baer, 93
Lebowitz, Israel, 243
Lekert, Hirsh, 144
Lemlich, Clara, 302–303
Lermontov, Mikhail Yuryevich, 113
Levin, I. L., 29
Levin, Shmarya, 154, 163
Levinsohn, Isaac Baer, 97
Libin, Z., 293

Libraries, self-education, 263–266
Liessin, Abraham, 140
Lilienblum, Moses Leib, 98, 126–127,
    136
Lilienthal, Max, 37
Lincoln, Abraham, 193
Linetsky, Isaac Joel, 101
Liptzin, Sam, 226, 233
Lisitzky, Ephraim E., 33, 47–48,
    53–54, 58, 217
Literature
    Hebrew and Yiddish, 96–106
    United States, 293–298
Lithuania
    Hasidism and, 89
    invasion of, 14
Lodge, Henry Cabot, 312, 313, 314
Loris–Melikov, Mikhail, 116, 117
Lowell, Abbot Lawrence, 311
Lower East Side (N.Y.C.)
    children's lives, 208–212
    cultural life, 285–288
    living conditions in, 197–207
    sweatshops, 220–229
Luther, Martin, 8

Madison House, 268
Mandelbaum, Herman, 243
Mandelkern, Solomon, 24–25
Marshall, Louis, 304
Marx, Karl, 113, 300
Marxism, Jewish labor and, 141
May Laws, 130
Mazzini, Giuseppe, 136
Melting pot ideology, 257–266
Mendelssohn, Moses, 21, 22
Merchants, Jews and, 4–5
Middle Ages, Western Europe, 4
Montefiore, Moses, 48–49
Morais, Nina, 194

Moslems, Christians and, 4–5
Mourning Journal, 284
Mowry, George E., 312
Muni, Paul, 293
Murray, Arthur, 269

Names. *See* Family names
Napoleon (e. of France), 19–20, 21
National Council of Jewish Women, 273
Nationalism, Talmudic law and, 21–22
Nativism, immigration and, 190
Newman, Pauline, 299, 301, 302
Newspapers, 282–285
New York City; *see also* United States
   immigrant living conditions in, 197–207
   immigrant populations, 190, 200–201
   sweatshops, 220–229
Nicholas I (c. of Russia), 26–27, 34, 36–39
Nicholas II (c. of Russia), 137
Novak, Michael, 259

Opatoshu, Joseph, 297, 298

Pale of Settlement
   establishment of, 24
   reactionary politics and, 111
   shtetl life, 44–50
Palestine, Jewish immigration to, 135
Palmer, A. Mitchell, 310
Palmer, Francis, 42–43
Pavlovna, Vera, 109
Peretz, I. L., 76, 94, 95, 96, 99, 101, 104–106, 293, 294–295
Perl, Joseph, 91
Perovskaya, Sophie, 118

Peter the Great (c. of Russia), 20
Pinsker, Leo, 135, 136
Pinski, David, 293
Pobedonostzev, Konstantin, 120
Poderovsky, Joseph, 232
Poetry, 293–298
Poland
   civil war in, 13–14
   Jewish life in, 9–18
   partition of, 19–20
Poliakov, Samuel Solomonovich, 70
Poole, Ernest, 228
Prosteh
   Hasidism and, 89
   shtetl social division, 62–70
Protestantism, anti–Semitism and, 8
Protocols of the Elders of Zion, 145, 312
Prussia
   Jews in, 23–24
   Polish partition, 19–20
Pulitzer, Joseph, 195, 235
Pushkin, Aleksandr Sergeyevich, 113

Rabbinic Judaism
   Hasidism versus Haskalah, 87–95
   Hebrew and, 96
Rabinowitz, Sholem. *See* Aleichem, Sholem
Racial theories
   immigration and, 191
   World War I, 310–311
Railroads, Russia, 70
Rashi, 73, 74–75
Red Scare, 310
Richman, Julia, 259
Riis, Jacob, 213, 233
Rischin, Moses, 166–167, 198
Roman Catholic Church; *see also* Christians
   anti–Catholic feelings, 192

Roman Catholic Church (continued)
  Cossacks and, 13
  immigrants and, 190
Rosenfeld, Morris, 225, 293,
  296–297, 305
Roskolenko, Harry, 218, 253, 268,
  284, 285, 288
Ross, Edward A., 311
Roth, Henry, 278
Russia; see also Eastern Europe; Shtetl
  anti–Semitism in, 99, 120–124
  assimilation policy of, 36–43
  conscription and, 26–35
  industrialization, 137–139
  Jewish assimilation in, 87, 91–92
  Jewish emigration from, 164–165
  Jewish persecution in, 160–164
  Jewish policy of, 22–25
  Jewish social achievement in,
    69–70
  Kishinev slaughter, 143–155
  origins of, 20
  pogroms encouraged by, 125–133
  Polish partition, 19–20
  political reform in, 40
  reactionary politics in, 107–115
  shtetl life in, 44–50
  terrorism in, 116–124
  Zionism and, 134–142
Russian Revolution (1917), 312
Russo–Japanese War, 150–151, 152
Russo–Turkish War (1877), 112
Ryan, John A., 238
Rysakov, 118

Sabbatai Zevi, 15
Sabbath, shtetl life, 83–86
Saltykov-Shchedrin, M. E., 127–128
Samuel, Maurice, 49, 75, 76–77, 81,
  104

Sanders, Ronald, 290
Sarnoff, David, 269
Schalit, A., 237
Schiff, Jacob, 304
Schneersohn, Menaham Mendel, 32
Schneiderman, Rose, 302
Schneour, Zalman, 83, 100
Scholarship, Poland, 12–13
Schwartz, J. R., 201, 216, 253
Schwartz, Maurice, 293
Schwartz, Samuel, 48
Schweitzer, Frederick M., 7
Self–help efforts, United States,
  267–274
Sephardim, origins of, 5
Serfs
  emancipation of, 40
  rebellion of, 109, 114
Shahn, Ben, 269
Shaler, Nathaniel, 313
Shazar, Zalman, 31, 59–61, 149
Sherman, C. Belzalel, 308
Sheyneh, shtetl social division,
  62–70
Sholem Aleichem schools, 280
Shtetl; see also Eastern Europe; Russia
  culture in, 80–86
  economics of, 51–61
  Hasidism versus Haskalah in,
    87–95
  Jewish education in, 71–79
  life in, 44–50
  social division in, 62–70
Shtif, Nokhum, 148
Silverman, Samuel, 243
Singer, I. J., 67–68, 75, 93, 137, 139,
  282
Slavic languages, Yiddish and, 97
Sliosberg, Henrik, 112
Smolenskin, Peretz, 98, 99

Socialism
 anti–Semitism and, 135
 Bund and, 140–141
 repression of, 309–310
 Russia and, 109
 United States, 282, 308
Socialist Party (U.S.), 301, 303
Socioeconomic class. *See* Economic factors
Soyer, Raphael, 160–161
Spain
 expulsion from, 7
 Jews in, 5–6
Starr, Ellen, 271
Statute of 1804 (Russia), 24
Steffens, Lincoln, 211, 282, 293
Stereotyping, anti–Semitism and, 193–194
Sterne, Maurice, 160, 161, 219
Stoddard, Lothrop, 311
Sweatshops, described, 220–229
Synagogues, United States, 273

Talmudic law, nationalism and, 21–22
Tarbell, Ida, 302
Taxation, Poland, 10
Tchernichovsky, Saul, 100
Teller, Judd, 246, 284
Tenements, described, 201–205
Theater, 289–293
Thomashefsky, Boris, 291, 292
Tolstoy, Lev, 127, 148
Townsend, Edward W., 222
Trepov, Fedor, 114
Triangle Shirtwaist Company, 299, 303, 304–307
Trotsky, Leon, 140
Trunk, Jehiel Isaiah, 105, 106
Turgenev, Ivan, 109–110, 127

Ukraine, Hasidism and, 89
Union movement. *See* Labor movement
United Hebrew Charities, 195
United Hebrew Trades, 300, 303
United States; *see also* New York City
 Americanization, 247–256
 anti–Semitism, 192–196
 child labor, 230–238
 cultural life
  actors and poets, 289–298
  newspapers and cafés, 281–288
 economic mobility, 239–246
 education, 251–256
 generational conflict, 275–280
 immigrant arrival conditions in, 182–188
 immigrant living conditions in, 197–207
 immigration restrictions, 191, 312–316
 immigration to, 164–165
 industrialization of, 189
 Jewish population of, 168, 179, 189–190, 200–201
 labor movement, 299–308
 melting pot ideology, 257–266
 self–help efforts, 267–274
 World War I, 309–310
University Settlement, 268

Von Plehve, 144, 145, 149

Wages, of immigrants, 235–238
Waksman, Selman, 44, 49–50
Wald, Lillian, 302
Walkowitz, Abraham, 269
Watson, Tom, 310
Weber, John B., 132

Weinstein, Bernard, 221–222
Weizmann, Chaim, 128
Wengeroff, Hanan, 68–69
Wengeroff, Pauline, 68–69
Western Europe; see also Eastern
    Europe
  expulsion from, 8
  French Revolution and, 21–22
  Jews in, 4
  political reform in, 38
Wiener, Leo, 297
Wilson, Woodrow, 309, 311, 314
Winchevsky, Morris, 113, 296
Wirth, Louis, 205
Wolwolff, Israel, 48, 54–55
Women
  labor of, 235
  shtetl life, 52–53
  tenement life, 206, 211–212
Women's Trade Union League, 302,
    303
Workmen's Circle, 280
World War I, 309

Yehuda, Eliezer Ben, 100
Yeshiva, shtetle life, 77–78
Yiddish; see also Language
  anti–Semitism and, 195
  Ashkenazi Jews, 3
  banning of, 268
  Haskalah and, 96
  Hebrew and, 96–106
  melting pot ideology, 258–259
  newspapers, 283, 284
  origins of, 13, 97
  theater, 289–298
  United States, 255–256

Zadels, Moisha, 53
Zasulich, Vera, 114
Zborowski, Mark, 49
Zeublin, Charles, 207
Zhelyabov, Andrey, 117
Zhitlowsky, Chaim, 280
Zionism
  Jewish education and, 280
  newspapers, 284
  Russia and, 134–142, 154
Zorach, William, 192, 231, 232, 247
Zunser, Eliakum, 65, 70, 74, 76, 91,
    101, 135, 294

About the Author

Milton Meltzer, distinguished biographer and historian, is the author of more than ninety books for young people and adults and has been the writer or editor for newspapers, magazines, books, radio, television, and films. Five of his books have been nominated for the National Book Award, and many have been chosen for the honor lists of the American Library Association, the National Council of Teachers of English, and the National Council for Social Studies. He is a member of the Authors Guild. He and his wife, Hildy, live in New York City. They have two daughters and two grandsons.